Fourth Edition

APPLYING PSYCHOLOGY
Individual and Organizational Effectiveness

Andrew J. DuBrin

College of Business
Rochester Institute of Technology

Prentice-Hall, International, Inc.

ISBN 0-13-176710-0

Printed in the United States of America

10 9 8 7 6 5 4 3

ISBN: 0-13-176710-0

Prentice-Hall International (UK) Limited, *London*
Prentice-Hall of Australia Pty. Limited, *Sydney*
Prentice-Hall Canada Inc., *Toronto*
Prentice-Hall Hispanoamericana, S.A., *Mexico*
Prentice-Hall of India Private Limited, *New Delhi*
Prentice-Hall of Japan, Inc., *Tokyo*
Prentice-Hall of Southeast Asia Pte. Ltd., *Singapore*
Editora Prentice-Hall do Brasil, Ltda., *Rio de Janeiro*
Prentice-Hall Inc., *Englewood Cliffs, New Jersey*

To Drew, Molly, Rosemary, and Clare

CONTENTS

Chapter 3 Individual Differences and Work Performance 47

part two Dealing with Individuals 72

Chapter 4 Understanding Yourself 72

Chapter 5 Motivating Yourself and Others 92

Chapter 6 Achieving Success through Goal Setting 118

Chapter 7 Solving Problems and Making Decisions 140

Chapter 8 Achieving Wellness and Managing Stress 168

Chapter 9 Managing Conflict and Frustration 199

PREFACE

An increasing number of students enrolled in business courses are demanding a satisfactory return on the time and money that they invest in education and training. Faculty members and administrators, too, are demanding textbooks that are useful in the development of practical insights and specific skills—yet still academically respectable. Virtually all applied psychology or human relations books contend that they "bridge the gap between theory and practice." Still, most students have difficulty walking across that bridge.

Applying Psychology: Individual and Organizational Effectiveness has been written to fill the need for a basic, career-oriented text with a variety of suggestions for personal improvement and effectiveness. Despite its emphasis on prescription, the book is based on empirical studies and established psychological concepts and theories. The research findings cited and the concepts mentioned are all illustrated with concrete, reality-based examples.

This text is designed to meet the curriculum needs of courses in business psychology, applied psychology, and human relations offered in various settings: postsecondary vocational and technical schools, business schools and institutes, and colleges. Previous editions of *Applying Psychology* have been widely used in programs in which business psychology or applied psychology is the only course the student takes. The current edition of the text remains a business psychology book with ample information about fundamentals of psychology.

The underlying design of this book is to present an overview of major psychological concepts and techniques that are relevant to the individual worker in attaining both good performance and personal satisfaction. Concise summaries are presented of major concepts of basic psychology, including learning, perception, personality, and motivation. The major classical theories of human behavior at work are summarized. Modern developments stemming from these classical theories (such as participative management, organizational behavior modification, and modified work schedules) are treated at greater length.

Current topics in the fields of business psychology and human relations, such as VDT stress, bias-free language, burnout, sexual harassment, and cross-cultural communication problems are also included. The literature cited in this text includes scholarly journals, magazines such as *Business Week, Success,* and *Psychology Today,* and professional books about business and self-help topics.

Changes in the Current Edition

Although the basic structure of the text remains the same, notable changes are included in this edition. A new emphasison positive thinking is reflected in five new chapter titles. Chapter 6 is now "Achieving Success through Goal Setting"; Chapter 10 is now "Building Relationships with Superiors, Co-workers, and Customers"; Chapter 14 is now "Leading and Influencing Others"; and Chapter 16 is now "Achieving High Personal Productivity and Quality."

New topics in this edition include the leader's role in building teamwork, total quality management, improving customer service, developing wellness, and working with cultural diversity. Much more emphasis is placed on how the brain influences job behavior and adjustment to technology. Fifty percent of the cases and exercises are new.

How This Book Will Benefit the Reader

A person who studies the information in this book and incorporates its suggestions into his or her way of doing things should derive the four benefits listed below. However, knowledge itself is not a guarantee of success. People vary so widely in learning ability, personality, and life circumstances that some people will be able to attain some objectives and not others. As a case in point, you might be so naturally effective at dealing with stress that the chapter on this topic is unnecessary from your viewpoint. Or you might be so shy at this stage in your life that you are unable to apply some of the confrontation techniques described for resolving conflict, Instead, you would benefit more from reading the information in the text about overcoming shyness.

The major benefits this book provides are the following:

1. *Awareness of relevant information.* Part of feeling comfortable and making a positive impression in any place of work is being familiar with relevant general knowledge about the world of work. By reading this book, you will become

conversant with many of the buzz words used on the job, such as autocratic manager, positive reinforcement, networking, and dressing for success.

2. Development of skills in dealing with people. Anybody who aspires toward higher-level jobs needs to develop proficiency in such interpersonal skills as how to motivate people, how to criticize others in a constructive manner, and how to overcome communication barriers.

3. Coping with job problems Almost everybody who holds a responsible job inevitably runs into human problems. Reading about these problems and prescriptions for coping with them could save you considerable inner turmoil. Among the job survival skills that you will learn about in the following chapters are managing job stress and dealing with conflict between yourself and your boss.

4. Capitalizing on opportunities. Many readers of this book will spend part of their working time taking advantage of opportunities, rather than resolving daily problems. Every career-minded person needs a few breakthrough experiences in order to make his or her life more rewarding. Toward this end, we devote attention to the subjects of creative decision making and methods of career advancement.

Instructor's Manual and Test Bank. The instructor's manual for this text is substantially enlarged and improved. It contains over 850 test questions, chapter outline and lecture notes, answers to discussion questions and case problems, and comments about the exercises. In addition, the manual includes step-by-step instructions for the use of computer-assisted scenario analysis (CASA).

CASA is a user-friendly way of using any word-processing program to assist in analyzing cases. The student enters an existing case into the computer and then analyzes it by answering the case questions in the text. Next, the student makes up a new scenario or twist to the case and **enters this scenario in boldface into the case.** The case questions are reanalyzed in light of this new scenario. Any changes in the answers are **printed in bold.** CASA gives the student experience in a creative application of word processing. Equally important, it helps students develop a "what-if" or contingency point of view in solving business psychology problems.

Acknowledgments

My primary thanks on this project are extended to the editorial, production, and marketing staffs at Prentice Hall Career & Technology. Elizabeth Sugg, Maria Klimek, and Penelope Linskey played key roles in launching the fourth edition. Thanks also to the other instructors who adopted the first three editions of the book, thus creating a demand for the fourth edition. Many of the changes made in this new edition are based on the suggestions offered by our adopters. Special thanks is owed our outside reviewers for the third and fourth editions, Margaret Squier of Kilgore College and Blaine Weller of Muskegon College.

Andrew J. DuBrin

part one *Business Psychology and Human Behavior*

Part one of the book introduces the field of business psychology in addition to presenting an overview of basic principles of human psychology. Chapter 1 defines the field of business psychology along with other major fields of psychology. You will learn about how business psychology is based on research. Chapter 2 overviews general principles of human behavior such as how people perceive and learn, along with basic concepts of motivation and values. This information examines the similarities among people. Chapter 3, in contrast, describes some of the many ways in which people differ from each other, and how these differences affect job performance.

Chapter 1

FOUNDATIONS OF BUSINESS PSYCHOLOGY

Learning Objectives _____

After reading and studying this chapter and doing the exercises, you should be able to

1. Define the term *business psychology* and explain what it means.
2. Describe several of the major fields within psychology.
3. Describe several of the major schools of thought within psychology.
4. Explain how business psychology fits into the human relations movement.
5. Understand why it is helpful to study business psychology even if you have a good amount of common sense.

What Is Business Psychology? _____

The study of psychology, as it applies to the workplace, can help you come to grips with the wide range of human problems encountered in any job. It can also help you to prepare for your career. An understanding of the basic principles of business psychology can help explain why people act as they do in certain situations and suggest what you can sometimes do to change their behavior.

In the chapters that follow, there are no sure-fire answers to getting along with employers and co-workers or making worthwhile things happen. However, there are specific guidelines that have proved to be true most of the time in the past. You can rely on these guidelines to help you in your relations with other people in the future. **Business psychology**, as the term is used in this book, refers to the application of organized knowledge about human behavior to improve personal satisfaction and productivity on the job. Business psychology can thus be used in any work setting, such as a company, government agency, community agency, hospital, or school.

Psychology is most accurately defined as the systematic study of behavior and all the factors that influence behavior. Almost any human activity might thus be the subject of study by a psychologist. Yet, in practice, psychology deals more with the mind than with the body. The term psychology has gained wide acceptance as the field associated with the scientific study of people and animals. It is important to recognize, however, that fields such as sociology, anthropology, political science, and economics are also concerned with the study of human behavior. Although these fields have useful insights to offer, the focus of this book is on the application of selected principles of psychology.

The meaning of psychology becomes clearer when you recognize that the field is both a science and a profession.[1] *Science* refers to the fact that many people engaged in psychology primarily conduct research about human behavior. The term *profession* means that many people engaged in psychology primarily provide services to (or help) people.

Before proceeding with the study of business psychology, it will be useful to examine psychology from two perspectives. First, we will describe what psychologists do by examining several fields within psychology. Second, we will describe the major schools of thought within psychology.

What Psychologists Do

Psychology touches our lives in thousands of ways. Among the best known contributions of psychologists to society have been mental tests, behavior modification, and helping people to work more effectively in groups. About 60,000 people are official members of the American and Canadian psychological associations. An even larger number of people are engaged in work that is closely related to the application of psychological knowledge to improve the lives of people. Among such specialists performing psychological work are human resource specialists, who conduct training programs on how to get along better with people; organization development specialists, who conduct programs for increasing the effectiveness of organizations; and guidance counselors, who advise students on how to cope with personal problems.

Here we will mention several of the more established specialty areas within modern psychology, along with two emerging ones.[2] Currently there are 48 specialty areas within psychology. One problem in dividing

TABLE 1–1. *MAJOR FIELDS OF PSYCHOLOGY* _____

1. Clinical and Counseling Psychology: includes psychotherapy
2. School Psychology
3. Child and Developmental Psychology
4. Experimental Psychology
5. Ergonomics: helps to design equipment and the workplace to fit human requirements
6. Industrial and Organizational Psychology: a scientific approach to business psychology
7. Health Psychology: helps to modify human behavior to prevent and treat physical illness

psychology into different specialties is that they show so much overlap. For instance, both industrial and clinical psychologists might conduct workshops to help employees work together more smoothly. Both school and child psychologists might try to determine what is preventing a specific child from learning how to achieve average reading skill. Table 1-1 outlines these fields.

Clinical and Counseling Psychology

About half of all practicing psychologists work within the fields of clinical and counseling psychology. These psychologists work with individuals or small groups to help them overcome personal problems and cope better with stress. Many clinical psychologists use biofeedback devices to help clients learn how to reduce tension. These devices give people feedback on stress signals such as rapid heartbeat and muscle tightness. Clinical psychologists also play an important role in diagnosing mental illness. Counseling psychologists tend to work with people with fewer major adjustment problems than clinical psychologists. Yet there is often very little distinction between the work of these two types of psychologists.

Psychiatry: A medical specialty that deals with the diagnosis and treatment of emotional problems and mental illness.

We often tend to confuse the work of psychiatrists, psychoanalysts, clinical psychologists, and psychotherapists. **Psychiatry** is a medical specialty that deals with the diagnosis and treatment of emotional problems and mental illness. Psychiatrists can legally treat people with drugs, electroshock, psychosurgery, or psychotherapy. Psychiatrists, however, rarely have a formal degree in psychology.

Psychoanalysis: A type of long-term psychotherapy in which patients are encouraged to explore early memories and their unconscious. Also a theory of motivation that focuses on unconscious motivation.

Psychoanalysis is a specialized type of psychotherapy in which the patient may spend up to three or four years, several times a week, working on personal problems. Psychoanalysts believe that psychoanalysis is the only valid way of getting to the root of emotional problems and reconstructing an individual's personality. To be certified as a psychoanalyst, the therapist must attend a specialized training program beyond regular medical or psychological training. Although the vast majority of psychoanalysts are psychiatrists, a few are clinical psychologists or psychiatric social workers.

Clinical psychologists have formal degrees in psychology, generally a doctor of philosophy (Ph.D.), and sometimes a doctor of education

(Ed.D.) or doctor of professional psychology (Psy. D.). In virtually all states and provinces, a certificate or license is required to call oneself a psychologist. Clinical psychologists work in hospitals, health maintenance organizations (HMOs), group practice with psychiatrists, and individual private practice. A growing number of clinical psychologists work with other mental health professionals in clinics that specialize in treating workers whose personal problems adversely affect their job performance.

Psychotherapist:
Any mental health professional who helps people with their emotional problems through conversation with them.

To confuse matters just a bit further, a **psychotherapist** is any mental health professional who helps people with emotional problems through conversation with them. All of the specialties we have described above include psychotherapy.

Clinical psychologists play an important role in occupational health. A primary reason is that stress-related conditions are among the most important health problems today for people at work. Psychological disorders are one of the ten leading work-related diseases and injuries in the country today.[3]

School Psychology

School psychologists work in elementary, junior high, and high schools to assist students with learning and/or emotional problems. Although these psychologists are generally not licensed mental health care providers, they are skilled at diagnosing problems, making referrals to appropriate agencies, and advising teachers how to help students with personal problems. A typical problem for a school psychologist is estimating if a given student has sufficient mental ability to benefit from a regular program of study.

Child and Developmental Psychology

Developmental psychologists study behavior and growth patterns from the prenatal period through maturity and old age. Child psychologists concentrate their efforts on the study of the person from birth through age 11. Many clinical psychologists specialize in dealing with the behavior problems of children. Research in child psychology sometimes helps understand work behavior. For example, one study showed that victims of childhood abuse and neglect may suffer long-term consequences. Among them are lower IQs and reading ability, more suicide attempts, and more unemployment and low-paying jobs.[4]

Many people today have become interested in the study of adult phases of human development. The work of developmental psychologists has led to widespread interest in the problems of the middle years, such as the mid-life crisis. A job-related problem of interest to developmental psychologists is why so many executives die earlier than expected after retirement. (A preliminary hunch is that some executives find it extraordinarily stressful to lose so much power and importance.)

Experimental Psychology

Experimental psychologists can be considered the most "scientific" of all psychologists. Their laboratories often rival those of biologists and medical scientists. Experimental psychologists are usually employed by colleges, universities, and research laboratories. Many of the principles of human behavior discussed in this book (such as those associated with learning, thinking, and perception) were developed by experimental psychologists. Experimental psychologists also help to design certain parts of computer software, such as commands, to make it easier for users to process information.

An unusual example of experimental psychology is a program to train astronauts how to avoid space motion sickness. Psychologist Pat Cowings teaches astronauts how to overcome the physiological stress response that causes nausea at zero gravity. Through self-suggestion, the space travelers go through exercises that develop their abilities to control the automatic responses of their nervous system. Sixty-five percent of the people who receive Cowing's training are able to completely eliminate symptoms of motion sickness.[5]

Ergonomics (or Human Engineering)

Ergonomics: The design of machinery, equipment, and the work environment to fit human characteristics, both physical and mental.

Ergonomics is the field of study that attempts to design machinery, equipment, and the work environment to fit human characteristics, both physical and mental. Ergonomics is closely associated with experimental psychology and is a combination of engineering and psychology. Specialists in this field are concerned with improving employee productivity by providing efficient work stations, appropriate lighting, good power tools, less environmental noise, and advice on the appropriate posture for a task. The accompanying box illustrates how human engineering psychologists are also involved in creating more productive office environments.

Ergonomics is now used to help lay out personal computers and desks to minimize the stress associated with working many hours in front of a video display terminal (VDT). When the chairs, desk, monitor, and keyboard are configured in the right way, a computer worker can often minimize various bodily problems. Of major significance, the disabling injury of repetitive motion disorder can often be prevented. Details about this important topic are presented in Chapter 11.

Industrial and Organizational Psychology

Industrial and organizational psychology: Basically, business psychology; the field of psychology that studies human behavior in a work environment. Overlaps considerably with organizational behavior.

Much of this book deals with the ideas and methods of industrial and organizational psychologists. Business psychology is a general term for the methods and ideas of industrial and organizational psychologists that are relevant to the individual who wants to succeed on the job. About 7 percent of psychologists list themselves in the **industrial and organizational psychology** category.

Among the major activities of specialists in this field are the design of employee selection methods (such as tests and interviews) and methods for training and developing employees at all job levels. Industrial and organizational psychologists have developed a number of methods for improving teamwork and cooperation in organizations. Among these techniques are production work teams that are given substantial authority to make a product on their own, working as a team, rather than in an assembly-line fashion.

Research in industrial and organizational psychology can solve practical problems. A representative example is an investigation of the relationship between certain personality traits and job success. The results of 117 different studies were combined to reach dependable conclusions. The personality traits studied were extroversion, emotional stability, agreeableness, conscientiousness, and openness to experience. The five occupational groups studied were professionals, police, managers, sales, and skilled and semiskilled workers.

Three different aspects of job success were measured. *Job proficiency* included ratings by supervisors and actual production records, such as number of sales. *Training proficiency* consisted of data about how well the employees performed in company training programs. *Personnel data* included data from employee files, such as salary level, promotion, and turnover.

One personality factor, conscientiousness, was associated with success on all three measures for all the occupational groups.[6] Employers can use this information by testing applicants for conscientiousness to predict job success. (However, an employer should investigate whether the job in question is comparable to the ones included in the study summarized here.) You can use this same information now, having scientific reassurance that being conscientious will indeed contribute to your career success.

Health Psychology

In modern Western societies, advances in health are more likely to stem from changes in behavior than from new medical discoveries. Most illnesses do not stem from infectious diseases, but from self-destructive behavior such as smoking, drug and alcohol abuse, and poor nutrition. Furthermore, many diseases stemming from infection (such as sexually transmitted diseases) can be prevented through changes in behavior.[7]

Health psychology: The study and practice of how human behavior can be modified to prevent and treat illness.

Recognition of the key role human behavior plays in preventing and curing disease has created a demand for health psychologists. **Health psychology** is the study and practice of how human behavior can be modified to prevent and treat illness. When practiced by physicians, the same field is referred to as *behavioral medicine*. Health psychology is concerned primarily with aspects of health and health care outside the area of mental health. However, emotional problems must often be dealt with to improve physical health. This brief case history illustrates how health psychologists can contribute to improved health care:

Over the course of a year, Linda G. made repeated visits to her HMO. One problem she complained of was a nagging cough, which she thought might be attributed to her cigarette smoking. When told by the physician to stop smoking, Linda said, "I can't, it's one of my few pleasures in life." She was also treated several times for skin infections traced to overexposure to sunlight. When told to stay out of the sun by a nurse, Linda replied, "I would rather take the medicine you give me; lying in the sun makes the summer worthwhile." A month later she was treated for a head wound she received as a passenger in a minor car accident. Asked by the physician if she was wearing a seatbelt, Linda replied, "No, it's a violation of my personal freedom."

The physician finally referred Linda to the mental health unit, where the health psychologist attempted to help Linda overcome her self-destructive behaviors. Without changing her behavior in regard to smoking, sunning, and the use of seat belts, Linda would inevitably return to be treated for physical problems.

Some health psychologists use their research skills to improve physical health in the workplace. For example, a study about quitting smoking was conducted among 15,000 Control Data employees. Among the findings were the following:

1. Employees who smoke a pack of cigarettes per day have 18 percent higher medical claim costs than do nonsmokers. (Reasons such as these have led to a ban on smoking in many workplaces.)
2. Employees who are physically inactive spend 30 percent more days in the hospital than do employees who engage regularly in physical exercise.
3. Seriously overweight employees are 48 percent more likely to have health claims exceeding $5,000 in one year.[8]

Health psychologists enhance workplace physical well-being in another important way. Many of them contribute to corporate fitness and wellness programs in such ways as teaching relaxation techniques to overcome work stress. In addition, health psychologists help employees overcome self-defeating behavior, such as food disorders, alcohol abuse, and tobacco use.

New Frontiers in Psychology

The demand for psychologists in colleges and universities has stabilized. Instead of psychology weakening as a science and profession, psychologists are expanding in fields in which they make a contribution. An example of a new frontier in psychology is research being conducted into ways of preserving the environment. The traditional concerns about protecting the environment have concentrated on soil conservation, preservation of wildlife habitat, and reducing air and water pollution. Environmental psychologists have contributed to these traditional concerns in such ways as developing motivational programs to help reduce litter.

A new frontier for psychologists is to develop ways of measuring natural scenic beauty.[9] Objective evidence about scenic beauty is useful in demonstrating that an activity, such as building a road, can actually mar the appearance of the environment.

One way to measure natural scenic beauty is to have people rate color slides of nature scenes, using an elaborate scale. For example, the raters might make judgments on "color harmony," "natural appearance," and "peacefulness." Perceived beauty indexes might appear subjective. Nevertheless, they have been remarkably consistent from one panel of observers to another, including environmental activists, college students, and the general public. Scenic beauty ratings have another useful application. They can measure *objectively* how much visibility-reducing air pollution harms the physical attractiveness of a specific environment.

With so much concern about preserving natural beauty, environmental psychology has a promising future. Many methods provide tangible evidence of physical harm to the environment through actions such as dumping toxins. Scenic beauty ratings can be used to demonstrate the psychological harm to the environment.

Schools of Thought in Psychology

To help explain the field of psychology, we have just described some of the major activities of psychologists. An equally important way of understanding psychology is to review the major schools of thought, or theoretical positions. These schools of thought help to influence which method a given psychologist will use to help solve a particular problem. For example, the cognitive school of psychology holds that people make rational decisions and are often driven by thoughts of self-fulfillment. An industrial and organizational psychologist who believes in the cognitive school would recommend an employee motivation program that gives employees a chance to have a voice in making decisions about their own work.

Here we will briefly describe five schools of thought in psychology: structuralism and functionalism, behaviorism, psychoanalysis, cognitive psychology, and humanistic psychology.[10] Business psychology today is influenced much more by behaviorism, cognitive psychology, and humanistic psychology than by the other two schools. Table 1-2 outlines the schools of thought in psychology.

TABLE 1–2. *SCHOOLS OF THOUGHT IN PSYCHOLOGY*

1. Structuralism and Functionalism: study the structure and the functions of the mind
2. Behaviorism: studies overt behavior
3. Psychoanalysis: studies inner motives and the unconscious part of personality
4. Cognitive Psychology: focuses on intellectual or mental aspects of behavior
5. Humanistic Psychology: emphasizes dignity and worth of people

Structuralism and Functionalism

Many historians believe that modern psychology began in 1879 when Wilhelm Wundt established a laboratory in Leipzig, Germany, to study human consciousness. Wundt aimed to discover the structure of the mind by analyzing conscious experiences of the senses and by reducing the mind to its basic elements. His most important contention was that you could take some object in the physical world, present it to a trained subject, and have the subject describe the fundamental elements of his or her conscious experience. For example, if you presented the subject a watermelon, she might say, "I see an elliptical shape, I see green and white, I feel a heavy weight." This method of looking into one's conscious experience is called **introspection**. By binding together the introspections of thousands of people, structuralists hoped to develop a science of conscious experience.

Introspection:
A method of looking into one's conscious experience.

Although historically important, structuralism lost momentum as a useful method of understanding human behavior. William James, an American student of Wundt's, extended the narrow limits of structuralism to the study of many topics that are still of current interest, including learning, motivation, and emotions. James was also concerned with the struggle of people to reach their goals or become reconciled to failure. His school of thought became known as **functionalism** because he tried to understand the functioning of the mind. In time, James became America's premier psychologist and some of his work is still quoted today. His book, *The Principles of Psychology,* should not be overlooked by any serious student of human behavior.

Functionalism:
An early school of psychological thought empahsizing the functions of the mind.

Behaviorism

Structuralism and functionalism soon came under fire because they focused too much on unscientific subjective experiences. In their place, John B. Watson proposed **behaviorism**, a school of thought based on the assumption that psychologists should study overt behavior, rather than mental states or other unobservable aspects of living things. He contended that mental life was something that cannot be seen or measured and thus cannot be studied scientifically. To Watson and to all subsequent behaviorists, the key to understanding human beings is their actual behavior, not their inner states.

Behaviorism:
A school of thought in psychology based on the assumption that psychologists should study overt behavior, rather than mental states or other unobservable aspects of living things.

Watson believed that everything we do is determined by our past experiences, and not by an ability to control our own destiny. In his thinking, all human behavior is a series of events in which a *stimulus* produces a *response*. According to behaviorists, almost any kind of stimulus can be made to produce any kind of response. Watson excited the imagination of millions of parents when he proclaimed, "I can take any dozen babies at birth and, by conditioning them in various ways, turn them into anything I wish—doctor, lawyer, beggar, or thief."[11] More will be said about conditioning in Chapter 2.

Modern-day Behaviorism. The next prominent leader of behaviorism was the experimental psychologist B. F. Skinner. His work led to improved methods of learning and motivation in schools, psychiatric wards, prisons, and industry. Skinner's name is closely associated with the terms positive reinforcement and behavior modification.

Skinner held that freedom is an illusion: the behavior of humans and animals is shaped by environmental influences, not internal ones. He championed the **law of effect**. According to this law, rewarded behavior tends to be repeated, while behavior that is ignored or punished tends not to be repeated. Feelings and other mental processes are simply the by-products of an endless cycle of pairings between stimuli and responses. Skinner believed strongly that a scientific analysis of human activity excludes the individual as the initiator of behavior.

Behaviorism has endured despite its many critics. Among their concerns are that behaviorism ignores the mind and is applicable only to animals and helpless children or in-patients.[12] Chapter 5 describes the use of behavior modification for motivating yourself and others.

Law of effect: In behavior modification, behavior that leads to a positive consequence for the individual tends to be repeated, while behavior that leads to a negative consequence tends not to be repeated.

Psychoanalysis

Another major approach to understanding human behavior is psychoanalysis, founded by Sigmund Freud and his key associate, Carl Jung. Psychoanalytic theory views men and women as constantly torn between internal unconscious forces and external social forces. People are born with powerful biological appetites and passions that demand constant satisfaction, despite the needs of others or themselves. Thus an employee with an urge toward self-punishment may insult his boss even though it will anger the boss and possibly cost him his job. Our major job in life is to direct these irrational motives and emotions into socially acceptable behaviors. A key point of psychoanalytic theory is that we must learn to control our inborn desires and achieve their fulfillment in ways that are harmonious with others.

The best known part of Freudian theory deals with the structure of the human **personality** (an individual's characteristic way of behaving, feeling, and thinking). It consists of three major forces interacting with each other:

Personality: An individual's characteristic way of behaving, feeling, and thinking.

1. *Id,* unconscious instincts such as sex and aggression.
2. *Ego,* the conscious, rational self, or intellect.
3. *Superego,* the social rules and values of society that govern our behavior.

The ego, or conscious self, is under constant pressure to fight off the pleasure-seeking desires of the id. At the same time, the ego is pressured by the reality forces of the environment and the moral dictates of one's upbringing—the superego. The healthy personality has an ego that does an effective job of coping with the urges of the id and the restrictions of the superego. Thus the well-adjusted employee refrains from punching his boss, but at the same time is able to challenge authority in an acceptable way.

The psychoanalytic school has had a major impact on understanding human behavior, particularly in regard to analyzing mental health problems. Its impact, however, has shown a rapid decline in recent years. Very little of business psychology deals directly with psychoanalytic theory. There are times, however, when the concept of unconscious behavior can be helpful in resolving a work problem. One example is when people procrastinate because of an inner fear of success (see Chapter 17). Ideas from psychoanalysis are useful in understanding how the emotional conflicts of top leaders can damage an entire organization.[13] For example, an executive might not share important information with key people because he or she is paranoid.

Cognitive Psychology

Cognitive:
Referring to the intellectual aspects of human behavior.

Another major movement in psychology is explaining the behavior of human beings in terms of their intellectual, rational selves. The term **cognitive** refers to the intellectual aspects of behavior. And a cognitive process is the means by which an individual becomes aware of objects and situations. It includes learning, reasoning, and problem solving. According to the cognitive school of thought, the mind processes information by producing new thoughts, making comparisons, and making decisions. **Cognitive psychology** focuses on the way our perception of events influences our actions. Thus, if an employee perceives it to be true that hard work will lead to a bonus, he or she will put forth extra effort. More will be said about the cognitive school of thought in relation to perception and motivation (Chapter 2).

Cognitive psychology:
A movement within, or branch of, psychology that attempts to explain the behavior of human beings in terms of their intellectual, rational selves.

Humanistic Psychology

Humanistic psychology:
An approach to psychology that emphasizes the dignity and worth of people, along with their many other positive but intangible or "soft" attributes.

Humanistic psychology emphasizes the dignity and worth of people, along with many other positive but intangible or "soft" attributes. The formal movement of humanistic psychology began about 25 years ago. Its official role was defined in these terms:

> Humanistic psychology is primarily an orientation toward the whole psychology rather than a distinct area or school. It stands for the respect and worth of persons, respect for differences of approach, openmindedness as to acceptable methods, and interests in exploration of new aspects of human behavior. As a new force in contemporary psychology it is concerned with topics having little place in existing theories and systems. Among them are love, creativity, self, growth, basic need gratification, self-actualization, higher values, being, becoming, spontaneity, play, humor, affection, naturalness, warmth, ego-experience, peak experience, courage, and related concepts.[14]

Humanistic psychology has had a substantial impact on business psychology and human relations, in terms of both theories and techniques. Abraham Maslow, who developed the need hierarchy, was also a founder of humanistic psychology. Among the humanistic techniques to be described in this book are wellness programs and assertiveness training. In many ways, business psychology is a blend of behaviorism and humanistic psychology.

Closely related in philosophy to humanistic psychology is another major influence on business psychology, the human relations movement.

The Human Relations Movement

Human relations movement:
A concentrated effort by managers and their advisors to become more sensitive to the needs of employees or to treat them in a more humanistic manner.

The **human relations movement** began as a concentrated effort by some managers and their advisors to become more sensitive to the needs of employees or to treat them in a more humanistic manner. In other words, employees were to be treated as human beings rather than as parts of the productive process. As explained by Robert Kreitner, the human relations movement was supported by three different historic influences: the Hawthorne studies, the threat of unionization, and industrial humanism (see Figure 1-1).[15]

The Hawthorne Studies

The human relations school of management is generally said to have begun in 1927 with a group of studies conducted at the Hawthorne plant of an AT&T subsidiary. These studies were prompted by an experiment carried out by the company's engineers between 1924 and 1927. Following the tradition of scientific management, these engineers were applying research methods to investigate problems of employee productivity.

Two groups were studied to determine the effects of different levels of illumination on worker performance. As prescribed by the scientific method, one group received increased illumination, while the other did not. A preliminary finding was that when illumination was increased, the level of performance also increased. Surprisingly to the engineers, productivity also increased when the level of illumination was decreased almost to moonlight levels. One interpretation made of these findings was that the workers involved in the experiment enjoyed being the center of atten-

FIGURE 1–1. *INFLUENCES SUPPORTING THE HUMAN RELATIONS MOVEMENT.*

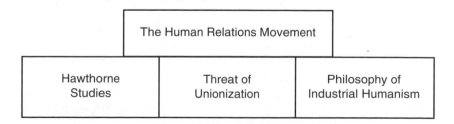

tion. In other words, they reacted positively because management cared about them. Such a phenomenon taking place in any work or research setting is now called the **Hawthorne effect**.[16]

As a result of these preliminary investigations, a team of researchers headed by Harvard professors Elton Mayo and Fritz J. Roethlisberger conducted a series of experiments extending over a six-year period. The conclusions they reached served as the foundations for later developments in the human relations approach to management. Business psychology has been equally influenced by these conclusions:

- Economic incentives are less important than generally believed in influencing workers to achieve high levels of output.
- Leadership practices and work-group pressures profoundly influence employee satisfaction and performance.
- Any factor influencing employee behavior is embedded in a social system. For example, to understand the impact of pay on performance, you have to understand the atmosphere that exists in the work group and how the leader approaches his or her job.

The Social Person Replaces the Economic Person. A major implication of the Hawthorne studies was that the old concept of an economic person motivated primarily by money had to be replaced by a more valid idea. The replacement concept was a social person, motivated by social needs, desiring rewarding on-the-job relationships, and more responsive to pressures from co-workers than to control by the boss.[17] Do you believe that workers are more concerned with social relationships than with money?

The Threat of Unionization

Labor union officials and their advocates contend that the benefits of unionization extend to many workers who themselves to not belong to unions. Managements in nonunion firms will often pay employees union wages in order to offset the potential advantages of unionization. A similar set of circumstances contributed to the growth of the human relations movement. Labor unions began to grow rapidly in the United States during the late 1930s. Many employers feared that the presence of a labor union would have negative consequences for their companies. Consequently, management looked aggressively for ways to stem the tide of unionization such as using human relations techniques to satisfy workers.[18]

The Philosophy of Industrial Humanism

Partly as a by-product of the Hawthorne studies, a new philosophy arose of human relations in the workplace. Elton Mayo was one of the two key figures in developing this philosophy of *industrial humanism.* He cautioned managers that emotional factors (such as a desire for recognition) were a more important contributor to productivity than physical and logical factors. Mayo argued vigorously that work should lead to personal satisfaction for employees.

Mary Parker Follett was another key figure in advancing the cause of industrial humanism. Her experience as a management consultant led her to believe that the key to increased productivity was to motivate employees, rather than simply ordering better job performance. The keys to both productivity and democracy, according to Follett, were cooperation, a spirit of unity, and a coordination of effort.[19]

We have described the growth of the human relations movement because it is so closely associated with many aspects of business psychology. Since many aspects of human relations border on common sense, it is important to bring this issue to the surface.

Theory X and Theory Y of Douglas McGregor

The importance of managing people through more effective methods of human relations was advanced by the writings of social psychologist Douglas McGregor. His famous position was that managers should challenge their assumptions about the nature of people. McGregor believed that too many managers assumed that people were lazy and indifferent toward work. He urged managers to be open to the possibility that under the right circumstances people are eager to perform well. If a supervisor accepts one of these extreme sets of beliefs about people, the supervisor will act differently toward them than if he or she believes the opposite. These famous assumptions that propelled the human relations movement forward are summarized as follows:

Theory X: Douglas McGregor's famous statement of the traditional management view that considers people as usually lazy and needing to be prodded by external rewards. A rigid and task-oriented approach to management.

Theory X assumptions
1. The average person dislikes work and therefore will avoid it if he or she can.
2. Because of this dislike of work, most people must be coerced, controlled, directed, or threatened with punishment to get them to put forth enough effort to achieve organizational goals.
3. The average employee prefers to be directed, wishes to shirk responsibility, has relatively little ambition, and highly values job security.

Theory Y: Douglas McGregor's famous statement of an alternative to traditional management thinking. It emphasizes that people seek to fulfill higher-level needs on the job, and that management must be flexible and human relations oriented.

Theory Y assumptions
1. The expenditure of physical and mental effort in work is as natural as play or rest.
2. External control and the threat of punishment are not the only means for bringing about effort toward reaching company objectives. Employees will exercise self-direction and self-control in the service of objectives to which they attach high valence.
3. Commitment to objectives is related to the rewards associated with their achievement.
4. The average person learns, under proper conditions, not only to accept but to seek responsibility.
5. Many employees have the capacity to exercise a high degree of imagination, ingenuity, and creativity in the solution of organizational problems.
6. Under the present conditions of industrial life, the intellectual potentialities of the average person are only partially utilized.[20]

How Do These Assumptions Influence a Manager's Actions? It is easy to visualize that a Theory X manager would treat employees quite differently than would a Theory Y manager. If a manager held Theory X assumptions about people, the manager would probably attempt to tightly control behavior. The manager might resort to frequent threats to keep workers in line and would make most decisions without consulting subordinates. A manager who held Theory Y beliefs would tend to grant subordinates more latitude and solicit their opinions before making important decisions. The Theory Y manager would also believe that subordinates are capable of governing their own behavior to a large extent.

The distinction between Theory X and Theory Y has sometimes been misinterpreted. McGregor was humanistic, but he did not mean to imply that being directive and demanding with employees is always the wrong tactic. Some people are under motivated and dislike work. In these instances, the manager has to behave sternly toward employees to motivate them. If you are a Theory Y manager, you size up your employees to understand their attitudes toward work.

Business Psychology and the Scientific Method

Much of the knowledge of business psychology is based on research following the scientific method. Experiments are conducted in both the laboratory (particularly with students) and in the field, or actual working

TABLE 1–3. *A RESEARCH DESIGN BASED ON THE SCIENTIFIC METHOD* ———

Procedures and Steps	Experimental Group	Control Group I	Control Group II
Assign women randomly to groups	Yes	Yes	Yes
Record current salary	Yes	Yes	Yes
Record current job level	Yes	Yes	Yes
Administer AT program	Yes	No	No
Conduct group discussions about careers	No	No	Yes
Allow time to pass without interacting with participants	Yes	Yes	Yes
Record salary level at one- and two-year periods	Yes	Yes	Yes
Record job level at one- and two-year periods	Yes	Yes	Yes

Field experiment: An attempt to apply experimental methods to real-life situations.

conditions. A **field experiment** is an attempt to apply experimental methods to real-life situations. Variables, or factors, can be controlled more readily in the laboratory. However, information obtained under actual working conditions is often more relevant.

Suppose a business psychologist were interested in studying the influence of assertiveness training (AT) on the career progress of women. Assertiveness training helps people to become more open in expressing their attitudes and feelings and in behaving more forcefully. One experimental method to investigate the impact of assertiveness training on career progress would be to measure how AT influences the salary growth and rate of promotion of women. A conventional research design, or scientific method, to study this problem is shown in Table 1-3.

The experimenter would make statistical comparisons of the salary progress and job-level progress of the experimental and control groups. The control group is used as a comparison. Members of the group receive no change in their routine. Assume that the women who underwent assertiveness training scored higher in salary and job level. It would be concluded tentatively that assertiveness training helped career progress more than did (1) no such training or (2) group discussions about career progress. Using the second control group helps to rule out the possibility that talking about improving one's career is as effective as assertiveness training.

Business Psychology and Common Sense ———————————

A student with several years of work experience commented after having attended the first few sessions of a class in business psychology, "Why should I study this field, since it's just common sense? You can't learn how to deal with people by reading a book." The attitudes expressed by this student are shared by many other people who study business psychology or human relations. However logical such an opinion might sound, common sense is not a fully adequate substitute for formal knowledge about business psychology for two major reasons.

Common Sense Is Uncommon

A small minority of people are truly effective in dealing with people or organizational forces. If **common sense** (meaning natural wisdom not requiring formal knowledge) were widely held, there would be fewer people problems on the job. The truth is that most organizations, even those that seem highly efficient to outsiders, are plagued with problems involving people. Five high-ranking executives from a business equipment company resigned within a one-year period. If common sense were so widespread, might not top management have prevented this chaotic situation?

Since few people have a high degree of common sense in matters dealing with people, a knowledge of business psychology (or a similar field such as human relations or organizational behavior) is necessary to improve on the chaos found in many business and not-for-profit organizations.

Business Psychology Sharpens and Refines Common Sense

People with an adequate degree of common sense often benefit more from a study of business psychology than do people who do not yet possess a well-developed degree of common sense. People who already have some experience tend to derive the most from specialized knowledge in most fields. They tend to build on strengths, which in general has a bigger payoff than overcoming weaknesses. A person with good common sense may already be making good use of his or her potential. With a few refinements, his or her ability to make good use of personal talents may multiply. One real estate broker is a case in point:

> Alison was doing well in her work, achieving above average commissions for people in her office. But she wasn't content with slightly better than average performance in the highly competitive real estate field. Alison wanted to make better use of her potential and in the process make more money. She applied some information she read in a business psychology text about the value of goal setting in raising performance. Alison then set a series of tough but sensible goals for herself. In the past she had "winged it" or "played it by ear." Primarily as a result of goal setting, Alison increased her sales performance and her commissions by 15 percent. By using realistic goal setting, Alison's effectiveness multiplied.

Summary of Key Points

❑ Business psychology is the application of organized knowledge about human behavior to improve personal satisfaction and productivity on the job. The general field of psychology is defined as the systematic study of behavior and all the factors that influence behavior. Among the many workers who practice business psychology, in addition to psychologists themselves; are human resource specialists and human relations trainers.

❑ Psychology has many different specialty areas, many of which overlap. The major specialties or sub fields include (1) clinical and counseling psychology, (2) educational psychology, (3) child and developmental psychology, (4) experimental psychology, (5) ergonomics, and (6) industrial and organizational psychology, and (7) health psychology.

❑ Another way of understanding psychology is to understand its major schools of thought or theoretical positions. Structuralism and functionalism are older schools that attempted to understand the workings of the mind. Behaviorism holds that behavior is shaped by its consequences (or the rewards and punishments we receive for our actions). Psychoanalysis views people as constantly torn between internal unconscious forces and external social forces. Cognitive psychology stresses the decision-making capabilities of people. Humanistic psychology focuses on the desirable qualities of people, such as love and creativity.

❑ The human relations movement was a concentrated effort to become more sensitive to the needs of employees, or to treat them in a more humanistic manner. The movement was supported by three different historic influences: the Hawthorne studies, the threat of unionization, and the philosophy of industrial humanism. One important conclusion reached by the Hawthorne studies was that showing concern for workers can increase their level of performance as much or more than improving physical working conditions. The Theory X and Theory Y of McGregor was an important force propelling the human relations movement forward.

❑ Many findings of business psychology are based on scientific methods, including experiments under actual working conditions. Business psychology is not simply common sense for two reasons: (1) common sense is uncommon, and (2) business psychology sharpens and refines common sense.

GUIDELINES FOR PERSONAL EFFECTIVENESS

1. Be careful about using common sense alone in solving problems you encounter at work. Most people do not have an abundance of common sense, and common sense is often wrong.
2. One important supplement to common sense and intuition in dealing with people is to use knowledge provided by business psychology. Specifically, you are likely to increase your personal effectiveness if you learn to use many of the concepts and techniques presented in this text.

Discussion Questions and Activities

1. What is the difference between the science and the practice of psychology?
2. How is business psychology different from psychology in general?
3. How might clinical psychology help an organization be more productive?
4. Ergonomics is more popular than ever. What developments in the workplace do you think have contributed to the importance of ergonomics?
5. Identify a piece of equipment for home or industrial use that you think is poorly designed for use by people. Explain the design flaw.
6. Explain why conscientiousness contributes to good job performance in so many occupations.
7. What relevance does health psychology have for employers?
8. What practical value do you see in techniques for measuring scenic beauty?

9. Explain how you could use the *law of effect* to get other people to do what you want them to do.

10. How might managers make use of the Hawthorne effect?

"We Can't Afford Business Psychology Around Here"

Tammy Phillips was happy to be hired by Bradbury Foods as a supervisor in the main processing plant. It was apparent to her that being a supervisor so soon after graduation would boost her career. After about a month on the job, Tammy began to make some critical observations about the company and its style of management.

To clarify her thoughts, Tammy requested a meeting with Adam Green, plant superintendent. The meeting between Tammy and Adam included a conversation of this nature:

ADAM: Have a seat, Tammy. It's nice to visit with one of our new supervisors. Particularly so when you didn't say you were facing an emergency that you and your boss couldn't handle.

TAMMY: (nervously) Mr. Green, I want to express my appreciation for your willingness to meet with me. You're right. I'm not facing an emergency. But I do wonder about something. That's what I came here to talk to you about.

ADAM: That's what I like to see—a woman who takes the initiative to ask questions about things that are bothering her.

TAMMY: To be truthful, I am happy here and I'm glad I joined Bradbury Foods. Yet I'm curious about one thing. I'm a business school graduate. A few of the courses I took emphasized using business psychology to manage people. It seems like the way to go if you want to keep employees productive and happy.

   Here at Bradbury it seems that nobody uses business psychology. I know that we're a successful company. However, some of the management practices seem out of keeping with the times. The managers make all the decisions. Everybody else listens and carries out the orders. Even professionals on the payroll have to punch time clocks. I've been here for almost two months and I haven't heard the term "business psychology" used once.

ADAM: Oh, I get your point. You're talking about using business psychology around here. I know all about that. The point you're missing, Tammy, is that business psychology is for the big profitable companies. That stuff works great when business is good and profit margins are high. But around here business is so-so, and profit margins in the food business are thinner than a potato chip. Maybe someday when we get very profitable we can start using business psychology. In the meantime, we've all got a job to do.

TAMMY: I appreciate your honest answer Mr. Green. Yet when I was in business school, I heard a different version of why companies use business psychology.

1. What is your evaluation of Adam's contention that business psychology is useful primarily when a firm is profitable?

2. To what extent should Tammy be discouraged?

3. What should Tammy do?

4. Based on your experiences, how representative of most managers is Adam's thinking?

Hard-working Sydney

Sydney Johnson felt good about his upcoming interview with the human resources director, Kathleen Corsini, at First Trust Company. He had already been through a screening interview, a second interview, and employment testing. Sydney assumed he would now receive a job offer to become a management trainee at First Trust. Sydney entered Corsini's office confidently.

"I'm glad to see you Sydney; have a seat," said Ms. Corsini. "I have some important things I want to review with you."

Sydney sat nervously on the edge of the chair, not quite sure what the bank human resources director was going to say next.

"Your credentials look generally quite good. We like your school record, and your references checked out quite well. Yet we do have one concern. You scored low on the psychological test measuring conscientiousness.

"Does that mean you aren't going to hire me?" asked Sydney.

"No, in fact we are going to make you a job offer. What it does mean, however, is that you will be hired as a temporary. If you prove to be a highly conscientious and honest employee, you will be made a permanent job offer in three months."

"I will certainly accept the temporary assignment and prove to you how conscientious I am. Yet I think the test is wrong. My teachers and my past employers have always said I was conscientious."

"I believe you Sydney, yet the test of conscientiousness has proved to be very accurate in the past. We hope that you can prove the test wrong in this instance."

1. Does First Trust Company have a right to offer Sydney a temporary job because he scores low on a test of conscientiousness?

2. Should Sydney have accepted the temporary assignment?

3. What should Sydney do to prove the conscientiousness test wrong?

A Business Psychology Exercise

The Well Employee

Individually or in a group, develop a list of 25 reasons why a well employee is an asset to a company. After the list is completed, sort out the list into about four different categories. Compare your list with those of other class members.

References

1. Stanley F. Schneider, "Psychology at a Crossroads," *American Psychologist*, April 1990, pp. 521–529.

2. A good general reference is Karen Huffman and Associates, *Psychology in Action*, 2nd ed. (New York: John Wiley, 1991).

3. J. Donald Millar, "Mental Health and the Workplace," *American Psychologist*, October 1990, p. 1165.

4. Peter Frieberg, "More Long-term Problems Seen for Abused Kids," *APA Monitor*, June 1991, p. 18.

5. Tina Adler, "Biofeedback May Quell Zero-gravity Sickness," *APA Monitor*, January 1990, p. 8.

6. Murray R. Barrick and Michael K. Mount, "The Big Five Personality Dimensions and Job Performance: A Meta-analysis," *Personnel Psychology*, Spring 1991, pp. 1–26.

7. Joseph D. Matarazzo, "The Status of Health Promotion in the Workplace," book review in *Contemporary Psychology*, January 1992, p. 7.

8. Stephen M. Weiss, Jonathan E. Fiedling, and Andrew Baum (eds.), *Health at Work* (Hillsdale, NJ: Erlbaum, 1991).

9. Terry C. Daniel, "Measuring the Quality of the Natural Environment: A Psychophysical Approach," *American Psychologist*, May 1990, pp. 633–637.

10. Special Issue: The History of American Psychology, *American Psychologist*, February 1992; Thomas Hardy Leahey, *A History of Psychology: Main Currents in Psychological Thought*, 2nd ed. (Englewood Cliffs, NJ: Prentice Hall, 1987).

11. Quoted in Jerome Kagan and Ernest Haveman, *Psychology: An Introduction*, 4th ed. (New York: Harcourt Brace Jovanovich, 1980), p. 30.

12. Alan E. Kazdin, *Behavior Modification in Applied Settings*, 4th ed. (Pacific Grove, CA: Brooks/Cole, 1989); B. F. Skinner, "Can Psychology Be a Science of Mind?" *American Psychologist*, November 1990, pp. 1206–1210.

13. Jay A. Conger, "The Dark Side of Leadership," *Organizational Dynamics*, Autumn 1990, pp. 44–55.

14. From the Articles of Association of the Association for Humanistic Psychology, 1980.

15. Robert Kreitner, *Management*, 5th ed. (Boston: Houghton Mifflin, 1992), pp. 51–52.

16. An original source of information about the Hawthorne studies is Elton Mayo, *The Human Problems of an Industrial Civilization* (New York: Viking Press, 1960).

17. James A. F. Stoner and R. Edward Freeman, *Management*, 4th ed. (Englewood Cliffs, NJ: Prentice Hall, 1989), p. 49.

18. Kreitner, *Management*, p. 50.

19. Kreitner, *Management*, p. 52.

20. Douglas McGregor, *The Human Side of Enterprise* (New York: McGraw-Hill, 1960), pp. 33–48.

Suggested Reading

Berk, Laura E. *Child Development*. Boston: Allyn & Bacon, 1989.

Bevan, William. "Contemporary Psychology: A Tour inside the Onion." *American Psychologist*, May 1991, pp. 475–483.

Bray, Douglas W., and Associates. *Working with Organizations and Their People*. New York: Guilford Publications, 1990.

Bugelski, B. R. *Psychology in the Common Cause*. Westport, CN: Praeger Publishers, 1989.

Corsini, Raymond J., and Wedding, Danny (eds.). *Current Psychotherapies*, 4th ed. Itasca, IL: Peacock, 1989.

——— (ed.) *Concise Encyclopedia of Psychology*. New York: Wiley, 1987.

Kimble, Gregory A., Wertheimer, Michael, and White, Charlotte (eds.). *Portraits of Pioneers in Psychology*. Washington, D.C.: American Psychological Association, 1991.

Special Issue: Organizational Psychology, *American Psychologist*. February, 1990.

Vischer, Jacqueline C., and Margulis, Stephen T. *Environmental Quality in Offices* New York: Van Nostrand Reinhold, 1989.

West, Jenny, and Spinks, Penny (eds.). *Clinical Psychology in Action: A Collection of Case Studies*. London: Wright/Butterworth Scientific, 1988.

Chapter 2

PERCEPTION, LEARNING, MOTIVATION, AND VALUES

Learning Objectives

After reading and studying this chapter and doing the exercises, you should be able to

1. Describe how perception influences job behavior.
2. Explain why our perceptions are often inaccurate.
3. Explain how people learn both simple skills and more complex activities.
4. Describe the need hierarchy and expectancy theories of motivation.
5. Illustrate several ways in which values and beliefs influence work behavior.

JOB TASKS RELATED TO THIS CHAPTER

In many instances, a knowledge of the basics of principles of human behavior can help you perform your job more effectively. Here are two possibilities. Imagine that you are asked to teach a complex skill to a co-worker. To get the job done properly and save time, you will want to choose the best teaching and learning method for that assignment. Another possibility is that you are trying to motivate somebody who reports to you, but he or she just won't get going. With the right explanation of human motivation, you should be able to diagnose the problem of low effort.

To understand and deal effectively with people in a job environment, you have to understand general principles about people that apply in a variety of situations. General principles help predict what will be the most probable behavior in a given situation. For instance, most people are conditioned to regard a flashing red light as a command to stop their forward movement completely or to proceed with extreme caution. When a flashing red light is placed over the entrance to an area within a factory, most people will sense that danger exists. Upon reading the sign under the flashing red light, "Protective gear must be worn in this area," most people will comply with the rule.

Despite the general success of conditioning people to learn the significance of a flashing red light, a few people will resist such conditioning. Some rebels who reject most authority will say to themselves, "I never pay attention to those kinds of things." A few other people will be so preoccupied with their own thoughts that they will have no particular response to the flashing red light. We therefore conclude that general principles do not work in every situation.

In this chapter we emphasize the general principles of four key aspects of behavior: perception, learning, motivation, and values. In Chapter 3 we emphasize how individual differences influence job behavior. We purposely use the term *emphasize*, because the distinction between gener-

al principles and individual differences is not always so clear-cut. How individual differences influence behavior often follows a general pattern. For example, people with good problem-solving ability (a source of individual differences) usually learn faster (a general principle).

Perception: The Science of First Impressions

The Nature of Perception

Most of us interpret what is going on in the world outside us as we perceive it—not as it really is. You do not usually experience a mass of colors, you experience a color photograph. You do not experience a thousand different vibrations in the air, you hear a favorite compact disc. When we answer a question, we answer in terms of our interpretation of what we hear.

An everyday happening, such as changes in air temperature, helps to illustrate the nature of human perception. Assume that you live in Vermont. A temperature of 52°F (11.1°C) would seem *warm* in January. The same temperature would seem *cold* in July. Our perception of temperature depends on many things going on inside our mind and body.

A standard psychology diagram is helpful in illustrating that "truth" depends on what we see as the "facts." Figure 2-1 was drawn by an anonymous artist to be intentionally ambiguous. Upon looking at this line drawing, many people will see an old woman with her chin tucked down, wearing a scarf around her head. Look at the drawing long enough, and you will see a young woman glancing away from you. Another curiosity about human perception is that the figure and the background switch back and forth in such a drawing.

FIGURE 2–1. *AN OLD WOMAN OR A YOUNG WOMAN? LOOK AGAIN.*

Perceptions on the job are very important. Many studies, for example, have investigated the consequences of employee job perceptions. The results show that employees who perceive their job to be challenging and interesting have high job satisfaction and motivation. In addition, these favorable perceptions lead to better job performance.[1]

In summary, **perception** deals with the various ways in which people interpret things in the external world and how they act on the basis of these perceptions. Those aspects of perception described here are (1) characteristics of the person influencing perception, (2) why perceptual problems exist, and (3) agreement about perceived events.

Characteristics of a Person That Influence Perception

Six major factors influence perception in general, as well as in a job situation. One or more of these factors may influence perception at a given time, and some of these factors are generally more influential than others. Perception is called a cognitive process since it relates to how we acquire knowledge.

Physiological and Anatomical Condition. A supervisor will have to speak loudly when giving direction to a hearing-impaired employee. Also, the supervisor must not use color-coded signals when dealing with a color-blind employee. A frail person might perceive lifting a 45-pound box to be a difficult task, while a physically strong person would perceive the task as pleasant exercise. Thus, basic body physiology and anatomy exert some influence on job perception and behavior.

Family Influences. A profound influence on the perception and behavior of most people is their family background, both present and past. A person reared in a family where parents have strong authority is likely to perceive a directive from a boss as a normal way of life. A person raised in a family where authority and power are shared with parents and children may have a more difficult time perceiving orders as legitimate. That particular employee may have a stronger need for freedom from supervision.

Cultural Influences. A person's cultural background influences his or her perception of stimuli on the job environment. People with strong work values, for example, tend to respond more positively to the opportunity to be productive. Much of the accomplishments of Japanese business and industry are believed to be attributed to the values held by Japanese managers and their employees. They believe strongly in commitment to the organization, perhaps more so than employees in many other countries.

Motives, Needs, and Goals. A major determinant of people's perception is their motivation at the time with respect to the object or experience to be perceived. A middle-aged manager who has just been laid off will take an active interest in a trade show exhibiting franchise opportunities (such as Subway Sandwiches). He may perceive purchasing a franchise as a good job opportunity. Previously, the same man ignored information about franchises.

Past Experiences. How a person perceives a stimulus today is heavily influenced by what happened when that stimulus was presented in the past. An older man may perceive a younger worker assigned to the department as a threat because in the past he was shown up by an energetic young worker. An employee who demands clarification on the smallest work rules, such as the limits to lunch hour, may be reacting to a past event: her last employer fired her for chronically returning late from lunch.

Personality Characteristics. How a person perceives an event is also influenced by his or her stable traits and characteristics, or personality. An optimistic, adventuresome individual might perceive a new boss as a welcome challenge, as another influential person to impress with his or her job competence. A pessimistic, cautious individual might perceive the same new boss as a threat, as another influential person who might think critically of his or her job performance.

Why Perceptual Problems Exist

Under ideal circumstances, people perceive information as it is intended to be communicated or as it exists in reality. For example, it is hoped that a union steward offered a promotion to a supervisory position will perceive it as an act of good faith on the part of management, not as a plot to get him or her out of the union. Both characteristics of the stimulus and the mental processes of people can lead to distorted perceptions.

Characteristics of the Stimulus. Perceptual problems are most likely to be encountered when the stimulus or cue to be perceived has an emotional meaning. Assume that Brian, an office supervisor, announces to his staff, "I would like you to meet Brenda. She's a temporary worker here to help us out this week." Announcing the presence of an office temporary could trigger several different perceptions. The specific perceptions would depend on many motives, needs, and the knowledge of department employees. Among the possible interpretations are these:

> "An office temporary? I wonder if this means the company is going to cut down the regular work force and use temporaries to help us through peak loads."
>
> "This seems to be a sure sign that business has picked up. The front office would never authorize extra help unless business were booming. Things look good for getting a decent raise this year."
>
> "I wonder if Brian has brought in a temporary worker to show us we had better get hustling or we could be replaced? I've heard a lot of these so-called temporaries usually wind up with a full-time job if they like the temporary assignment."

Mental Processes of People. The devices people use to deal with sensory information play a major role in creating perceptual problems. Several of these can also be classified as defensive behavior.

Denial. If the sensory information is particularly painful to us, we often deny to ourselves and others that the information even exists. A secretary was confronted with the fact that her use of the office copying machine to make copies of her shrimp creole recipe was against company regulations. She replied, "I never saw that regulation," even though she had word processed the company policy manual just six months previous to the confrontation. Similarly, many people use denial when reading the message from the surgeon general printed on each pack of U.S.-made cigarettes.

Stereotyping. A common method of simplifying the perceptual process is to evaluate an individual or thing on the basis of our perception of the group or class to which he, she, or it belongs. One production employee said he preferred not to accept a transfer to the quality-control department, giving as his reason, "I don't want to work for a nit picker."

Halo Effect. A tendency exists to color everything that we know about a person because of one recognizable favorable or unfavorable trait. When a company does not insist on the use of objective measures of performance, it is not uncommon for a supervisor to give a favorable performance rating to people who dress well or smile frequently. The fine appearance or warm smile of these people has created a halo around them. Employees often create a negative halo about a supervisor simply because he or she is gruff or stern in manner or speech.

Projection. Another shortcut in the perceptual process is to project our own faults onto others instead of making an objective appraisal of the situation. A manager might listen to a supervisor's request for one additional office assistant because of what the supervisor perceives as a heavy workload within her department. The manager might mutter, "Who does she think she is, trying to build an empire for herself?" In reality, the manager might be the empire builder and is projecting this undesirable characteristic onto her supervisor.

Selective Perception. People use this mechanism when they draw an unjustified conclusion from an unclear situation. A feedback memo from the boss might be interpreted as a letter of documentation to help the company build a case for firing the individual. Selective perception can have negative consequences when it leads to self-deception about potentially bad news:

> Jim Fixx, the man who made running an obsession, died of a heart attack while on his daily jog. Fixx knew he was at risk for heart disease: his father

had died of heart trouble at the age of 43. And for the few days before his death, Fixx had experienced fatigue and a tight pain in his throat while running—both possible signals of a heart condition. Yet several times shortly before his death he had declined to take a stress test, a test that would have revealed the seriousness of his heart condition.[2]

Perceptual Defense. Once we hold a perception of something or somebody, we tend to cling to that perception by making things that we see, hear, smell, or touch consistent with that belief. All the previous perceptual shortcuts are involved in perceptual defense. For example, if an employee is perceived to be a poor performer by his or her manager, it will take a long time for that employee to change how he or she is perceived. Some of his or her good performance might be attributed to luck or the efforts of other people.

Perceptual Congruence

Perceptual congruence:
The degree to which people perceive things the same way.

The discussion of perception so far has focused on perceptual errors. At times, most people in the organization perceive an event in the same way. **Perceptual congruence** refers to the degree to which people perceive things the same way.[3] High congruence generally implies valid perception, but people can also agree on a distorted perception. For example, many American, European, and Japanese automobile executives perceived South Korean automotive companies as nonserious competitors. The ascendance of the Hyundai demonstrated the inaccuracy of their high congruence.

Despite the reservation cited, high congruence generally leads to more positive consequences for the organization than low congruence. A case in point is that it is beneficial for managers and subordinates to perceive the subordinate's task in the same manner.

You can apply directly the information about perception. After your first attempt at interpreting an object or message, ask yourself, "How accurate is my perception? Which perceptual errors might have made my interpretation inaccurate?" If possible, ask another person for feedback to clarify whether your perception is accurate.

How People Learn

Learning:
A relatively permanent change in behavior based on practice or experience.

Much of learning takes place on the job simply because people spend such a large proportion of their lives in a job setting. **Learning** is a relatively permanent change in behavior based on practice or experience. A person does not learn how to grow physically, hear sounds, or see light. These are innate, inborn patterns of behavior. But a person does learn how to wire a circuit board, program a computer, cut hair, fix flat tires, or balance a checkbook. Unless new learning takes place, almost no person would be able to perform his or her job in a satisfactory manner.

Here we will describe several different methods of learning, beginning with classical conditioning, the simplest type. Then we will describe learning of an intermediate level of complexity, operant conditioning. Finally, we will describe the learning of complicated skills, called shaping and modeling. Complicated learning, particularly modeling, is called a cognitive process because it requires the learner to make a number of judgments and observations.[4]

Classical Conditioning: Learning Simple Habits and Reflexes

Classical conditioning: A basic form of learning in which a stimulus that usually brings forth a given response is repeatedly paired with a neutral stimulus. Eventually the neutral stimulus will bring forth the response when presented by itself.

In the late 1890s a Russian physiologist, Ivan Pavlov, conducted a long series of experiments about digestion. While studying a dog, he noticed that the dog salivated not only to the presence of food in the mouth, but at the sight of the food, the sound of the food trays, and even the footsteps of the experimenter The principles of **classical conditioning** stemming from his experiments help us to understand the most elementary type of learning—how people acquire uncomplicated habits and reflexes. Since most of work behavior involves more than reflexes and simple habits, classical conditioning itself is not of major consequence to the supervisor or individual worker. Yet its basic principles and concepts are included in more complicated forms of learning.

Classical conditioning works in this manner. Kurt takes an entry-level, unskilled job in a factory. His first day on the job a bell rings in his department at 11:34 A.M. Suddenly, every other worker stops working and opens a lunch box or heads out to the company cafeteria. Kurt says to himself, "The bell must mean it's time for lunch. By the third day on the job, Kurt develops stomach pangs and begins to salivate as soon as the bell rings. Prior to this job, Kurt was in the habit of eating lunch at 1 P.M. and did not begin to have stomach pangs until that time.

Looking at the essentials of classical conditioning, here is what happened to Kurt. Because the food naturally and automatically elicits (brings forth) stomach pangs and salivation, it is referred to as the *unconditioned stimulus* (UCS). Salivating to the food in Kurt's lunch box or in the cafeteria occurs automatically, without any learning. It is therefore called the *unconditioned response* (UCR). The sound of the department bell was originally neutral with respect to the salivary or hunger pang response, since it did not naturally elicit the UCR. Conditioning has taken place when the previously neutral stimulus (the department bell in Kurt's case) acquires the capacity to bring forth hunger pangs and salivation. The previously neutral stimulus is now called the *conditioned stimulus* (CS), and the hunger pangs and salivation to the sound of the bell are known as *conditioned response* (CR).

Two other conditioning concepts are also of major importance. If the department bell rings frequently when it is not time for lunch, Kurt's hunger pangs and salivation responses will gradually cease or extinguish. (An important exception is that time alone or the empty feeling in his stomach can also serve as a stimulus to Kurt.) As he goes through life, Kurt will learn not to salivate or experience hunger pangs to every bell that sounds like the one used in his department. At first he may generalize his learning by salivating to many different bells and experiencing hunger pangs in response to a variety of bells. After a while, he will discriminate and only make such responses to the bell in his department (or any other bell that signals food time).

Classical conditioning helps to explain such elementary job behaviors as how people learn to avoid being conked on the head by cranes and low hanging pipes. By classical conditioning, people also learn how to avoid being burned twice by a hot pipe or shocked twice by inserting a screwdriver into an electric outlet.

Operant Conditioning: Learning through the Consequences of Our Behavior

Operant conditioning is learning that takes place as a consequence of behavior. In other words, a person's actions are instrumental in determining whether or not learning takes place. Operant conditioning is the cornerstone of behaviorism, as reflected first in the work of John B. Watson and then later by B. F. Skinner. The process by which a person learns the maximum temperature for safe operation of a personal computer illustrates operant conditioning. (The person in question lacked air conditioning.) Several times on warm days disturbing things begin to happen, such as files disappearing and unusual symbols appearing on screen. In desperation one day, the person shuts off the computer and returns late at night when the room temperature is much cooler. Because the computer now operates correctly, from that time on the person operates the computer only when the temperature is 90°F (32°C) or lower. In this case the operant is waiting for the temperature to drop or turning a fan in the direction of the computer. The person adopted checking the temperature on warm days because that person received reinforcement for the initial effort—the computer performed properly when the room temperature was lowered.

Operant conditioning is also referred to as **instrumental learning** because the behavior of the individual is instrumental in bringing forth the reward, absence of a reward, or punishment. Similarly, operant conditioning can be called **trial and error learning.** If you happen to do something right (such as making the right movement while water skiing) and it leads to a reward (such as a smooth turn), you will continue to practice that response.

Learning versus Motivation. Motivation and learning are separate but closely related processes. You cannot motivate people to perform a task they do not know how to perform. Yet you can motivate a person to want to learn how to perform that task. Managers are frequently faced with the problems of (1) helping group members to learn, and (2) motivating them to repeat the learned behaviors.

Operant conditioning:
Learning that takes place as a consequence of behavior. Also known as behavior modification or reinforcement learning.

Instrumental learning:
A type of learning in which the behavior of the individual leads to a specific consequence.

Trial and error learning:
A type of learning in which the person tries different approaches until one works.

Positive and Negative Reinforcement. The distinction between positive and negative reinforcement is very important. Positive reinforcement adds something rewarding to a situation, such as praise or a gift certificate. **Positive reinforcement** is thus receiving a reward for making a desired response. Negative reinforcement is effective because it takes away something unpleasant from a situation. It is a form of *avoidance learning or motivation*. **Negative reinforcement** is thus being rewarded by being relieved of discomfort. The personal computer incident described above included negative reinforcement. Adjusting the room temperature took away the unpleasant situation of the computer malfunctioning.

Note carefully that negative reinforcement is not the same thing as punishment. Negative reinforcement is pleasant and therefore a reward. Punishment, by definition, is something unpleasant, unless the person involved likes to be punished. With masochists, the reward is to be punished!

Punishment. Being punished for your mistakes can be an important part of learning. **Punishment** can be regarded as the introduction of an

Positive reinforcement: Receiving a reward for making a desired response.

Negative reinforcement: Receiving a reward by being relieved of discomfort.

Punishment: The introduction of an unpleasant stimulus as a consequence of the person having done something wrong.

YOU'VE BEEN OUR TOP PRODUCER FOR TWO YEARS, JIMMY. IN APPRECIATION, WE'RE NOW MOVING YOU INTO A DEPARTMENT WITH AIR CONDITIONING.

unpleasant stimulus as a consequence of the learner having done something wrong (in the eyes of the person in control of the situation). Or the threat of punishment can be used instead of actually punishing people for the wrong response in a learning or motivational situation. Punishment assists the operant conditioning process because it weakens the particular response. You tend not to repeat a response because of its negative consequences. Yet some people continue to repeat behavior that leads to severe punishment, such as individuals who receive a series of speeding tickets. One behavioristic explanation of this occurrence is that the thrill from speeding is so rewarding that it overpowers the punishment of getting caught. (And one psychoanalytic explanation is that the speeder has a death wish!)

For punishment to facilitate operant conditioning, it must be of appropriate intensity. If the punishment is too mild, such as simply having to punch a delete key every time you make an input error with a computer, it will have a small impact on learning. However, if you wipe out a file with an input error, such as turning off the computer before you stored your file, you probably will not repeat that mistake very often. If the punishment is too severe, you may withdraw from the situation and strike back with aggressive behavior of your own. For instance, if you flunked a computer utilization course simply because you wiped out one file by accident, you might knock the terminal off the desk and never voluntarily use a computer again.

The purpose of punishment is to extinguish or eliminate a response. The same result can often be accomplished by simply ignoring the undesirable behavior. One way to stop the class clown from acting up is for the teacher and classmates to ignore that person's antics.

Primary and Secondary Reinforcers. Another important distinction in operant conditioning is between primary reinforcers and secondary reinforcers. A **primary reinforcer** is one that is rewarding by itself, without any association with other reinforcers. Food, water, air, and sex are primary reinforcers. A **secondary reinforcer** is one whose value must be learned through association with other reinforcers. It is referred to as secondary not because it is less important, but because it is learned. Money is a secondary reinforcer. Although money is paper or metal, through its association with food, clothing, shelter and other primary reinforcers, money becomes a powerful reward.

Schedules of Reinforcement. An important issue in operant conditioning (and in motivation) is how frequently to reward people when they make the correct response. So much experimentation has been conducted on this topic that some accurate guidelines are available. Two broad types of *schedules of reinforcement* are in use, continuous and intermittent.

Under a *continuous schedule*, behavior is reinforced each time it occurs, such as saying "good job" every time a bank teller comes out even at the end of a day. Continuous schedules usually result in the fastest learning, but the desired behavior quickly diminishes when the reinforcement stops. Under an *intermittent schedule*, the learner receives a reward after some instances of engaging in the desired behavior, but not after

Primary reinforcer:
A reinforcer that is rewarding by itself without association with other reinforcers, such as food.

Secondary reinforcer:
A reinforcer whose value must be learned through association with other reinforcers, such as money.

S_1	R_1	S_2	R_2
Memo from supervisor informing sales representative to prepare inventory report	Prepares monthly report	Receives praise from superior	A sense of achievement and satisfaction
Conditioned stimulus	Conditioned operant response	Reward or reinforcing stimulus	Unconditioned response

FIGURE 2–2. *EXAMPLE OF OPERANT CONDITIONING.*

each instance. Intermittent reinforcement is particularly effective in sustaining behavior, because the learner stays mentally alert and interested. At any point in time, the behavior might lead to the desired reward. Slot machines in gambling casinos operate on this principle.

In practice, learning through operant conditioning proceeds as a sequence of interrelated events, as illustrated in Figure 2-2.[5] A sales representative receives a memo from his supervisor to prepare a monthly report of customer inventories on the company's line of ski equipment. The memo is the conditioned stimulus. His conditioned operant response is to prepare the report. The operant response is referred to as conditioned because the sales representative did not spontaneously think of preparing the report. His boss generously praises the first report for its thoroughness and clarity. Such praise acts as a reward; the sales representative has received positive reinforcement. His unconditioned responses to this reward are feelings of achievement and self-satisfaction.

Modeling and Shaping: Learning Complicated Skills

When you acquire a complicated skill such as speaking in front of a group, photography, preparing a budget, or taking a store inventory, you learn much more than just a single stimulus–response relationship. You learn a large number of these relationships, and you also learn how to put them together in a cohesive, smooth-flowing pattern. Two important processes that help in learning complicated skills are modeling and shaping.

Modeling:
A form of learning in which a person learns a complex skill by watching another person perform that skill. Also called learning by imitation.

Modeling occurs when you learn a skill by observing another person perform the skill. Modeling is considered a form of *social learning* because it is learned in the presence of others. The process is classified as cognitive learning because it is a complex intellectual activity. Modeling or imitation often brings forth behaviors people did not previously seem to have in their repertoire. Many apprentices learn part of their trade by modeling an experienced craftsperson who practices the trade. Modeling is widely used in teaching sports through videotapes that give the viewer an opportunity to observe the skill being performed correctly. Although modeling is an effective way of learning, the learner must also have the proper capabilities and motivation.

Shaping of behavior (behavior shaping): The process of learning through approximations until the total skill is learned.

Shaping (or **behavior shaping**) is the process of learning through approximations until the total skill is learned. Behavior is shaped by the reinforcement of a series of small steps that build up the final or desired behavior. Shaping is an aspect of operating conditioning and therefore can be classified as noncognitive learning. At each successful step of the way, the learner receives some positive reinforcement. Unless the learner receives positive reinforcement at each step of the way, that person will probably not acquire the total skill. As the learner improves in his or her ability to perform the task, more skill is required to receive the reward. A woman might be shaped into an automobile mechanic through a series of small skills beginning with changing tires. She receives a series of rewards as she moves along the path from a garage helper to a mechanic who can diagnose an engine malfunction and repair the problem.

Among the forms of positive reinforcement she received along the way were approval for acquired skills, pay increments, and the feeling of pride as new minor skills were learned. The negative reinforcement she received was fewer bruised knuckles. When this series of small skills has been put together through a complicated pattern of response, the woman has been converted from a fledgling garage assistant to a full-fledged mechanic. Shaping is a concept that applies to both learning and motivation. It will therefore be reintroduced in Chapter 5.

Information about learning can help you when attempting to teach yourself or somebody else a skill or knowledge. Remember that learning is improved when rewards are present. Be aware that classical conditioning and operant conditioning work best for tasks that are not too complicated. Also, use learning by imitation for complicated skills. When the task is complex, it may be necessary to shape behavior by giving rewards for progress.

Two Key Explanations of Motivation

Understanding why people carry out certain actions and how to make them carry out actions that you want them to are both included in the study of motivation. The term *motivation*, in general, is used in two related senses. First, it is a trait or disposition that prompts people to attain certain goals. Second, this disposition to engage in actions must be prompted by an outside force (such as an encouraging boss or a possible reward).[6]

Motivation: Work motivation is essentially motivation directed toward the attainment of organizational goals.

Motivation, as it applies to the job, refers to why workers behave as they do and how much effort they will put into reaching organizational goals. Motivation is a major contributor to **productivity**—the amount of useful output achieved in comparison to the amount of input. Therefore, motivation has always been of interest to managers and business psychologists. Here we will describe two cognitive explanations of human motivation: (1) the classical theory of Abraham Maslow, and (2) a currently popular theory called expectancy theory. In Chapter 5 we will describe several specific methods of motivating other people and yourself.

Productivity: The amount of useful output achieved in comparison to the amount of input.

Maslow's Need Hierarchy

The most widely quoted explanation of human motivation was developed by psychologist Abraham Maslow.[7] He reasoned that human beings have an internal need pushing them toward self-actualization and personal superiority. However, before higher-level needs are activated, physiological needs must be satisfied. Physiological needs are therefore **prepotent** over all other needs. This means that when physiological needs, such as the need for water, are not met, they take over and direct behavior.

According to **Maslow's need hierarchy**, a poor person thinks of finding a job as a way of obtaining the necessities of life. Once these are obtained, that person may think of achieving recognition and self-fulfillment on the job. When a person is generally satisfied at one level, he or she looks for satisfaction at a higher level. As Maslow describes it, a person is a "perpetually wanting animal." Very few people are totally satisfied with their lot in life, even the rich and famous.

The Five Sets of Needs. Maslow arranged human needs into a five-rung hierarchy or ladder, as shown in Figure 2-3. Each of the first four rungs refers to a group of needs, not one need for each rung. The need for self-actualization is sometimes considered a solitary need. These groups of needs are described next in ascending order.

1. *Physiological needs* refer to bodily needs, such as the requirements for food, water, shelter, and sleep. In general, most jobs provide ample opportunity to satisfy physiological needs. Nevertheless, some people go to work hungry or in need of sleep. Until that person gets a satisfying meal or takes a nap, he or she will not be concerned about finding an outlet on the job for creative impulses.

2. *Safety needs* include actual physical safety, as well as a feeling of being safe from both physical and emotional injury. Many jobs frustrate a person's need

Prepotent:
In reference to needs, one that must be satisfied before higher needs are activated.

Maslow's need hierarchy:
A widely quoted and accepted theory of human motivation developed by Abraham Maslow, emphasizing that people strive to fulfill needs. These needs are arranged in a hierarchy of importance—physiological, safety, belongingness, esteem, and self-actualization. People tend to strive for satisfaction of needs at one level only after satisfaction has been achieved at the previous level.

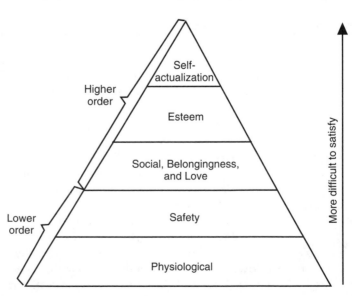

FIGURE 2–3. *MASLOW'S NEED HIERARCHY.*

for safety (police officer, taxi cab driver). Therefore, many people would be motivated by the prospects of a safe environment. People who do very unsafe things for a living (such as racing-car drivers and tightrope walkers) find thrills and recognition more important than safety. Many people are exceptions to Maslow's need hierarchy.

3. *Social needs* are essentially love or belonging needs. Unlike the two previous levels of needs, they center on a person's interaction with other people. Many people have a strong urge to be part of a group and to be accepted by that group. Peer acceptance is important in school and on the job. Many people are unhappy with their job unless they have the opportunity to work in close contact with others.

4. *Esteem needs* represent an individual's demands to be seen by others—and to appear to himself or herself—as a person of worth. Esteem needs are also called ego needs, pointing to the fact that people want to be seen as competent and capable. A job that is seen by yourself and others as being worthwhile provides a good opportunity to satisfy esteem needs.

Self-actualization: Making maximum use of the potential in oneself; like *self-fulfillment*.

5. *Self-actualization needs* are the highest level of needs and include the needs for self-fulfillment and personal development. True **self-actualization** is an ideal to strive for, rather than something that automatically stems from occupying a challenging position. A self-actualized person is somebody who has become what he or she is capable of becoming. Few of us reach all our potential, even when we are so motivated.

The Extent of Need Satisfaction. Not everybody can have as much need satisfaction as he or she wishes. Maslow estimated that the typical adult satisfies about 85 percent of physiological needs; 70 percent of safety and security needs; 50 percent of the belongingness, social, and love needs; 40 percent of the esteem need; and 10 percent of the self-actualization need.[8] There are substantial individual differences in the amount of need satisfaction. Some construction jobs, for example, frustrate both physiological and safety needs. Ordinarily, there is much more opportunity for approaching self-actualization when a person occupies a prominent position, such as a top executive or famous athlete. However, a person with low potential could approach self-actualization by occupying a lesser position.

The Need Hierarchy in Perspective. Maslow's need hierarchy is a convenient way of classifying needs and has spurred thousands of people to take the subject of human motivation more seriously. Its primary value has been the fact that it highlights the importance of human needs in a work setting. A practical application of the need hierarchy is that, when a manager wants to motivate a subordinate, he or she must offer the individual a reward that will satisfy an important need.

The Expectancy Theory of Motivation

Expectancy theory: An explanation of human motivation that centers around the idea that people will expend effort if they believe the effort will lead to a desired outcome.

How much effort you expend to accomplish something depends on how much you expect to receive in return, according to **expectancy theory.** The theory assumes that people are rational decision makers. Based on mental calculations, they choose from among the alternatives facing them the one that appears to have the biggest personal payoff at the time. A specific example is that most people will choose an occupation they think will bring them the rewards they are seeking, providing they believe they can overcome the hurdles necessary to get into that occupation. Here we will examine several basic aspects of this cognitive explanation of the why of employee behavior.[9]

Basic Components. The expectancy theory of motivation has three major components: expectancy, instrumentality, and valence. A summary of expectancy theory is presented in Figure 2-4.

Expectancy is the probability assigned by the individual that effort will lead to performing the task correctly. An important question rational people ask themselves before putting forth effort to accomplish a task is this: "If I put in all this work, will I really get the job done properly?" Each behavior is associated in the individual's mind with a certain expectancy or hunch of the probability of success. Expectancies range from 0 (no chance at all) to 1.0 (guaranteed success).

Expectancies thus influence whether you will even attempt to earn a reward. Self-confident people have high expectancies, and being well trained will increase your subjective hunch that you can perform the task.

Instrumentality is the probability assigned by the individual that performance will lead to certain outcomes or rewards. When people engage in a particular behavior, they do so with the intention of achieving a desired outcome or reward. Instrumentalities also range from 0 to 1.0. If you believe there is no chance of receiving the reward, the assigned probability is 0. If you believe the reward is certain to follow from performing correctly, the assigned probability is 1.0. For example, "I know for sure that if I show up for work every day this two-week period I will receive my paycheck."

Valence is the attractiveness of an outcome. In each work situation there are multiple outcomes, each with a valence of its own. For instance, if you make a substantial cost-saving suggestion for your employer, potential outcomes include cash award, good performance evaluation, promotion, recognition, and status. Most work situations include outcomes with both positive and negative valences. For instance, a promotion may have many positive outcomes, such as more pay and responsibility. Yet it may also have the negative outcomes of less time for family and friends and being envied by some people.

In the version of expectancy theory presented here, valences range from −100 to +100. A valence of +100 means that you strongly desire an outcome. A valence of −100 means that you are strongly motivated to avoid an outcome, such as being fired from a job. A valence of 0 means that you are indifferent toward an outcome. An outcome with a 0 valence is therefore of no use as a motivator.

Person will be motivated under these conditions

{
A. Expectancy is high: person believes he or she can perform the task.

B. Instrumentality is high: person believes that performance will lead to certain outcomes.

C. Valence is high: person highly values the outcomes.
}

FIGURE 2–4. *A BASIC VERSION OF EXPECTANCY THEORY.*

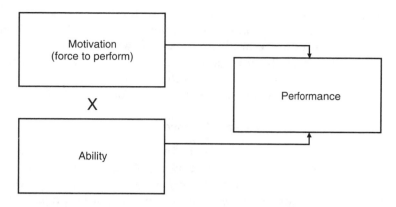

FIGURE 2–5. *HOW MOTIVATION AND ABILITY INFLUENCE PERFORMANCE.*

How Motivation and Ability Are Linked to Performance. Another important contribution of expectancy theory is that it helps to explain how motivation and ability are linked to job performance. As depicted in Figure 2-5, to achieve performance (actual job results), both motivation and ability must be present. If one is absent, no performance will be possible. It is important to recognize the contribution of ability in bringing about performance, because our culture tends to overdramatize the contribution of motivation to performance. Too many people uncritically accept the statement, "You can achieve anything you want if you try hard enough." In reality, a person also needs the proper education, ability, tools, and technology.

Motivation is often the key to attaining good results. Yet at other times, factors other than motivation come into play. For example, as a member of a work group you might want to be a high producer, but group pressures may keep you from producing much more work than the group standard.

One way to use the information presented about motivation is to diagnose why you or another person is not well-motivated in a given situation. Ask questions such as these: (1) Is there an opportunity to satisfy an important need? (2) Are the expectancies high enough? Does the person believe he or she can accomplish the task? (3) Are the instrumentalities high enough? Does the person believe that hard work will lead to a reward? (4) Is the reward meaningful to the person?

How Values and Beliefs Influence Job Behavior

Value:
The importance a person attaches to something, such as education, religion, or sports.

Another group of factors influencing how a person behaves on the job is that person's values and beliefs. A **value** refers to the importance a person attaches to something. Values are also tied in with enduring beliefs that one's mode of conduct is better than an opposite mode of conduct. If you believe that good interpersonal relations are the most important part of your life, your humanistic values are very strong. Similarly, you may think that people who are not highly concerned about interpersonal relations have poor values.

Values are closely tied in with **ethics**, or the moral choices a person makes. A person's values influence which kinds of behavior he or she believes are ethical. An executive who strongly values profits might not find it unethical to raise prices more than are needed to cover additional costs. Another executive who strongly values family life might suggest that the company invest money in an on-premises child care center.

How Values are Learned

A person is not born with a particular set of values. He or she learns them in the process of growing up, and many values are learned by the age of 4. One important way we acquire values is through observing others, or modeling. Often, a person who places a high value on reading was reared around people who valued reading. Models can be parents, teachers, friends, brothers and sisters, and even public figures.

If we identify with a particular person, the probability is high that we will develop some of his or her major values. One woman from a family of poor farmers moved to a large city and became a caseworker. Asked why she chose casework as an occupation, she explained:

> About once a year this kindly old woman would visit our farm to see how we were doing. She was sent by the county. My mother and father thought she was snooping into our business. Because of it, they almost hated her. I admired the kindness that she had for poor people like ourselves. I decided to do the same thing when I grew up.

Another major way in which values are learned is through the communication of attitudes. The attitudes that we hear expressed directly or indirectly help shape our values. Assume that using credit to purchase goods and services was talked about as an evil practice among your family and friends. You might therefore hold negative values about installment purchases.

Unstated, but implied, attitudes may also shape your values. If key people in your life showed no enthusiasm when you talked about spectator sports, you might not place such a high value on watching sports. If, on the other hand, your family and friends centered their lives around watching sports on television, you might develop similar values. (Or you might rebel against such a value because it interfered with other things that you might have wanted to do with your free time.)

Many key values are also learned through religion and thus become the basis for society's morals. A basic example is that all religions emphasize treating other people fairly and kindly. To "knife anybody in the back" is considered immoral both on and off the job.

Clarifying Your Values

The values that you develop early in life are directly related to the kind of person that you are now and will be and to the quality of the relationships that you form.[10] A recognition of this fact has led to hundreds of exercises designed to help people clarify and understand some of their own values. Almost all these value-clarification exercises ask you, in one

DIRECTIONS: Rank from 1 to 10 the importance of the following things to you as a person. The most important thing receives a rank of 1; the least important a rank of 10. Use the space next to "Other" if we have left out the most important thing in your life.

___ Having my own place to live
___ Having a child
___ Having an interesting job and career
___ Owning a car
___ Having good health
___ Being a religious person
___ Helping people less fortunate than myself
___ Loving and being loved by another person
___ Making an above-average income
___ Other _____

1. Discuss and compare your ranking of these things with the person next to you.
2. Perhaps your class, assisted by your instructor, can arrive at a class average on each of these things or values. How does your ranking compare to the class ranking?

FIGURE 2–6. *A METHOD OF EXAMINING YOUR PERSONAL VALUES.*

way or another, to compare the relative importances that you attach to different things. One such exercise is presented in Figure 2-6.

Values Lead to Goals

Values and goals are closely related. The values that people hold create needs that can be best satisfied by establishing certain goals. People who value status will also have needs for status. The needs, in turn, will lead to setting goals that mesh with one's values and satisfy the need for status. Here is an industrial example. Some organizations place a high value on cleanliness. These values are converted into goals of cleanliness, which often make a difference in performance. Consultant Tom Peters elaborates on this point:

> Milliken & Company, which I recently honored as one year's best managed company in America, will go to any length to entice a customer into the plant. "We never lose an order once we get a visitor into the plant," a senior manager boldly asserts. Many companies keep the customer as far away from the plant as possible, often on the flimsy pretense of protecting production secrets. The real reason is usually the plant's questionable appearance. It's impossible to earn credibility with high quality and timely delivery when your plant or distribution center looks—as many do—more like a garbage dump than a hospital operating room.[11]

The Mesh between Individual and Job Values

Under the best of circumstances, the values of employees mesh with those required of the job. When this state of congruence exists, job performance is likely to be higher. A national survey of managers investigated the fit between the values of managers and their organizations.[12] (One such mesh would be a highly ethical person working for a highly ethical firm.) A major finding was that managers who experienced a good fit were more successful and more likely to believe they could reach their career goals. They were also more confident about remaining with their present firm and more willing to work long hours.

When the demands made by the organization or a superior clash with the basic values of the individual, that person suffers from **person–role conflict**. He or she wants to obey orders, but does not want to perform an act that seems inconsistent with his or her values. A situation such as this might occur when an employee is asked to produce a product that he or she feels is unsafe or of no value to society. A sales associate in a retail furniture store resigned, giving her boss this explanation:

> I'm leaving because I don't think we're doing right by our customers. We sell mostly to poor people who can't get credit elsewhere. The furniture we sell them is shoddy, overpriced merchandise. But that's only half the problem. We're really in the finance business but we don't admit it to our customers. If people paid cash or obtained bank financing for the furniture they bought from us, we would make no profits. Most of our profits come from interest paid by our customers. I'm very disturbed about what we're doing to people.

Person–role conflict: A situation that occurs when the role that an organization assigns to an individual conflicts with his or her basic values.

BACK TO THE JOB TASK

In attempting to teach a complex skill to a co-worker, a good starting point is to use modeling. Reading a manual will certainly be helpful to your co-worker, but also offer him or her the opportunity to observe you perform the task correctly. Use expectancy theory to handle the motivational problem. In overview, check to see if the person is confident enough to perform the task. Ask if the person believes the reward will be forthcoming for doing the job. Also, see if the reward you are offering is the right one for this person.

Summary of Key Points

To understand and deal effectively with people on the job, you have to understand general principles about people that apply in many situations. Here we describe some general principles of four key aspects of behavior: perception, learning, motivation, and values.

❑ Perception, the organization of sensory information into meaningful experiences, influences job behavior. Perception is influenced by factors within the person, such as physiological and anatomical condition; family influences; cultural influences; motives, needs, and goals; past experiences; and personality characteristics.

❑ Perceptual problems stem from both a stimulus with an emotional meaning and the mental processes of people. These mental processes or shortcuts include denial, stereotyping, the halo effect, projection, selective perception, and perceptual defense.

❑ Perceptual congruence refers to the degree to which people perceive things the same way. High congruence generally leads to more positive consequences for the organization than low congruence.

❑ Classical conditioning is the most elementary form of learning. It occurs when a previously neutral stimulus is associated with a natural (unconditioned) stimulus.

Eventually, the neutral stimulus brings forth the unconditioned response. For example, a factory whistle blown just prior to the lunch break induces employees to salivate and experience hunger pangs.

❏ Operant conditioning (or instrumental learning) occurs when a person's spontaneous actions are rewarded or punished, which results in an increase or a decrease in the behavior. Much of human learning occurs through operant conditioning. Complicated sets of skills are frequently learned by modeling or imitation. Such skill repertoires are also learned by behavior shaping, a form of learning in which approximations to the final skill are rewarded. Eventually, only the final skill is rewarded.

❏ Theories of motivation attempt to explain why people behave as they do. Maslow's need hierarchy is widely used to explain work motivation. It contends that people have an internal need pushing them on toward self-actualization. However, needs are arranged into a five-step ladder. Before higher-level needs are activated, certain lower-level needs must be satisfied. In ascending order, the groups of needs are physiological, safety, social, esteem, and self-actualization (such as self-fulfillment).

❏ Expectancy theory is a currently popular explanation of work motivation. It assumes that people are decision makers who choose among alternatives by selecting the one that appears to have the biggest personal payoff at the time. The expectancy model has three major components: expectancies (can I do the job?); instrumentality (will getting the job done lead to a reward?); and valence (how valuable is the reward?). Motivation is calculated by multiplying the numerical values for all three. Expectancy theory also points out that both motivation and ability are necessary for performance.

❏ Values are learned in the process of growing up. Two methods of measuring values are described in the chapter. Values and beliefs influence job behavior in several ways: (1) People's values lead to goals; (2) work assignments may mesh with values, leading to high performance; (3) work assignments may conflict with personal values and cause stress and inaction.

GUIDELINES FOR PERSONAL EFFECTIVENESS

1. An important strategy for helping others to learn is to use operant conditioning, with an emphasis on positive reinforcement. The most basic approach is to give the learner encouragement when he or she makes the right response. At the same time, it is helpful to tactfully point out mistakes to the learner.

2. A generally effective way of helping people to learn complicated skills is for you to serve as an effective model. At the same time, make sure that the learner has the opportunity to observe you.

3. A generally effective strategy for motivating people is to identify the needs that they are trying to satisfy and then to give them an opportunity to satisfy those needs. An important way of improving this process is to apply expectancy theory. Do what you can to increase the expectancies, instrumentalities, and valences of the people you are trying to motivate. Specifically, you might:

   a. Help them to improve their skills so that their expectancies increase.

   b. Explain how performance will lead to a reward so that their instrumentalities will increase.

   c. Increase the attractiveness of the rewards in order to increase their valences.

1. Give an example of a problem to which general principles of human behavior might be applied.

2. How might a person's family background influence his or her perception of the importance of earning a high income?

3. Describe two different perceptions people might have about a boss? What might be the reason for these differences in perception?

4. Describe some of the principles of learning involved when a person learns to run a word-processing program.

5. How do your psychological needs influence the amount of effort you put forth on the job or in school?

6. Give an example of a person you think is self-actualized. Explain your reasoning.

7. Identify two rewards that have a very strong positive valence for most people getting started in their careers.

8. Using expectancy theory, explain whether you will strive for an A in this course.

9. Give an example of how a person's sense of ethics influences his or her behavior on the job.

10. Ask an experienced supervisor or manager how he or she trains people. Relate his or her answer to learning theory.

A BUSINESS PSYCHOLOGY PROBLEM

The Police Misspellers

Sergeant Maureen O'Brien grabbed a crime investigation report from her desk and placed it in front of her boss, Lieutenant Jose Lugo. Pointing to the report, she said to Lugo, "See all those circled words? They indicate spelling errors. Officer Gaudion made twenty-eight spelling errors in one investigation report. I wish I could say that Gaudion is an exception. The truth is that he is far from the worst speller in our platoon. I wish I could get the officers in my platoon to make fewer spelling errors on their daily reports."

With a concerned expression on his face, Lugo commented, "What steps have you taken so far to improve the spelling of your officers?"

"I've done about what I think is feasible. As you know, there is no money in the budget for purchasing word processors. The electronic spell checkers on those rigs would be a big help. I've made sure that our department has given each officer a pocket dictionary. I've also given them clear instructions to use the dictionary when needed. We've even supplied phonetic dictionaries in case an officer has no idea how to spell a word. Another step I've taken is to schedule a training program in report writing for all platoon members. The sessions will be held this spring. I'm hoping that will cure the problem of so many misspellings."

"Maureen, I'm not so sure the report writing workshop will do the trick. Your officers are adults. If they haven't learned to be good spellers yet, I doubt a one-day workshop will cure their problems. Your real problem might be that your officers have no desire to be better spellers. Have you thought about that?"

"I have given some thought to the matter. In fact, I've told each officer with a spelling problem that I want very much for him or her to commit fewer spelling errors on police reports."

"Maureen, between now and the next time we talk, I want you to develop a better plan for motivating your officers to make fewer spelling mistakes," concluded Jose.

1. To what extent do you think the frequent spelling errors made by the officers reflect a motivational problem?
2. What approach would you recommend Sergeant O'Brien to take to motivate her platoon to become better spellers?

A BUSINESS PSYCHOLOGY PROBLEM

The Socially Conscious Restaurant

You work as a restaurant manager for a large chain of quality restaurants. The owner says to you one day, "Let's do something good for society. We'll find 25 people recently released from prison, or on parole, who are likely to have a difficult time finding employment. We'll put them to work in one of our restaurants. You'll be the manager in this new restaurant. Your only employees will be those ex-convicts."

You ask, "Which ex-cons shall we hire?" Your boss answers, "The first 25 to show up for the job. First come, first hired. I don't care about sex, age, race, appearance, size, schooling, or reasons for conviction. Just put them on the payroll, train them, and run a first-class, profitable restaurant."

1. What will be your biggest challenge in this assignment?
2. What cautions should you exercise in using general learning principles in training your employees?
3. Is this any way to run a restaurant? Explain.

A BUSINESS PSYCHOLOGY ROLE PLAY

The Laid-back Ex-con

The scenario in the case just presented serves as the background material for conducting this role play. Role players project themselves into the role to be played, using the information presented as a general guideline. Much like extemporaneous acting, the role player has to assume the role of the person he or she represents.

In this role play, one person plays the role of the profit-minded manager who is trying to deal with an employee who has a casual attitude toward work. In fact, the worker is seen frequently sitting on the loading dock, smoking a cigarette. Another student plays the role of an ex-convict hired for this position. Your attitude is that you have experienced enough discipline during incarceration. You now value freedom and independence and want to set your own work pace. You wonder why your boss wants to see you today. The basic role play consists of the interchange between restaurant manager and employee.

References

1. Ricky W. Griffin, "Effects of Work Redesign on Employee Perceptions, Attitudes, and Behaviors: A Long-term Investigation," *Academy of Management Journal,* June 1991, p. 426.
2. Daniel Goleman, "Who Are You Kidding? *Psychology Today,* August 1989, p. 24.
3. John B. Miner, *Organizational Behavior: Performance and Productivity* (New York: Random House, 1988), p. 101.

4. Barry Schwartz, *Psychology of Learning and Behavior,* 3rd ed. (New York: Norton, 1989).

5. James L. Gibson, John M. Ivancevich, and James H. Donnelly, Jr., *Organizational Behavior, Structure, Processes*, 6th ed. (Homewood, IL: Irwin, 1988), p. 142.

6. Richard S. Lazarus, "Progress on a Cognitive–Motivational–Relational Theory of Emotion," *American Psychologist*, August 1991, p. 820.

7. A current synthesis of Maslow's ideas is Abrahman H. Maslow, *Motivation and Personality*, 3rd ed. (New York: Harper & Row, 1987).

8. Gibson, Ivancevich, and Donnelly, *Organizations: Behavior, Structure, Processes,* p. 111.

9. Donald A. Nadler and Edward E. Lawler, "Motivation: A Diagnostic Approach." In John R. Hackman, Edward E. Lawler, & Lyman W. Porter (eds.), *Perspectives on Behavior in Organizations* (New York: McGraw-Hill, 1977), pp. 26–34; Joseph W. Harder, "Equity Theory versus Expectancy Theory: The Case of Major League Baseball Free Agents," *Journal of Applied Psychology*, June, 1991, p. 458.

10. David C. McClelland, "How Motives, Skills, and Values Determine What People Do," *American Psychologist*, July 1985, p. 815

11. Tom Peters, "Cleanliness Is Next to Profitability," syndicated column, February 8, 1987.

12. Barry Z. Posner, James M. Kouzes, and Warren H. Schmidt, "Shared Values Make a Difference: An Emprical Test of Corporate Culture," *Human Resource Management*, 1985, pp. 293–309.

Suggested Reading

Evans, Phil. *Motivation and Emotion.* London: Routledge, 1989.

Hall, John F. *Learning and Memory,* 2nd ed. Boston: Allyn & Bacon, 1989.

Houston, John P. *Fundamentals of Learning and Memory*, 4th ed. New York: Harcourt Brace Jovanovich, 1991.

Lazarus, Richard S. "Cognition and Motivation in Emotion." *American Psychologist,* April 1991, pp. 352–367.

Ormond, Jeanne Ellis. *Human Learning: Principles, Theories, and Educational Applications.* Columbus, OH: Merrill, 1990.

Reed, Edward S. *James J. Gibson and the Psychology of Perception.* New Haven, CT: Yale University Press, 1988.

Sidowski, Joseph B. (ed.) *Conditioning, Cognition, and Methodology: Contemporary Issues in Experimental Psychology.* Lanham, MD: University Press of America, 1989.

Stadden, J. E. R., and Ettinger, R. H. *Learning: An Introduction to the Principles of Adaptive Behavior.* New York: Harcourt Brace Jovanovich, 1989.

Wakefield, Jerome C. "The Concept of Mental Disorder: On the Boundary between Biological Facts and Social Values." *American Psychologist*, March 1992, pp. 373–388.

Weiner, Bernard. "Metaphors in Motivation and Attribution." *American Psychologist*, September 1991, pp. 921–930.

Chapter 3

INDIVIDUAL DIFFERENCES AND WORK PERFORMANCE

Learning Objectives

After reading and studying this chapter and doing the exercises, you should be able to

1. Understand how individual differences affect job performance.
2. Describe the nature of intelligence and how to make effective use of your mental ability.
3. List some skills that account for individual differences in job performance.
4. Identify some major personality traits and describe how they relate to job performance.
5. Describe how sex roles can lead to individual differences in performance.
6. Recognize how cultural factors can lead to individual differences in job performance.

JOB TASKS RELATED TO THIS CHAPTER

Understanding individual differences can help you to perform jobs better that involve being responsible for the results of other people's work. If your job includes helping to select job candidates or team members, a knowledge of individual differences is essential. A broader reason for understanding individual differences is to promote better communication and understanding of each other. This will enable us to work together more productively and respond more humanly.

Business psychology began with the awareness that individual differences in personal characteristics influence how people will perform on the job. A study of individual differences is as vital today as it was at the turn of the century. A person's basic traits and characteristics have a profound influence on job behavior. The situation in which a person works is also important, but a person often influences the situation. Job behavior is always the combined influence of both the person and the situation.

How individual differences influence job performance is illustrated by the mysterious finding that a small percentage of the work force in many fields contributes to most of the extremely good or bad performances. Marketing specialists find consistently that 20 percent of the sales force contributes 80 percent of the sales. A handful of the people who submit suggestions win the big awards. On the negative side, a small proportion of the work force creates turnover, absenteeism, accidents, and formal complaints.

In this chapter we examine some aspects of human nature that have a direct bearing on how well people perform in their jobs and careers. Among the topics discussed will be mental ability, personality, sex-role differences, and culturally based individual differences. First, however, we look at the general idea of how individual differences affect work behavior.

Implications of Individual Differences on the Job

It is well known that individual differences exist and that organizations must pay attention to these differences to stay competitive. Individual differences moderate or influence how people respond to many aspects of their job. A company might install new lighting, considered to be badly needed by 80 percent of the work force. Twenty percent of the employees would probably grumble that the work area is too brightly lit. Six illustrative ways in which individual differences have important implications for working with people are noted here.

1. People differ in productivity. A thorough analysis of individual differences illustrates the magnitude of human variation in job performance. The researchers pulled together studies involving over 10,000 workers. They found that, as jobs become more complex, individual differences have a bigger impact on work output.[1] An outstanding industrial sales representative might produce 100 times as much as a mediocre representative. In contrast, an outstanding data-entry technician might produce only twice as much as a mediocre one. (An industrial sales job is more complex than the work of a data-entry technician.)

2. People differ in ability and talent. Factors such as ambition, desire, self-confidence, a favorable appearance, and the ability to play office politics are not sufficient for getting the job done. People also need the right abilities and talents to perform any job well. Ability is thus a major source of individual differences that influence job performance.

3. People differ in the importance that they attach to interesting work. People with a love of work are looking for stimulating, exciting, or enriched jobs. About one-third of the work force is not looking for stimulating, exciting work. They prefer jobs that require a minimum of mental involvement and responsibility. Some people prefer to daydream on the job and find their self-ful-fillment through recreational and family life. For such individuals (the opposite of work addicts), a repetitive job is the most pleasing.

4. People differ in the style of leadership that they prefer and need. Many individuals like as much freedom as possible on the job and can function well under such leadership. Other individuals want to be supervised closely by their manager. People also vary with respect to the amount of supervision that they require. In general, less competent, less motivated, and less experienced workers need more supervision. One of the biggest headaches facing a manager is to supervise people who need close supervision but who resent it when it is administered.

5. People differ in their need for contact with other people. As a by-prod-uct of their personality traits and vocational interests, people vary widely in how much people contact they need on the job to keep them satisfied. Some people can work alone all day and remain highly productive. Others become restless unless they are engaged in business or social conversation with another employ-ee. Sometimes a business luncheon is scheduled more out of a manager's need for social contact than out of a need for discussing job problems.

6. People differ in their amount of commitment and loyalty to the firm. Many employees are so committed to their employers that they act as if they were part owners of the firm. As a consequence, committed and loyal employees are very concerned about producing quality goods and services. And they main-tain very good records of attendance and punctuality, which helps reduce the cost of doing business. At the other extreme, some employees feel very little commitment or loyalty toward their employer. They feel no pangs of guilt when they produce scrap or when they miss work for trivial reasons.

Mental Ability

Mental ability, or intelligence, is one of the major differences among peo-ple that affects job performance. As common sense would suggest, there is an advantage to being bright in performing a complex job. If a job is dra-matically uncomplex, such as stuffing envelopes seven hours per day, being not so bright would be an advantage. The term intelligence, as it is used here, refers to problem-solving ability. Intelligence quotient, or IQ, is in reality just one measure of intelligence, just as classifying a person as having superior intelligence is a measure of intelligence. Because the par-ticular test score called IQ is so widely known, many people regard IQ as synonymous with intelligence.

Here we describe two important aspects of mental ability: the com-ponents of intelligence and practical intelligence.

Components of Intelligence

g (general) factor: A major component of intelligence that contributes to problem-solving ability.

s (special) factors: Specific components of intelligence that contribute to problem-solving ability.

Intelligence is not a pure characteristic. The preponderance of evi-dence suggests that it consists of a **g (general) factor** along with **s (spe-cial) factors** that contribute to problem-solving ability.[2] The g factor helps explain why some people seem to perform so well in so many different mental tasks. Although the specific components of intelligence are debatable, at a minimum it is composed of verbal and numerical abilities.

One widely used employment test, The Employee Aptitude Survey, is based on the idea that intelligence is composed of many components or factors. It is worth noting these components, because they are a source of individual differences related to job performance. Seven of the components measured by the survey relate closely to mental ability, as follows:

1. *Verbal comprehension*. The ability to use words in thinking and in both spoken and written communication. Good verbal skills are an asset in a wide variety of occupations, including sales representatives, executives, and advertising specialists.

2. *Numerical ability*. The ability to handle numbers, engage in mathematical analysis, and do arithmetic calculations. Among the occupations calling for good numerical comprehension are financial analysis, computer programming, tax advising, and engineering.

3. *Space visualization*. The ability to visualize forms in space and manipulate objects mentally, particularly in three dimensions. This ability is a critical requirement for drafting technicians, engineers, and other technical personnel. Space visualization is also an important component of mechanical aptitude.

4. *Numerical reasoning*. The ability to analyze logical relationships and discover principles underlying such relationships. Numerical reasoning is basically the same process as *inductive reasoning*—making valid generalizations from specific instances, or discovering principles. Most higher-level occupations and some medium-level ones require inductive reasoning. For example, an insurance claims adjuster uses inductive reasoning when she assembles facts to reach conclusions about the probable cause of a fire.

5. *Verbal reasoning*. The ability to analyze verbally stated facts and to make valid judgments on the basis of the logical implications of such facts. Also, the ability to know when a conclusion is unjustified on the basis of available facts. The ability to organize, evaluate, and utilize information is required for administrative and technical decision making.

6. *Word fluency*. The ability to use words quickly and easily, without an emphasis on verbal comprehension. This ability is called for in positions requiring extensive oral or written expression, such as technical writer and tour guide.

7. *Symbolic reasoning*. The ability to manipulate abstract symbols mentally and to make judgments and decisions that are logically sound. Symbolic reasoning also involves the ability to evaluate whether adequate information is available to make definite decisions. This ability is required in high-level positions, particularly in those classified as technical or scientific.

Tests of mental (or cognitive) ability have proved useful in understanding the nature of intelligence, as described above. The same tests have also proved valuable in predicting job performance of many different occupations.[3] Despite their contribution to selecting people for jobs, mental ability tests have received considerable criticism. Many people believe that mental ability tests are biased against people with limited opportunity for good education. Another criticism is that people whose cultural values are opposed to learning will perform poorly on these tests.

Practical Intelligence

Many people, including psychologists, are concerned that the traditional way of understanding intelligence as described above inadequately describes mental ability. An unfortunate implication of intelligence testing is that intelligence is largely the ability to perform tasks related to scholastic work Thus a person who scored very high on an intelligence test could follow complicated diagrams but might not be "street smart."

Practical intelligence: The concept that intelligence is composed of several aspects, including academic intelligence and skills, creativity, and adaptation to the environment.

To overcome the limited idea that intelligence involves mostly the ability to solve abstract problems, the concept of **practical intelligence** has been proposed. It means that intelligence is composed of several varieties or aspects. Practical intelligence therefore does not exclude the type of intelligence measured by intelligence tests, but it also includes other types of intelligence. The message is that intelligence is exhibited in mental activities of various kinds and that the study of intelligence must entail the study of these mental activities.

The theory underlying practical intelligence is that there are three different subtypes of intelligence. One subtype is *componential:* the traditional type of intelligence needed for solving difficult problems. The second subtype is *experiential:* the type of intelligence required for imagination and combining different things in creative ways. The third subtype is *contextual:* the type of intelligence required for adaptation to your environment or changing your environment to suit your needs. Contextual intelligence is necessary to be street smart.[4]

The idea of practical intelligence helps explain why a person who has a difficult time getting through school can still be a successful businessperson, politician, or athlete. Practical intelligence seems to incorporate the ideas of common sense and wisdom. One reservation about practical intelligence is the implication that people who are highly intelligent in the traditional sense are not practical thinkers. In truth, most executives and other high-level workers score quite well on tests of mental ability.

How To Make Good Use of Your Mental Ability

In Chapter 2 we explained *how* people learned. Here we will look at key principles of learning and a specific study method that will help you make good use of your intelligence in school and on the job. Both the general principles and the specific study method relate to remembering what you have learned.

Principles of Learning

The principles of learning described in the following paragraphs are based on hundreds of experiments and are widely used in school systems and training programs and by serious students.

1. Concentrate. Not much learning takes place unless you concentrate carefully on what you are learning. Concentration is basically thinking. Many failures in school are due more to poor concentration than to low mental ability. Concentration improves your ability to do both mental and physical tasks.

Walter Pauk notes that one enemy of concentration is indecision: "Indecision about when to study and which subject to study first is not only a great time-waster, but also a sure way to create a negative attitude toward studying."[5] The same idea has relevance to the job. If you spend time wondering which job task (if any) you should do for the balance of the day, you will probably do a poor job.

2. Use motivated interest. You learn best when you are interested in the problem facing you. If your answer is, "This subject bores me," or "So far I don't know what interests me," this principle still applies. In any situation, you will probably be able to find something of interest to you. Look for some relationship between the information at hand and your personal welfare. For instance, as you read this chapter you might say to yourself, "Where do I fit in? What is my mental makeup?" and so on.

3. Use selectivity. William James, the famous philosopher and psychologist, said, "The essence of genius is to know what to overlook." You cannot learn everything brought to your attention in school or on the job. Be selective. Try to determine which is the most important. Your course instructor will often alert you to the most important information in a course. Your boss will often alert you to the most important parts of your job.

4. Intention to remember. I have played cards with people who seem brilliant in terms of their ability to remember which cards in the deck have been played. One of the best of these players told me her secret of knowing which cards have been played: "As each card is turned up, just look at it carefully and try to remember it." With practice, most people can apply this simple method to their schoolwork or jobs. Remember the names of important people in your company. It will impress other people.

5. Use meaningful organization. When you have to learn large batches of information, the best method is to organize it into chunks that make sense to you. For instance, in studying portions of this book, you might make such arbitrary groupings as "Ideas I can use for self-development" versus "Ideas that can help me deal with other people."

6. Rely on the magic number seven. Most people can remember up to about seven categories of most things. It is probably not coincidental that we have seven days of the week, seven primary colors, seven deadly sins, and seven notes on the musical scale. When you are trying to learn new information, arrange it into seven large chunks. New bits of information can be added on to these seven chunks. An example: If you are forced to give a speech without using notes, organize it into seven major parts.

7. Acquire the right background. The more you know about a subject, the easier it is to acquire new information. Knowledge gives you certain "hooks" on which to hang new information. If your hobby is studying antique automobiles, it will be easy for you to learn the names and identifying information about the next generation of automobiles.

8. Use rehearsal. The leading principle for remembering things is rehearsal. If you want to retain information for just a minute or two, the most effective device is **rote rehearsal.** You recite the information to yourself silently or out loud, several times. By using rote rehearsal constantly, information can be stored in short-term memory almost indefinitely, providing there is an intention to learn.

For longer-term retention, it is usually necessary to use **elaborative rehearsal**—relating something to information we already know. Suppose you first encounter the term *hydroponic* in relation to growing plants. You decide to store the term in long-term memory because it seems important (it refers to growing

Rote rehearsal:
In learning, reciting the information to yourself silently or out loud, several times.

Elaborative rehearsal:
Relating something to information we already know.

plants with water but no soil). You therefore make the association of hydroponic to water because *hydro* refers to water.

9. Use distributed practice. An effective way of learning something is a little bit at a time. Most people retain more, and thus make better use of their intelligence, when they break up learning with frequent rest periods. (Some students overdo this principle and use too many rest periods.) Assume that you are trying to learn some difficult company procedures. It would be best to study these for about 15 minutes at a time and then do something on the job that is relatively easy for you. The principle of distributed practice helps to explain why cramming for exams is inferior to studying over a longer period of time.

10. Let things jell in your mind. Your long-term memory is likely to improve if you allow one set of facts to jell in your mind before attempting to learn another set of facts. Psychologists call this principle *consolidation.* It helps to explain the value of reviewing material immediately after your first exposure to it.

The SQ3R Method

SQ3R method:
A method of studying written material: survey, question, read, recite, and review.

Charles G. Morris says that the most effective method for studying written material is the **SQ3R method,** known for the first letters of its five steps.[6]

Step 1: Survey. Before starting to read, glance quickly at the learning objectives or chapter outline, the headings of various sections in the chapter, and the chapter summary. This provides an overview and makes it easier for you to organize and interrelate the material in the chapter.

Step 2: Question. Also before you begin to read, translate each heading in the chapter into questions about the text to follow. Questioning helps you to get actively involved in the reading and forces you to attempt to understand what you read. It also helps you to relate the new material to things you already know. A question you might have asked in this chapter is "What are the different components of intelligence?" Writing out these questions is helpful.

Step 3: Read. Now read the first section in the chapter. Look for answers to your questions. If you find information not related to your questions, make up questions to cover the new material.

Step 4: Recite. After you have completed reading the section, close the text and recite answers to your questions and any other major points you can remember from memory. Jot down your answers in outline form. Repeat steps 2, 3, and 4 for each section of the chapter.

Step 5: Review. After completing the chapter, review your notes and recite your questions and answers from memory. Relate the material to familiar things in your life.

The SQ3R method forces you to have a dialogue with the text. This interaction makes material more interesting and meaningful and improves the chances of recollection. Organizing the material and relating it to what you know is important for transferring the material into long-term memory. Although the SQ3R method is time consuming in the short range, it saves time in the long run because studying for exams goes more quickly.

Learning Styles

Learning style:
The fact that people learn best in different ways.

Another strategy for making the best use of your mental ability is to recognize your **learning style,** the fact that people learn best in different ways. Some people, for example, acquire new material best through passive learning. Such people quickly acquire information through studying texts, manuals, and magazine articles. They can juggle images in their mind as they read about abstract concepts such as the law of gravity, cultural diversity, or customer service. Others learn better by doing rather than studying, such as those who learn best about customer service by dealing with customers in many situations.

Another key dimension of learning styles is whether you learn best working alone or cooperatively, such as in study groups. Learning by oneself allows for more intense concentration, and you can proceed at your own pace. Learning in groups and through classroom discussion allows you to exchange viewpoints and perspectives. Another advantage of cooperative learning is that it is more likely to lead to changes in behavior. Assume your instructor holds group discussions about individual differences based on culture. You are more likely to respond to such differences on the job than if you only studied these differences by yourself.

Skills and Job Performance

Mental ability can be considered a general skill that contributes to individual differences in performance. Many other skills are also important for accomplishing work. Skills are also the basis for a career. The greater the number of useful skills a person possesses, the greater the chance of securing employment and job advancement. Skills are also another major source of individual differences on the job. People vary widely in such skills as mathematics, keyboarding, selling, and providing customer service.

Figure 3-1 presents a useful way of categorizing skills developed by Julie Griffin Levitt.[7] As you study these skills areas and specific skills, take the opportunity to note your areas of strength. Making these notations may help you appreciate your capabilities and identify areas where training is needed.

FIGURE 3–1. *SKILLS PROFILE.*

Directions: Review the following skills areas and specific skills. In the space provided, write down each one you believe is a strong skill for you. You can also add a specific skill that was not included in the skill area listed at the left.

Skill Area	Specific Skills	A Strong Skill for Me
Communication	writing, speaking, knowledge of foreign language, telephone skills, persuasiveness, listening	_____
Creative	originating ideas, thinking up novel solutions	_____

Interpersonal relations	ability to get along well with others, being a team player, diplomacy, conflict resolution, understanding others	_____
Management	ability to lead, organize, plan, motivate others, make decisions, manage time	_____
Manual and mechanical	mechanically inclined, build, operate, repair, assemble, install, drive vehicles	_____
Mathematics	math skills, computers, analyzing data, budgeting, using statistical techniques	_____
Office	keyboarding, filing, business math, bookkeeping, spread sheets, word processing, database management, record keeping	_____
Sales	persuading others, negotiation, promoting, dressing fashionably	_____
Scientific	investigating, researching, compiling, systematizing, diagnosing, evaluating	_____
Service of customers	serving customers, handling complaints, dealing with difficult people	_____
Service of patients	nurturing, diagnosing, treating, guiding, counseling, consoling, dealing with emergencies	_____
Other skill area:_____	_____	_____

Source: Abridged and adapted from Julie Griffin Levitt, *Your Career: How to Make It Happen,* 2nd ed. (Cincinnati, OH: South-Western Publishing Co., 1990), pp. 19–21.

Most failures on the job are not attributed to a person's intelligence or technical skills, but to personality characteristics. The subject of personality must therefore be given some consideration in any serious study of business psychology.

A recent analysis of many studies concluded that personality characteristics are related to job performance. The relationship is the strongest when a personality factor is related to a person's job description.[8] For example, the trait of extroversion is a reliable predictor of success in sales.

In the popular sense, the concept of personality is used to evaluate an individual's manner of relating to people. An effective way to insult another person is to say, "Don't ask me to work with him. He has a horrible personality." A psychologist uses the term **personality** not to make value judgments, but to describe those persistent and enduring *behavior patterns* of an individual that tend to be expressed in a wide variety of situations. Your personality is what makes you unique as an individual. Your walk, your talk, your appearance, your speech, and your inner values and conflicts all contribute to your personality.

> **Personality:**
> An individual's characteristic way of behaving, feeling, and thinking.

Our discussion of personality emphasizes how individual differences in personality influence job performance and behavior. Toward this end, we will describe personality traits and needs, the Big Five personality factors, other key personality traits, and how personality type influences occupational choice.

Personality Traits and Needs

Among the many ways to study individual differences in personality is to observe how people differ on important traits. Many years ago, Henry Murray developed a list of human needs that led to personality traits.[9] A need is an internal striving or urge to do something. Thus, if you have a strong **need** to dominate people, a noticeable personality trait of yours will be dominance.

> **Need:**
> An internal striving or urge to do something.

Personality traits and needs influence people to act in certain ways. The dominant person will gravitate toward leadership positions or frequently get into arguments with others. Table 3-1 describes nine important personality needs. To the right of each need is a sampling of the type of behavior that corresponds to that particular need. Each need results in a propensity to behave in a particular way. The needs we have chosen to include in this list are those most likely to influence you in your work and personal life.

The Big Five Personality Factors

Many psychologists believe that the basic structure of human personality is represented by five broad factors: I. Extroversion, II. Agreeableness, III. Conscientiousness, IV. Emotional Stability, and V. Openness to

TABLE 3–1. *How Personality Traits Based on Needs Influence Behavior* _____

Personality Trait Based on Particular Need	Description	Example of Type of Behavior Shown by Person Who Has Strong Need
Achievement	To accomplish something difficult; to win over others office; sets up own business	Tries hard in competitive sports; runs for political
Affiliation	To seek out close relationships with others; to be a loyal friend	Joins many social groups; tries to be "one of the gang" at work
Aggression	To attack, injure, or punish others; to overcome people into fights with people off the job	Uses hard-sell tactics as a sales representative; gets
Autonomy	To act independently and be free of constraints able when closely super	Takes job as insurance claims adjuster; feel uncomfortvised
Deference	To admire and support a superior or other person in authority; to conform to custom	Prefers to call older people by title (Mister, Professor, Doctor); makes excellent soldier and respectful subordinate
Dominance	To influence others toward your way of thinking often by forceful methods	Often takes over in meetings; volunteers to be the leader; good at the hard sell
Nurturance	To help, support, take care of weak and needy people	Works well with disadvantaged people; often overprotective of children or subordinates
Order	To put things in order; to achieve arrangement, balance, neatness, and precision	Keeps work area neat; writes careful reports; keeps good files; works well with computer
Power	Strong need to control other people and resources; wants fame and recognition	Orients life around rising to the top; likes to look and act powerful through choice of clothing and car

Experience. People develop these factors partially from inborn tendencies and partially from being raised in a particular environment. For example, a person might have a natural tendency to be agreeable. Growing up in an environment in which agreeableness was encouraged would help the person become even more agreeable.

The Big Five personality factors were mentioned in passing in Chapter 1 and will be described more fully here.[10] The Big Five are very useful for business psychology because all factors influence job performance.

The interpretations and meanings of the Big Five personality factors

Most failures on the job are attributed to personality characteristics.

provide useful information because they can help you to pinpoint important areas for personal development. Although these characteristics are partially inherited, most people can improve their standing on them.

I. *Extraversion*. Traits associated with this personality factor include being social, gregarious, assertive, talkative, and active. An outgoing person is often described as extroverted, while a shy person is described as introverted. (Note that extraversion and intraversion in everyday language are spelled extroversion and introversion.)

II. *Emotional stability*. Traits associated with this factor include being anxious, depressed, angry, embarrassed, emotional, and worried. A person with low emotional stability is often referred to as neurotic or emotionally unstable.

III. *Agreeableness*. An agreeable person is friendly and cooperative. Traits associated with the agreeableness factor include being courteous, flexible, trusting, good natured, cooperative, forgiving, soft hearted, and tolerant.

IV. *Conscientiousness*. A variety of meanings has been attached to this personality factor, but it generally implies being dependable. Traits associated this factor include being careful, thorough, responsible, organized, and planful. Other related traits include being hard working, achievement oriented, and persevering.

V. *Openness to experience*. People who score high on the openness to experience factor have well-developed intellects. Traits commonly associated with this factor include being imaginative, cultured, curious, original, broad minded, intelligent, and artistically sensitive.

Depending on the job, any one of these personality factors can be very important for success. As described earlier, conscientiousness relates to job performance for many different occupations. Another important research finding is that extroversion is associated with success for managers and sales representatives. The explanation, of course, is that managers and salespeople are required to interact extensively with people.[11]

Other Key Personality Traits

Key personality traits in addition to those described so far include beliefs about fate being under the individual's control, honesty, craving for excitement, and positive or negative mood tone. All four traits can influence job performance.

Locus of Control. Some people believe they are responsible for the rewards and punishments they receive, while others blame what happens to them on luck and fate. People with an **internal locus of control** are those who believe that fate is pretty much under their control. People with an **external locus of control** believe that external forces control their fate.

In general, internals perform better in technical professional, and managerial jobs. For instance, a sales representative with an internal locus of control would feel personally responsible for making a quota even if general business conditions were poor. Externals tend to perform better when the work requires compliance and conformity and when pay is not tied to performance This is true because the person with an external locus of control is interested in controlling how many rewards he or she receives.[12]

Honesty and Dishonesty. An important personality dimension for many jobs is degree of honesty. Dishonest employees engage in such behaviors as stealing merchandise and cash, selling trade secrets, trading stocks on inside information, cheating on time cards, sneaking off from work during regular working hours, falsifying production records, and blaming others for their mistakes. Employee dishonesty is such a problem that several industries—particularly banking, securities, and retailing—use **honesty testing.**[13]

Both polygraphs (lie detectors) and paper and pencil tests are used to measure employee honesty. Polygraphs are very controversial and are banned in most places. Federal legislation has been passed that limits the use of honesty tests to screening employees in highly sensitive occupations such as those dealing with national security. Paper and pencil honesty tests ask people questions that directly or indirectly measure their tendency not to tell the truth. A direct question would be, "Should a person be fired for stealing $5 worth of merchandise from the employer?" (A dishonest person would answer "No.") An indirect question would be, "Do you read the editorial page of the newspaper every day?" (Only a dishonest person would answer "Yes." Almost nobody can claim a perfect record in this regard.)

Internal locus of control:
The belief that fate is pretty much under one's control.

External locus of control:
A belief that external forces control one's fate.

Honesty testing:
A method of determining if job applicants and present employees are telling the truth.

Thrill Seeking. Our discussion of personality so far does not explain why some people crave constant excitement on the job and are even willing to risk their lives to achieve thrills. The answer may lie in the **Type T personality,** an individual driven to a life of constant stimulation and risk taking.

A strong craving for thrills may have some positive consequences for the organization, including willingness to perform such dangerous feats as setting explosives, capping an oil well, controlling a radiation leak, and introducing a product in a highly competitive environment. The Type T personality also creates some problems for employers. These individuals may be involved in a disproportionate number of accidents, drive while intoxicated just for the added excitement and risk, and take risks with company property or money. One of the people caught in a check-kiting scheme at a large brokerage firm appeared to be a Type T personality: he talked about enjoying the thrill of seeing how far his firm could go without getting caught.

A person who uses thrill seeking for constructive purposes is a *T-plus*. The counterpart who gets into trouble with thrill seeking is a *T-minus*. T-plus people can be quite productive because they are often creative.[14] The famous dealmaker Donald Trump appears to be a T-plus person. Can you think of another T-plus person?

Type T personality:
An individual driven to a life of constant stimulation and risk taking.

Affective tone:
A person's
predisposition to be
positive or negative.

Affective Tone. Another personality trait with implications for job behavior and performance is **affective tone**, a person's predisposition to be positive or negative. A person with a positive affective tone is positive and agreeable in most situations. In contrast, a person with a negative affective tone has a negative outlook in most situations. Positive and negative affectivity therefore relate quite closely to the agreeableness factor described earlier.

The relationship of affective tone to work behavior was studied among 300 salespeople. It was found that, when group members had above average negative affectivity, the group took on a negative tone. Furthermore, negative affectivity interfered with good customer service and led to increased absenteeism.[15]

Personality Types and Occupational Choice

Individual differences in personality can also influence our choice of occupation. According to the theory of John Holland, people tend to choose a career to match their personalities.[16] Furthermore, if people are able to find a career matching their personalities, they are likely to be happier on the job and stay longer with their work.[17] An elementary example is that, if your personality type is classified as *artistic,* you will be happier as a photographer than as an accountant. Table 3-2 lists and defines Holland's personality types and a sampling of occupations associated with each type.

TABLE 3–2. *Holland's Personality Types and Corresponding Sample Occupations*

Personality Type	Description	Sample Occupations
Realistic	Likes work requiring physical strength; tends to avoid interpersonal and verbal types of work; prefers task problems that are concrete rather than abstract	Engineer, carpenter, architect, forester, machinist, printer, agriculturist
Intellectual	Prefers tasks involving the intellectual processes such as thinking and comprehension; tends to avoid work activities that require domination and persuasion of people or close interpersonal contact; tends to be more introverted than extroverted	Physician, home economist, paramedic, anthropologist, veterinarian, biologist, medical radiographer
Social	Exhibits skill in interpersonal relations and chooses work situations requiring interpersonal relationships; prefers work activities that help other people such as teaching or therapeutic service; tends to avoid high-stress, intellectual problem-solving work activities	Minister, teacher, psychologist, counselor, dental assistant, nurse, social worker

TABLE 3–2. *(CONTINUED)*

Artistic	Tends to dislike structure, to be more introverted than extroverted, and to exhibit a high degree of femininity; expresses feelings and may act on impulse	Actor or actress, musician, photographer, artist, journalist, cosmetologist
Enterprising	Desires power and status and likes work activities that involve manipulating and dominating others; tends to have good verbal skills economist	Attorney, salesperson, politician, manager, administrator, real estate agent, public relations worker,
Conventional	Prefers structure and order with rules and regulations governing the work activities; exhibits much self-control; identifies with power and status	Secretary, accountant, business teacher, clerk, data-processing worker, financial advisor

Source: Synthesis of Holland's work prepared by A. Christine Parham, *Psychology: Studying the Behavior of People,* 2nd ed. (Cincinnati: South-Western Publishing Co., 1988), pp. 370–371. See also John L. Holland, *Self-Directed Search™*, 1985 revision (Odessa, FL: Psychological Assessment Resources, Inc.)

One important criticism of this theory of personality type and occupational choice is that it is too simplistic. Some occupations require a combination of two or more personality types. For example, an accountant who sets up his or her own firm would need to be both "Enterprising" and "Conventional."

Sex Roles and Individual Differences

A topic of debate and continuing interest is whether men and women differ in aspects of behavior related to job performance. An undisputed fact is that males and females are biologically and genetically different, as evidenced by male cells possessing X–Y chromosomes, and female cells the X–X chromosome. A much disputed issue, however, is whether males and females show consistent differences in behavior. In other words, do men and women occupy different **sex roles**? A sex role is a pattern of behavior attributed to being male or female. Also, if sex-role differences do exist, are they attributed mostly to heredity or to learning?

Sex role:
A pattern of behavior attributed to being male or female.

The tentative answer offered here is that sex-role differences are more pronounced in personal than in work behavior. Although some sex-role differences can be found on the job, they are not consistent. Furthermore, the sex-role differences that do exist can be attributed more to learning than to heredity (or nurture rather than nature).[18] Here we will summarize some of the evidence about sex-role differences.

Influence Tactics. Several findings that do not fit common sense have emerged in the study of differences in influence tactics between men and women. A study of 225 supervisors and 224 subordinates examined a variety of influence tactics, including assertiveness and making bargains with subordinates. Men and women chose about the same influence tactics. Also, the tactics chosen did not differ whether the person being influenced was a man or woman.[19]

A more recent survey investigated the self-reports of influence tactics chosen by 176 men and 161 women in mostly higher level jobs. As in the previous study, many similarities were found in the influence tactics chosen by both sexes. Important differences were also noted. The findings contradicted some popular beliefs about how men and women go about gaining advantage. Men were significantly more likely than women to perceive themselves as relying on charm, manipulation, and personal appearance to achieve results and gain advantage.[20]

A follow-up study found that men make far more use of joking and kidding to influence others, according to the perceptions of both men and women. Women were more likely to use compliments.[21]

Cooperation versus Competition. Males tend to be more competitive and less cooperative than females. These differences were particularly pronounced before women entered the work force. Recent observations suggest that career women tend to compete more than cooperate with other career women. In fact, they are sometimes prone to engage in devious tactics to block the success of women co-workers.[22]

Creativity. Few differences in creativity are found among boys and girls, and this pattern continues through adulthood.[23] In some situations women are more creative than men because women tend to be more emotionally expressive (a stimulant to creativity).

Stress. Consistent evidence exists that men and women show different stress symptoms. The most pronounced difference is that women tend to exhibit symptoms of low emotional well-being to a greater extent than men. For instance, women are more likely to get depressed and also report higher rates of emotional discomfort. Men are more prone to serious and incapacitating illness, such as heart disease and cirrhosis of the liver, in response to stress. Be aware, however, that some researchers do not believe that these sex differences exist.[24]

Absenteeism. Mothers of young children tend to be absent from work more frequently than male or female workers without children. However, mothers of grown children probably do not have higher absenteeism rates than do male workers. Furthermore, when adequate child-care facilities are available, these differences in male and female absenteeism rates shrink. Absenteeism differences between men and women thus reflect differences in the roles of men and women rather than in their characters.[25]

The culture in which a person is reared influences his or her work behavior, as we noted in Chapter 2 in relation to perception. Although culture may be regarded as a group rather than an individual factor, it functions as a source of individual differences. People from different cultural backgrounds may respond quite differently to the same stimulus. For example, workers from large urban areas tend to be much more skeptical than people from rural areas. This is one reason that programs designed to offer employees more responsible work tend to fare better in nonurban areas.

The internationalization of workplaces has made an awareness of culturally based individual differences more important than ever. For example, a substantial number of sales associates positions in New York City and Los Angeles are held by people from the Far and Middle East. A retail store manager raised in the United States, who worked in New York City, would therefore have to be sensitive to cultural differences. For example, a sales associate from India might regard the manager as abdicating responsibility if the manager asked the associate for her opinion about how to handle a customer problem.

Another major cultural difference in job behavior occurs between Americans and Canadians and Asians. Americans and Canadians are predisposed by culture to welcome confrontation and conflict in the workplace, while Asians tend to avoid confrontation and conflict. This cultural difference helps to explain why Asians often smile even when they strongly disagree with the other person's position on a work issue.[26]

The general principle for handling cultural differences is to be sensitive to their existence. Be aware that culturally based differences in work behavior exist and be ready to make some adjustments to these differences. A specific example: an employee raised in Taiwan will be more predisposed to accept a manager's authority than an employee from Sweden. Figure 3-2 illustrates mistakes, or *cultural bloopers*, to avoid should you be on assignment in various countries. Some of the same ideas would apply if you were dealing with people from a foreign land in your native land. We will return to the topic of the internationalization of the workplace and cultural diversity at several places in the text.

FIGURE 3–2. *CULTURAL MISTAKES TO AVOID IN SELECTED COUNTRIES.*

- Insisting on getting down to business quickly in most countries outside the United States. (In most countries, building a social relationship precedes closing a deal.)
- Licking postage stamps in India. (Indians regard this practice as offensive.)
- Telling Indians you prefer not to eat with your hands. (If the Indians are not using cutlery when eating, they expect their guest to do likewise.)
- Misinterpreting "We'll consider it" as "Maybe" when spoken by a Japanese. (Japanese negotiators mean "No" when they say "We'll consider it.")
- Thinking that a business person from England is unenthusiastic when he or she says, "Not too bad at all." (English people understate positive emotion.)
- Giving small gifts to Chinese people when conducting business. (Chinese are offended by these gifts.)

- Not giving small gifts to Japanese when conducting business. (Japanese are offended by not receiving these gifts.)
- Appearing in shirt sleeves at a business meeting in West Germany. (Germans believe that a person is not exercising proper authority when he or she appears at a meeting in shirt sleeves.)
- Being overly rank conscious in Scandinavian countries. (Scandinavians pay relatively little attention to a person's rung on the organizational ladder.)
- Appearing perturbed when somebody shows up late for a meeting in most countries outside the United States. (Time is much less valued outside the United States.)
- Pressuring an Asian job applicant or employee to brag about his or her accomplishments. (Boasting about his or her professional achievements makes Asians feel self-conscious. They prefer to let the record speak for itself.)
- Greeting a French customer or other business contact for the first time in a French-speaking country and saying "Glad to meet you." (French is a polite language. It is preferable to say, "Glad to meet you, sir (or madame or miss).")

Source: Several of these errors are based on Sandra Thiederman, "Overcoming Cultural and Language Barriers," *Personnel Journal,* December 1988, pp. 34–40; and Jon Pepper, "U.S. Exec Often Doesn't Fit in at Japanese Firm," Gannett News Service Story, March 29, 1990.

BACK TO THE JOB TASKS

If you have full or partial responsibility for selecting job candidates or team members, search for individual differences that could affect their productivity. The human resources department may have a screening process that includes interviewing and testing. Combine that information with your own impressions. Above all, do not assume that, because two candidates have similar education and experience, they will perform equally well. Speak to other people who have worked with the candidate, and ask questions about how productive the person was in the past.

Use your understanding of individual differences to work more productively and with better understanding of others. For example, if a team member learns better in groups than alone, contribute to his or her opportunity for cooperative learning.

Summary of Key Points

❑ Business psychology began with the awareness that individual differences in personal characteristics influence how people will perform on the job. A study of individual differences is still of major importance today. This chapter concentrates on dimensions of human behavior that have a big impact on job performance, except for the discussion of sex roles.

❑ The implications of individual differences on the job include the fact that people differ in these ways: (1) how productive they are on the job, (2) ability and talent, (3) the importance they attach to interesting work, (4) the style of leadership they prefer and need, (5) their need for people contact, and (6) their degree of loyalty and commitment.

❑ Mental ability, or intelligence, is related to performance in a wide variety of medium- and higher-level occupations. Intelligence consists of a general factor and specific factors. The components of intelligence described here are verbal comprehension, numerical ability, space visualization, numerical reasoning (including inductive reasoning), verbal reasoning, word fluency, and symbolic reasoning. The idea of practical intelligence means that intelligence is exhibited in mental activities of various kinds and that the study of intelligence must entail the study of these mental activities.

❏ One way of making good use of your mental abilities is to practice good habits of learning and remembering. Among the more important habits described here are (1) learn to concentrate, (2) use motivated interest, (3) try to remember, and (4) use rote and elaborative rehearsal. An effective method for studying written material is the SQ3R method (survey, question, read, recite, and review). Understanding your learning style, such as cooperative learning, also helps improve mental ability.

❏ Many other skills in addition to mental ability are important for job performance and career building. Among these important skills are communication, creative, interpersonal relations, sales, scientific, and customer service.

❏ Personality refers to those persistent and enduring behavior patterns of an individual that are expressed in a wide variety of situations. Individual differences in personality influence job performance and behavior. Certain needs of people, such as the need to be dominant over others, are often transformed into personality traits. Such traits then influence them to behave in certain ways, such as trying to control others.

❏ Many psychologists believe that the basic structure of personality is represented by five broad factors: extroversion, agreeableness, conscientiousness, emotional stability, and openness to experience. All these factors are partly inherited and partly learned.

❏ Four other important personality traits of consequence for job performance are locus of control, honesty and dishonesty, thrill seeking, and affective tone. Your personality type can be influential in determining the occupation you will find satisfying, as summarized in Table 3-2.

❏ Sex roles also have some influence on job behavior. Although sex-role differences can be found on the job, they are not highly consistent. One reasonably consistent sex difference is that men are more likely to suffer severe consequences from job stress.

❏ The culture in which a person is reared influences work behavior. Although culture is a group rather than an individual factor, it functions as a source of individual differences. People from different cultures may respond quite differently to the same stimulus.

GUIDELINES FOR PERSONAL EFFECTIVENESS

1. If you are an exceptionally good problem solver (a very bright person), it should help you to perform well in most high-level jobs. However, it is important to recognize that most problems in business call for concrete solutions rather than abstract discussion.

2. Dimensions of personality may have as big an impact on your job performance as your skills. It is therefore important to attempt to modify your traits to match job requirements. For example, if you rely too much on external circumstances to control your performance, you might have to develop a stronger take-charge attitude.

3. Your main concern with your basic intelligence should be in making the best use of your capability. The suggestions in this chapter about improving your retention of information should be helpful in this regard. Information presented in other chapters in this book should also help you to make the best use of your intelligence (particularly, information about communication skills and work habits).

4. As the work force continues to become more internationalized, it will help your career to become more sensitive to cultural differences. A sensitivity to such differences will help you to develop good working relationships with people from different cultures. Significant differences in culture can be found from one country to another and within a large country such as the United States.

Discussion Questions and Activities

1. Assume that an organization pays extra careful attention to individual differences in ability. How might this make the organization less democratic?

2. What is the underlying reason that people who do well in school and score high on mental ability tests generally tend to do better in their careers?

3. Do you know anybody who seems to be very intelligent, yet is not effective in his or her job? What seems to be that person's problem?

4. Why is job performance so heavily influenced by personality factors?

5. Assume that a student has an extreme external locus of control. What reasons is the student likely to give for having failed a course?

6. Draw a profile of an ideal supervisor, using all the personality factors in the Big Five. To draw the profile, indicate whether the supervisor should be high, low, or medium on each of the factors.

7. Draw your own profile on the Big Five. Ask a family member or close friend for his or her assistance in rating you.

8. What is your opinion of the accuracy of the survey finding that many men use charm to gain advantage on the job?

9. Why should you have to adjust to cultural differences of a person from another country who is working in your country? Why shouldn't he or she be making the adjustments?

10. Ask two experienced working people what they think is the major source of individual differences on the job. Be prepared to discuss your findings in class.

A BUSINESS PSYCHOLOGY CASE

Flipping Burgers in Yugoslavia

Belgrade, Yugoslavia, was the location of the first McDonald's to open in a Communist country. Management ran into an unexpected problem. Turnover is high because employees find they have to work like Westerners but get paid like East Europeans. During the first few months of operation, 40 employees, about one-third of the operation, have quit their jobs despite a high unemployment rate.

Predrag Dostanic, managing director of the restaurant, blames misperceptions about the West gathered from American movies shown on Yugoslav television. Dostanic said, "That is all a result of drastically incorrect concepts about international businesses, implanted in people's minds by such American TV series as *Dynasty*."

"Those who have left us thought they would earn high wages only by virtue of working for an American enterprise," said an official from a state enterprise that entered into a joint venture agreement with McDonald's.

Dostanic added, "Those young people who quit probably also expected they could do their jobs the Yugoslav way—relax at work but still receive their wages."

The fast food outlet, located on a downtown square, has drawn large crowds since it opened, selling an average of 6,000 meals daily in its first month.

"The work was so hard that I could not stand it any more," said a former employee. "If my salary was adequate to the work, I might have stayed."

The McDonald's employees, mostly young people trained to work at counters and in the kitchen, receive about $170 a month, which is slightly above the average Yugoslavian wage.

"Maybe there is something good in all these unexpected staff problems," said the state enterprise official. "Only the best workers will survive."

1. How does this case relate to individual differences?
2. How does this case relate to values?
3. What recommendations would you make to the managing director of McDonald's (Belgrade) to decrease turnover and get the restaurant workers to work harder?

Source: As reported in Dusan Stojanovic, "Belgrade McDonald's Hits Snag," Associated Press story, May 26, 1988.

A BUSINESS PSYCHOLOGY SELF-EXAMINATION EXERCISE

What Controls Your Destiny?

What determines the outcome of events in your life? Do you believe that it is luck, chance, or fate that actually determines what happens to you and that there is nothing you can do to influence your life? Or are you at the other extreme, believing that your lot is mainly the result of your own actions and judgments? Take the following quiz developed by psychologist Salvatore Didato to help determine whether you lean toward inner (self) determination or toward outside social influences.

Answer "yes" or "no" to the left of each of the following items.

_____ 1. When I am certain I am right, I can convince others.
_____ 2. It's probably silly to think that I can change someone else's basic attitudes.
_____ 3. Success in school or work is due mainly to my own efforts and frame of mind.
_____ 4. Whether I make a lot of money in life is mostly a matter of luck.
_____ 5. There's not much that a poor person can do to succeed in life unless the person educates himself or herself.
_____ 6. Assuming that there are two teams of equal skill, the cheering of a crowd is more important than luck in determining the winner.
_____ 7. Most problems work themselves out.
_____ 8. I sometimes get a feeling of being lucky.
_____ 9. I own a good luck charm.
_____10. It's better to be smart than lucky.

Explanation: The subject of the quiz is locus of control. As described in the chapter, the term refers to an individual's belief that he or she is inner or outer directed. Internals believe that they have control over what happens to them, while externals think that they are at the mercy of fate or the power of others.

Scoring: Give yourself 1 point toward being an internally directed person for each answer as follows: 1. yes; 2. no; 3. yes; 4. no; 5. no; 6. yes; 7. no; 8, no; 9, no; 10, yes.

7 to 10 points: You are highly internally (self) directed. You don't usually rely on chance to achieve your goals.

4 to 6 points: You have a balance between inner and outer directedness.

0 to 3 points: You tend to lean toward being outer directed. This could mean you are discouraged about life, or you are quite young, or you lack self-confidence. You rely too much on luck to determine your destiny. To build your self-confidence, perhaps it would be a good idea to set goals and give yourself credit when you reach them. By doing so, you will be more able to realize that you have the power to achieve results alone and that you do not have to rely on outer sources.

Source: Salvatore Didato, Ph.D., psychologist and columnist.

References

1. John E. Hunter, Frank L. Schmidt, and Michael K. Judiesch, "Individual Differences in Output Variability as a Function of Job Complexity," *Journal of Applied Psychology,* February 1990, pp. 28–42.

2. Linda S. Gottfredson (ed.), "The g Factor in Employment," Journal of Vocational Behavior, Special Issue, Vol. 29, No. 3 (Duluth, MN: Academic Press with the Johns Hopkins University Project for the Study of Intelligence and Society, 1986); Charles C. Spearman, *The Nature of "Intelligence" and the Principles of Cognition* (London: Macmillan, 1923).

3. "Employee Aptitude Survey (EAS)," © 1952–1983, *The Psychological Corporation Harcourt Brace Jovanovich, Inc.,* 1992 Catalog.

4. Robert J. Sternberg, *Beyond IQ: A Triarchic Theory of Human Intelligence* (New York: Cambridge University Press, 1985).

5. Walter Pauk, *How to Study in College,* 2nd ed. (Boston: Houghton Mifflin, 1974), Chaps. 2, 5; Point 8 is from Charles G. Morris, *Psychology: An Introduction,* 6th ed. (Englewood Cliffs, NJ: Prentice Hall, 1988), pp. 234–235.

6. Paraphrased from Morris, *Psychology: An Introduction,* p. 249.

7. Julie Griffin Levitt, *Your Career: How to Make It Happen,* 2nd ed. (Cincinnati, OH: South-Western Publishing, 1990), pp. 11–21.

8. Robert P. Tett, Douglas N. Jackson, and Mitchell Rothstein, "Personality Measures as Predictors of Job Performance: A Meta-Analytic Review," *Personnel Psychology,* Winter 1991, p. 703.

9. Henry A. Murray, *Explorations in Personality* (New York: Oxford University Press, 1938).

10. Murray R. Barrick and Michael K. Mount, "The Big Five Personality Dimensions and Job Performance: A Meta-Analysis," *Personnel Psychology,* Spring 1991, pp. 1–26.

11. Barrick and Mount, "The Big Five," p. 19.

12. John B. Miner, *Organizational Behavior: Performance and Productivity* (New York: Random House, 1988), p. 83.

13. Tori DeAngelis, "Honesty Tests Weigh in with Improved Ratings," *APA Monitor,* June 1991, p. 7.

14. Research cited in John Leo, "Looking for a Life of Thrills," *Time,* April 15, 1985, pp. 92–93.

15. Jennifer M. George, "Personality, Affect, and Behavior in Groups," *Journal of Applied Psychology,* April 1990, pp. 107–116.

16. John L. Holland, *Making Vocational Choices: A Theory of Careers* (Englewood Cliffs, NJ: Prentice Hall, 1973).

17. A. Christine Parham, *Psychology: Studying the Behavior of People*, 2nd ed. (Cincinnati, OH: South-Western Publishing, 1988), p. 370.
18. B. L. Benderly, *The Myth of Two Minds: What Gender Means and Doesn't Mean* (Garden City, NY: Doubleday, 1987).
19. David Kipnis, Stuart M. Schmidt, and Ian Wilkinson, "Intraorganizational Influence Tactics: Explorations in Getting One's Way," *Journal of Applied Psychology*, August 1980, pp. 440–452.
20. Andrew J. DuBrin, "Sex Differences in Endorsement of Influence Tactics and Political Behavior Tendencies," *Journal of Business and Psychology*, Fall 1989, pp. 3–14.
21. Andrew J. DuBrin, "Sex and Gender Differences in Influence Tactics," *Psychological Reports*, 1991, pp. 635–646.
22. Judith Briles, *Women to Women: From Sabotage to Support* (New York: New Horizon Press, 1988).
23. H. Joseph Reitz, *Behavior in Organizations* (Homewood, IL: Irwin, 1987), p. 443.
24. Reitz, *Behavior in Organizations*, p. 176.
25. Todd D. Jick and Linda F. Mitz, "Sex Differences in Work Stress," *Academy of Management Review*, July 1985, pp. 410–412; Joseph J. Martocchio and Anne M. O'Leary, "Sex Differences in Occupational Stress: A Meta-Analytic Review," *Journal of Applied Psychology*, June 1989, pp. 495–501.
26. Jon Pepper, "U.S. Exec Often Doesn't Fit in at Japanese Firm," Gannett News Service Story, March 29, 1990.

Suggested Reading

Behrens, Gary M., and Halverson, Ronald R. "Predicting Successful Territory Sales Performance." *Journal of Business and Psychology*, Winter 1991, pp. 273–277.

Derlega, Valerian, and Associates (eds.). *Personality: Contemporary Theory and Research*. Chicago: Nelson-Hall, 1991.

Giambra, Leonard M., and Quilter, Reginald E. "Sex Differences in Sustained Attention across the Adult Life Span." *Journal of Applied Psychology*, February 1989, pp. 91–95.

Kennedy, Jim, and Everest, Anna. "Put Diversity in Context." *Personnel Journal*, September 1991, pp. 50–55.

Lowenberg, Geula, Lowenberg, Benjamin H., and Dowhower, Daniel P. "Individual Differences in Perception of Appropriate Pay Differentials in the U.S. and Sweden." *Journal of Business and Psychology*, Spring 1990, pp. 343–356.

Maddi, Salvatore R. *Personality Theories: A Comparative Analysis*, 6th ed. Chicago: Dorsey Press, 1993.

"Researchers Search for Trustworthy Employees through Testing." *Human Resource Measurements* (Supplement to April 1992 *Personnel Journal*), p. 4.

Salter Ainsworth, Mary D., and Bowlby, John. "An Ethological Approach to Personality Development." *American Psychologist*, April 1991, pp. 333–341.

Wong, Alan, and Carducci, Bernardo J. "Sensation Seeking and Financial Risk Taking in Everyday Money Matters." *Journal of Business and Psychology*, Summer 1991, pp. 525–530.

part two   *Dealing with Individuals*

Part two of the book provides information about a major segment of business psychology, understanding and dealing with individuals in the workplace. Chapter 4 helps you take the first step toward understanding individuals—achieving self-understanding. Chapter 5 builds further on the information about motivation presented in Chapter 2 by describing various approaches to motivating others and yourself. Chapter 6 takes the study of motivation one step further. We describe how workers and organizations set goals to improve performance.

Chapter 7 provides information to improve problem solving and decision making, with an emphasis on creativity. Chapter 8 describes what you can do to stay physically and mentally well, and properly manage stress. We also explain the employer's role in wellness and stress management. Chapter 9 deals with the perennial topic of managing conflict and frustration. Learning how to resolve conflict is one of the most useful skills you can acquire in your study of business psychology.

Chapter 4

UNDERSTANDING YOURSELF

Learning Objectives _____

After reading and studying this chapter and doing the exercises, you should be able to

1. Identify and describe ways of learning about yourself.
2. Understand how personality and the self-concept relate to each other.
3. Describe the impact of self-esteem on work and personal life.
4. Pinpoint the importance of self-disclosure.
5. Describe tactics for building and increasing your self-confidence.

JOB TASKS RELATED TO THIS CHAPTER

Many jobs require above-average self-confidence to succeed. You will need high self-confidence for such job tasks as selling, dealing with customer complaints, supervising people, and negotiating with suppliers and vendors. Also, asking for a raise or promotion requires self-confidence.

The process of self-examination is an important starting point in applying knowledge in general to yourself. Suppose that, instead of a book about business psychology, this were a book all about presentation skills. It would be valuable to read about what other people making presentations do right and wrong. But reading about principles of presentations would be of greater benefit to you if you first took a candid look at your own presentation style. Videotaping several of your presentations would be useful. You might also want to receive comments and suggestions from others about your oral presentations.

In achieving self-understanding, it is helpful to recognize that the **self** is a complicated idea. It generally refers to a person's total being or individuality. The ego is another word that approximates the meaning of the self. A distinction is sometimes made between the self a person projects to the outside world, and the inner self. The **public self** is what the person is communicating about himself or herself and what others actually perceive about the person. The **private self** is the actual person that one may be.[1] To avoid making continuous distinctions between these two selves throughout this book, we will use the term *self* to refer to an accurate representation of the individual.

Because an entire chapter is devoted to the self, it does not imply that other chapters in this book do not deal with the self. Most of this book is geared toward using business psychology for self-development and self-improvement. Only Chapters 1 to 3 and 13 deal more with general psychological information than with information specifically geared toward personal improvement and self-understanding.

Self:
The total being of the individual or the person. Also one's own interests, welfare, or advantage. It is important to understand yourself in order to understand others.

Public self:
What the person communicates about himself or herself and what others actually perceive about the person.

Private self:
The actual person one may be.

Ways of Learning about Yourself

To achieve self-understanding, you need to gather accurate information about yourself. Here we will discuss five general methods of gathering information for self-understanding: (1) acquiring general information about human behavior, (2) feedback from psychological tests, (3) feedback from superiors, co-workers, and friends, (4) feedback from personal growth groups, and (5) insights gathered in career counseling and psychotherapy.

General Information about Human Behavior

As you read about or listen to facts and systematic observations about people in general, you should also be gaining knowledge about yourself. This book and all other books about human behavior discuss many things that have relevance to you as an individual. At times, the author will explain how this information applies to you. At other times, it is your responsibility to relate the general information to your particular case.

Among the many general topics discussed in Chapter 2 is perception. To improve your self-understanding with respect to perception, you will have to relate that information to yourself. For example, one aspect of perception is selective perception, a tendency to see things according to our need at the time. In reading about selective perception, you might arrive at a self-insight such as, "Maybe that is why I didn't listen when people said I was too young to get married. If I had listened, I wouldn't have the problems I do today."

Feedback from Standardized Tests and Questionnaires

Methods are available for gathering systematic knowledge about your aptitudes, interests, and skills. Thousands of people in the last several decades have discovered through aptitude testing that they had the potential to become computer programmers. Many of these people are now engaged in a satisfying career because of the self-understanding they achieved from these tests. However, test results can also be inaccurate and misleading. You might be functioning as a confident and outgoing individual. If you take a personality test and discover that you rated low on self-confidence and high on introversion, you should not be concerned about the results. In your particular case, the test results are misleading. The most effective way to gain self-understanding from mental ability, personality, and interest tests is to have the results interpreted to you by a professional in the field of mental measurement.

In addition to receiving feedback from standardized tests, you might derive self-understanding from other self-examination instruments, such as the self-knowledge questionnaire presented later in this chapter. A standardized test or questionnaire has the advantage of having been constructed on the basis of scientific principles. Other self-examination instruments offer less certain results, but they are still valuable for purposes of introspection. A number of such self-examination instruments are presented in this book to help you understand yourself better. Extremely high or low scores on these questionnaires may provide useful clues to self-understanding.

Feedback from Superiors, Co-workers, Subordinates, and Friends

A valuable source of information for understanding yourself is to learn what significant people in your life think of you. Feedback of this nature sometimes hurts or makes you feel uncomfortable; but when it is consistent, it gives you an accurate picture of how you are perceived by others. In many organizations, systematic feedback is offered to people during the process of appraising their performance.

If you are seriously interested in feedback about yourself from others, it is better to act independently than to wait for a yearly performance appraisal. One problem is that not all performance appraisal systems provide candid feedback. A simple, but effective, approach is to ask people who know you for such feedback. One man enrolled in a personal improvement seminar obtained valuable information about himself on the basis of a questionnaire he sent to 15 people. His directions were:

I am hoping you can help me with one of the most important assignments of my life. I want to obtain a candid picture of how I am seen by others. What they think are my strengths, weaknesses, good points, and bad points. Any other observations about me as an individual would also be most welcome.

Write your thoughts on the enclosed sheet of paper. The information that you provide me will help me develop a plan for personal improvement that I am writing for a course in career management. Mail the form back to me in the enclosed envelope. It is not necessary for you to sign the form.

Inevitably, when this method of obtaining feedback is mentioned, a few skeptics will argue that friends will not give you a true picture of yourself. Instead, they will say flattering things about you because they value your friendship. Experience has shown, however, that if you impress others with the importance of their opinions they will generally give you some constructive suggestions. Not everybody will give you helpful feedback. You therefore may have to sample a wide range of opinion.

Feedback from Personal Growth Groups

Personal growth group:
Small training or development groups similar in design and intent to encounter groups. People usually attend personal growth groups to learn more about themselves and "get in touch with their feelings."

A formal method of improving your self-understanding is to obtain feedback about yourself in the process of participating in a **personal growth group.** Groups of this nature are designed to help people improve their self-awareness and learn how to express their feelings. The major reason personal growth groups (or encounter groups) have persisted over the years is that so many people recognize that they need to become more open with their feelings. Too often, we are taught from early childhood to suppress our feelings. Three specialists in the area of feeling-expression put it this way:

> Emotional suppression is everywhere. The social groups we live in—family, friends, work groups, and neighbors—make frequent demands on us to curb feeling-expression. These demands, rational and irrational, are frequent, at times subtle, and often extremely persuasive. Growing children learn under what circumstances feelings can be expressed fully, covertly, or not at all. Even the freest children quickly learn that many feelings must be at least partially suppressed. For example, if a child gets angry and begins to yell in a supermarket, his or her parents are liable to become extremely embarrassed. In most cases, parents will forcibly stop the child from yelling. Few will be so composed as to explain, "I need you to stop yelling. Feel angry if you want, but don't show it."[2]

As a starting point in the growth group, you usually receive feedback on how you are perceived by other members of the group. Such perceptions by others have a positive impact on self-understanding. Feedback can occur at any phase in the life of the personal growth group. A sample of the type of feedback from others that took place at an early stage of one such group is presented next.

GROUP LEADER: To get things started, everybody will tell everybody else what kind of first impression they have made. We'll do this clockwise, starting with Jeanne sitting on my left. Everybody, beginning with Jack, will tell Jeanne what he

	or she thinks of her. Of course, if Jeanne has made absolutely no impression on you, if she is the invisible woman, you can pass [group laughs]. Okay, Jack, look Jeanne straight in the eye and tell her what you think.
JACK:	My first impression of you, Jeanne, is that you're kind of cool. The type of woman I'd like to know better.
MERYL:	Jeanne, I would guess that you have a lot of friends. No doubt you are a nice person. But those eyes of yours give me something to worry about. They look a little shifty. I wouldn't trust you fully until I got to know you better. [Nervous laughter from the group.]
MAGGIE:	I think you try to give the impression that you are very casual. But underneath, you have worked very hard to create that impression. I know for sure that your jeans cost about three times as much as the usual type you find in the discount store. I'll bet you worked hours on your hair to achieve that casual look.
GEORGE:	Don't take Maggie too seriously. I think you're attractive. You also give me the impression of being very intelligent. I like the way you talk. I think you should "go for it" in life. There's nothing stopping you.
TERRY:	I can see those good points about you, too. I think the real you, however, is a fun-lover. I can see Jeanne out on a sailboat taking long weekends. I think that underneath you're the party type. Am I wrong?
CAROL:	So long as we're being candid, I'll make this comment. You're kind of pushy in a nice way. I noticed it was you who manipulated things so you could be right next to the group leader. You've also got this look about you that you're superior to other people. Maybe it's that you're a natural leader.
JEFF:	It's tough to be last. All the good comments have been used up. I'll have to go along with the good comments made about Jeanne. She's terrific. I wish I wasn't already in a committed relationship. Jeanne would be a lot of fun to go out with.
GROUP LEADER:	Jeanne, tell us how you feel about what has just happened to you.
JEANNE:	I feel terrific. Thanks for all the compliments. Even your negative comments were helpful. Maybe I do come on a little too strong at times. I like to be on top of situations. This is the first time anything like this has happened to me. Thanks again.

How might this session have benefited Jeanne? First, she perceived the tone of the feedback to be positive. This would probably give her at least a temporary boost in self-confidence. Second, the session might give her some ideas for self-improvement, even if they are somewhat superficial. She can't do much about the alleged "shifty eyes," but she might try not to appear standoffish *when she does not want to be perceived in this manner.* If Jeanne leaves the session with a boost in self-confidence and one valid suggestion for self-improvement, we can conclude that the session was worthwhile for her.

Insights Gathered in Career Counseling and Psychotherapy

An advanced method of achieving self-understanding is to obtain feedback about yourself from a career counselor or psychotherapist. Counseling centers located in schools often provide career counseling. The counselors obtain their information from interviews, tests, and questionnaires. A valuable service they provide is to collect information that you have revealed about yourself and gather in into a meaningful whole. Some career counselors provide the counselee with written suggestions. A 27-year-old woman who entered into career counseling received a report with the following conclusion:

> Based on our interview and test findings, it appears you show aptitude for and an interest in managerial work. You have excellent problem-solving ability and organizing ability, and you are interested in working closely with people. You combine these characteristics with above-average needs for getting things accomplished and holding a powerful position.
>
> We recommend that you stay in your present field and take any opportunities offered for supervisory experience. Obtaining a degree or certificate in management would enhance your chances for becoming a manager.

In addition to career counseling, many people seek self-understanding through discussions with a psychotherapist. Most people enter into psychotherapy with the intention of coping better with personal problems. However, many people choose psychotherapy for the purpose of gaining insight into themselves. A representative area of insight would be for the therapist to help the client detect patterns of self-defeating behavior. For example, some people unconsciously do something to ruin a personal relationship or perform poorly on a job when things are going really well. The therapist might point out this self-defeating pattern of behavior. Self-insight of this kind often, but not always, leads to useful changes in behavior.

Your Self-concept: What You Think of You

Self-concept:
What you think of you
and who you think
you are.

Another aspect of self-understanding is your **self-concept,** or what you think of you and who you think you are. A successful person, one who is achieving his or her goals, usually has a positive self-concept. In contrast, an unsuccessful person often has a negative self-concept. Such differences in self-concept can have a profound influence on your career.[3] If you see yourself as a successful person, you will tend to engage in activities that help you to prove yourself right. If you have a limited view of yourself, you will also tend to engage in activities that prove yourself right. You will find ways to not be particularly successful.

A strong self-concept leads to **self-confidence,** which in turn is an important requirement for being successful as a leader. Why some people develop strong self-concepts, while others have average or weak self-concepts, is not entirely known. One important contributing factor is the life-long feedback you receive from other people. If at 2 years old your parents, other children in your family, and playmates consistently told you that you were great, it would probably lead to strong self-concept. A 4-year-old may occasionally look in the mirror and utter statements such as "I like me," "I'm cute," or "I'm a good girl." It would appear that in later life she will have a strong self-concept.

In summary, much of what we call the self-concept is a reflection of what others have said about us. If enough people tell you that you are "terrific," after a while you will have the self-concept of a "terrific" person. When enough people tell you that you are not a worthwhile person, after a while your self-concept will become that of a not worthwhile person.

Self-confidence:
A basic belief in your ability to achieve the outcome you want in many situations or in a specific situation.

If enough people tell you that you are terrific, after awhile you will have the concept of a terrific person.

People who say "I'm OK" are expressing a positive self-concept. People who say "I'm not OK" have a negative self-concept.

Here we describe several important topics related to the self-concept: how personality influences the self-concept, body image as part of the self-concept, and how self-esteem contributes to the self-concept.

How Personality Influences the Self-concept

What you think of yourself depends in part on your basic traits and characteristics, a major part of your personality. Here is how the tie-in between the development of your personality and your self-concept might work in practice.

Keith began life as an active human being, even before he was born. In his prenatal days, Keith made his mother quite aware of his presence through his frequent kicking and squirming. His father was often invited by his mother to rest his hand on her abdomen to feel Keith making his presence known.

Keith's high activity level continued into his crib life. His squirming and kicking made him an attractive object of affection to his mother, father, and older sister. They enjoyed playing with him because of his responsiveness to them.

The affection and attention Keith attracted through his physical movement helped reinforce his energetic action. As a toddler, his exceptional physical condition brought him continued attention from adults. Keith's personality in early life was characterized by a high energy level. As the growing (maturation) process continued, Keith learned new ways of making good use of his abundant energy. He played several sports, studied hard, and helped his parents and older sister take care of household chores.

By the time Keith was 14, he had already developed the self-concept of an energetic, confident person. A self-concept of this nature helped direct Keith toward activities requiring a high degree of energy. When Keith was 17, he had the chance to work for a distant relative as a roofer's assistant. The money offered was outstanding for a person of his age. Yet the work would be physically exhausting to most people and require extreme courage. Keith thought to himself, "Why not take the job. I'm a 'heavy' who can handle almost any tough job."

As an adult, Keith completed technical training beyond high school. Today he runs a successful home improvement business and plays semiprofessional football. He has four children and a happy wife. As Keith sees himself, he works hard and plays hard. His high natural energy level is one of the factors that has contributed to such a self-concept.

Your Body Image as Part of Your Self-Concept

Body image:
A person's perception of his or her own body.

Our discussion of the self-concept so far has emphasized mental traits and characteristics. Your **body image,** or your perception of your body, also contributes to your self-concept.[4] The current emphasis on physical fitness stems largely from a desire on the part of people to be physically fit and healthy. It is also apparent that being physically fit contributes to a positive self-concept. Being physically unfit can contribute to a negative self-concept. The relationship between the self-concept and physical fitness also works the other way: if your self-concept is positive,

it may push you toward physical fitness. Conversely, if you have a negative self-concept, you may allow yourself to become physically unfit.

A positive body image can be important on the job. Employees who have a positive body image are likely to feel confident performing jobs that require customer contact, like sales work. Many business firms today expect their managers to appear physically fit and to present a vigorous, healthy appearance. Managers with these qualities would generally have positive body images.

Criticism has been voiced about the body image having such a large influence on the self-image. One problem is that a focus on body image leads to superficiality. People judge themselves and others too readily on their physical features. A 37-year-old single mother of three who had breast implants after cancer surgery commented:

> You're always being judged on all sorts of superficial things—how skinny you are, how pretty you are, how old you are. It's not your personality, it's your body, your looks. More women are working, but we haven't progressed much in our thinking. It's not just women though. I think men tend to be judged superficially too.[5]

Self-esteem: The Key To a Good Self-concept

Self-esteem:
The sense of feeling worthwhile.

Although the different ways of discussing the self may seem confusing, these various approaches to the self strongly influence your life. **Self-esteem,** the sense of feeling worthwhile, plays a particularly important role. It will enhance understanding of the topic to regard self-esteem as a judgment people make about themselves. Self-esteem is a major part of the self-concept. People with positive self-esteem have a deep-down, inside-the-self feeling of their own worth.[6] Consequently, they develop a positive self-concept and do not find it necessary to put down or discriminate against others. In contrast, the person with low self-esteem (one who is self-rejecting) tends to reject many other people.

Self-esteem has an important influence on the job. Employees have a fundamental need to regard themselves positively. When managers frustrate this need, workers become defensive and uncooperative. For example, employees whose suggestions are ignored will suffer a blow to their self-esteem. On the positive side, management actions that enhance self-esteem trigger a cycle of success. Employees work harder, achieve success, and feel even better about themselves. Consequently, they strive for even higher achievements.[7]

One of the many on- and off-the-job benefits of high self-esteem is that it is associated with good mental health. People with low self-esteem are often depressed, and many people who appear to have paranoid personalities are suffering from low self-esteem. A store manager who continually accused store associates of talking behind his back finally said to a mental health counselor, "Face it, I think I'm almost worthless, so I think people are saying negative things about me."

Our attention here is directed toward two plausible methods of increasing your self-esteem and self-acceptance: increasing your self-disclosure and taking an inventory of your strengths. Exercises will be presented for using both of these methods.

Self-disclosure and Self-esteem

Self-disclosure:
The process of revealing your inner self to others.

One method of increasing your self-esteem and self-acceptance is to engage in the right amount of **self-disclosure,** the process of revealing your inner self to others. Self-disclosure assists self-acceptance because revealing more of oneself provides more of you for others to accept. As acceptance by others increases, so does self-esteem. Conversely, if you keep yourself hidden from others, there is little opportunity to be accepted by them.

Nevertheless, you must be careful of excessive self-disclosure. Many people feel uneasy if another person is too self-revealing. The overly candid person thus risks rejection. For instance, if you communicate all your negative feelings and doubts to another person, he or she may become annoyed and pull away from you.

Figure 4-1 presents a questionnaire to assist you in assessing your level of self-disclosure. A person with a high degree of self-disclosure is open, while a person with a low degree of self-disclosure is closed.

Awareness of Strengths and Self-acceptance

Another method of improving your self-esteem is to develop an appreciation of your strengths and accomplishments. Research with more than 60 executives has shown that their self-concept becomes more positive after

FIGURE 4–1. *THE SELF-DISCLOSURE QUESTIONNAIRE*

Directions

The following quiz may indicate how much of yourself you reveal to others. Think about the person closest to you, whether he or she is a spouse, parent, or close friend. Using the list of responses provided, review the questions and select the number of the response that best describes you.

1. I have not mentioned anything about this.
2. I have talked about this to some degree.
3. I have confided this to a large degree.
4. I have disclosed practically all there is to know about this.

Quiz

_____ 1. Traits I am ashamed of, such as jealousy, daydreaming, and procrastination
_____ 2. Pet peeves or prejudices about others
_____ 3. Facts about my love life, including details about flirting, dating, and sexual activity
_____ 4. Things I have done or said to others that I feel guilty about
_____ 5. What it takes to make me extremely angry
_____ 6. My feelings about my attractiveness and sex appeal, and my insecurities about how my romantic interests perceive me
_____ 7. Aspects of myself I wish I could improve, such as my figure or physique, mental abilities, shyness
_____ 8. What I worry about most, such as illness, job loss, death, etc.
_____ 9. Impulses I fear will get out of control if I "let go," such as drinking, gambling, sex, and anger
_____ 10. My very deepest sensitivities, dreams, and goals

Scoring and Interpretation

To tally your score, add the numbers that correspond with the answers you gave to the quiz questions.

10 to 17 points: You are a closed person. You may feel satisfied with the level of intimacy you have established with others, but it's likely you would benefit from sharing your feelings more openly. Doing so allows others to give you feedback on your feelings and goals, helping you to get a clearer picture of yourself. Begin to change your style by making small disclosures at first. Perhaps it will be easier to start by talking about your goals.

18 to 28 points: You are average on self-disclosure and have a good balance between your private self and your openness.

29 to 40 points: You are a very open type of person, but beware. Sometimes indiscriminately revealing too much can be a sign of personal insecurity, guilt, or the need for acceptance by others. If others take advantage of you, look down on you, or feel uncomfortable with you, you may be telling more than the listener wants or cares to handle.

Source: Reprinted with permission from Salvatore Didato, "Self-Disclosure Isn't Easy But It's Necessary to Bring People Together." Copyrighted feature appearing in newspapers, April 1985; updated June 1988.

one month of practicing this exercise for a few minutes every day.[8] A good starting point is to list your strengths and accomplishments on paper. The list is likely to be more impressive than you expected. The list of strengths and accomplishments requested in the Self-knowledge Questionnaire presented at the end of the chapter can be used for building self-esteem.

An exercise used in personal growth groups helps you build self-esteem through knowledge of your strengths. After group members have compiled their lists of strengths, each person discusses his or her list with the other group members. Each person then comments on the list. Group members sometimes add to your list of strengths or reinforce what you have to say. Sometimes you may find some disagreement. One man told the group, "I'm handsome, intelligent, reliable, athletic, self-confident, very moral, and I have a good sense of humor." A woman in the group retorted, "And I might add that you're unbearably conceited."

A Checklist for Self-awareness

One problem in becoming more aware of ourselves is the problem of semantics. Think of the first time that you were asked to describe a painting, perhaps for a class in art appreciation. At first you might have been stymied in terms of what to say about the painting. Adjectives such as "interesting," "colorful," and "imaginative" might have been your first thoughts. Describing yourself, similar to describing a painting, requires skill. Describing yourself is important because it leads to more self-awareness and self-knowledge.

A useful exercise in developing self-awareness is the adjective list[9] shown in Figure 4-2. Read through this list and circle the seven adjectives that you think best describe you. You have now formed a brief self-description composed of seven adjectives such as "aggressive, courageous, extroverted, friendly, greedy, tenacious, and zestful." Next discuss your list with a friend. Your friend should be encouraged to discuss his or her list with you. The process should result in feedback about the accuracy of your self-perceptions.

Another recommended use of the adjective list is to discuss your list of adjectives with others in a group setting. Each group member has a chance to read his or her list to the other members and receive feedback from them.

Building Your Self-confidence

A practical use of knowledge about the self is to use it as a method of strengthening your self-confidence. Several of the ideas already presented in this chapter relate to developing self-confidence. For instance, hearing positive things about yourself from others is a good confidence builder. Here we will describe easy-to-implement tactics that will often lead to a strengthening of one's self-confidence.[10] As you read them, look for tech-

FIGURE 4–2. *ADJECTIVE LIST*

able	happy	overconfident	self-aware
accepting	hard	overconforming	self-conscious
adaptable	helpful	overemotional	self-effacing
aggressive	helpless	overprotecting	self-indulgent
ambitious	honorable	passive	selfish
annoying	hostile	paternal	self-righteous
anxious	idealistic	patient	sensible
authoritative	imaginative	perceptive	sensitive
belligerent	immature	perfectionist	sentimental
bitter	impressionable	persuasive	serious
bold	inconsiderate	petty	silly
calm	independent	playful	simple
carefree	ingenious	pleasant	sinful
careless	innovative	pompous	skillful
caring	insensitive	powerful	sly
certain	insincere	pragmatic	sociable
cheerful	intelligent	precise	spontaneous
clever	introverted	pretending	stable
cold	intuitive	pretentious	strained
complex	irresponsible	principled	strong
confident	irritable	progressive	stubborn
conforming	jealous	protective	sympathetic
controlled	jovial	proud	taciturn
courageous	juvenile	questioning	tactful
cranky	kind	quiet	temperamental
critical	knowledgeable	radical	tenacious
cynical	lazy	rational	tender
demanding	learned	rationalizing	tense
dependable	lewd	reactionary	thoughtful
dependent	liberal	realistic	tough
derogatory	lively	reasonable	trusting
dignified	logical	reassuring	trustworthy
disciplined	loving	rebellious	unassuming
docile	malicious	reflective	unaware
dogged	manipulative	regretful	uncertain
domineering	materialistic	rejecting	unconcerned
dreamy	maternal	relaxed	uncontrolled
dutiful	mature	reliable	understanding
effervescent	merry	religious	unpredictable
efficient	modest	remote	unreasonable
elusive	mystical	resentful	unstructured
energetic	naive	reserved	useful
extroverted	narcissistic	resolute	vain
fair	negative	respectful	vapid
fearful	nervous	responsible	visionary
foolish	neurotic	responsive	vulnerable
frank	noisy	retentive	warm
free	normal	rigid	willful
friendly	objective	sarcastic	wise
genial	oblivious	satisfied	wishful
gentle	observant	scientific	withdrawn
giving	obsessive	searching	witty
greedy	organized	self-accepting	worried
gruff	original	self-actualizing	youthful
guilty	overburdened	self-assertive	zestful
gullible			

MS. KELLY IS REALLY MOVING UP IN THE COMPANY...

You work up to a level that fits your self-image.

Success cycle:
A situation in which each little success builds self-confidence, leading to more success and self-confidence.

Positive self-talk:
Saying positive things about oneself to oneself.

Positive visual imagery:
Imagining yourself doing well in an upcoming situation that represents a challenge.

niques that you think would make sense in terms of your personality and life circumstances.

1. *Score a few easy victories.* Self-confidence builds as a direct result of success. The more little victories you achieve in life, the more likely your self-confidence will be strong. A little victory could include such things as learning to operate a new electronic instrument, receiving a favorable grade on a term paper, or running a mile 10 seconds faster than you did last month. The easy victory is based on the **success cycle.** Each little success builds up your self-confidence, which leads to a bigger success, which leads to more self-confidence, and so on.

2. *Use positive self-talk.* To appear and be self-confident, negative statements about oneself must be replaced by **positive self-talk,** that is, saying positive things about oneself to oneself. It is particularly important to make these positive self-affirmations in front of others. Examples include, "I know I can do it." "Give me a chance, and you will be pleased with the outcome." "My success ratio is very high."

3. *Use positive visual imagery.* To use **positive visual imagery,** imagine yourself performing well in an upcoming situation that represents a challenge. For exam-

ple, if you will be asking for a loan, visualize yourself making a convincing argument about your credit-worthiness. Think of the loan officer smiling agreeably and getting the papers ready for your signature. Positive visual imagery helps you appear self-confident because your mental rehearsal has helped you prepare for the challenge.

4. *Become self-directing.* If you develop an internal locus of control, your self-confidence will increase. When you take responsibility for events around you, others regard you as being self-confident and in control.

5. *Talk with optimism.* Optimistic people, almost by definition, project an image of self-confidence. It will not be necessary to overhaul your personality if you are naturally pessimistic. Nevertheless, you can learn to keep some of your pessimistic thoughts to yourself and search for optimistic comments to fit the situation. When you have struggled through a rough assignment and finally completed it, talk about how you have benefited from experience and will do even better next time.

6. *Dress and act professionally.* If you are proud of your clothing and mannerisms, you will project more self-confidence than if you are self-conscious about how you are dressed and act. Dress in a manner that makes you feel good about yourself to achieve a boost in self-confidence. Review your general behavior and mannerisms to decide which facets make you feel the most professional.

7. *Develop a solid knowledge base.* A bedrock for projecting self-confidence is to develop a base of knowledge that enables you to provide sensible alternative solutions to problems. Intuition is important, but working from a base of facts helps you project a confident image. Both formal education and day-by-day absorption of information related to your career are necessary for increasing your knowledge base.

8. *Develop and publicize new skills.* Most people realize it takes courage and confidence to learn a complex, new skill. Learning new skills and letting others know about it will therefore project self-confidence and make you feel confident.

9. *Show intense pride in your work.* The saying, "Every piece of work you complete (or service you provide) is a self-portrait" is truer than ever. A by-product of being proud is that you project self-confidence. Feeling proud creates a warm inner glow that leads to facial expressions and posture that project self-confidence.

10. *Take risks.* Risk taking is associated with self-confidence. The risk taker consequently projects an image of self-confidence. Taking sensible risks, such as offering an offbeat solution to a problem, will make one appear self-confident.

11. *Be flexible and adaptable.* Self-confident people can adapt to change quickly for the good of the organization. In contrast, people with low self-confidence want to preserve the status quo. If you show a willingness to accept change readily, you will project an image of self-confidence. Of greater significance, adapting to change will enhance your self-confidence.

BACK TO THE JOB TASKS

If you need to elevate your self-confidence to perform your job better, carefully study the 11 suggestions made above. The results will not be immediate, but at least you can begin the journey toward higher self-confidence by taking such steps as scoring a few easy victories and using positive self-talk.

Summary of Key Points

❏   Methods of learning about yourself include (1) acquiring general information about human behavior and applying it to yourself, (2) obtaining feedback from psychological testing, (3) feedback from superiors, co-workers, subordinates, and friends, (4) feedback from personal growth groups, and (5) insights gathered in career counseling and psychotherapy.

❑ Your self-concept is basically your attitude toward yourself. A successful person usually has a positive self-concept. An individual's personality traits and characteristics help form the self-concept. Body image is an important part of the self-concept, and a positive body image can improve confidence on the job.

❑ A high degree of self-esteem contributes to a positive self-concept. One way to increase self-acceptance is to disclose more of yourself to others. Another is to develop an appreciation of your strengths and accomplishments.

❑ One problem in becoming more aware of yourself is that you may not know enough terms to describe yourself. An aid to developing self-awareness is the adjective list presented in this chapter. After you prepare a self-description based on adjectives, you can share this profile with a friend.

❑ Knowledge about the self can be used to strengthen one's self-confidence. Among the tactics for accomplishing this end are (1) score a few easy victories, (2) use positive self-talk, (3) become self-directing, (4) develop a solid knowledge base, (5) develop and publicize new skills, (6) be proud of your work, and (7) take risks.

GUIDELINES FOR PERSONAL EFFECTIVENESS

1. A major step that you can take toward improving your effectiveness as an individual is to strengthen your self-concept and self-esteem. A series of successes, however small, will improve your self-concept and help you to feel more self-confident.
2. Your self-concept will also be strengthened as you become more self-accepting. You can achieve increased self-acceptance by the process of being more open in expressing your feelings. Another approach to increased self-acceptance is to learn to appreciate your strengths and accomplishments.
3. To enhance your career and personal effectiveness, strive toward increasing your self-confidence. Recognize that self-confidence builds gradually over time, but it can be strengthened little by little by performing well in a variety of situations.

Discussion Questions and Activities

1. Assume that a manager asks employees in the department for feedback. In what ways might this feedback be biased?
2. Give an example of self-defeating behavior that you have observed among friends or within yourself.
3. Describe your self-concept in 25 words or less.
4. When asked, "What do you do?" many people respond, "I'm just a ...." What does this tell you about their self-concepts?
5. To what extent do you think many people study psychology in order to increase their self-understanding?
6. What are some of the potential problems created by a strong concern about one's body image?
7. At what point do you draw the line in being open with people?

8. It is often said that most people who commit crimes have low self-esteem. Why might this be true?

9. How might you go about increasing the self-confidence of a co-worker?

10. Ask a manager or supervisor how he or she decides whether or not an employee is self-confident.

A BUSINESS PSYCHOLOGY PROBLEM

The Office Clown

Jack Conway, the director of customer service at the bank, called a Saturday morning meeting. The purpose of the meeting was to conduct a lengthy problem-solving session about improving the bank's telemarketing program. By 9 A.M., everybody scheduled to attend was present, except Melissa Mandarin. At 9:05 in walked Melissa, wearing a beanie with two spring-like antennae extending from its base. The antennae bobbed up and down as Melissa moved toward the conference table.

"Okay, Melissa," said Jack. "Join us at the table, and please take off your beanie. We all appreciated the humor, but it's time to get back to work."

With a deadpan expression, Melissa replied, "Sorry Jack, I couldn't possibly take off my beanie. It's my thinking cap." With her expression changed to a smile, Melissa said, "Okay, the meeting can begin. I'm here to be a source of inspiration to you all."

During the beverage and food break at 10:30, Melissa went into an exaggerated impersonation of the bank president. In a haughty and overdignified tone, Melissa said, "Members of our wonderful financial institution, I'm *so* glad you have voluntarily given up your Saturday morning to help make our great institution even greater.

"It is obvious you take exceptional pride in providing outstanding customer service. It fills my heart with delight to know that we have such dedicated team members here at First Federal. Your true rewards will come from the smiles you will receive from our wonderful customers.

"I am so happy to share this exciting moment with all you members of our warm and friendly, First Federal family."

Jack, who watched Melissa's presentation, said, "Okay, tone it down, Melissa. It's time to get back to work. Besides that, I think you've created enough disruption for the morning."

"Sorry about that," replied Melissa. "I was just trying to lighten things up a little."

1. Should Melissa be subjected to a formal reprimand?
2. How might Melissa's behavior be tied in with her self-esteem?
3. Referring back to Chapter 3, identify several of Melissa's key personality traits.

A BUSINESS PSYCHOLOGY PROBLEM

The Struggling Service Technician

Throughout his childhood and early adulthood, Rick Sanchez believed he had a self-confidence problem. As he explains, "I don't know why, but I never had much faith in myself. I did not think I was incompetent, but I never believed I was as capable as some of my friends. My lack of total confidence showed up even in my social life. I usually hesitated to ask a woman for a date who was my first choice. I figured she would reject me. I tended to ask out women who I thought would most likely not refuse me. The same tendency is with me today.

"Despite my low self-confidence, I was able successfully to complete a degree program in electronics technology, a field that has always interested me. I was hired by an importer of business machines made in the Far East to work as a service technician. The company put me through an extensive training program designed to teach me how to repair disabled machines located on customer premises. Although I was receiving good training and good support from my boss, I still had some concerns about how well I could perform under field conditions. It was the old self-confidence problem surfacing again.

"To phase me into my job, the firm sent me out on repair assignments with my boss. Soon it was my turn to troubleshoot customer problems on my own. One Friday morning I was sent out on my first solo assignment. A customer was having problems with one of our biggest copiers. The machine seemed to chew up paper and create a jam that the customer could not fix.

"Trembling somewhat inside, I arrived at the customer office to lend my expertise. I poked around inside the machine but I couldn't locate the cause of the problem. By the end of the hour I had made no progress and I was becoming uptight. My armpits were soaked and I developed an uneasy feeling in my stomach. Much to my embarrassment, I had to call my boss to help me locate the root of the problem. What a blow to my self-confidence! However, my boss was very helpful. He patiently explained to me where I went wrong."

1. How might Rick have used his first solo assignment to build his self-confidence?
2. How might Rick's boss have used the situation to help Rick build his self-confidence?
3. How can Rick use future assignments to build his self-confidence?

A Business Psychology Self-examination Exercise

The Self-knowledge Questionnaire

DIRECTIONS: Complete the following questionnaire for your personal use. You might wish to make up a worksheet before putting your comments in final form.

I. Education
   1. How far have I gone in school?
   2. What is my major field of interest?
   3. Which are (or have been) my best subjects?
   4. Which are (or have been) my poorest subjects?
   5. What further educational plans do I have? Why?
   6. What extracurricular activities have I participated in?
   7. Which ones did I enjoy? Why?
II. Work Experience
   8. What jobs have I held since age 16?
   9. What aspect of these jobs did I enjoy? Why?
   10. What aspect of these jobs did I dislike? Why?
   11. What were my three biggest accomplishments on the job?
   12. What kind of employee am (was) I?
   13. What compliments did I receive from my bosses or co-workers?
   14. What criticisms or suggestions did I receive?
   15. What would be an ideal job for me?
III. Attitudes toward People
   16. The kind of people I get along best with are:
   17. The kind of people I clash with are:

18. How many close friends do I have? What is it I like about each one?
19. Would I prefer working mostly with men or women? Why?
20. How much contact with other people do I need?
21. My arguments with other people are mostly about::

IV. Attitudes toward Myself
22. What are my strengths?
23. What are my weaknesses or areas for improvement?
24. What do I think of me?
25. What do I worry about the most?
26. What is my biggest problem?
27. What things in life do I dislike?
28. What have I accomplished in life so far?
29. Has this been enough accomplishment?
30. So far, what has been the happiest period of my life? Why?
31. What gives me satisfaction in life?
32. In what ways do I punish myself?
33. What motivates me?

V. How Others See Me
34. What is the best compliment my spouse (or a good friend) has paid me?
35. In what ways would my spouse (or a good friend) like me to change?
36. What do my friends like best about me?
37. What do my friends dislike about me?

VI. Hobbies, Interests, Sports
38. What activities, hobbies, interests, sports, and so forth do I actively participate in?
39. Which one of these do I really get excited about? Why?

VII. My Future
40. What are my plans for further education and training?
41. What positions would I like to hold within the next five years?
42. What are my career goals beyond five years?
43. Where would I like to be at the peak of my career?
44. What activities and interests would I like to pursue in the future?
45. What goals do I have relating to friends, family, and marriage?

Additional Thoughts

1. What other questions should have been asked of you on this questionnaire?
2. To what use can you put some or all of this information?
3. What impact did completing this questionnaire have on your self-understanding?

References

1. C. R. SYNDER, "So Many Selves," *Contemporary Psychology,* January 1988, p. 77.
2. Adapted from ROBERT A. PIERCE, MICHAEL P. NICHOLS, AND JOYCE R. DuBRIN, *Emotional Expressions in Psychotherapy* (New York: Gardner Press, 1983), p. 2.

3. Daniel L. Aroz, "The Manager's Self-Concept," *Human Resources Forum,* July 1989, p. 4.

4. Thomas F. Cash, Barbara A. Winstead, and Louis H. Janda, "Your Body, Yourself," *Psychology Today,* July 1985, pp. 22–26.

5. Susan McNamara, "Self-image Goes Bust," Rochester *Democrat and Chronicle,* February 16, 1992, p. 1D.

6. Wolf J. Rinke, "Maximizing Management Potential by Building Self-esteem," *Management Solutions,* March 1988, p. 11.

7. Robert L. Dipboye, "Understanding and Managing Self-esteem in the Workplace," *Contemporary Psychology,* July 1990, pp. 680–681.

8. Aroz, "The Manager's Self-Concept," p. 4.

9. David W. Johnson, *Human Relations and Your Career: A Guide to Interpersonal Skills,* 2nd. ed. (Englewood Cliffs, NJ: Prentice Hall, 1987). Reprinted with permission.

10. Adapted from Andrew J. DuBrin, *Stand Out! : 330 Ways to Gain the Edge with Bosses, Subordinates, Co-Workers and Customers* (Englewood Cliffs, NJ: Prentice Hall, 1993), pp. 1–21.

Suggested Reading

Bednar, Richard L., and Associates. *Self-esteem: Paradoxes and Innovations in Clinical Theory and Practice.* Washington, DC: American Psychological Association, 1991.

Canfield, John V. *The Looking Glass Self: An Examination of Self-awareness.* New York: Praeger, 1990.

Goldberg, Arnold (ed.). *Dimensions of Self Experience.* Hillsdale, NJ: Analytic Press, 1989.

Guidano, Vittorio F. *The Self in Process: Toward a Post-rationalist Cognitive Therapy.* New York: Guilford Press, 1991.

Hermans, Hubert J. M., and Associates. "The Dialogical Self: Beyond Individualism and Rationalism." *American Psychologist,* January 1992, pp. 23–33.

Krueger, David W. *Body Self and Psychological Self: A Developmental and Clinical Integration of Disorders of the Self.* New York: Brunner/Mazel, 1989.

Lapsley, Daniel K., and Power, F. Clark (eds.). *Self, Ego, and Identity: Integrative Approaches.* New York: Springer-Verlag, 1988.

Steffhagen, R. A. *Self-esteem Therapy.* Westport, CT: Praeger, 1990.

Ulman, Richard B., and Brothers, Doris. *The Shattered Self: A Psychoanalytic Study of Trauma.* Hillsdale, NJ: Analytic Press, 1988.

Wylie, Ruth C. *Measures of Self-Concept.* Lincoln: University of Nebraska Press, 1989.

Chapter 5

MOTIVATING YOURSELF
AND OTHERS

Learning Objectives _____

After reading and studying this chapter and doing the exercises, you should be able to

1. Explain how the work ethic influences motivation on the job.
2. Explain how your manager's expectations of you can influence your motivation.
3. Describe how to motivate people through recognition and the work itself.
4. Describe how empowerment and employee participation are used as a motivational strategy.
5. Develop a strategy for motivating yourself.

JOB TASKS RELATED TO THIS CHAPTER

Many job tasks require motivating people, including customers. Among these tasks are getting a subordinate to be more productive, getting a co-worker to give you more assistance, getting a customer who is vascillating to make a purchase, and motivating yourself to work harder at a task you dislike.

We have already described how the job behavior of people is influenced by their needs, motives, and the meaning they attach to work. In addition, two major theories of work motivation were explained in Chapter 2. An understanding of the psychology of motivation alone, however, will not enable you to motivate others or yourself to accomplish results. To improve motivation on the job, you must translate this underlying knowledge into methods and techniques. A variety of field-tested motivational methods and techniques will be discussed in this chapter. But, first, it will be helpful to explore further the nature and meaning of motivation.

The Meaning of Motivation

Motivation is concerned with the "why" of behavior, the reason people do things. Many psychologists believe that all behavior is motivated behavior: there is a reason for doing everything you do. Following this logic, if you misplace your car keys, it could mean that you want to be late for work. Perhaps you think today's tasks will be boring; or perhaps you are trying to punish yourself.

Human motivation, in general, can be defined as an *inner state that activates or moves a person toward a goal*. It includes all those inner striving conditions described as wishes, desires, and drives. **Work motivation** is more specific. It refers to a person expending effort toward the accomplishment of a goal considered worthwhile by the organization. A drafting technician studying computer-assisted design (CAD) on her own time to improve her job skills shows high work motivation. Motivation also refers to the process of trying to get someone else to do something. For example, a manager might use a motivational technique to influence a worker to do high-quality work.

Work motivation: The expenditure of effort toward the accomplishment of a goal considered worthwhile by the organization.

If you want to succeed in your career, you must have strong work motivation. If you become (or are) a manager, you will often be placed in the position of trying to motivate others.

Self-interest plays a key role in motivation. People ask themselves, "What's in it for me?" before engaging in any form of behavior.[1] In one way or another, people act in a way that serves their self-interest. It can even be argued that when people act in a way that helps others they are doing so because helping others helps them! A person, for example, may give money to poor people because this act of kindness makes him or her feel wanted and powerful.

Both the need hierarchy and expectancy theories of motivation include the underlying idea of self-interest as a motivator. According to Maslow's theory, people strive to achieve goals that will satisfy their needs of the moment. And expectancy theory contends that people will put forth effort if they believe the outcome will benefit them in some important way.

A major influence on whether people show high motivation on the job is their **work ethic,** a firm belief in the dignity of work. People with a strong work ethic are well motivated because they value hard work. To not work hard clashes with their values. If the **organizational culture,** the predominant values of a firm, encourage hard work, most employees will be highly motivated. Similarly, if the organizational culture does not emphasize hard work, many employees will have average or low motivation.

The society in which people live and the subgroups in society that they identify with contribute heavily to the work ethic. A major controversy is whether people from the United States have a weak or strong work ethic. Many people argue that the United States is at a competitive disadvantage with many other countries because so many Americans have a weak work ethic. Robert Eisenberger, for one, argues that nineteenth-century America was characterized by people with a strong work ethic, including pride in accomplishment. However, this work ethic has weakened because so many Americans are preoccupied with leisure and see no direct payoff to hard work. One recent problem is that so many hardworking people lose their jobs.

By easy access to credit, many Americans reward themselves with consumer goods they cannot afford. Instead of working hard and saving, they obtain the rewards of hard work by using consumer credit. As a result of all this, we have a poorly motivated work force (according to this viewpoint).[2]

Another point of view is that Americans have been misjudged. In reality, U.S. employees work much longer hours than in years past, and they have to work extra hard just to pay for leisure activities, such as VCRs and memberships in athletic clubs. Juliet Schor, a Harvard professor, conducted a comprehensive study of the work habits of Americans. Schor found that the average American puts in nearly three more weeks at the office per year than he or she did in 1970. Furthermore, factory workers in the United States and Canada spend two months longer on the job than their European counterparts. The average work week for managers and professionals today is about 55 hours.[3]

Whether Americans are generally lazy or generally overworked, the message is clear. How hard a given person works is heavily influenced by his or her values, particularly the work ethic. The type of work ethic a person displays is often a factor in determining whether that person will receive a job offer. A case in point is America Works, a company that specializes in finding jobs for welfare recipients. Before welfare recipients are offered to companies as a potential employee, they must first attend classes preparing them for work, including learning job skills and productive attitudes.

America Works "screens by motivation." If candidates miss or are late for even one session without calling ahead, they are eliminated from the program. The welfare recipients who remain are determined to succeed: they have a strong work ethic.[4]

Pygmalion effect:
People perform according to expectations of them, particularly with respect to superior–subordinate relationships.

The simplest way of motivating other people is to set high expectations for them. This mysterious phenomenon of a manager's expectations influencing employee motivation and performance has been labeled the **Pygmalion effect.** According to Greek mythology, Pygmalion was a sculptor and king of Cyprus who carved an ivory statue of a maiden and fell in love with the statue. The statue was soon brought to life in response to his prayer. The point of the Pygmalion effect is that you may be able to convert an undermotivated person into a high producer by the simple method of believing that he or she can improve.

The Pygmalion effect on the job works in a subtle, almost unconscious way. When a manager believes that a subordinate will succeed, that manager communicates this belief to the subordinate without realizing that the belief is being transmitted. Conversely, when a manager expects an employee to fail, the subordinate will usually not disappoint the manager. The manager's expectation of failure has become a self-fulfilling prophecy. Because the manager believed that the employee would fail, the manager contributed to the failure.

Holding high expectations for employees can help overcome some of the motivational problems of a low work ethic. Many employees with a low work ethic will change their attitude and behaviors if management expects these people to perform well.[5] The Pygmalion effect is also useful in explaining why effort-to-performance expectancies (part of expectancy theory) are important. A worker who believes he or she can accomplish the work will actually perform better. The belief thus becomes a self-fulfilling prophecy.

High expectations are effective motivators also because they form an expectation cycle, as shown in Figure 5-1. As the manager increases his or her expectations of the worker, the worker performs better. As the worker

FIGURE 5–1. *THE EXPECTATION AND PERFORMANCE CYCLE.*

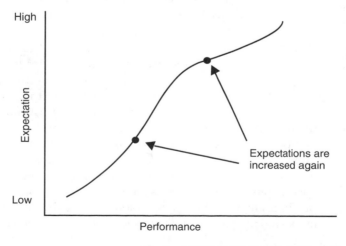

performs better, the manager further raises the expectations. In turn, the worker performs even better, and the cycle continues.

Although the Pygmalion effect has been shown to increase motivation in many settings, it does not always work. Two researchers studied the impact of supervisory expectations on the job performance of 259 sales associates in two new department stores. The sales managers in the study were given a list of specific employees. They were told that these associates had been identified by a test as having "exceptional sales potential." In reality, these associates were chosen at random by the researchers.

The results showed that the group for whom expectations were high did not perform better than the other associates. However, there was slight evidence that the Pygmalion effect worked for the male sales associates.[6] A possible limitation to the study is that perhaps the sales managers were not convinced that the test was an accurate predictor of sales ability. They therefore did not project much confidence in this "select group" of sales associates. What do you think?

Later in the chapter, we will examine the possibility that you can turn the Pygmalion effect inward. If you raise your level of self-expectations, your motivation and performance will sometimes increase.

Motivation through Behavior Modification

Behavior modification:
Changing behavior by rewarding the right responses and/or punishing or ignoring the wrong responses.

A widely used technique of work motivation is **behavior modification**— changing behavior by rewarding the right responses and/or punishing or ignoring the wrong responses. Behavior modification is therefore a form of operant conditioning.

Behavior Modification Focuses on Behavior and Its Consequences

Law of effect:
In behavior modification, behavior that leads to a positive consequence for the individual tends to be repeated, while behavior that leads to a negative consequence tends not to be repeated.

Environmental determinism:
The doctrine of behaviorism stating that our past history of reinforcement determines, or causes, our present behavior.

A program of behavior modification is concerned with the actual job behavior of an employee (such as making a sale) and the consequences of that behavior (such as getting a commission for making the sale). This emphasis on behavior and its consequences is based on two important principles: (1) the law of effect, and (2) environmental determinism. According to the **law of effect,** behavior that leads to a positive consequence for the individual tends to be repeated, whereas behavior that leads to a negative consequence tends not to be repeated.

The law of effect is a basic principle of psychology. **Environmental determinism** is a belief that stems from this principle. It contends that our past history of reinforcements (rewards and punishments) determines, or causes, our current behavior. Thus, behavior modification makes no references to internal states such as needs or motives that influence behavior. Reinforcers shape our lives. If doing little favors for people brought you the appreciation you craved in the past, you will do favors for people again when you want to be appreciated.

Behavior modification (or behavior mod) programs in organizations generally rely on positive reinforcement rather than negative reinforcement, punishment or extinction (ignoring or not rewarding the undesired behavior). The use of behavior mod in the workplace is therefore likely to be called positive reinforcement. The information about operant conditioning presented in Chapter 2 applies to motivation as well as learning.

Rules for Using Positive Reinforcement

To use positive reinforcement effectively on the job, certain rules or procedures must be followed. The best results will be achieved if these rules are combined with a genuine interest in the welfare of workers. The following rules are presented from the standpoint of the manager.

Rule 1: State Clearly What Behavior Will Lead to a Reward. The nature of good performance, or the goals, must be agreed to by both manager and team member. Clarification might take this form: "I need delivered units that are returned by no more than 1 percent of our customers because of complaints about quality."

Rule 2: Focus on the Positive Aspects of Job Performance. To use a popular phrase, "Catch the employee doing something right." Most negative job behaviors have a positive counterpart. To improve performance, reward the employee for engaging in positive behavior. When the team member just mentioned has a month in which 99 percent of goods are not shipped back for quality problems, the manager should offer a compliment. Many managers would only complain about the 1 percent of returned units.

Rule 3: Use Appropriate Rewards. An appropriate reward is an effective one because it is valued by the person being motivated. As you examine the list of rewards in Table 5-1, note that some have more appeal to you than do others. The best way to motivate people is to offer them their preferred rewards for good performance, so it is helpful to discuss with employees what they are interested in attaining.

Rule 4: Administer Rewards Intermittently. As explained in Chapter 2, intermittent reinforcement is more effective than continuous reinforcement for sustaining the right behavior. If you worked as a shoe store manager, it might be rewarding to you if, on an occasional visit to your store, your boss told you, "Everything looks just fine around here. The customers seem pleased. Your volume is up and the store looks first class. Keep this up and you'll notice a difference in your salary." If your boss gave the same pep talk every week, the reward would lose its impact. Worse, you might come to depend on the reward to perform good work. No pep talk, no good performance.

TABLE 5–1. *REWARDS SUITABLE FOR POSITIVE REINFORCEMENT ON THE JOB*

Monetary	Social and Pride Related
Salary increase or bonus	Compliments
Gift certificates	Encouragement
Discount coupons	Access to confidential information
Time off from work with pay	Pat on the back
Profit sharing	Expression of appreciation in front of
Paid personal holiday (such as	others
birthday)	
Movie or athletic event passes	

Job and Career Related	Recognition and Status Symbols
Challenging work assignments	Elegant job title
Job security	Bigger work area or office
Favorable performance review	Bigger desk
Freedom to choose own work activity	Company-paid cellular telephone
Promotion	Wall plaque indicating accomplish
Improved working conditions	ment
Opportunity to perform more of	Special commendation (e.g.,
preferred task	employee of the month)
Chance to fill in for boss when boss	Company recognition pin, watch,
is away	or ring
Job rotation	

Food and Dining
Business lunch paid by company
Company picnics
Department picnics
Department parties
Holiday turkeys and fruit baskets

Rule 5: Vary the Size of the Reward with the Size of the Accomplishment. Big accomplishments deserve big rewards; small accomplishments deserve small rewards. Rewards of the wrong magnitude lose some of their motivational power. An important corollary of this principle is that people become embarrassed when praise is overlavish. If an employee reloads a jammed printer, he or she should not be told, "Incredible job! This should boost department productivity immensely." A more realistic compliment would be, "Thanks for helping us out of a jam."

Rule 6: Administer Rewards Shortly after They Are Deserved. The proper timing of rewards will often be difficult because the manager is not present at the time of good performance. In this case, a telephone call or note of appreciation within several days of the good performance would be appropriate.

The way to motivate people is to use a reward that is meaningful to each particular person.

Rule 7: Change Rewards Periodically. Rewards grow stale quickly, making it necessary to change them periodically. A related problem is that a repetitive reward can become an annoyance. How many times can one be motivated by the phrase, "Fabulous job"? How many recognition plaques can one wish to receive for making quota?

We discuss next a reward that is unlikely to grow stale for the vast majority of people.

At several places in this chapter, examples are given of the use of behavior modification and positive reinforcement to motivate people. An additional example will help explain how supervisors use behavior modification on a daily basis. Marla Chevalier, a customer service supervisor at a utility company, explains how she uses behavior modification:

> The job of a customer service rep in a gas and electric company has its rough moments. Customers scream at reps when they think their bill is too high or if their service is discontinued because of a delinquent account. Suppose I notice that a rep has handled a nasty customer in a tactful and constructive way. I congratulate him or her on the spot. Or sometimes I will write the rep a note by hand, send a kind word through E-mail, or write a memo to the file.

My best reinforcer of all is to mention the rep's handling of the tough incident when we hold a department meeting. If I wait until performance evaluation time to talk about good performance, the motivational impact is lost.

I think my motivational program is working. After a rep receives one of my little rewards, he or she seems even more determined to iron out customer problems.

Using Money to Motivate People

A controversy has raged for several decades about the effectiveness of money as a motivator. At one extreme are those who point to studies showing that employees rank money low in importance in comparison to such job factors as challenging work, opportunities for advancement, and recognition. At the other extreme are those who argue that people are still primarily motivated by money.

Current research and opinion indicate that money is a powerful motivator, even for creative people. A review was made of all the systematic studies available about the use of money as a motivator. Overwhelming support was found for the traditional belief that money is still a top motivator. The researcher concluded, "There is no more effective way to improve productivity than by financial incentives."[7] The current emphasis on variable pay and bonus pay, as described later, suggests that financial incentives are still powerful motivators.

For money to live up to its potential as an effective reward, certain conditions must exist or be met. To the extent that the several conditions described next apply to your situation, you will probably be motivated by money.

Money Is a Good Motivator When You Need It Badly Enough. Money has a motivational pull for most people who perceive themselves to have a strong need for money. Once people have enough money to pay for all those things they think are important in life, money may lose its effectiveness. There are tremendous individual differences in what people classify as "necessities." If, for example, somebody thinks owning three cars and having two residences is a necessity, that person will be motivated by money for a long time. The following case example sheds some insight on the use of financial rewards with a person of modest tastes:

> A supervisor was busily signing up people to work overtime hours for the holiday season. A 23-year-old woman said to not include her on the list. In disbelief, the supervisor said to her, "How can anybody turn down overtime work during the holidays?" She replied, "Money is no big hassle for me. I lead a simple life. I make all my friends and relatives presents. I'd rather spend holiday time with my loved ones than working overtime in a factory, hustling a few extra dollars."

A Financial Incentive Tends to Be an Effective Motivator When It Can Change Your Life-style. Many people will work hard to earn enough money to change they way they live, whether that change involves the purchase of a yacht or a used car. A surveyor took on a part-time job installing vertical venetian blinds in addition to his regular job. Asked why he was willing to tie up so many nights and weekends for relatively modest pay, he replied, "My part-time job enables my family and I to live in a much larger house than if I only brought home money from one job."

Money Motivates You When Your Compensation Is Related to Your Performance. Many employers make a systematic effort to link some portion of pay to performance to make pay more motivational. Such practices are based on reinforcement theory. Good performance leads to the reward of a salary increase, while poor performance leads to punishment or no increase.

To relate pay to performance, many companies today have shifted to variable pay as a method of motivating people with money. **Variable pay** is an incentive plan that intentionally pays good performers more money than poor performers. Employees receive more money by excelling on performance measures such as number of sales or number of computer programs completed. Traditionally, variable pay has been referred to as *merit pay*. Whatever the specific plan, employees receive a base level of pay along with a bonus related to performance.[8] Table 5-2 presents an example of guidelines for variable pay used in a private hospital. The specific merit increase percentage varies from year to year, depending on the cost of living.

Pay can also be related to the performance of groups in an attempt to motivate large numbers of employees at once. Under a **gainsharing program,** for example, employees are allowed to participate financially in the productivity gains they have achieved. Gainsharing plans have a 50-

Variable pay:
An incentive plan that intentionally pays good performers more money than poor performers.

Gainsharing program:
A profit-sharing plan in which employees are allowed to participate financially in the productivity gains they have achieved.

TABLE 5–2. *GUIDELINES FOR PERFORMANCE-BASED MERIT INCREASES AT A HOSPITAL*

Performance Level	Merit Percent
Staff members who have demonstrated exceptional performance and who have made outstanding contributions during the year	5.75–6.50
Staff members with consistently productive performance that has met standards and exceeded some	4.75–5.74
Staff members with consistently productive performance that meets expectations	3.00–4.74
Staff members who demonstrate performance that is not wholly satisfactory, even though some expectations may be met or even exceeded	1.00–2.99
Staff members who generally fail to meet key expectations and standards; substantial improvement is necessary and essential	0.00

year history of turning unproductive companies around and making successful companies even more productive. The gainsharing bonus in these plans can be relatively uncomplicated, such as awarding employees a bonus for exceeding a targeted level of productivity (often defined as a ratio of labor costs to units produced). The size of the bonus varies with the amount of improvement, thus enhancing the motivational properties of the gainsharing plan.[9]

Financial payouts to workers under a gainsharing program can be exceptional. The best-publicized of these plans is the Scanlon Plan used at Lincoln Electric, a large manufacturer of arc-welding machines and electric motors. For the last 50 years, bonuses have averaged 95 percent over base pay.[10] In addition to strong motivation provided by financial incentives, gainsharing programs offer another key advantage. Employees become highly involved in improving productivity and develop a strong sense of teamwork.

Motivation through Recognition

Another old-fashioned motivator, giving people recognition for good performance or loyalty to the organization, is also of current interest.[11] Recognition is listed in Table 5-1 as a feasible motivator in a job setting. To maximize the power of recognition, it should suit the preferences of the individual. One employee, for example, might prefer a hand tool over a watch or crystal vase as a reward. Recognition awards that are given for seniority rather than performance may increase loyalty to the firm, but they do not necessarily improve performance.

Recognition Symbols. The first step in a formal recognition program is to develop an attractive symbol of service, which usually involves the company logo. The second element in the program is an attractive accessory or gift that carries the symbol. Among these items would be jewelry, pocket knives, pens, and key chains. Presenting these awards in a ceremony attended by a top organizational official is highly recommended.

It is also possible for managers to give recognition to good performers in a much less formal way. Assume that you achieved something very important on the job (such as handling a major customer problem or snuffing out a small fire). Your manager might write a memo attesting to this fact and place the memo in your personnel file. Which would motivate you better? An expensive recognition pin or a memo to the file documenting your good deed?

Does Recognition Lead to Increased Motivation or Satisfaction? The study in question evaluated the results of 1,000 recognition award programs as perceived by the program administrators.[12] According to these administrators (who were probably biased toward these programs), the five most frequent benefits were as follows:

1. Increases employee recognition
2. Instills company pride
3. Emphasizes individual importance
4. Improves morale
5. Enhances company team spirit

Notice that these five benefits seem to relate to how people feel about themselves and the company, but not necessarily to how much effort they put forth or how productive they are. Stated in the language of business psychology, recognition award programs seem to be doing more for job satisfaction than job motivation. The same is true of many other programs designed to increase motivation: they demonstrate the fact that it is easier to make people happier than to make them work harder or smarter!

The accompanying box describes a program of employee motivation and satisfaction that combines positive reinforcement, financial incentives, and recognition.

WELLS FARGO EMPLOYEES BANK ON INDIVIDUALIZED GIFTS

When Wells Fargo Bank wanted to show appreciation to employees for performing well, it looked into its vault for an appropriate gift. The bank initiated the two-phase In Good Company program with a $500 bonus check for salaried, full-time employees. Part-time employees received a prorated portion of $500, and hourly employees received $50. Top executives were ineligible.

In phase two of the program, each full-time and part-time employee received a coupon to present to a co-worker. These awards were worth $35 and the reasons for presenting them varied. "Everybody appreciated the $500, but employees clearly treasured the chance to support their co-workers who had helped them through difficult times and made their job a little easier," said vice-president Connie Matsui.

To identify reasons for the gift, givers could check boxes on the coupon, such as "always putting in that extra effort," "helping get the job done," or "inspiring me to excel." A personalized memo could also be included.

Thirty-one employees received at least seven coupons, and one person received thirteen. To recognize this accomplishment, the bank listed 101 gifts that ranged from season tickets to a sporting event to a Dalmatian puppy. Among the other choices were five shares of Wells Fargo stock, airline tickets, one mortgage payment, and paid days off.

"We realize that everybody's needs are different," Matsui said. "So when we put the list together, we wanted a wide variety of gifts to appeal to these different needs."

The top winners were flown to the San Francisco headquarters for a special celebration. The next morning some winners were chosen to take part in a round-table discussion with both the bank president and chairman. Participants were encouraged to ask questions about the bank and provide input for making the bank run more smoothly. The discussion was videotaped and then distributed to all branches.

Source: As reported in "Wells Fargo Employees Are in Good Company," *Personnel Journal,* October 1989, pp. 100–102.

Motivating Others through the Work Itself (Intrinsic Motivation)

Intrinsic motivation: Motivation stemming from a person's belief about the extent to which an activity can satisfy his or her needs for competence and self-determination.

Self-determination theory: The idea that people are motivated when they experience a sense of choice in initiating and regulating their actions.

Many management experts contend that, if you make jobs more interesting, there may be less need for motivating people with external rewards. Also, attempting to motivate people by external rewards may not be sufficient. Motivating people through interesting work is based on the principle of **intrinsic motivation.** It refers to a person's beliefs about the extent to which an activity can satisfy his or her needs for competence and self-determination. Intrinsic motivation is therefore also referred to as **self-determination theory,** the idea that people are motivated when they experience a sense of choice in initiating and regulating their actions. Instead of looking to somebody else for rewards, a person is motivated by the intrinsic or internal aspects of the task. Here we describe the rationale behind intrinsic motivation and two of its applications: job enrichment and the flow experience.

The Rationale behind Intrinsic Motivation Theory

Intrinsic motivation and self-determination go hand in hand. According to the theory of intrinsic motivation, individuals are active agents rather than passive recipients of environmental forces. Two factors can affect perceptions of intrinsic motivation. Certain characteristics of the task (such as challenge, autonomy, and feedback) can promote intrinsic motivation because they allow for satisfaction of needs for competence and self-determination. An individual's perceptions of why he or she performs a task can also affect intrinsic motivation. Specifically, intrinsic motivation may increase when people perceive that they perform tasks for themselves rather than for an external reward. This is true because such perceptions provide individuals with the opportunity to satisfy their self-determining needs.

In contrast, when an individual performs a task to achieve an external reward (such as money or recognition), the perceived cause of behavior shifts from within the individual to the external reward. Money or recognition is literally controlling the person's actions. In this instance, the individual no longer perceives that he or she is self-determining and, as a result, intrinsic motivation may decrease.[13]

Job Enrichment

Job enrichment refers to making a job more motivational and satisfying by adding variety and responsibility. A job is considered enriched to the extent that it demands more of an individual's talents and capabilities. As the job becomes more meaningful to you, you become better motivated and it is hoped more productive. Unless you *want* an enriched job, these positive results may not be forthcoming. One angry worker had this comment to make about a job-enrichment program in his department:

> My job is more exciting, but it's also more taxing. I'm doing more things now, which means I have to learn more skills. I'm more tired at the end of the day. What really gripes me though is that my paycheck hasn't gotten any bigger. If management enriches the job, let them also enrich the paycheck. I don't want to be taken advantage of.

General Characteristics of an Enriched Job. A good deal of research and practical experience has gone into enriching jobs. Industrial psychologist Frederick Herzberg, for example, has supervised the programs for enriching the jobs of over 100,000 employees in both the military and private industry. His work shows that an enriched job has eight important characteristics.[14]

1. *Direct feedback.* A worker should get immediate knowledge of the results he or she is achieving. This evaluation of performance can be built into the job (such as a highway patrol person catching a speeder) or provided by a supervisor.
2. *Client relationships.* An employee with an enriched job has a client or customer to serve, whether that client is inside or outside the organization. In this regard, both a hair stylist and a staff photographer have enriched jobs.
3. *New learning.* An enriched job allows its incumbent to feel that he or she is psychologically growing. In contrast, an impoverished job allows for no new learning.
4. *Scheduling.* Employees should have the freedom to schedule some part of their own work, such as deciding when to tackle which assignment.
5. *Unique experience.* An enriched job has some unique qualities or features, such as custodial assistants having the opportunity to report on building damage to management.
6. *Control over resources.* Groups of workers might have their own minibudgets and be responsible for their own costs. Or individual workers might be authorized to order as many supplies as needed to get the job done.
7. *Direct communication authority.* An enriched job allows the worker to communicate directly with other people who use his or her output, such as a quality-control technician handling customer complaints about quality.
8. *Personal accountability.* A good job makes workers accountable for their results. In this way they can accept congratulations for a job well done and blame for a job done poorly.

A superenriched job would have all eight of these characteristics, whereas an impoverished job would have none. The more of these characteristics present, the more enriched the job. High-level managers usually have enriched jobs. At times their jobs are too enriched: they have too much responsibility and too many different tasks to perform. Production workers are generally thought to have unenriched jobs. Today, however, many production workers are encouraged to make suggestions about quality improvement. In addition, a dominant trend is to organize workers into teams in which they have more responsibility. These work teams are described later and can be considered a form of group job enrichment.

The Flow Experience

Flow experience:
The phenomenon of total absorption in one's work.

The ultimate form of job enrichment is a task so intriguing to the job holder that it is capable of totally absorbing the individual's attention. The **flow experience** is the phenomenon of total absorption in one's work. It is akin to "being in the zone" in athletics. When you are in the zone, you are achieving peak performance largely because your concentration is so complete. When flow occurs, things go just right. The person feels alive and fully attentive to what he or she is doing. In flow, there is a sense of being lost in the action.

The common features of flow experience are high challenge, clear goals, a focus of psychic energy and attention, and continuous feedback. There is also a loss of self-consciousness. People experiencing flow are not concerned with themselves.[15] A person who experiences flow is well motivated, whether or not status, prestige, or large amounts of money are associated with the job. The comments of famous writer Ray Bradbury about his work characterize the flow experience:

> If you are writing without zest, without gusto, without love, without fun, you are only half a writer. It means you are so busy keeping one eye on the commercial market, or one eye peeled for the avant-garde coterie that you are not being yourself. You don't even know yourself. For the first thing a writer should be is—excited.[16]

Flow is found frequently in creative jobs and in athletics. A singer is often totally absorbed in his or her singing. A soccer player may receive total enjoyment from twirling a soccer ball on his or her foot. Fortunately, for purposes of job motivation, flow can be experienced by people in other work. A carpenter can experience flow while hammering a nail if the carpenter basically enjoys the activity of hammering nails. A secretary can experience flow in the process of carefully word processing a document.

The feedback a person receives from doing a task correctly serves as a signal that things are going well. As the tennis player hits the ball squarely in the middle of the racket, there is an immediate sound (a delightful thud), indicating that things are going well. In addition, a pleasant vibration moves up the arm. As the truck driver maneuvers properly around a curve, he or she receives a road-hugging feeling up through the wheels, indicating that the turn has been executed properly.

Despite the importance of control and feedback, the person who is experiencing flow doesn't stop to think what is happening. It is as if you are an onlooker and the precise actions are taking place automatically. Your body is performing pleasing actions without much conscious control on your part. When you are totally absorbed in reading a book, you do not realize you are turning the pages—your fingers take over for you.

Motivation through Empowerment and Employee Participation

A comprehensive strategy for employee motivation is to grant workers more power by allowing them to participate in decisions affecting themselves and their work. Employees experience a greater sense of self-efficacy (effectiveness) and ownership of their jobs when they share power. **Empowerment** is the process by which a manager shares power with team members, thereby enhancing their feelings of self-efficacy.[17] Because the worker feels more effective, empowerment contributes to intrinsic motivation. Sharing power with team members enables them to feel better about themselves and perform at a higher level.

Empowerment:
The proces by which a manager shares power with team members, thereby enhancing their feelings of self-efficacy.

People tend to be better motivated when they participate in decision making because they become *ego involved* in the matter. For example, if it was your suggestion to purchase a particular machine for the office, you would probably be motivated to use that machine. Empowerment and participation also have a positive effect on job satisfaction. Workers typically enjoy having more decision-making authority.

Empowerment is the major new thrust both in motivating employees and managing organizations. Here we describe four specific ways in which employees are empowered to participate in decisions about their work: work teams, participation in technical suggestions, decision making about administrative matters, and participation in setting working hours. Participation in goal setting, as described in Chapter 6, is but another of many empowerment methods.

Work teams:
A small group with total responsibility for a task that manages itself to a large extent.

Work Teams. The most dramatic change in modern organizations is to organize activity into **work teams,** a small group with total responsibility for a task that manages itself to a large extent. Members of the team perform a variety of tasks in contrast to the high specialization of an assembly line. Work teams are empowered to perform many traditional management functions, including assigning tasks, solving quality problems, and selecting, training, and counseling team members.

Among the positive results of these work teams have been higher productivity, improved attendance, less turnover, and improvement in both product quality and the quality of work life for employees.[18] All these benefits stem in part from the high motivation associated with being part of a work team.

A favorable example of a work team took place at United Electric Controls Co., a manufacturer of temperature and process instrumentation. The company reorganized the production work floor into cells as one step to deal with increasing competition and low profits. Employees were assigned to work together in small teams on similar products and were encouraged to become more flexible in which jobs they could perform. Within three years the company experienced a 60 percent decrease in inventory and a 90 percent reduction in the time required to complete a project. In addition, the on-time delivery rate rose from 65 to 95 percent.[19]

Participation in Technical Suggestions. A natural way to encourage employee participation is to give employees a chance to make suggestions about the technical details of their jobs. Often this takes the form of employees giving their advice on how to improve the workings of the job. For instance, a server might be asked her opinion about what management can do to better please the customers. Bit by bit, as large numbers of employees throughout the organization contribute technical suggestions, the work force becomes better motivated and satisfied. A Westinghouse executive puts it this way: "Participative management is most of all a way of releasing the natural, inherent enthusiasm of and creativity of the entire organization."[20]

Decision Making about Administrative Matters. Many employees like to provide their input into decisions about topics that go beyond the confines of their particular job. These nontechnical matters are often termed administrative work and could involve such things as general working conditions, the assignment of offices, or department budgets. Scandinavian workers participate extensively in such general matters. Much of the high quality of Scandinavian goods and services has been attributed to involving employees in all phases of decision making. William Starbuck makes this observation: "Scandinavian managers are often quite apologetic about putting themselves into leadership positions. They think that members of the group should have more say."[21]

Participation in Setting Working Hours. A large number of firms grant their employees some say in setting working hours. The arrangement is called **flexible working hours,** or **flextime.** Flexible working hours are more frequently found in offices than in factories, mills, or stores. Employees on flexible working hours are required to work certain core hours such as 10 A.M. to 3:30 P.M. However, they are able to choose which hours they work during the workday period from 7 A.M. to 10 A.M. and from 3:30 P.M. to 6:30 P.M. A basic model of flexible working hours is shown in Figure 5-2. Time recording devices are frequently used to monitor whether employees have put in the total number of required hours for the week.

Flexible working hours sometimes increase motivation because employees perceive that they have more control over their hours of work.

Flexible working hours (flextime): A method of organizing hours of work so that employees have flexibility in choosing their own hours.

FIGURE 5–2. *TYPICAL FLEXIBLE WORKING HOURS SCHEDULE*

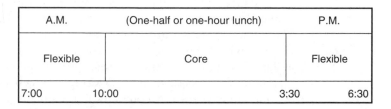

A.M.	(One-half or one-hour lunch)	P.M.
Flexible	Core	Flexible
7:00 10:00		3:30 6:30

The underlying psychology is that being in control satisfies higher-level needs. Although flexible working hours do sometimes increase motivation, the method is much more likely to increase job satisfaction.

Techniques for Motivating Yourself

Many students of business psychology and practicing managers often interpret theories and techniques of work motivation as a way to motivate other people. Of equal importance, a study of work motivation should help you to energize yourself to accomplish worthwhile tasks. In general, applying the techniques discussed in this chapter (and the motivation topics in Chapter 4) to yourself should help you to understand the conditions under which you are likely to work and study hard. Described next are six techniques for motivating yourself, all based on theory and research about human behavior.

Set Goals for Yourself. Goals are fundamental to human motivation. Set yearly, monthly, weekly, daily, and sometimes even morning or afternoon goals for yourself. For example, "By noontime I will have emptied my in-basket and made one suggestion to improve safety practices in our shop." Longer-range, or life, goals can also be helpful in gathering momentum in spurring yourself on toward higher levels of achievement. However, these have to be buttressed by a series of short-range goals. You might have the long-range goal of becoming a bank vice-president, but first it would be helpful to earn an A in a business law course. The contribution of goal setting to your career is explained again in Chapter 6.

Identity and Seek out Your Motivators. Having read this chapter, combined with some serious introspection, you should be able to identify a few personal motivators. Next find a job that offers you them in ample supply. You might have good evidence from your past experience that the opportunity for close contact with people (comradeship or good interpersonal relationships) is a personal motivator. Find a job that involves working in a small, friendly department.

Owing to circumstances, you may have to take whatever job you can find, or you may not be in a position to change jobs. In such a situation, try to arrange your work so you have more opportunity to experience the reward(s) that you are seeking. Assume that solving difficult problems excites you, but your job is 85 percent routine. Develop better work habits so that you can more quickly take care of the routine aspects of your job. This will give you more time to enjoy the creative aspects of your work.

Get Feedback on Your Performance. Few people can sustain a high level of drive without getting an objective or subjective opinion on how well they are doing. Even if you find your work exciting, you will need feedback. Photographers may be enamored with aspects of their work. Yet photographers, more than most people, want their work displayed. A display delivers the message, "Your work is good enough to show to other people."

If your boss or company does not recognize the importance of feed-back (or simply forgets to tell people how they are doing), don't be hesi-tant to ask an occasional question such as:

"Is my work satisfactory so far?"

"How well am I doing in meeting the expectations of my job?"

"I haven't heard anything good or bad about my performance. Should I be worried?"

Apply Behavior Modification to Yourself. The information pre-sented earlier in this chapter about others using behavior modification to motivate you can also be applied to self-motivation. To boost your own motivation through reinforcement principles, you have to (1) decide whether you should be rewarded or punished for your behavior, and (2) administer those rewards or punishments. You become both the jury and the judge.

One method of using behavior mod for self-motivation would be to decide which of the rules for positive reinforcement would make the most sense in your particular situation. A lot depends on the particular motiva-tional problem you are facing. The representative example presented next will help to direct you toward an approach that might work for you.

Eric is a client representative for a company that buys accounts receivable from business firms at a discount. His firm then collects the money that was originally owed to the firm with the accounts receivables. Although *factoring,* as this business is called, is not well known, it is very competitive. Eric realizes being late for appointments with clients is an important work-habit problem. He annoys and angers both prospective and present clients with his lateness. Eric might try this approach:

First, he should make a list of all the good things that might be forthcoming from being punctual for appointments. Among the many items on his list might be increased sales, higher commissions, and fewer customer complaints about him sent back to the office.

Second, Eric should force himself to make a logical plan for arriving promptly for appointments. His plan might include allowing more time for travel, not booking appointments too closely together, and making more careful use of a pocket calendar.

Third, Eric should reward himself for any progress he makes toward the goal of almost 100 percent promptness. He might purchase himself a new sweatshirt for having arrived on time for all appointments for three days; he might buy himself a new tie; he might cook himself a nice meal. Eric should chart his progress, perhaps making simple notations of being early, on time, or late for appointments.

Eric, however, should not reward himself all the time. A fantasy reward now and then could be helpful. Eric might say to himself, "If I continue to be prompt for my appointments I might someday become a vice-president in my company."

Fourth, Eric might develop a plan of administering himself occasional punishments for lack of progress or for slipping backward to even more lateness for appointments. If he is late for several appointments in one week, Eric might punish himself by not watching his favorite sport on television for two weeks. (If the timing is right, he might punish himself by not watching the Super Bowl or the finals of the NCAA men's basketball tournament.)

Many people have used a plan such as Eric's to overcome counterproductive habits such as nail biting and cigarette smoking. With some modification to suit your particular circumstances, you should be able to use behavior modification to motivate yourself toward some worthwhile end.

Increase Your Expectancies. A practical way of using expectancy theory (see Chapter 2) is to increase the subjective probability that your effort will lead to good performance on a given task. One way to increase your expectancy is to increase your level of skill with respect to a task for which you want to be highly motivated. If a person has the necessary skills to perform a particular task, that person will usually raise his or her subjective hunch about the chances of getting the task accomplished.

A recommended strategy for increasing your expectancies in a wide variety of situations is to raise your general level of self-confidence. Self-confident people, by definition, tend to have high subjective hunches that they can perform well in many situations. Raising your self-confidence is a long and gradual process.

Raise Your Level of Self-expectation. A final important strategy for increasing your motivational level has to do with the Pygmalion effect turned inward, or setting up a self-fulfilling prophecy to guide your own behavior. Instead of someone else having high expectations of your performance, you set up these high expectations for yourself. You expect to succeed, so you do succeed. Often this phenomenon is called developing a **positive mental attitude.** Since you expect to succeed, you do succeed, so the net effect is the same as if you increased your level of motivation.

Positive mental attitude:
Expecting to succeed in a given undertaking.

Although the concepts of expectancies and self-expectations are not identical, they are related. If you have many high expectancies, you are a self-confident person. And if you raise your level of self-expectation, you begin to behave in a self-confident manner.

BACK TO THE JOB TASKS

If faced with the job task of motivating another person or yourself, an excellent starting point is to use positive reinforcement. First, think through which reward will be effective for that person, and administer that reward when he, she, or yourself engages in productive behavior. You will, of course, need to follow the other suggestions for using positive reinforcement described in this chapter.

❑ This chapter describes techniques and methods for increasing the motivation of other people and yourself. Work motivation refers to expending effort toward an organizational goal. Motivation also refers to the process of trying to get somebody else to do something. Given a choice, most people are motivated by the prospects of serving their self-interest.

❑ A major influence on whether people show high motivation is their work ethic, a firm belief in the dignity of work. The organizational culture has a strong influence on an employee's work ethic and so does the influence a person's subculture. Opinion is mixed as to whether Americans have a weak or a strong work ethic.

❑ A manager's expectations of team members can influence their actual performance, known as the Pygmalion effect. Employees tend to live up to, or down to, a supervisor's expectations of them.

❑ Behavior modification, particularly positive reinforcement, is a standard motivation program in the workplace. Seven rules are presented here for the use of positive reinforcement. They include (1) stating clearly what behavior will be rewarded, (2) focusing on the positive aspects of performance, (3) using appropriate rewards, and (4) changing rewards periodically.

❑ Financial incentives are effective in increasing motivation and productivity, particularly under these conditions: (1) You need the money. (2) The amount of money can change your life-style. (3) The amount of money you receive is related to your performance. (4) You are tense and anxious about your lack of money.

❑ Giving employees recognition for a job well done can be an effective motivator and lead to increased productivity. Recognition programs involve developing an attractive recognition symbol and making formal award ceremonies. It is possible that, in reality, these programs do more for job satisfaction than motivation.

❑ Another major motivational strategy is motivating people through the work itself, or intrinsic motivation. The theory of intrinsic motivation, or self-determination, emphasizes that people are active agents, rather than recipients of environmental forces. Intrinsic motivation is tied in with needs for competence and self-determination.

❑ Job enrichment capitalizes on intrinsic motivation by adding variety and responsibility to the job. Dimensions of an enriched job include direct feedback, client relationships, control over resources, and personal accountability. An ideal state of job enrichment is when the job holder experiences flow, a feeling of total absorption in the job at hand. It is characterized by intense concentration and effortlessness in performing the job.

❑ A comprehensive strategy for employee motivation is to grant workers more power by allowing them to participate in decisions affecting themselves and their work. Empowerment is the process by which a manager shares power with team members, thereby enhancing their feelings of self-efficacy. Four methods of empowerment and employee participation described here are (1) work teams, (2) participation in technical suggestions, (3) decision making about administrative matters, and (4) participation in setting working hours (flexible working hours).

GUIDELINES FOR PERSONAL EFFECTIVENESS

1. One critical factor related to success in all occupations is motivation—the expenditure of effort toward goals. To increase or sustain your level of motivation, it is recommended that you pick and choose from the techniques described previously.
2. A relatively easy way of increasing your motivation and performance is for others to raise their expectations of you. Raising your self-expectations might be helpful in increasing your own motivation. However, it is not easy to raise your self-expectations.
3. A well-documented and highly recommended approach to motivating others is systematically to apply positive reinforcement. PR can also be helpful in self-motivation.
4. Your level of satisfaction and motivation will increase substantially if you find a job activity so interesting that you experience flow—total absorption in what you are doing.
5. A general strategy for motivating others is to find ways to empower them through participation in decision making. If you are a team member and you want to demonstrate that you are motivated, ask to be empowered.

Discussion Questions and Activities

1. If people in a given country do have a work ethic problem, how does this affect the importance of motivational techniques?
2. How could your instructor make good use of the Pygmalion effect in this course?
3. Give two examples of how you could communicate high expectations to somebody working for you.
4. For what reasons is focusing on the positive aspects of performance more motivational for most people than focusing on the negative aspects?
5. Which of the rewards listed in Table 5-1 are the most appropriate for motivating you? How do you know?
6. How does motivating people through money tie in with behavior modification?
7. What evidence can you provide that recognition is one of the most important motivators in our society?
8. Which personal characteristics of people might influence the effectiveness of empowerment and participation as a motivational tactic?
9. What kind of work has given you, or would give you, the flow experience? Would you take a lower-paying job to get that flow?
10. Ask two managers what they think is the most effective technique of employee motivation. Be prepared to discuss your findings in class.

The Stale Rewards

Charlie Adamski is the postmaster of a large mail-processing facility. One factor in his annual performance review is the number of accidents occurring during the work year. Most accidents typically occur either on the workroom floor, where the mail is processed, or on the street, during mail delivery. On occasion, a postal employee in a more sedentary job will experience an accident.

Adamski keeps on the lookout for ways to reduce work-related accidents without incurring costs that will adversely affect other measures of his performance. Several years ago he instituted a program of providing coffee and doughnuts to any unit that did not have a chargeable accident within the previous quarter. Adamski would arrive in the conference room with the coffee and doughnuts and a plaque commemorating that quarter's achievement. Usually, he would then give a brief speech congratulating the unit before he hurried off to his next appointment. This motivational program has been in place for about three years.

The employees in the accounting section had had only one accident in all the time Barbara Catrett was their manager. One winter day Connie Raven broke her wrist after slipping and falling in the parking lot when it had not been adequately cleared of snow. As a result of this low-accident record, the walls of the accounting section were cluttered with plaques.

Relevant facts about the department employees include the following:

Barbara Catrett, manager. Mid-thirties, health and fitness conscious, a casual dieter.

John Valvano, supervisor. Mid-thirties, has a mild diabetic condition, generally passes on sweets.

Connie Raven, technician. Early forties, very overweight, not on a serious diet.

Ed Small, technician. Late fifties, still relatively trim, will eat one of anything.

Linda Yang, technician. Early twenties, just discovering that she can no longer eat everything, constantly dieting.

Frieda Fromholtz, technician. Late forties, hates sweets.

Cheryl Friedman, technician. Early forties, watches her weight, but will not refuse sweets.

Bob Gambrelli, technician. Late forties, has a medical condition that prevents him from eating most sweets.

One day Charlie arrived with the usual fanfare in the accounting section to deliver his quarterly rewards. About halfway through his typical speech, he stopped and said: "I'm getting pretty tired of these things. Aren't you? Hasn't everybody had enough doughnuts? These aren't even that good. I wish someone would come up with another way to reward the areas that have done a good job of avoiding accidents."

Barbara looked around the room and observed everybody looking pensive. Each employee was jotting down ideas, waiting for Charlie to give the cue to speak. Charlie then said, "If you think of anything, let me know," and walked out of the conference room.

1. What concerns do you think the department members are likely to have about Adamski's program of behavior modification?
2. What rules for applying behavior modification did Adamski violate?
3. How can Adamski revitalize his motivational program?

Source: Case researched by Barbara P. Catrett, Rochester Institute of Technology.

How Do You Motivate a Coupon Sorter?

The R. G. Blair Company specializes in the distribution and redemption of grocery store discount coupons. At the heart of its operation is a huge coupon sorting department. The task of sorting coupons into appropriate boxes is performed manually by men and women employees of different ages. Each coupon sorter is surrounded by a never-ending supply of thousands of coupons. Each day, each hour, the work is the same—sorting coupons into their appropriate boxes and sending the boxes on to the next department responsible for their processing.

One day Jennie Kent, manager of the coupon sorting department, was visited by Lance McGraw, her counterpart in another location of the firm. "Thanks so much for allowing me to visit your operation," said Lance. "As I mentioned over the phone, I am really curious about how you folks are running your coupon sorting department. You seem to be doing well, and we're having lots of trouble."

"Thanks for the compliment," said Jennie. "But what kind of trouble are you having?"

"Our problem is turnover. It's vicious. We're having a tough time keeping employees on the job for more than a few months. We only have three satisfactory employees in the department who have stayed with us over a year."

"Lance, what do you see as the basic problem?" said Jennie.

"It must obviously be the job itself. It's a nightmare for the average person. The job isn't even clean. After a while a lot of the ink on those coupons comes off on your hands and clothing. The employees are forced to wear smocks and gloves unless they want stained clothing and hands. The job reminds me of raking leaves after a fall rainstorm. There's no end to it. Just nonstop coupons."

"What screening devices has your personnel department used for the employees?" inquired Jennie.

"We try to be as thorough as we can in terms of the type of people we hire for the job of coupon sorter. We check references. We even use personnel tests. We look for solid citizens who are fairly bright."

Jennie responded, "Lance, I think I've located your problem. You are setting your mental ability requirements too high. I suspect the best coupon sorters would have average to below average intelligence. People brighter than that would become restless sorting coupons."

Lance McGraw took Jennie Kent's advice and did install new screening procedures for hiring coupon sorters. After eight months of using these procedures, it seemed that some of Lance's earlier problems were under control. Turnover was down and the newly hired employees seemed to enjoy their work. Several of the new employees even took the initiative to thank management for having given them a job that is just right for them. Lance noticed, however, that productivity within the group was below company standards. Although the coupon sorters seemed to be enjoying their work, they were too relaxed. They did not seem to pay much attention to the output figures suggested by the company.

Lance paid another visit to Jennie. The substance of his comments was, "Jennie, this time I have another tale of woe. The personnel procedures you suggested have helped me reduce turnover. And some of the new people we hired are good workers. But I think we have a bunch of contented farm animals. They like what they are doing, but they are working at a pace below what R. G. Blair Company wants.

"What advice can you give me to get these coupon sorters to hustle a little? As you know, there are strict limits on what we can pay them."

1. What program of employee motivation do you suggest be used to increase the productivity of these coupon sorters?
2. Do you think that management should adopt a philosophy of "shape up or ship out"? Why or why not?

A Business Psychology Role Play

Motivating a Coupon Sorter

Lance McGraw decides to attempt an individual motivation program with the coupon sorters. He plans to identify the psychological needs of each employee and then give each employee a chance to satisfy his or her needs using positive reinforcement. Lance has a motivational meeting this morning with Bertha Kelp, a contented but not so productive coupon sorter. One student plays the role of Lance. Another student plays the role of Bertha, who wonders why her boss wants to speak to her. She hopes she might be getting a raise.

References

1. STEPHEN P. ROBBINS, *Organizational Behavior: Concepts, Controversies, and Applications,* 4th ed. (Englewood Cliffs, NJ: Prentice Hall, 1989), p. 147.

2. ROBERT EISENBERGER, *Blue Monday: A Loss of the Work Ethic in America* (New York: Paragon House, 1989).

3. JULIET SCHOR, *The Overworked American: The Unexpected Decline of Leisure* (New York: Basic Books, 1992).

4. KAREN MATTHES, "From Welfare to the Workplace: America Works," *Personnel,* August 1991, p. 23.

5. DOV EDEN, *Pygmalion in Management: Productivity as a Self-fulfilling Prophecy* (Lexington, MA: Lexington Books, 1990).

6. CHARLOTTE D. SUTTON AND RICHARD W. WOODMAN, "Pygmalion Goes to Work: The Effects of Supervisor Expectations in a Retail Setting," *Journal of Applied Psychology,* December 1989, pp. 943–950.

7. RICHARD E. KOPELMAN, "Linking Pay to Performance Is a Proven Management Tool," *Personnel Administrator,* October 1983, p. 68.

8. STUART FELDMAN, "Another Day, Another Dollar Needs Another Look," *Personnel,* January 1991, p. 9.

9. KEVIN M. PAULSEN, "Lessons Learned from Gainsharing," *HRMagazine,* April 1991, p. 70.

10. NANCY J. PERRY, "Here Come Richer, Riskier Pay Plans," *Fortune,* December 1988, p. 51.

11. DAVID J. CHERRINGTON, "Follow through on Award Programs," *HRMagazine,* April 1992, pp. 52–55; BOB MARTIN, "A Case for Rewarding Recognition," *Personnel Journal,* December 1986, pp. 66–68.

12. MARTIN, "A Case for Rewarding Recognition."

13. EDWARD L. DECI, JAMES P. CONNELL, AND RICHARD M. RYAN, "Self-determination in a Work Organization," *Journal of Applied Psychology,* August 1989, pp. 580.

14. FREDERICK HERZBERG, "The Wise Old Turk," *Harvard Business Review,* September–October 1974, pp. 70–80.

15. MICHAEL CSIKSZENTMIHALYI, *Flow: The Psychology of Optimal Experience* (New York: Harper & Row, 1990).

16. Quoted in JOAN CROWDER, "Prolific Ray Bradbury Busy Teaching Enthusiasm," *The New York Times* syndicated story, March 8, 1990.

17. JAY A. CONGER AND RABINDRA N. KANUNGO, "The Empowerment Process: Integrating Theory and Practice," *Academy of Management Review,* July 1988, pp. 473–474.

18. Frank Shipper and Charles C. Manz, "Employee Self-management without Formally Designated Teams: An Alternative Road to Empowerment," *Organizational Dynamics,* Winter 1992, p. 48.

19. Dawn Gunsch, "Employees Team up with HR," *Personnel Journal,* October 1991, p. 68.

20. E. J. Cattabiani and Randall P. White, "Participative Management," *Issues & Observations,* August 1988, p. 2.

21. Ron Zembe, "Scandanavian Management—A Look at the Future?" *Management Review,* July 1988, p. 46.

Suggested Reading

Belohlav, James A. *Championship Management: An Action Model for High Performance.* Cambridge, MA: Productivity Press, 1990.

Byham, William C. *Zapp! The Lightening of Empowerment.* New York: Harmony Books, 1991.

"Farewell, Fast Track: Promotions and Raises Are Scarcer—So What Will Energize Managers?" *Business Week,* December 10, 1990, pp. 192–200.

Friedman, Myles, II, and Lackey, George H., Jr. *The Psychology of Human Control: A General Theory of Purposeful Behavior.* Westport, CT: Praeger, 1991.

Grensing, Lin. *Motivating Today's Workforce.* Vancouver, British Columbia: Self-counsel Press, 1991.

Huret, Judy. "Paying for Team Results." *HRMagazine,* May 1991, pp. 39–43.

Newsom, Walter B. "Motivate, Now!" *Personnel Journal,* February 1990, pp. 50–55.

Pritchard, Robert D. *Measuring and Improving Organizational Productivity: A Practical Guide.* Westport, CT: Praeger, 1990.

Schwisow, C. Ronald. "Tools for Your Motivational Campaign." *HRMagazine,* November 1991, pp. 63–64.

Weber, Joseph. "A Big Company That Works." *Business Week,* May 4, 1992, pp. 124–132.

Wellins, Richard S., Byham, William C., and Wilson, Jeanne M. *Empowered Teams: Creating Self-directed Work Groups That Improve Quality, Productivity, and Participation.* San Francisco: Jossey-Bass, 1991.

Chapter 6

ACHIEVING SUCCESS THROUGH GOAL SETTING

Learning Objectives

After reading and studying this chapter and doing the exercises, you should be able to

1. Understand the contribution of goal setting to achieving success.
2. Explain the basics of goal–setting theory.
3. Identify various types of goals.
4. Specify the characteristics of effective goals.
5. Understand how goals are used to increase productivity on the job.
6. Prepare a tentative set of career goals.
7. Pinpoint the problems sometimes created by goals.

JOB TASKS RELATED TO THIS CHAPTER

Goal setting is related to numerous job tasks. The most frequent opportunity for goal setting is to jointly establish productivity goals with your manager. As a member of a work team, you might be asked to establish goals for increasing quality or reducing defects. In many jobs, a person might be asked to set goals for reducing costs.

Almost all successful people use goal setting to help them organize their lives and achieve success. Some goals of successful people are lofty, such as the captain of a basketball team declaring that her "Lady Longhorns" will be national champions this year. Others are more modest, such as the sales manager aiming to have lunch with each of his sales representative once during the next two months.

Goals lie at the core of many motivational theories and approaches to work improvement. This chapter can therefore be regarded as an extension of the discussion of motivation. Our study of goals and success begins with an overview of their advantages, followed by such topics as goal-setting theory, different types of goals, actions plans, effective goals, and the use of goals to enhance productivity and career planning.

The Contribution of Goal Setting To Success

Goal:
The object or aim of a person's actions.

A **goal** is the object or aim of a person's actions. Goals give us direction and help us to focus our efforts in a consistent direction. Without a goal, our effort is often scattered in a variety of directions. We keep trying, but it leads us nowhere unless we are very lucky.

Despite the contribution of goals to success, technically speaking, they are not motivational by themselves. Rather, the discrepancies created by what individuals do and what they aspire to do creates self-dissatisfaction. The dissatisfaction in turn creates a desire to reduce the discrepancy between the real and the ideal.[1] The tension created by not having already achieved your goal spurs you to reach your goal. If your goal is to prepare a 25-page report for your boss by 10 days from now, your dissatisfaction with not having started should propel you into action. The specific contributions of goal setting are described next.

Goals Consistently Lead to Improved Performance. Research indicates that goal-setting programs are a highly effective technique for improving performance. The effectiveness of goal setting as a motivational tool is seldom questioned.[2] People who set goals increase their chances of receiving better performance appraisals, getting more work accomplished, and earning more money.

Part of the contribution of goal setting to performance is that goals serve as self-fulling prophecies. Once you set a goal that you accept, you will gear your actions toward making that goal come true. Assume that a sales representative sets a goal of $100,000 in sales for the week. If the representative's sales are less than $50,000 on Wednesday, he or she will engage in a flurry of activity on Thursday and Friday to reach the $100,000 target.

Setting Goals and Reaching Them Brings Personal Satisfaction. Attaining a goal you perceive as worthwhile is a sure route to satisfaction. This is one reason a sport like basketball or soccer can be so exhilarating. Each time you score a goal you receive an emotional lift.

Attaining Goals Is a Confidence Builder. The most potent way of building self-confidence is to set and reach goals. Each act of goal attainment bolsters your belief in your own capabilities.

Setting Goals Gives You a Sense of Mission. Like an organization, each career person can benefit from a mission or purpose. Establishing goals gives you a sense of mission and a purpose that serve as guidelines for your career. A financial consultant (stockbroker) might say, "My mission is to help my clients improve the quality of their lives. I will therefore make available to them the financial products best suited to their particular needs."

Goal Setting Theory

Thousands of studies have been conducted about the relationship between goal setting and work performance. Enough consistency is found in these findings to provide guidelines for motivating people.[3] The best established facts about goal-setting theory are outlined in Figure 6-1. The basic premise underlying goal-setting theory is that behavior is regulated by values and goals. Our values create within us a desire to do things consistent with them. The goals are what we want to accomplish.

Goal-setting theory also contends that difficult goals lead to a higher level of performance than do easy goals. Although setting difficult goals is effective, goals should not be set so unrealistically high that they result in frustration due to failure.

It is also important to make goals specific, such as "reduce billing errors to less than 1 percent," rather than "do your best with the billing problem." The goals people work toward tend to lead to improved performance regardless of whether these goals are set by them or the organization—provided that the individual accepts the goal.

FIGURE 6–1. *THE BASICS OF GOAL-SETTING THEORY.*

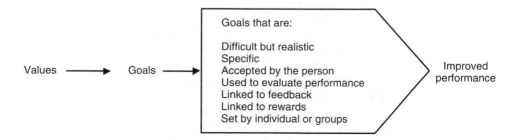

Values ⟶ Goals ⟶

Goals that are:

Difficult but realistic
Specific
Accepted by the person
Used to evaluate performance
Linked to feedback
Linked to rewards
Set by individual or groups

Improved performance

Goals are also more effective when the person knows that they will be used to evaluate performance. Furthermore, the person should receive feedback on the goals and should be rewarded for reaching them.[4] Goal setting combined with financial rewards is thus a powerful motivator, as implied in our discussion of motivation. When goals are set for both individuals and their work groups, goals lead to even higher levels of performance.[5]

Goal Setting According To Difficulty Level and Time Period

Two basic ways of setting goals are according to when they will be accomplished and how difficult they are to accomplish. Goal setting is likely to be more effective when both dimensions are included in the goals.

Difficulty Level

Most jobs and careers involve a mixture of routine and nonroutine activities. Therefore, divide your goals into three categories based on how difficult they are to attain: routine, challenging, and breakthrough.

Routine Goals. Routine goals refer to the day-to-day activities that make up so much of life, even of the busy executive. Quite often they represent the contents of a daily activity (to do) list. Routine activities include such matters as "Authorize expense voucher for Jennifer," "Inspect valve on acid tank," "Reorder magazine subscription," "Get telephone repaired," and "Renew lease." Observe carefully that routine should not be confused with unimportant: a career can be ruined by not taking care of such routine items as inspecting a valve or renewing a lease.

Challenging Goals. Your goals should also include those that help you grow and prosper. These challenging goals expand your horizon and are personally uplifting; they stretch your capability to a reasonable extent. To derive much payoff from goal setting, you must establish some challenging goals. Challenging goals call for prudent risks, such as borrowing money for a new business venture—but not so much that you will go bankrupt if your investment does not yield a quick return.

What constitutes a challenge depends on your capabilities and past accomplishments. Learning how to use a new software package might be a challenge to a person with limited computer experience. A computer buff might classify this as a routine goal.

Breakthrough Goals. The highest level of goals is referred to as breakthrough or fantasy. Attaining it brings you substantial recognition, power, influence, and often wealth. Breakthrough goals take you to the outer limits of your capabilities. Attaining them requires talent, careful planning, hard work, and a few good breaks. Breakthrough goals are also referred to as fantasy goals because they are positive dreams that goad you toward high levels of accomplishment. Fantasy goals are good for mental health because they help you to cope with an unpleasant situation by giving you hope for the future.

According to a strict interpretation of goal-setting research, goals will be more helpful in attaining routine than challenging or breakthrough goals. Nevertheless, goals still make some contribution to reaching complex goals.[6]

The Time Dimension in Goal Setting

Many of the goals mentioned in this chapter include a date for their attainment. It also helps the goal-setting process to classify goals into a time frame roughly as follows: long range, medium range, short range, daily, and immediate.

Long-range goals relate to the overall life-style that you wish to achieve, including your highest level of career accomplishment and the family situation you hope to have. A hospital might set the long-term goal of becoming "the biggest and most influential general hospital in this region by the year 2000."

Medium-range goals relate to events that will take place in the next five years or so. They concern things such as the type of education or training you plan to undertake and the next step in your career. An example of a medium-range goal is "Become a supervisor within this company within four years." You usually have more control over medium- than long-range goals and you can tell how well you are achieving them. If you are falling behind in reaching a medium-range goal, you can adjust your actions accordingly.

Short-range goals cover the period from about one month to one year into the future. Many short-range goals are used on the job, as illustrated in the preceding section.

Daily goals relate to what you intend to accomplish today. Most successful people establish daily goals for themselves in the form of a "to do" list (see Figure 6-2). We will return to this topic in Chapter 16.

Immediate goals are concerned with the next 15 minutes to an hour. No one can accomplish long-range, medium-range, short-range, or daily goals without paying attention to immediate goals. A successful philosophy of goal setting contends, "The only kind of planning you have direct control over are the modest little goals; the trick of planning a successful life is to stack together these smaller goals in a way that increases your chances of reaching the long-range goals you really care about."[7]

Suggestions for Setting Effective Goals

Setting a goal that leads to success is not so simple. The following paragraphs offer some suggestions for establishing goals that are likely to result in successful outcomes.

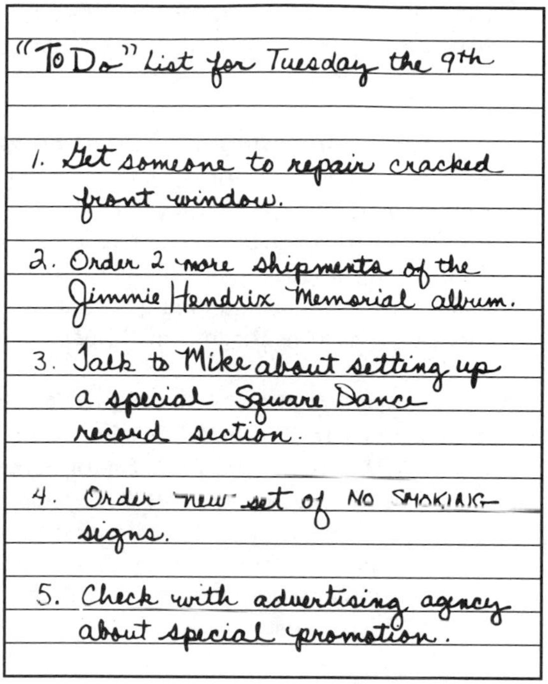
"To Do" List for Tuesday the 9th

1. Get someone to repair cracked front window.

2. Order 2 more shipments of the Jimmie Hendrix Memorial album.

3. Talk to Mike about setting up a special Square Dance record section.

4. Order new set of NO SMOKING signs.

5. Check with advertising agency about special promotion.

FIGURE 6–2. *DAILY WORK GOALS OF ASSISTANT MANAGER OF RECORD STORE.*

1. Formulate Clear, Concise, and Unambiguous Goals. A misunderstood goal can have negative consequences. An understandable, and therefore useful, goal can be expressed in a concise statement much like a computer message. Such a goal might be "Develop an inventory control system that reduces inventory costs by 25 percent by June 30 of this year."

2. Describe What You Would Actually Be Doing if You Reached Your Goal. A vague goal for a data-entry specialist would be "to become a better data-entry specialist." A more useful goal would be "to increase current speed" from 40 wpm to 65 wpm. The meaning of "better data-entry specialist" needs to be narrowed down as much as possible.

3. Imagine How It Would Feel To Accomplish Your Goal. An exciting way of improving your ability to work with goals is to use visual imagery. Imagine what it would be like to achieve your goal. Create a mental image of activities such as making an excellent presentation to management or winning a sales contest. Imagery is so useful that it has become a standard training technique for improving work performance.

4. The Goal Must Be Consistent with Organizational Policies and Procedures. A goal that violates company policy only leads its setter into trouble. One caseworker established the objective of making night calls to agency clients in order to facilitate communication with them. She was later reprimanded by higher management for violating an agency restriction about after-hours work.

5. Set Interesting and Challenging Goals Whenever Possible. It is important to recognize that trivial goals are not motivational. At the same time, goals that are too far beyond your capability may lead to frustration and despair because there is a good chance you will fail to reach them. Realistic goals fall somewhere between the two. An income tax specialist might find challenging a goal that stated, "Successfully complete income tax returns for my small business clients by April 15 of this year."

6. Specify What Is Going to Be Accomplished, Who Is Going to Accomplish It, When It Is Going to Be Accomplished, and How It Is Going to Be Accomplished. Establishing the "what," "who," "when," and "how" in your goals reduces the chance for misinterpretation. Here is a work goal meeting these requirements: "The waterbed sales manager will increase sales by 50 percent within 12 months. Returns will be subtracted from the dollar amount of sales. Waterbeds will not be offered to the public at or below cost."

7. Review Your Goals from Time to Time. An experienced goal setter realizes that all goals are temporary to some extent. In time, one particular goal may lose its relevance for you and may therefore no longer motivate you. At one period in your life you may be committed to earning an income in the top 10 percent of the population. Along the way toward achieving that goal, some other more relevant goal may develop. You might decide that the satisfactions of being self-employed are more important than earning a particular amount of money. You might therefore open a retail store with the simple financial goal of "meeting my expenses."

Up to this point we have described the advantages of goal setting, goal-setting theory, different types of goals, and characteristics of effective goals. Before proceeding further, do the exercise in Figure 6-3. It gives you an opportunity to think through your readiness to accept goals as part of your life.

Action Plans To Support Goals

Action plan:
A series of steps to be taken to achieve a goal.

Goals alone often fail to achieve their intended purpose of accomplishing something worthwhile. To accomplish a purpose, it is usually necessary to support goals with **action plans**—a series of steps to be taken to achieve a goal. The major reason you need an action plan for most goals is that, without a method for achieving what you want, the goal is likely to slip by.

One goal mentioned in the preceding section concerned a data-entry specialist who intended to "increase current speed from 40 wpm to 65 wpm. per hour." Action planning to achieve this goal might include such

FIGURE 6–3. *ARE YOU READY FOR GOAL SETTING?*

Answer each of the following questions spontaneously and candidly. As with all self-help quizzes, if you try to answer the question in a way that will put you in a favorable light, you will miss some potentially valuable diagnostic information. For each question answer 1 for strongly disagree, 2 for disagree, and 3 for a neutral attitude, 4 for agree and 5 for strongly agree.

1. I almost always know what day of the month it is. _____
2. I regularly prepare "to do" lists. _____
3. I make good use of my "to do" lists. _____
4. I can tell you almost precisely how many times I engaged in my favorite sport or hobby this year. _____
5. I keep close tabs on the win and lose record of my favorite athletic team. _____
6. I have a reasonably accurate idea of the different income tax brackets. _____
7. I use a budget to control my personal expenses. _____
8. I know how much money I want to be making in five years. _____
9. I know what position I want to hold in five years. _____
10. Careful planning is required to accomplish anything of value. _____

Total _____

Scoring and Interpretation: Add up your point score. If your score is 40 points or higher, you are probably already convinced of the value of goal setting. If your score is between 20 and 39 points, you are in the middle range of readiness to incorporate goal setting into your life. You probably need to study more about goal setting to capitalize on its value. If your score is between 10 and 19 points, you are far from ready to accept goal setting. Carefully review the information about the advantages of goal setting mentioned previously. Until you change your attitudes about the contribution of goals to your life, you will not become an active goal setter and planner.

things as (1) taking a refresher training course, (2) participating in a stress management workshop to improve mental concentration, and (3) getting more sleep on a regular basis to increase mental alertness.

Some goals are so difficult to reach that your action plan might encompass hundreds of separate activities. You would then have to develop separate action plans for your major subgoals. If your goal were to have a rewarding and satisfying career, the techniques presented in this book could help you formulate many of your action plans. Among these skill-building techniques are assertiveness, resolving conflict, solving problems and making decisions, and developing good work habits.

Some very short term goals do not really require an action plan. A mere statement of the goal may point to an obvious action plan. If your goal were to get your computer account number from your school or employer today, it would not be necessary to draw up a formal action plan, such as "Go to office of student services, speak to office assistant, ask for computer account number form, take ball pen from pocket, fill out form, return same."

A standard way of increasing productivity on the job is through a goal-setting program. Employees at all levels set goals and develop action plans. Their performance is then judged in terms of how well they have achieved these goals. To explain how goals contribute to organizational productivity, we describe a goal-setting program in general, an elaborate goal-setting program in one company, and some research pendings.

Management by Objectives

Management by objectives (MBO): A formal program of goal setting and review of performance against goals that is applied on an organizationwide basis.

Management by objectives (MBO) is a formal program of goal setting and review of performance against goals that is applied on an organizationwide basis. It is fundamentally an application of goal theory to help individuals and organizations be more productive. Although MBO is not nearly as popular as in the past, many firms now use a less rigid version of the original system.

MBO is used in both private and public organizations, and the specific format varies considerably. A modern application of management by objectives, "Turbo MBO," is described in the accompanying box. Despite the variation, one key element can be found in most programs: an MBO program typically involves people setting many objectives for themselves. However, management frequently imposes important objectives on people. The top management of a hospital might impose the following objective on all ward personnel: "All prescription drugs must be accounted for with 100 percent accuracy."

A sample set of objectives is shown in Figure 6-4. The caseworker who set these objectives took into account the requirements of her boss and the agency. Even if you set objectives, they still take into account the needs of your employer.

FIGURE 6–4. *FORM USED IN SOCIAL AGENCY FOR STATEMENT OF OBJECTIVES.*

Job Title and Brief Job Description
Caseworker: Responsible for interviewing applicants for public assistance. Serve as liaison person between agency and client. Provide clients assistance on matters of managing personal resources.

Objectives for Wanda Benjamin
1. By December 31, 1996, fifteen percent of my clients will be able to live adequately without benefit of public assistance. I will accomplish this by helping them to find employment or additional help from close relatives.
2. Improve my handling of working with difficult clients by using forml techniques to achieve this end. I will attend a workshop on handling difficult people in February.
3. Decrease by 75 percent the number of case reports that I submit to my manager past their due date.
4. Increase by 20 percent the number of clients that I serve by spending less time with my most troubled clients.
5. Will coordinate my efforts more closely with utility company to ensure that my clients do not spend cold nights without heat.

TURBO MBO: THE ULTIMATE SYSTEM TO KEEP A COMPANY ON TARGET

In a darkened conference room in the San Jose, California, headquarters of Cypress Semiconductor Corp., the company's seven vice-presidents sit in tense silence. Today is Wednesday, the day of reckoning. Every Wednesday at noon sharp, T. J. Rodgers, president and CEO, assembles his top management team for a status report on the goals of each department. In the confines of this corporate boardroom, there is no escaping a late report or a delinquent budget. The harsh light of a computer-generated projector beams down detailed charts on the status of each executive's weekly goals.

Today, Fred Jenne, vice-president of research and development, is on the spot. An electrical failure is cropping up in one of the company's new prototype chips, and Rodgers wants to know why. There is a good chance that the glitch can be traced to one of two potential sources—an error in the chip's design specifications or a mistake made by the chip designer himself. Jenne is quick to demonstrate that he has a handle on the problem. Cypress's extensive goal-setting system allowed him to pinpoint a flaw in the software used to help test the chip, and Jenne announces proudly that it is already being corrected.

Rodgers refers to Cypress's version of MBO as a Turbo MBO—a souped-up, computer-driven monster that tracks the goals of every company employee. For example, the vice-president of finance and administration is responsible for 5 to 7 of his own goals every week, plus another 100 goals on behalf of the 20 people reporting to him.

Rodgers has the soul of his entire company at his fingertips. With the touch of a few keys on his personal computer, Rodgers can call up any one of about 4,500 weekly goals for his 670 employees. It is a system that keeps Rodgers on top of the company's day-to-day operations. "Just by looking at my computer or a computer printout, I can take any project at our company, put it under a microscope, and find out exactly what is going on," says the 39-year-old CEO.

The Turbo MBO is revved up every Monday morning at Cypress. Project leaders sit down with their staff and jointly decide which jobs need attention that week. At the end of the day, the new goals are put into a minicomputer that is linked to managers via personal computers. Spreadsheet software is used to display employee goals and continually update their status. By the pivotal Wednesday meeting, any manager delinquent on more than 35 percent of his or her goals will have some explaining to do. A company executive says that to work effectively with this system you have to be the kind of person who "can make commitments and be accountable for them all the time. There are no excuses for not executing well."

A major component of the Cypress performance measurement system is "killer software." Assume, for example, that a manager has ordered a product from an outside supplier. The order does not arrive on time, but no one has provided senior management with an explanation. A computer program then shuts down all the computer systems in purchasing. To get the system back up, the offending manager has to contact the supplier, obtain a new delivery date, and report the news back to the Cypress chief financial officer.

Rodgers believes that the benefits gain from increased productivity outweigh the costs of an occasional shutdown. After a shutdown, employees say, "What happened, and how can we make sure it never happens again?" The Cypress system of electronic bloodhounds has now been copied by a number of other companies.

Source: Based on facts as reported in Steve Kaufman, "Going for the Goals," *Success,* January–February 1988, pp. 39–41; Richard Brandt, "Here Comes the Attack of the Killer Software," *Business Week,* December 9, 1991, p. 70.

Research Evidence about Management By Objectives

Management by objective systems are widely used in both private and public organizations. Often, government agencies are required to use MBO to receive funding because goal setting is associated with being efficient. The

contribution management by objectives makes to improving organizational productivity varies considerably. In some programs studied, the productivity increases have been huge. In others the increases in productivity have been small, and in some instances productivity has actually decreased.

A major reason that MBO usually increases productivity is that it is a combination of three techniques of proven ability to improve performance: goal setting, participation in decision making, and objective feedback.[8]

The extent of top-management commitment is a deciding factor in whether or not an MBO program is successful. If top-level managers really want the program and participate in it themselves, the program has a good chance of success. Bausch and Lomb Corporation, a successful manufacturer of optical and health-care products, is a case in point. Top executives in several of the divisions make their goals known to staff members, thus demonstrating their commitment to MBO.

Meta-analysis:
A study of studies, combining quantitative information from them all.

Two researchers conducted a **meta-analysis** of 70 studies evaluating the contribution of management by objectives to organizational productivity. (A meta-analysis is basically a study of studies, combining quantitative information from them all.) The effect of MBO on an entire organization was evaluated in some studies. In others, the impact of MBO on a single department, division, or plant was studied.

Sixty-eight out of the 70 studies showed productivity gains, and only two studies showed losses. The mean productivity gain was 44.6 percent. In studies where costs were used to measure the effectiveness of MBO, costs decreased an average of 26 percent. In organizations with high commitment from top management, the average productivity gain was 56.5 percent. In the organizations with moderate commitment, the average gain was 32.9 percent. In the organizations with low commitment, the average gain was 6.1 percent.[9]

In conclusion, goal setting in organizations is an effective way to increase productivity, especially when top management is committed to the program.

Ethical Concerns about MBO Programs. The MBO approach to goal setting has aroused a good deal of controversy, despite the many solid contributions it has made to organizations. Among the criticisms of MBO is that it manipulates employees and is therefore unethical. MBO programs are sold to employees as being organizationwide programs of participative management. Yet, in practice, not much participation takes place.

After interviewing several hundred managers in an MBO program, one researcher reached this conclusion: "Managers may feel forced to accept objectives that they honestly feel are unrealistic or undesirable because they are unable to argue effectively against them."[10] The argument here is that your input is important if you are going to be measured in terms of how well you achieved these objectives.

A stronger ethical argument against MBO is that they are systems of phony participation. The fiction is maintained that the subordinate is making a real input into planning work goals and procedures. Yet he or she is forced into setting goals that fit exactly what the company wanted in the first place.

Of course, not all employees working under an MBO (or similar) system feel they are being manipulated. Do you see any ethical problems with management by objectives?

Setting Goals for Your Career

Career goal:
A specific position, type of work, or income level that a person aspires to reach.

Career path:
A sequence of positions necessary to achieve a career goal.

Target position:
The ultimate goal of a career path.

Your chances of achieving career success increase if you establish carefully formulated goals. If your goals are laid out systematically to lead to your ultimate **career goal,** you have established a career path. A **career path** is thus a sequence of positions necessary to achieve a goal. The ultimate goal you are seeking is called a **target position.**

If a career path is laid out in one firm, it must be related to the present and future demands of that firm. If you aspire toward a high-level manufacturing job, it would be vital to know the future of manufacturing in that firm. Many U.S. firms, for example, plan to conduct more of their manufacturing in the Pacific Rim and Mexico. If you were really determined, you might study the appropriate language and ready yourself for a global position.

While laying out a career path, it is also helpful to list your personal goals. They should mesh with your work plans to avoid major conflicts in your life. Some life-styles, for example, are incompatible with some career paths. It would be difficult to develop a stable home life (spouse, children, friends, community activities, garden) if a person aspired toward holding field positions in international marketing. Contingency ("what if") plans should also be incorporated into a well-designed career path. For

A person's chances of finding career satisfaction increase if he or she establishes clear-cut goals.

instance, "If I don't become an agency supervisor by age 35, I will seek employment in the private sector." Or, "If I am not promoted within two years, I will enroll in an advanced degree program."

Lisa Irving, an ambitious 20-year-old, formulated the career path shown below prior to receiving an associate degree in business administration. After she presented her tentative career path to her classmates, several accused Lisa of shooting for the moon. Lisa's career goals are high, but she has established contingency plans. Presented as an example, not as an ideal model, here is Lisa's career path:

Work

1. Purchasing trainee for two years
2. Assistant purchasing agent for three years
3. Purchasing agent for five years (will join Purchasing Manager's Association)
4. Purchasing supervisor for five years
5. Purchasing manager for six years
6. Manager, materials handling for five years
7. Vice-president, procurement, until retirement

Personal Life

1. Rent own apartment after one year of working
2. Attend college evenings until receive B.S. in business administration
3. Marriage by age 27 (plan only one marriage)
4. One child by age 30
5. Live in private home with husband and children by age 33
6. Volunteer work for Downs syndrome children
7. Travel to India before age 50

FIGURE 6–5. *A CAREER PATH.*

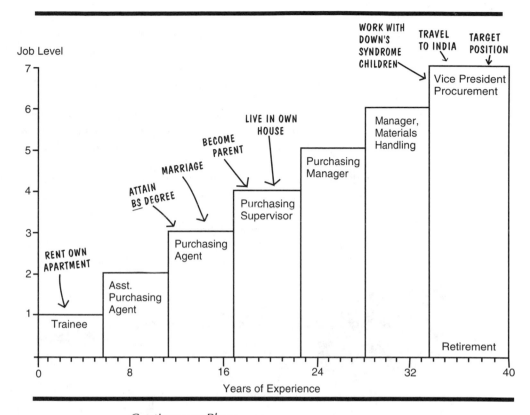

Contingency Plans

1. Will seek new employment by stage 3 if not promoted to purchasing agent.
2. If not promoted to vice-president by stage 6, will consider opening small retail business.
3. If I encounter sex discrimination at any stage, will look for employment with firm that has large government contracts (where discrimination is much less likely).
4. If I develop stress disorder at any point, will seek nonsupervisory position in purchasing field.

Career paths can also be laid out graphically, as shown in Figure 6-5. One benefit of a career path laid out in chart form is that it gives a clear perception of climbing steps toward your target position. As each position is attained, the corresponding step can be shaded in color or cross-hatched.

Most of the goals just mentioned include a time element, which is crucial to sound career management. Your long-range goal might be clearly established in your mind (such as regional manager of a hotel chain). At the same time, you must establish short-range (get any kind of job in a hotel) and intermediate-range (manager of a hotel by age 27) goals. Goals set too far in the future that are not supported with more immediate goals may lose their motivational value.

Personal goals enter heavily into the formulation of career goals. For this reason alone, it is well worth setting personal goals and objectives in conjunction with career goals. Ideally, there would be an integration of career and personal goals. Several examples are in order.

One person may have a strong interest in visiting museums, shopping at retail stores, dancing at night clubs, and dining at a variety of restaurants. One personal goal he formulates is to have enough money and to live in an area where he can lead such a cosmopolitan life. His occupational goals should then include developing job skills that are needed in large cities.

Another person might develop an early preference in life for the outdoors, with an emphasis on bird watching, fishing, and camping. She might also be interested in raising a large family. Part of her career planning should include developing skills that are in demand in rural areas where her preferences are easier to satisfy than in a city. She then learns that in recent years many manufacturing facilities have been developed in rural and semi-

Some people find it exciting to add an element of fantasy into their personal goal setting.

rural areas. Her career planning might then include the goal of developing job skills that are in demand in a factory or mill. Secretarial skills, of course, are in demand everywhere. Another alternative for her would be to develop technical and professional skills that would enable her to find a manufacturing job. For instance, she might seek a job as a production planner.

Career Goals Can Influence Personal Goals. In many situations a person's career goal exerts a heavy influence on personal goals. A 22-year-old man decided that he wanted to become a commercial artist. One of his major personal goals was to become a successful motorcycle racer. After careful deliberation, he decided to give up on his motorcycle goals. The reason he offered was this: "Without a good right hand and a good mind, I'll never make it as a commercial artist. Too many of my buddies have been smashed up racing their bikes. My art means more to me, so I'll find some other off-the-job thrills. Maybe golf or model airplane racing."

Other individuals have postponed marriage or raising families in order to better establish themselves in their career. A heavy travel schedule, for instance, might place too many strains on a young marriage or a young family. Some people with heavy travel schedules have postponed raising a family until that phase of their career has passed.

Fantasy and Personal Goal Setting. Fantasy goals and their benefits were mentioned previously in relation to work goals. Some people find it exciting to add an element of fantasy to personal goal setting. Fantasy goals offer the additional advantage of bridging the gap between personal and career goal setting. Here is a sampling of fantasy goals found in the career reports of people age 21 or under.

> "Someday I would like to own a stable of horses and have one of them win the Kentucky Derby."
>
> "I would like to take a year off from work and go big-game hunting in Africa."
>
> "Once my children are grown, I would like to travel around the world taking nature photographs for fun and profit."
>
> "Before I retire I would like to be a millionaire and buy a major league hockey team."

Problems Goals Can Create

Despite the positive aspects of goals discussed in this chapter, they are not without flaws. Three major criticisms of goal setting will be discussed next.

Goals Often Neglect Achieving a Balance between Quality and Quantity. If you set difficult goals on the job, quantity may be given priority over quality. You might, for example, turn out shoddy products just to meet your quota. An example from personal life is that you might set an arbitrary goal of dating six new people over the next three months. In your quest to date six people you might fail to recognize that the fifth person you date would make an excellent long-term companion for you. In short, in addition to setting goals, you should set priorities as to the relative importance of quantity and quality.

Goals Sometimes Become Obsessions. In some instances people become so obsessed with reaching particular goals that they cannot react to emergencies or they fail to grasp real opportunities. Many sales representatives neglect to invest time in cultivating a prospective customer simply because of the pressure to achieve a specific sales quota.

Short-range goals sometimes backfire for another reason. Long-term negative consequences are sometimes ignored for the sake of the short range. The argument has been advanced, for example, that saving the taxpayer money by cutting back on youth programs could incur more expense in the long run. Some of the young people no longer enrolled in the youth program might turn to crime. It can cost society as much as $35,000 per year to imprison one convicted criminal.

When goals become obsessions, they lead to neglect in another way. Sensing that reaching goals is the only thing the company cares about, an individual might neglect other important aspects of his or her job. Suppose you are a sales representative in a furniture store. You are paid strictly by commission. To maximize your pay, you might concentrate on selling fast-moving merchandise (such as inexpensive desk lamps). In the meantime, you might neglect trying to sell slower-moving items such as high-quality bedroom sets. Some students find themselves facing a similar situation when taking a course. They might be tempted to concentrate on the details they think will be on a test and neglect to review other important aspects of the course.

Goals Can Interfere with Relaxation. Finally, a preoccupation with goals makes it difficult for a person to ever relax. Instead of improving one's life, goals become a source of stress. In the words of one ambitious sales representative, "Ever since I caught on to goal setting as a way of life, I feel like I'm a basketball player running from one end of the court to another. Even worse, nobody ever calls a time out."

Despite the problems that can arise in goal setting, goals appear to be a valuable tool for managing your work and personal life. Used with common sense and the ideas presented in this chapter, goals can have a major impact on your life.

BACK TO THE JOB TASKS

Before you set work goals by yourself or jointly with your manager, review the suggestions in this chapter for setting effective goals, such as "describe what you would actually be doing if you reached your goals." Make sure to include action plans to support your goals. Otherwise, you are unlikely to produce the expected results.

❑ A goal is the object or aim of a person's actions. The potential contributions of goals include improved work performance, personal satisfaction, confidence building, and providing a sense of mission.

❑ According to goal-setting theory, behavior is regulated by values and goals. Also, difficult and specific goals improve performance. The goals should be accepted by the person and be related to feedback and rewards. Group goals are also important.

❑ Goals can be set according to difficulty level, such as routine, challenging, and breakthrough (or fantasy). It is also helpful to set goals for different time periods, such as long range, medium range, short range, daily, and immediate.

❑ An effective goal has the following characteristics: (1) It is clear, concise, and unambiguous. (2) It describes what the person will be doing when the goal is reached. (3) It is consistent with organizational policies and procedures. (4) It is interesting and challenging. (5) It specifies "what," "who," "when," and "how." (6) It is subject to periodic review. Every goal should be backed up by an action plan—a series of steps or actions that will be taken in order to achieve the goal.

❑ Goal setting is a standard way of increasing organizational productivity. Such goal setting often takes the form of management by objectives (MBO). It involves both individual and organizational goals and can also be considered a system of management. Substantial evidence exists that management by objectives programs increase productivity. The results are more impressive when top management is committed to the MBO program. Management by objectives has been criticized as being unethical because it imposes goals on people while pretending to be participative.

❑ Career goals play a significant role in achieving success and satisfaction. When you set career goals, or a career path, it is advisable to set contingency plans. Personal goals enter heavily into the formulation of career goals. Ideally, there should be an integration of career and personal goals.

❑ Despite their advantages, goals sometimes create problems. Three potential problems include (1) pursuing quantity over quality; (2) that reaching goals becomes so obsessional that unplanned opportunities may be ignored and short-range considerations are given too much importance; and (3) that relaxation becomes difficult.

GUIDELINES FOR PERSONAL EFFECTIVENESS

1. A major improvement that you can probably make in your career or personal life is to set realistic goals. In addition, you must develop action plans for attaining these goals.
2. Even if your place of work does not have a formal system of goal setting, you will personally benefit by setting work goals for yourself. Such goals will generally lead to improved performance.
3. Although goals are very beneficial, be careful not to become obsessed with attaining them. The obsession, in turn, will limit your flexibility in exploring new opportunities and alternatives.

1. How effective have goals been for you in attaining the grades that you would like?

2. Explain how the learning objectives in the first page of a text chapter can be classified as goals.

3. What could you say to somebody working for you to use the Pygmalion effect on that person?

4. How can the look on a boss's face become a self-fulfilling prophecy?

5. Where do goals enter into behavior modification?

6. How useful would goal-setting theory be to a small-business owner?

7. Why do you think some managers and professionals are hesitant to put challenging and breakthrough goals into writing?

8. Why might some employees dislike "Turbo MBO" and "killer software"?

9. What is a potential disadvantage of developing a career path at the beginning of one's career?

10. Ask an experienced worker what he or she thinks of the contribution of goal setting to work performance. Be prepared to discuss your findings in class.

A BUSINESS PSYCHOLOGY PROBLEM

The Enthusiastic Bank Manager

Brookside Savings Bank, like other financial institutions, experienced a growth in pension plans. The growth was attributed to both company and individual pension plans. Recent government legislation made it mandatory for businesses to pay more careful attention to the management of their pensions, particularly with respect to making sure that adequate reserves were on hand. The growth in individual plans resulted from legislation in the late 1970s that made it possible for self-employed people, those partially self-employed, and those employed full time to establish their own pension plans. (The pension plans in question are Keogh plans, Individual Retirement Accounts, and Simplified Employee Plans.)

After ten years of increased pension business, Chris Talbot, president of Brookside Savings, proposed to the board of directors that the bank form a new subsidiary, Financial Planning Associates, Inc. The new subsidiary would handle all the individual retirement accounts, plus counsel individuals on a wide range of financial matters. In the past, much of this work had been performed by the investment department. Company pension plans would continue to be handled by Brookside Savings. The board agreed to the proposal, and the new subsidiary, FPA, was formed shortly thereafter. FPA was assigned separate offices of its own, and six managers from the bank were transferred to the new subsidiary.

To justify the additional overhead, including office space, salaries, and advertising, the new president of FPA, Sue Wong, had to make business projections. Wong and the people she consulted projected a 25 percent increase in business per year for the next three years.

As a starting point in achieving these projections, Wong held a meeting with the other managers from FPA and all the financial counselors. Part of her presentation contained these words: "FPA is committed to a 25 percent increase in revenues each year for the next three years. Such growth is our breakeven point. This new venture is a costly one for the bank, but I know we can reach our goal of 25 percent growth per year.

"The goal I just stated translates quite simply into 25 percent growth for each of the departments in FPA. No excuses, no apologies, no tears. Just let me see the new business roll in. If you want, I will personally meet with any employee who thinks this target is unreasonable."

A brief discussion followed of how the increase in business would be achieved, including a description of the advertising campaigns planned to help bring in new business.

After two years of operation, the total revenues of FPA reflected only a 2 percent increase over the amount of business the bank was doing in individual investments before FPA was formed. The board then voted to discontinue FPA as a separate entity and collapse its business back into Brookside Savings.

1. What criticism can you make of the goal setting carried out by FPA?
2. How might goal setting have made a bigger contribution to the productivity of FPA?

A BUSINESS PSYCHOLOGY PROBLEM

The Honest Career Path

Tony Pareto was proud of his job as a human resources specialist at a large financial services company. The company's product line included insurance policies for life, health, and automobile and homeowner liability. The company also sold a diversified line of investments. Tony worked at company headquarters in Indianapolis, Indiana. His duties as a human resources specialist centered around recruiting employees for sales and staff support positions.

As Tony began his second year of employment, he was eligible to participate in the Career Builder program. The program gave each participant the opportunity to develop a career path and to discuss the career path with his or her manager. In many instances, the participant would be directed toward career-building activities that would facilitate goal attainment. For example, some employees would be given the chance to rotate to other jobs and take appropriate courses.

The sequence of jobs in Tony's career path was as follows: human resources specialist (3 years); division human resources manager (3 years); manager of college recruiting (4 years); self-employment as owner of employment agency (until retirement).

Three weeks after submitting his career plan, Tony asked his manager when he would be given some of the experiences open to many others in the Career Builder program. Tony's manager replied, "I doubt you will be getting any special privileges other than the opportunity to take a course or two. Why should our company invest money on a person who will be leaving us in ten years to form his own business?"

"Wait a minute," pleaded Tony. "I thought this was an honest program. I thought being truthful was an asset. I'm being penalized for being honest about my plans. I didn't say I would be leaving in ten years for sure. Those are just my tentative plans.

"Even if I were to leave in ten years, that's a long time to stay with one company."

"Will you give me a chance to prepare another career path?"

"No," replied Tony's manager. "We already know your true plans."

1. Is the company being fair with Tony?
2. Was Tony naive in being so honest about his career path?
3. What would you recommend Tony do now?

Goal Sharing and Feedback

Each person writes down one occupational (or school) and one personal goal that he or she would be willing to share with other members of the class. In turn, every class member presents these two goals to the rest of the class exactly as they are written down. Other class members have the privilege of providing feedback to the person sharing his or her goals. Here are some questions you should ask yourself about the goals you have written down to avoid common errors in goal setting.

1. Is the goal too lengthy and complicated? Is it really a number of goals rather than one specific goal?
2. Is the goal so vague that the person will be hard pressed to know if he or she has reached that goal? (Such as, "I intend to become successful.")
3. Does the goal sound sincere? (This is admittedly a highly subjective judgment on your part.)

References

1. P. Christopher Earley and Terri R. Lituchy, "Delineating Goal and Efficacy Effects: A Test of Three Models," *Journal of Applied Psychology,* February 1991, p. 83.
2. Patrick M. Wright, "Operationalization of Goal Difficulty as a Moderator of the Goal Difficulty–Performance Relationship," *Journal of Applied Psychology,* June 1990, p. 227.
3. Edwin A. Locke and Gary P. Latham, *A Theory of Goal Setting and Task Performance* (Englewood Cliffs, NJ: Prentice Hall, 1990), p. 46.
4. F. Christopher Earley and associates, "Impact of Process and Outcome Feedback on the Relation of Goal Setting to Task Performance," *Academy of Management Journal,* March 1990, pp. 87–105.
5. Terence R. Mitchell and William S. Silver, "Individual and Group Goals When Workers Are Interdependent: Effects on Task Strategies and Performance," *Journal of Applied Psychology,* April 1990, p. 191.
6. Locke and Latham, *A Theory of Goal Setting,* p. 307.
7. David Campbell, *If You Don't Know Where You're Going, You'll Probably Wind up Somewhere Else* (Niles, IL: Argus Communications, 1974), pp. 36–40.
8. Robert Rodgers and John E. Hunter, "Impact of Management by Objectives on Organizational Productivity," *Journal of Applied Psychology,* April 1991, p. 322.
9. Rodgers and Hunter, "Impact of Management by Objectives," p. 329.
10. Charles D. Pringle and Justin Longenecker, "The Ethics of MBO," *Academy of Management Review,* April 1982, p. 306.

BOLLES, RICHARD N. *The 1994 What Color Is Your Parachute: A Practical Manual for Job Hunters and Career Changers.* Berkely, CA: Ten Speed Press, 1994.

CHANICK, RICHARD. "Career Growth for Baby Boomers." *Personnel Journal,* January 1992, pp. 40–44.

EARLEY, P. CHRISTOPER, AND EREZ, MIRIAM. "Time-dependency Effects of Goals and Norms: The Role of Cognitive Processing on Motivational Models." *Journal of Applied Psychology,* October 1991, pp. 717–724.

MORRISON, ROBERT F., AND ADAMS, JEROME (eds.). *Contemporary Career Development Issues.* Hillsdale, NJ: Erlbaum, 1991.

MUCZYK, JAN P., AND REIMANN, BERNARD C. "MBO as a Complement to Effective Leadership." *Academy of Management EXECUTIVE,* May 1989, pp. 131–138.

SAWYER, JOHN E. "Goal and Process Clarity: Specification of Multiple Constructs of Role Ambiguity and a Structural Equation Model of Their Antecedents and Consequences." *Journal of Applied Psychology,* April 1992, pp. 130–142.

SOLOMON, CHARLES MARMER. "Managing the Baby Busters." *Personnel Journal,* March 1992, pp. 52–59.

WRIGHT, PATRICK M. "Test of the Mediating Role of Goals in the Incentive–Performance Relationship." *Journal of Applied Psychology,* October 1989, pp. 699–705.

Chapter 7

SOLVING PROBLEMS AND MAKING DECISIONS

Learning Objectives

After reading and studying this chapter and doing the exercise, you should be able to

1. Improve your problem-solving and decision-making skills.
2. Summarize the stages in decision making.
3. Pinpoint important factors that influence decision making.
4. Explain how creativity contributes to decision making.
5. Increase your creative problem-solving ability.
6. Explain what organizations are doing to enhance creativity.

JOB TASKS RELATED TO THIS CHAPTER

Being able to make good decisions and thinking more creatively will increase your effectiveness for performing unique (or nonroutine) tasks. Good decision-making skills and creative thinking are required for such tasks as figuring out (1) how much credit to a give customer, (2) how to increase sales, (3) how to cut costs, (4) whether or not to purchase a new piece of equipment, and (5) how to resolve conflicts.

Making decisions to solve difficult problems is an important part of all jobs that are not routine. The higher the level of the job is, the greater the decision-making skill required. Executives, for example, are expected to make decisions that have far-reaching consequences for an organization. In contrast, an office supervisor is usually expected to make decisions that deal with the short range.

We begin our study of decision making and problem solving with a situation facing Raul. He has worked many years in a large company and saved a substantial sum of money in order to go into business for himself. Raul is faced with a **problem,** a gap between an existing and a desired situation. His career is proceeding satisfactorily, but not with quite the challenge and excitement he thinks might be present in self-employment. To solve this problem, Raul has a heavy decision to make. A **decision** is a choice among two or more alternatives. There are many alternatives facing a person who contemplates self-employment. To arrive at the best alternative, it is necessary to engage in **decision making,** the thought processes that lead to a decision.

Our study of decision will include the stages of decision making, factors that influence decision making, creativity, and what organizations are doing to enhance creativity.

Problem:
A gap between an existing and a desired situation.

Decision:
A choice among two or more alternatives.

Decision making:
The thought processes that lead to a decision.

Decision-making Stages

Your decision-making effectiveness increases when you use a systematic approach to solving problems and making decisions, such as the one presented in Figure 7-1. It summarizes the explanation of solving problems and making decisions presented here.[1] The diagram implies that decision making should take place in an orderly flow. However, there will be times when even good decision makers deviate from this step-by-step sequence. The decision faced by Raul will be used to illustrate the process of solving problems and making decisions.

Awareness of Problem. Problem solving and decision making begin with an awareness that a problem exists. Raul is aware that, although he enjoys his work as an office manager, he would like to attempt self-employment. Solving a major problem such as this simultaneously involves solving a series of other problems. For example, Raul might have to borrow money to start a business.

In most instances of decision making, problems are given or assigned. Somebody hands us a problem for which a decision has to be made. For example, your manager might ask you to decide whether the company should convert from telephone answering machines to voice mail.

Analyze the Problem. The second step in problem solving and

FIGURE 7–1. *Stages in Problem Solving and Decision Making.*

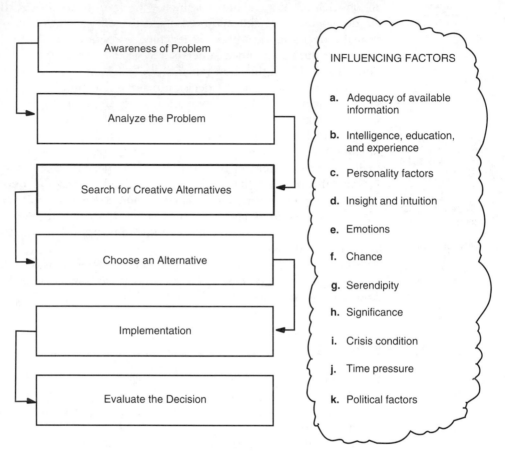

decision making is to analyze the problem and its causes. Raul must ask himself why he wants to be self-employed. He should ask such questions as, "What seems so attractive about self-employment? Am I looking for more money? Is it more challenge that I'm really after? Is being my own boss that is really important to me?"

Part of good decision-making practice is to diagnose the true decision being faced. Many decisions prove to be poor decisions because a decision was not made about the real problem. Management might observe that company morale is low. The antidote that they choose to boost morale is to build a new company cafeteria, at a cost of $600,000. After completion of the project, morale might decrease. The underlying cause of low morale might be that employees have so little voice in the affairs of the company. Constructing a new cafeteria without consulting the employees simply aggravated the problem.

When faced with a problem, a typical behavior is to use scripts to help deal with the situation. In this meaning, a **script** is a program in the brain that orients a person in a particular direction toward solving a prob-

Script:
A program in the brain that orients a person in a particular direction toward solving a problem.

lem. Scripts both enable individuals to understand situations and guide behavior appropriate to these situations.[2] The individual may have multiple scripts in his or her brain that pave the way toward coping with a problem. For example, Raul may have one or two scripts in his brain that will help guide him toward solving discontent.

Search for Creative Alternatives. The essence of creativity and effective problem solving is found in this step: Search for and generate a number of sensible alternatives to the problem at hand. Intellectual free-wheeling is therefore called for at this stage. A sound decision is more likely when the decision maker chooses among a number of plausible alternatives. Conversely, many people make poor decisions simply because they did not search long enough for a good alternative. The trap at this stage of decision making is to think of only a few obvious alternative solutions. It is preferable to stretch one's imagination for many different possibilities.

In Raul's case, he might explore such alternatives to self-employment as establishing a brand new business, purchasing an existing business, becoming a franchise operator, or running his own business part time.

Choose an Alternative. In this stage the pros and cons of each alternative are weighed, and one of them is chosen. In facing a major decision, each alternative would have to be given serious consideration. Raul is facing a major career decision and thus must weigh each alternative carefully. A useful mechanical aide for weighing alternatives is to list each on a separate piece of paper. The sheet is then divided into two columns. Advantages are listed on the left side and disadvantages on the right.

An alternative that has many more advantages than disadvantages would usually be considered a favorable alternative. Once in a while a disadvantage could be so striking that it would outweigh the larger number of advantages. For example, purchasing a McDonald's franchise for $500,000 would be out of the question for many people however good the prospects. After an analysis of the pros and cons of each alternative is made, one is chosen. The alternatives always include taking no action. Raul, for example, may finally decide to stay with his corporate job.

Implementation. Implementing an alternative is a logical extension of the previous step. Implementation can also be regarded as converting a decision into action, such as exploring the purchase of a franchise and then speaking to his lawyer. Implementing a solution requires time, effort, and money. In large organizations, many more possible solutions to problems are generated than are ever implemented. As noted by Brian Dorval, of the Center for Studies in Creativity, "Brainstorming will generate a lot of novelty, but what do you do with all those tons of flip-chart papers filled with ideas? How do you get them implemented and accepted by others?"[3]

Evaluate the Decision. The final stage of problem solving and decision making involves evaluating the quality of the decision made. Answering the deceptively simple question "How effective is the decision I made?" is complex. If the decision made clearly achieves what it was supposed to, evaluating the decision is easy. Assume that Raul wanted self-employment to feel more independent. If self-employment does bring him a feeling of independence, Raul has made a good decision.

Evaluating the outcome of a decision is important for another basic reason. Feedback of this type can improve decision-making skills. One might say, for example, "This time around I chose an alternative without giving careful thought to how difficult it would be to implement."

To begin developing your skill in making major decisions, do Exercise 7-1. You will receive additional practice in using the problem-solving method in the end-of-chapter case "A Bad Day at Citron Beverages."

EXERCISE 7-1 USING THE PROBLEM-SOLVING PROCESS

Imagine that you have just received $375,000 in cash with the gift taxes already paid. The only stipulation is that you will have to use the money to establish some sort of enterprise, either a business or a charitable foundation. Solve this problem, using the worksheet provided below. Describe what thoughts you have or what actions you will take for each stage of decision making.

I. *Awareness of the problem:* Have you found your own problem or was it given to you?

II. *Analyze the problem:* What is the true decision that you are facing? What is your underlying problem?

III. *Search for creative alternatives:* Think of the many alternatives facing you. Let your imagination flow and be creative.

IV. *Choose an alternative:* Weigh the pros and cons of each of your sensible alternatives.

	Alternatives	Advantages	Disadvantages
1.			
2.			
3.			
4.			
5.			

V. *Implementation:* Outline your action plan for converting your chosen alternative into action.

VI. *Evaluate your decision:* Do the best you can here by speculating how you will know if the decision you reached was a good one.

Problem-solving ability:
Mental ability or intelligence used to solve problems.

Many factors can influence a person's **problem-solving ability** and ability to make decisions, as depicted by the "cloud" in Figure 7-1. For example, an individual's ability to discover a problem is related to many traits and characteristics, such as perceptiveness and practical intelligence. These same factors are closely related to a person's ability to make decisions. In combination, these influencing factors help to account for individual and situational differences in decision-making ability. Some people are much better at making decisions than others and because of this achieve a higher quality of work and personal life. Here we explore a number of important factors that influence problem solving and decisions.

Adequacy of Available Information. Having ready access to current, relevant information places you in a good position to identify problems and make decisions. In Raul's situation, his decision would probably be of higher quality if he consulted a source such as the Small Business Council of the local Chamber of Commerce. Speaking to a variety of self-employed people and reading about self-employment might also yield information to help Raul make an informed decision.

Intelligence, Education, and Experience of Decision Maker. In general, intelligent, well-educated, and experienced people are more likely to find problems and make good decisions than their counterparts of lesser intelligence, education, and experience. Common sense would suggest that this statement would go unchallenged because it is obviously true. Subtle exceptions, however, exist. People without a well-developed facility for abstract reasoning will sometimes see a problem or opportunity in the most rudimentary form:

> A company was embarking on a study to determine the root causes of low morale and high turnover in the organization. A worker at the very bottom level of the company made a spontaneous comment that proved to be the crux of the problem: "There's only one thing wrong with this place. The president is a cheapskate. He tries to squeeze every penny he can out of the workers. He has us skimp on ridiculous things like making it almost impossible to replace a broken broom."

Personality Factors. Traits and behavioral characteristics can also influence an individual's ability to find problems and make decisions. Rigid people will have difficulty finding problems even when they are intelligent, well educated, experienced, and have access to good information. Perfectionism can also inhibit problem finding. A scientist was hired because of his presumed inventive talents. After one year had passed, this man had not only discovered nothing, he had failed to even completely define what kind of project he would like to pursue. His perfectionistic tendencies led him to rework one fundamental experiment until (in his words) its "scientific integrity is unquestionable." Similarly, cautious individuals have some difficulty in finding problems. Discovery of new opportunities requires an entrepreneurial or risk-taking flare.

Decisiveness is another personality factor that exerts a strong influence on decision making. Decisive people make decisions rapidly, but not impulsively, and do not agonize over decisions that did not prove to be effective. Figure 7-2 provides an opportunity to examine your own degree of decisiveness.

FIGURE 7–2. *HOW DECISIVE ARE YOU?*

Not all of us are free enough to make decisions. We are blocked or inhibited in our decision making by emotional factors, usually fear of a wrong choice. How decisive are you? Do you waver in the face of action? The following quiz about decisiveness is based on the decision-making research of Dr. Martin Seidenfeld. Answer the items as follows: 1—often; 2—sometimes; 3—rarely.

1. I tend to go over things a lot until all the flaws are ironed out.
2. I forget to do the things I am supposed to do.
3. I change my mind at the last moment about what to wear when I go out.
4. I repeat my New Year's resolutions from year to year.
5. I buy clothes with enthusiasm, but a short time later I lose interest in wearing them.
6. When dining out with friend, I am the last to select from the menu.
7. I usually have a list of projects to do which is more than six months old.
8. I still have an undesirable habit I decided to stop over six months ago, such as nail biting, smoking, going to bed late.

Score Total up all numbers corresponding to your answers. The meaning of your scores is as follows: 20–24 points—You are a highly decisive person. Study your options carefully, for you may have a tendency to be too sure of yourself.

13–19 points—You are about as resolute in decision-making as the average person.

8–12 points—Your lack of resolve may seriously hamper your chances of happiness.

Explanation Being an indecisive person doesn't have to be a permanent state of affairs. Sometimes we are so swamped by pressing problems and setbacks that we hesitate to make a decision lest we add yet another burden (of failure) on ourselves. If you find that you score low on this test, examine your current situation. Are you under unusual stress now? Have there been some pretty serious mistakes which you've recently made in money matters, social affairs, job functions? If you have, they can indeed contribute to your indecisiveness now. When your living pattern gets back to an even keel, you probably will resume more of your normal ability to make decisions.

Source: Salvatore Didato, "Are You Having Trouble Making Decisions, or Aren't You?" syndicated column, August 1, 1987.

Intuition:
A method of arriving at a conclusion by a quick judgment or "gut feel."

Intuition. Effective decision makers do not rely on careful analysis alone. Instead, they also use their **intuition,** a method of arriving at a conclusion by a quick judgment or "gut feel." In recent years, considerable attention has been drawn to the importance of intuition for managers.[4] Managers must still analyze many problems systematically. However, they also need to be able to respond to situations rapidly. Developing intuition requires cultivation over many years of experience and training.

To use intuition to your advantage, you have to know when to rely on facts and figures and when to rely on intuitive skills. Intuition is often required when the facts and figures in a situation still leave you with

uncertainty. One way of honing your intuition is to keep an idea journal. Whenever an insight comes to you, record it on paper. If you notice that you shut off these insights without carefully processing them, you will know that you must learn to give them more careful thought.[5]

Emotional Factors. Problem finding and decision making are not entirely rational processes. Instead, emotion plays a key role in all stages of decision making. Have you ever decided to take a weekend vacation instead of studying for an exam, although all the facts in the situation suggested that you stay home and study? Intellect, reason, *and* **emotion** enter into most decisions. Even when decisions appear to be based almost entirely on hard data, *which* data are selected for inclusion in the decision-making process is influenced to some degree by emotion and feeling.

Fear of making the wrong decision is another significant emotional factor that influences decision making. Each time you make a decision, you run the risk that someone will disagree with you or not like your decision. A person who is too fearful will hesitate to make important decisions. Keep in mind that you will never please everyone, so use facts and intuition to make the best possible decision.[6]

Emotion:
Any strong agitation of the feelings triggered by experiencing love, hate, fear, joy, and the like.

Intuition, or educated hunch-making, enters into most decisions about non-routine matters.

Chance Factors. Problems and opportunities are sometimes found or correct decisions made on the basis of luck or other unpredictable factors. Research conducted at the Center for Creative Leadership confirms the idea that there is a good deal of luck involved in decision making. A researcher there notes that the all-knowing decision maker who decides on the basis of logic alone and with knowledge of all the facts simply does not exist. Decisions made by managers have been and will continue to be a product of judgment and luck, as well as expertise.[7]

Serendipity: The gift of finding valuable things not sought for while looking for something else.

Serendipity. **Serendipity** is the gift of finding valuable things not sought for. It is thus a special type of luck and an unpredictable factor that enters into problem solving and decision making. Observe the serendipity involved in this example:

Several years ago, James R. Leatherman and some friends were driving around Los Angeles trying to find a movie of interest to them. Leatherman had just finished shooting a television advertisement for an 800-line teleprocessing service. It occurred to him that there should be a phone number you could call for complete movie listings.

He brought his idea to the movie studios, and they were enthusiastic. He invested the next six months in building a prototype system. Leatherman remortgaged his house, and he and his partner made credit-card loans to raise $250,000 for equipment. Just at the point when the two partners faced bankruptcy, a commodities firm in New York read an article about their high-tech idea in the *Hollywood Reporter.* The firm signed on as partners and MovieFone was born. The company now operates in seven cities and is prospering. In addition to offering information about movies, tickets can be ordered over the phone.[8]

Significance. The more significant a decision, the more important it is to plod methodically through the decision-making stages. Four characteristics of a business decision greatly influence its significance. First is the number of people affected; the more people affected by a decision, the more significant the decision. Second is the relative impact of the dollar amounts involved. A decision is highly significant if it affects the survival or profitability of an organization. Third is the amount of time needed to acquire the knowledge necessary to make a proper decision. For example, it might take a retail executive ten years of experience to make sound decisions about whether to open a new branch.

Crisis Conditions. Under crisis or extremely high pressure conditions, many decision makers panic. They become less rational and more emotional than they would in a calmer environment. Decision makers adversely affected by crisis conditions exhibit symptoms of severe stress, including poor concentration, poor judgment, and impulsive thinking. Decision makers facing a crisis may be aware of conflicting opinions, but be too pressured to reach a solution to exploring these differences and incorporating them into their choices.[9]

Decision making under crisis conditions has become so frequent that many organizations provide training in crisis management. For example, the Environmental Protection Agency conducts earthquake preparedness training programs. An EPA official notes that these sessions have been taken more seriously since the San Francisco earthquake of 1989.[10]

Time Pressures. The quality of decisions may suffer when the decision making is hurried. An exception is that some people make their best decisions when faced with a tight deadline. For most people, tight time pressures make it difficult for them to identify enough alternatives to make a good decision. A laboratory study of business students forced the subjects to make decisions under varying degrees of pressure and distraction. Under heavy time pressure and many distractions, the students place much more weight on negative than positive evidence in arriving at decisions. The particular decision that they faced was something of interest to most people about to graduate from business school: making an automobile purchase.

Making quick decisions about such matters as introducing a new product often gives companies a competitive advantage.[11] Thinking quickly can also help you in your career by helping you to get more work done and by impressing superiors.

Political Factors:
Factors other than merit that influence a decision, such as favoritism or attempting to please a key person.

Political Factors. A serious discussion of decision making would be incomplete and naive if it ignored the importance of **political factors.** A political factor in this context is the potential reaction to the decision by an influential person. Specific political factors include favoritism, alliances, or the desire of the decision maker to stay in favor with the people who wield power.[12] Political factors sometimes influence which data are given serious consideration in evaluating alternatives. The decision maker may select data supporting the position of the influential person he or she is trying to please. Similarly, political factors are sometimes used to help a person to evaluate the effectiveness of a decision.

Despite the importance of political factors, a person with high professional integrity arrives at what he or she thinks is the best decision. A diligent attempt should then be made to convince management of the merits of the chosen alternative.

Creativity in Decision Making

Creativity:
The ability to develop novel ideas that can be put into action.

Creative problem solving:
The ability to overcome obstacles by approaching them in novel ways.

Creativity is helpful at any stage of decision making, but is essential for identifying problems, analyzing them, and searching for creative alternatives. **Creativity** is the ability to develop novel ideas that can be put into action. **Creative problem solving** stems from creativity. It is the ability to overcome obstacles by approaching them in novel ways.[13] Being creative is important for your career, and imagination is required to solve most difficult problems. Our discussion of creativity will encompass measuring creative potential, characteristics of the creative worker, the conditions necessary for creativity, how to improve your creativity, and what organizations are doing to foster creativity.

What Is Your Creative Potential

A logical starting point in studying creativity is to gain a tentative awareness of your creative potential. Here we confine our measurement of creative potential to two illustrative exercises (Figures 7-3 and 7-4). Do not be overly encouraged or dejected by any results you achieve on these tests. They are designed to give only preliminary insights into whether your thought processes are similar to those of creative individuals.

Characteristics of the Creative Worker

Creative workers tend to have different intellectual and personality characteristics from their less creative counterparts. A large number of studies point toward one distinguishing overall characteristic. Creative people are in general more mentally flexible than others, which allows them to overcome the traditional way of looking at problems. This flexibility, or "looseness," often manifests itself in practical jokes and other forms of playfulness. A case in point is Terry, a physician's assistant. One Halloween he encouraged three of his friends to join him in an outlandish prank. The first part of their prank was to borrow a coffin from an undertaker known to Terry. He also arranged to borrow four operating room uniforms. On Halloween day the four pranksters carried the coffin around downtown Cleveland during midday. Terry's playful idea worked. The foursome brought laughter to some people and shock to others.

FIGURE 7-3

WORD HINTS TO CREATIVITY[14]

The object of this exercise is to find a fourth word that is related to all three words listed below. For example, what word is related to these?

cookies	sixteen	heart	___________

The answer is "sweet." Cookies are sweet; sweet is part of the word "sweetheart" and part of the phrase "sweet sixteen."

What word is related to these words?

poke	go	molasses	___________

Answer: slow.

Now try these words:

1.	surprise	line	birthday	___________
2.	base	snow	dance	___________
3.	rat	blue	cottage	___________
4.	nap	rig	call	___________
5.	golf	foot	country	___________
6.	house	weary	ape	___________
7.	tiger	plate	news	___________
8.	painting	bowl	nail	___________
9.	proof	sea	priest	___________
10.	maple	beet	loaf	___________
11.	oak	show	plan	___________
12.	light	village	golf	___________
13.	merry	out	up	___________
14.	cheese	courage	oven	___________
15.	bulb	house	lamp	___________

If you were able to think of the "correct" fourth word for ten or more of these combinations of words, your score compares favorably to that of creative individuals. A very low score (about one, two, or three correct answers) suggests that performing such remote associations is not yet a strength of yours. Here are the answers:

1. party	5. club	9. high	13. make
2. ball	6. dog	10. sugar	14. Dutch
3. cheese	7. paper	11. floor	15. light
4. cat	8. finger	12. green	

The characteristics of creative workers can be grouped into three broad areas: knowledge, intellectual abilities, and personality. The following information incorporates the thinking of several writers and researchers.[15]

Knowledge. Creative thinking requires a broad background of information, including facts and observations. Knowledge is the storehouse of building blocks for generating and combining ideas. This is particularly true because some experts say that creativity always boils down to com-

FIGURE 7–4

Creative Personality Test. The following test will help you to determine if certain aspects of your personality are similar to those of a creative individual.

		Mostly True	*Mostly False*
1.	Novels are a waste of time. If you want to read, read nonfiction books.	_____	_____
2.	You have to admit, some crooks are very clever.	_____	_____
3.	People consider me to be a fastidious dresser. I despise looking shabby.	_____	_____
4.	I am a person of very strong convictions. What's right is right; what's wrong is wrong.	_____	_____
5.	It doesn't bother me when my boss hands me vague instructions.	_____	_____
6.	Business before pleasure is a hard and fast rule in my life.	_____	_____
7.	Taking a different route to work is fun, even if it takes longer.	_____	_____
8.	Rules and regulations should not be taken too seriously. Most rules can be broken under unusual circumstances.	_____	_____
9.	Playing with a new idea is fun even if it doesn't benefit me in the end.	_____	_____
10.	As long as people are nice to me, I don't care why they are being nice.	_____	_____
11.	Writing should try to avoid the use of unusual words and word combinations.	_____	_____
12.	Detective work would have some appeal to me.	_____	_____
13.	Crazy people have no good ideas.	_____	_____
14.	Why write letters to friends when there are so many clever greeting cards available in the stores today?	_____	_____
15.	Pleasing myself means more to me than pleasing others.	_____	_____
16.	If you dig long enough, you will find the true answer to most questions	_____	_____

Scoring the Test. The answers in the *creative direction* for each question are as follows:

1.	Mostly False	7.	Mostly True	13.	Mostly False
2.	Mostly True	8.	Mostly True	14.	Mostly False
3.	Mostly False	9.	Mostly True	15.	Mostly True
4.	Mostly False	10.	Mostly True	16.	Mostly False
5.	Mostly True	11.	Mostly False		
6.	Mostly False	12.	Mostly True		

Give yourself a plus one for each answer you gave in agreement with the keyed answers.

How Do You Interpret Your Score? Extremely high or low scores are probably the most meaningful. A score of 12 or more suggests that your personality and attitudes are similar to that of a creative person. A score of 5 or less suggests that your personality is dissimilar to that of a creative person. You are probably more of a conformist (and somewhat categorical) in your thinking, at least at this point in your life. Don't be discouraged. Most people can develop in the direction of becoming a more creative individual.

1. How does your score on this test compare to your own evaluation of your creativity?
2. Describe a person who you think would probably score 15 or 16 on this test. Identify him or her.
3. Do the same for a person whom you think would score 0 or 1 on this test.

bining two existing things in a new and different way. For example, a fax machine is a combination of a telephone and a photocopier.

Intellectual Abilities. Cognitive abilities such as general intelligence and abstract reasoning are included under the category of intellectual abilities. In general, creative workers tend to be bright rather than brilliant. Extraordinarily high intelligence is not required to be creative, but creative people are good at generating alternative solutions to problems in a short period of time. Creative people also maintain a youthful curiosity throughout their lives. And the curiosity is not centered just on their own field of expertise. Instead, their range of interests encompasses many areas of knowledge, and they generate enthusiasm toward almost any puzzling problem. It has also been observed that creative people are open and responsive to feelings and emotions and the world around them.

Personality. Included here are the emotional and other nonintellectual aspects of an individual that facilitate being creative.

- Creative people tend to have a positive self-image. They feel good about themselves but are not blindly self-confident. Because they are reasonably self-confident, creative people are able to cope with criticism of their ideas.
- Creative people have the ability to tolerate isolation. Isolation is useful because it helps put a person into a receptive mood for ideas. Working alone also helps creative people avoid the distraction of talking to others. Creativity, however, is often facilitated by interaction with others.
- Creative people are frequently nonconformists. They value their independence and do not have strong needs to gain approval from the group.
- Creative people often have a Type T personality. Their thrill-seeking tendencies often lead to outstanding creativity because finding imaginative solutions to problems is thrilling.
- Creative people are persistent. Persistence is important because finding creative solutions to problems is hard work and requires intense concentration.
- Creative people are resistant to frustration in the sense that they have a high toleration for ambiguity and chaos.

Synthesizing these lists leads to a general picture of the creative person. He or she is more flexible than rigid, open than closed, playful than always serious, adventuresome than safety-seeking. Several of these characteristics support the popular stereotype of the creative person as somewhat of a maverick, both intellectually and socially. Later we will present some suggestions for helping you to develop into a more creative person.

The Conditions Necessary for Creativity

Creativity is not just a random occurrence. For creativity to occur, ability, intrinsic motivation, and certain cognitive activities are needed.[16] These necessary conditions are not surprising considering our discussion of creativity up to this point. *Ability* is the knowledge in the area in which the individual works, combined with the skills to process information to produce a useful, novel solution. A mind disciplined through study is therefore a major contributor to creativity.

Intrinsic motivation, as described in Chapter 4, is a fascination with the task. Even if you have the potential, you are unlikely to be creative unless you are inherently interested in the task. Creative people usually enjoy their work intensely.

Finally, for creativity to occur, the person must engage in certain *cognitive activities.* Most of these cognitive activities are included in the decision-making stages outlined in Figure 7-1. For example, to be creative the individual must define the problem, gather data, implement the solution, and evaluate the solution. Added to these cognitive activities is unconscious activity about the problem. To reach a creative solution, a person has to be unconsciously thinking about the problem. If you are seriously interested in solving a problem, the unconscious thinking may take place automatically.

In addition to these conditions for creativity, an environmental need must stimulate the setting of a goal.[17] (To quote an old adage, "Necessity is the mother of invention.") For example, an information systems specialist might be confronted with the problem of linking personal computers together in his or her company. No standard solution is available. The specialist then sets a goal of making the links and must be creative to reach that goal.

Improving Your Creativity

Because of the importance of becoming a creative problem solver, many techniques have been developed to improve creativity. Here we describe both specific techniques and general strategies for becoming more creative. The goal of these experiences is to think like a creative problem solver. Such a person lets his or her imagination wander. In addition, he or she makes deliberate jumps in thinking and welcomes chance ideas whenever they come along. The creative problem solver ventures beyond the constraints that limit most people.

Brainwriting (brainstorming): Arriving at creative ideas by jotting them down oneself.

Brainwriting. In its usual format, brainstorming involves group members thinking of multiple solutions to a problem. **Brainwriting,** or solo brainstorming, is arriving at creative ideas by jotting them down yourself.[18] An important requirement of solo brainstorming is that you set aside a regular time (and perhaps place) for generating ideas. The ideas discovered in the process of routine activities can be counted as bonus time. Even five minutes a day is much more than most people are accustomed to invest in creative problem solving. Give yourself a quota with a time deadline. A good way to get started with solo brainstorming is to use the method for your next work, school, or personal problem that requires an imaginative solution.

Forced-association Technique. A widely used method of releasing creativity is to make forced associations between the properties of two objects in order to solve a problem. The method works in this way. You select a word at random from a dictionary. Next you list all the properties and attributes of this word. You then force-fit these properties and attributes to the problem you are trying to solve. The properties of the random object are related to the properties of the object involved in your problem. A new way of delivering medicine was supposedly developed by listing the properties of a time bomb. One key property was "slow release," leading to medicine that goes to work several hours after it was taken—a time capsule.[19]

Develop a Synergy between Both Sides of the Brain.

Neurological and psychological studies of the brain have shed light on creativity. Researchers have been able to demonstrate that the left side of the brain is the source of most analytical, logical, and rational thought. It performs the tasks necessary for well-reasoned arguments. The right side of the brain grasps the work in a more intuitive, overall manner. It is the source of impressionistic, creative thought. People with dominant right brains thrive on disorder and ambiguity—both characteristics of a creative person.

But the argument that the left side of the brain controls logic and the right side of the brain controls intuition has been disputed by biopsychologist Jerre Levy and other researchers. Levy's studies show that any mental activity is carried out by both sides of the brain simultaneously. Joined by the corpus callosum, the two hemispheres work together in harmony.[20]

Whether you believe that both sides of the brain work independently or interdependently, the message for creativity improvement is the same. Both logical and intuitive thinking are required. The creative person needs a fund of accessible facts in order to combine them to solve problems. He or she also needs to rely on hunches and intuition to achieve flashes of insight.

Synergy:
A phenomenon of group effort whereby the whole is greater than the sum of the parts.

The highly creative person achieves a synergy between the two sides of the brain. **Synergy** is a combination of things with an output greater than the sum of the parts. The unique capabilities of both sides of the brain are required. Robert Gundlach, a leading inventor (and a person who endorses brainwriting), explains it this way:[21]

> Being creative means developing a synergy between the left half of the brain—the analytical half—and the right half of the brain—the creative half. I learned that at home during my childhood. My mother was an artist, a painter of landscapes. My father was a chemist, and inventor of Wildroot hair oil. Both my parents influenced me equally well.

The Raudsepp Exercises and Principles.

Eugene Raudsepp has developed a set of 12 exercises and principles as a guide to creative growth. Based on his many years of research, they are summarized as follows:[22]

1. *Keep track of your ideas at all times.* Keeping an idea notebook at hand will help you to capture a permanent record of flashes of insights and good ideas borrowed from others.
2. *Pose new questions every day.* If your mind is questioning and inquiring, it will be creatively active. It is also a mind that constantly enlarges the circumference of its awareness. "Have fun, and enjoy your creative probings and experiences."
3. *Maintain competence in your field.* The information explosion makes knowledge become obsolete quickly. Having current facts in mind gives you the raw material to form creative links from one bit of information to another.

4. *Read widely in fields that are not directly related to your field of interest.* Look for the relationship between what you read and what you already know. Once you learn how to cross-index the pieces of information you gather, you will be able to cross-fertilize seemingly unrelated ideas.

5. *Avoid rigid patterns of doing things.* Strive to overcome fixed ideas and look for new viewpoints. Experiment and always generate several alternative solutions to your problems. Develop the ability to let go of one idea in favor of another.

6. *Be open and receptive to your own as well as to others' ideas.* Seize on tentative, half-formed ideas and hunches. A new idea seldom arrives in finished form. Entertain and generate your own farfetched or silly ideas. If you are receptive to the ideas of others, you will learn new things that can help you behave creatively.

7. *Be alert in observation.* Search for the similarities, differences, and unique features of things and ideas. The greater the number of new associations and relationships you form, the greater your chances of arriving at creative and original combinations and solutions.

8. *Engage in creative hobbies.* Develop hobbies that allow you to produce something with your hands. You can also keep your brain tuned up by playing games and doing puzzles and exercises. "Creative growth is possible only through constant and active use of your mind."

9. *Improve your sense of humor and laugh easily.* Humor helps to relieve tension, and most people are more productively creative when they are relaxed. Also, humor is an everyday expression of creativity.

10. *Adopt a risk-taking attitude.* The fear of failure suppresses creativity, so be willing to fail on occasion.

11. *Have courage and self-confidence.* Move ahead on the assumption that you can solve your problems or achieve your goals. Many people surrender just when they are on the brink of a solution, so persist when you are seeking a creative solution to a problem.

12. *Learn to know and understand yourself.* "Creativity is an expression of one's uniqueness. To be creative, then, is to be oneself."

An underlying message to these suggestions is that self-discipline is required to develop more creative behavior. The advice offered also assumes that you have sufficient control over emotions and intellect to develop new habits and break old ones. Assuming you have such control, following these suggestions over time would most likely help you to become a more creative person.

Be an Explorer, Artist, Judge, and Lawyer. A method for improving creativity has been proposed that incorporates many of the suggestions already made. The method calls for you to adopt four roles in your thinking.[23] *First,* be an explorer. Speak to people in different fields and get ideas that you can use. For example, if you are a telecommunications specialist, speak to salespeople and manufacturing specialists.

Second, be an artist by stretching your imagination. Strive to spend about 5 percent of your day asking "what if" questions. For example, a sales manager at a fresh-fish distributor might ask, "What if some new research suggests that eating fish causes intestinal cancer in humans?" Also, remember to challenge the commonly perceived rules in your field. An example is that a bank manager challenged why customers needed their canceled checks returned each month. This questioning led to some banks not returning canceled checks unless the customer paid an additional fee for the service.

Third, know when to be a judge. After developing some wild ideas, at some point you have to evaluate these ideas. Do not be so critical that you discourage your own imaginative thinking. However, be critical enough to prevent attempting to implement weak ideas.

Fourth, achieve results with your creative thinking by playing the role of a lawyer. Negotiate and find ways to implement your ideas within your field or place of work. The explorer, artist, and judge stages of creative thought might take only a short time to develop a creative idea. Yet you may spend months or even years getting your brainstorm implemented. For example, it took a long time for the developer of the electronic pager to finally get the product manufactured and distributed on a large scale.

What Organizations Are Doing to Foster Creativity

To achieve creative solutions to problems and to think of new opportunities, an organization needs more than creative people. Creativity is the combined influence of people with creative potential working in an environment that encourages creativity. Here we examine four related ways in which organizations contribute to creativity: having a favorable climate for creativity, conducting creativity training programs, suggestion programs, and skunk works.

A Favorable Climate for Creativity. Organizations that are able to capitalize on much of the creative potential of their members have a general characteristic in common. Employees are given encouragement and emotional support for attempts at creativity. Encouragement also involves managers at the top of the organization supporting innovation and imagination. Of considerable importance, employees are not penalized for taking sensible risks and trying new ideas.

> An employee who worked for a catalog shopping service proposed that the company use popcorn as shipping filler because it is biodegradable and would therefore not harm the environment. The company received so many sarcastic letters and outright complaints from customers that it was forced to return to Styrofoam as packing material. The company president then wrote a letter to the employee responsible for the popcorn packing suggestion. She was told not to be discouraged, that any progressive company will have a few ideas that meet with resistance at first.

Training Programs. One third of medium- and large-size U.S. companies provide some sort of creativity training. Several, including Du Pont and Eastman Kodak Company, have in-house creativity departments. Many of these programs involve traditional brainstorming, solo brainstorming, and specific techniques such as forced association.

Mind mapping:
A creativity tool tool that produces a physical and conceptual map of a project.

A training program currently gaining attention is **mind mapping,** a creativity tool that produces a physical and conceptual map of a project. A mind map uses words, colors, and pictures to pack information onto one page. The mind map, as shown in Figure 7-5, winds up resembling

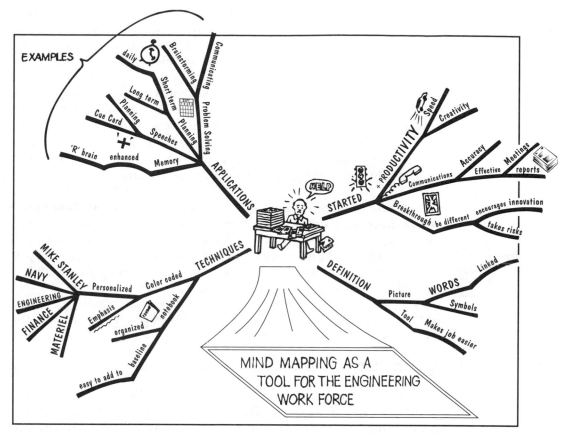

FIGURE 7–5. *MIND MAPPING.*
Source: James Braham, "Eureka!" *Machine Design,* February 6, 1992, p. 32. Reprinted with permission.

a giant spider's web. The main idea is drawn first in the center, with main spokes springing from the idea. An increasing number of details are added as a speech, conference, or problem-solving meeting unfolds. The system developed by Michael Stanley uses eight different colored pens. For example, an action item is drawn in red, while a quote appears in blue.

Mind mapping emphasizes a synergy between both halves of the brain. The full range of the brain's abilities is used. The image placed in the center facilitates memorization and the creative generation of ideas. Subsequently, the mind map branches out in associate networks that mirror externally the brain's internal structure. The payoff from the technique is supposed to be a large number of ideas, rather than a brief list.[24]

Suggestion programs:
A formal method for collecting and analyzing employee suggestions about processes, policies, product, and services.

Suggestion Programs. To encourage creative thinking, many companies use **suggestion programs,** a formal method for collecting and analyzing employee suggestions about processes, policies, product, and services. Many companies offer financial rewards for useful suggestions. Among the criteria for usefulness are whether the suggestions saves money, earns money, or increases safety. Suggestion awards have run as high as $50,000. For example, a group of American Airline mechanics received a $37,500 award for developing a tamper-proof airport security door.

In addition to stimulating creative thinking, suggestion programs help to get employees involved in the success of their organization.[25] Suggestion programs are sometimes criticized, however, because they collect loads of trivial suggestions and pay small awards just to pacify employees. One employee, for example, was paid $50 for suggesting that the company dust light bulbs more frequently to increase illumination.

Establishment of Skunk Works and Other Small Innovative Organizational Units. An important principle of encouraging creativity is to conduct innovative work in small organizational units. The best publicized example is **skunk works,** a secret place to conceive new products. The term derives from the fact that something secret and perhaps unpleasant (for the status quo) is thought to be going on in these off-site locations. Major products conceived in skunk works include jet fighter technology, a small photocopier for engineering applications, and the IBM family of personal computers.

Skunk works:
A secret place to conceive new products.

Computer-assisted Decision Making

An increasing number of managers and professionals are using computers to help them make higher-quality decisions, including thinking more creatively. Three such uses of technology in decision making are decision-making software, expert systems, and brainwriting by computer.

Decision-making Software

A modern development in computer-assisted decision making is software that actually helps you to reach valid alternative solutions to your problem. **Decision-making software** is any computer program that helps the decision maker to work through the problem-solving and decision-making steps. In addition, such programs ask questions about values, priorities, and the importance you attach to such factors as price and quality. The decision-making process used in these programs is referred to as intuitive because the programs rely more on human judgment than heavy quantitative analysis.[26] The intent is to improve the quality of decisions, rather than just make computations or generate data. A decision-making program, for example, might help an executive decide where to locate a new plant.

Decision-making software:
Any computer program that helps the decision maker work through the problem-solving and decision-making steps.

Expert Systems (Artificial Intelligence)

A promising development in computer-assisted decision making is **expert systems,** computer programs that can "reason" and manipulate data in a manner similar to humans. Expert systems are a direct application of the more

Expert systems:
Computer programs that can "reason" and manipulate data in a manner similar to humans.

general field of artificial intelligence (the technology to make computers think). Expert systems are used to support decision making, rather than to automate the decision-making process and replace managers and professionals.

Expert systems were developed originally to help physicians make medical diagnoses. The reasoning capability of these systems is based on rules of thumb used by human experts to make decisions in a wide range of business situations. Among these situations are inventory control, financial forecasting and investments, and credit analyses. The rules of thumb are in the form of "if this, then that" statements. When asking advice from the system, the user provides known information or hunches. The expert system than draws conclusions that appear as computer output.

An example of an expert system is MUDMAN, created to analyze the drilling fluids or "muds" that are pumped down the shaft to make drilling easier by such means as lubricating and carrying shavings back to the surface. On deep or complex wells, an engineer often has to sample and analyze the mud a minimum of twice daily. MUDMAN helps the engineer do the job more consistently. The software evaluates the data provided by the engineer and by combining these data with historical data for the well, identifies trends. MUDMAN then recommends adjustments to the mud composition and alerts the engineer to potential problems.

An example of MUDMAN's effectiveness is that at one site in the North Sea it correctly diagnosed a mud contaminant that human experts had misdiagnosed for more than a decade. The oil company customer was so impressed that the drilling service company that developed MUDMAN was invited to bid on extra business.[27]

Brainwriting by Computer

A computer program, *IdeaFisher,* has been developed to facilitate brainwriting. The software contains a list of over 3,000 specific questions designed to help the user to think of solutions to business problems. Typical problems include developing a marketing strategy or inventing a new product or service. A book editor in New York City uses *IdeaFisher* to help her think of catchy book titles. As part of the program, over 60,000 words, expressions, people, places, and things are cross-referenced in over 700,000 ways. Associations to your key word are broken down into subcategories.[28] Assume that you were trying to develop a new marketing campaign for frozen yogurt. *IdeaFisher* would help you develop a giant list of things and ideas associated with the concepts of yogurt and frozen.

BACK TO THE JOB TASKS

The information in this chapter can help you to make better decisions and think more creatively. The next time you endeavor to solve a nonroutine problem, apply several ideas from this chapter to solve the problem more readily. For example, in conducting a job campaign remember to go through the decision-making steps. By following carefully the decision-making steps, your percentage of high-quality decisions will increase.

❏ A problem is a gap between an existing and a desired situation. A decision is a choice among two or more alternatives to solve that problem. Decision making consists of six continuous and somewhat overlapping stages: awareness of problem, analyzing the problem, searching for creative alternatives, choosing an alternative, implementing the alternative, and evaluating the decision.

❏ At any stage of problem solving and decision making, certain factors influence our thinking. Those factors described here are adequacy of available information; intelligence, education, and experience; personality factors such as decisiveness; intuition; various emotions; chance; serendipity; crisis conditions; time pressures; and political factors.

❏ Creativity is the ability to develop novel ideas that can be put into action. Creative potential can sometimes be measured through questionnaires. Creative workers tend to have intellectual and personality characteristics that are different from their less creative counterparts. In general, they are more mentally flexible than others, thus allowing them to overcome traditional ways of looking at problems. Creative people also tend to be intellectually playful and adventuresome.

❏ For creativity to occur, ability, intrinsic motivation, and certain cognitive activities are needed. Among the cognitive activities are going through the problem-solving process and unconscious thinking about the problem. An environmental need must also be present to stimulate the setting of a creativity goal.

❏ People can improve their creativity by engaging in a variety of activities. Among them are brainwriting, using the forced-association technique, developing a synergy between both halves of the brain, and engaging in the Raudsepp's exercises. Another useful approach to creativity improvement is to be an "explorer, artist, judge, and lawyer."

❏ Because creativity is so important, organizations support creativity in many ways. Among them are setting up a favorable climate for creativity, training programs (including mind mapping), suggestion programs, and the establishment of skunk works.

❏ Computers can be used to improve decision making, including creativity. One form of computer-assisted decision making is decision-making software that helps one work through the steps in problem solving and decision making, yet emphasizes qualitative factors. Another form is expert systems (an application of artificial intelligence) that simulate human reasoning. Software has also been developed to assist in brainwriting.

GUIDELINES FOR PERSONAL EFFECTIVENESS

1. Use a deliberate, systematic approach, such as following the stages in the decision-making process, when making major decisions in business and personal life. An impulsive, hasty decision will often neglect some important information that should have been included before you reached your decision.

2. Although a systematic approach to decision making is highly recommended, it does not mean that you should avoid using your insight and intuition. Intuition is particularly helpful in finding a problem to work on and in selecting from among the available alternatives. Top-level decision makers still rely heavily on intuition.

3. Improving your creativity can improve your chances for success in your career. When faced with a problem or decision, discipline yourself to search for several alternatives, since this is the essence of creative behavior.

4. Be alert to software that can help improve the quality of your decisions. You might be at a competitive disadvantage if you neglect such software because an increasing number of higher-level workers are using computer-assisted decision making.

Discussion Questions and Activities

1. Explain the relationship between problem solving and decision making.

2. Give three examples of problems for which it would be helpful to go through the decision-making stages outlined in Figure 7-1.

3. What standards should a person use to determine if a decision he or she made was a good one?

4. Why does having too much information available sometimes hamper decision making?

5. Give two examples of major crises faced by executives in recent years.

6. A man who escaped a fire in a skyscraper told a newspaper reporter, "I survived because I used the information I learned in business school about making decisions." What do you think he learned about decision making that saved his life?

7. To what extent do you think the divorce rate would be lower if people used the stages in problem solving and decision making to help decide whether to marry their prospective mate?

8. A student said to his instructor in a business psychology course, "I'm not an artist, an advertising specialist, or a scientist, so why should I study creativity?" How would you respond to this student if you were the instructor?

9. Think of the most creative person you know. How well does he or she fit the characteristics of a creative worker summarized on pages 150 to 156?

10. Ask one creative person and one not-so-creative person to take the creativity tests (Figures 7-3 and 7-4). Report their scores back to the class and average them to determine if creative people score higher than less creative people.

A Business Psychology Case

A Bad Day at Citron Beverages

Julia Anderson worked as the production manager at Citron Beverages, a manufacturer of lemon-flavored soft drinks. She looked forward to another fast-paced workday this Monday morning. Although Citron was not a major player in the vast soft-drink market, it had a solid group of loyal customers in the Northwest United States and Canada. A warm spell had increased demand for its top seller, "Citron Power." However, production was able to keep up with demand.

At 9:15 A.M., Ramesh Sharma, a production supervisor, rushed into Anderson's office. "We've got to talk, Julia," said Ramesh with a worried look on his face. Anderson motioned for Sharma to sit down.

"Something awful may have happened on the production line," said Ramesh. "One of the maintenance workers said he found an empty container of lemon-scented liquid cleaner next to a production vat. He's worried that somebody may have dumped the cleanser into the vat as a joke or as sabotage.

"I had one of the quality control technicians test the vat for impurities. Her tests were inconclusive. We use so much artificial lemon flavoring in Citron Power, anyway, that it makes the testing more difficult."

"Oh my God," said Julia. "You mean to say a vat of Citron Power syrup might have been contaminated with liquid cleanser?"

"We don't know for sure. But it seems too late to do much about it now. We've already bottled and canned several hundred cases of Citron Power from the batch of syrup in question. Besides that, one bottle of liquid cleaner in one vat of Citron Power syrup might not be detectable to the consumer."

"Ramesh, I question your judgment. All it takes is one foamy-mouthed Citron drinker to lodge a complaint. Then the place will fall apart."

"Julia, keep in mind that if we attempt to recall any possible contaminated shipment the company will really fall apart."

"Okay, Ramesh. Let me just think this problem through for ten minutes or so."

1. Why is this case problem included in a chapter on problem solving and decision making?
2. Which factors are present that could influence the quality of Anderson's decision about this problem?
3. Offer Julia Anderson a creative suggestion.

A Business Psychology Case

The Food Company Skunk Works

Melrose Foods is a large food manufacturer and processor consisting of 21 divisions. Many of these divisions are smaller companies purchased in recent years. The executive office, headed by Gardner Appelby, recently decided to establish a research and development group whose responsibility it would be to develop new food products. Appelby explained it in these words to the corporate staff and division heads.

"The time as arrived for Melrose to copy the high-tech approach to R&D [research and development]. Effective July 1 of this year, we are building our own skunk works. The executive office has chosen Manuel Seda for this key assignment. As you recall, Manuel was a dynamically successful entrepreneur who established Tangy Tacos. Starting in his mother's kitchen, he built up a national distribution for his product in three years. We bought Tangy Tacos for its growth and profitability. But even more important, we bought the talent of Manuel Seda.

"Tangy Tacos will be headed by Wanda Morales while Manuel is on indefinite assignment as a manager of our skunk works. Manuel will begin with six competent associates. He and his group can have all the budget they need, so long as it looks like they are on the path to developing successful products."

At this point in Appelby's presentation, Garth Laidlaw, division head of Tiger Pet Foods, waves his hand. "We need clarification, Gardner. You mention that the skunk works will be funded as long as it looks like they are about to develop successful products. Developing a successful new food product is a risky business. About 90 percent of new product ideas never make it to the marketplace. And about half of the 10 percent that do arrive on the market fail within one year."

"I'm aware of those dismal statistics," said Appelby. "But without a push on new product development, Melrose Foods is doomed to stagnation and mediocrity.

"Members of the management team, let us all move forward toward a successful skunk works. And let us all wish Manuel the best of luck."

Three months after the skunk works was established, Seda received a visit from Appelby. After a brief tour of the facility, Appelby said to Seda: "Manuel, I do get the impression that there is a lot of activity going on here, but it does not seem to be focused activity. Could you give me an update?"

"Gardner, it's premature to expect results. We have been set aside so we can think at our own pace. This is not a crash program. Don't forget, I had been working in the food business for three years before I thought of the idea for Tangy Tacos."

"It's true, we are not expecting immediate results from the skunk works, but you are a pretty well-funded group. Could you please give me a hint of any new product idea you have developed so far?"

Seda answered, "Actually, we are pretty excited about one new idea. It's a form of instant fish called Sudden Seafood. Today's busy and health-conscious professional will love it. You add boiling water to pulverized sea food, and you get a mashed-potato-like substance that is actually tasty seafood. We would certainly be the first on the market."

"Revolting," responded Appelby. "I would definitely turn thumbs down on Melrose investing money to market instant fish. Maybe you could interest our Tiger Pet Foods division in that idea. It could be used when traveling with cats."

Three months later, Appelby revisited Seda at the skunk works. The president said, "I'm just doing an informal check again. What new product idea is the skunk works toying with these days?"

"I think we have a real winner on the drawing board," said Manuel. "The country is sick of wimpy soft drinks that have no real flavor, no gusto, and give no boost to the psyche. We have been experimenting with a raspberry-flavored soft drink that has four times the caffeine and three times the sugar of anything on the market. It's tentative name is Razzle Razzberry. It's destined to be a winner."

"Hold on, Manuel. You're getting carried away. You're running counterculture. The country is moving away from heavy soft drinks and you're suggesting a product that's practically a narcotic. It sounds like our skunk works might be getting carried away."

"Gardner, it's too bad you don't like this promising idea. Maybe I could meet with you and other members of the executive office to discuss the mission of the company skunk works. I don't think things are going right."

"It sounds to me like you're getting a little touchy," said Appelby.

1. How would you evaluate Appelby's approach to evaluating the output of the skunk works?
2. Are Appelby's review sessions justified?
3. What do you think of Seda's request to review the mission of the skunk works with the executive office?
4. What is your hunch about the potential success of Sudden Seafood and Razzle Razzberry?

A BUSINESS PSYCHOLOGY EXERCISE

Brainwriting

A problem for which many useful alternative solutions are sought is the water crisis faced by industry. Water is becoming scarcer in supply and more costly. To help solve this problem, each class member will write down five water-saving suggestions for business and industry. After devoting about 10 minutes to the task, each class member makes a 2-minute presentation of his or her suggestions to the rest of the class. By listening to the other class member's suggestions, students can gauge their originality.

Although somebody else may have already presented a suggestion identical to yours, present it anyway. It gives others a chance to learn which ideas are more obvious.

References

1. The decision-making approach outlined here follows the logic of the approach used at such diverse places as the Center for Creative Leadership and Xerox Corporation.

2. J. C. WOFFORD AND VICKI L. GOODWIN, "Effects of Feedback on Cognitive Processing and Choice of Decision Style," *Journal of Applied Psychology,* December 1990, p. 603.

3. JAMES BRAHAM, "Eureka!" *Machine Design,* February 6, 1992, p. 36.

4. ORLANDO BEHLING AND NORMAN L. ECKEL, "Making Sense out of Intuition," *Academy of Management Executive,* February 1991, p. 46.

5. "When to Go with Your Intuition," *Working Smart,* May 27, 1991, pp. 1–2.

6. ELEANOR DAVIDSON, "Overcoming the Fear of Decision Making," *Supervisory Management,* October 1991, p. 12.

7. "The Stream of Decisions," *Issues and Observations,* August 1982, p. 3.

8. JASON FORSYTHE, "Idea Bulletins," *Success,* October 1991, p. 22.

9. DEAN TJOSVOLD, "Effects of Crisis Orientation on Manager's Approach to Controversy in Decision Making," *Academy of Management Journal,* March 1984, p. 137.

10. LUCIA W. LANDON, "We Didn't Fall through the Cracks," *HRMagazine,* November 1991, p. 49.

11. WILLIAM Q. JUDGE AND ALEX MILLER, "Antecedents and Outcomes of Decision Speed in Different Environmental Contexts," *Academy of Management Journal,* June 1991, p. 449.

12. BERNARD M. BASS, *Organizational Decision Making* (Homewood, IL: IRWIN, 1983), pp. 9–11.

13. DAVID R. WHEELER, "Creative Decision Making and the Organization," *Personnel Journal,* June 1979, p. 394.

14. This test, developed by EUGENE RAUDSEPP, is from "Ideas: Test Your Creativity," *Nation's Business,* June 1965, p. 80.

15. ROBERT R. GODFREY, "Tapping Employees' Creativity," *Supervisory Management,* February 1986, pp. 17–18; JOHN A. GLOVER, ROYCE R. RONNING, AND CECIL R. REYNOLDS (eds.), *Handbook of Creativity* (New York: Plenum Press, 1989), p. 10; FRANK FARLEY, "The Big T in Personality," *Psychology Today,* May 1986, p. 48.

16. CHRISTINA E. SHALLEY, "Effects of Productivity Goals, Creativity Goals, and Personal Discretion on Individual Creativity," *Journal of Applied Psychology,* April 1991, pp. 179–180.

17. DANIEL G. TEAR as quoted in *Issues & Observations,* February 1981, p. 5.

18. TREVOR THOMAS, "Knowing When to Brainstorm Solo," *Supervisory Management,* October 1991, p. 5.

19. EDWARD GLASSMAN, "Creative Problem Solving: New Techniques," *Supervisory Management,* March 1989, p. 16.

20. JERRE LEVY, "Right Brain, Left Brain: Fact and Fiction," *Psychology Today,* May 1985, p. 44; TERENCE HINES, "Left Brain/Right Brain Mythology and Implications for Management and Training," *Academy of Management Review,* October 1987, pp. 600–606.

21. DAVID DORSEY, "The Curious Cowboy," *Upstate,* April 20, 1986, pp. 6–7.

22. EUGENE RAUDSEPP, "Exercises for Creative Growth," *Success,* February 1981, pp. 46–47.

23. "Be a Creative Problem Solver," *Executive Strategies,* June 6, 1989, pp. 1–2.

24. Our description of mind mapping follows closely the description in Braham, "Eureka!" p. 32.

25. DOREEN MANGAN, "It's Just a Suggestion," *Small Business Reports* (Saranac Lake, NY: American Management Association, 1992).

26. "Programs That Make Managers Face the Facts," *Business Week,* April 8, 1985, p. 74.

27. DOROTHY LEONARD-BARTON AND JOHN J. SVIOKLA, "Putting Expert Systems to Work," *Harvard Business Review,* March–April 1988, pp. 92–93.

28. BRYAN W. MATTIMORE, "Mind Blasters," *Success,* June 1990, p. 46.

Suggested Reading

ANDERSON, VALERIAN. "Kudos for Creativity." *Personnel Journal,* September 1991, pp. 90–93.

BASADUR, MIN. "Managing Creativity: A Japanese Model." *The Executive,* May 1992, pp. 29–42.

CONNOR, PATRICK E. "Decision-making Participation Patterns: The Role of Organizational Context." *Academy of Management Journal,* March 1992, pp. 218–231.

DACEY, JOHN S. *Fundamentals of Creative Thinking.* Lexington, MA: Lexington Books, 1989.

GLASSMAN, EDWARD. "Creative Problem Solving: Habits That Need Changing." *Supervisory Management,* February 1989, pp. 8–12.

JANIS, IRVING L. *Crucial Decisions: Leadership in Policy Making and Crisis Management.* New York: Free Press, 1989.

KLAAS, BRIAN S., AND WHEELER, HOYT N. "Managerial Decision Making about Employee Discipline: A Policy Capturing Approach." *Personnel Psychology,* Spring 1990, pp. 117–134.

SAUNDERS, CAROL, AND JONES, JACK WILLIAM. "Temporal Sequences in Information Acquisition for Decision Making: A Focus on Source and Medium." *Academy of Management Review,* January 1990, pp. 29–46.

SINNOTT, JAN D. (ed.). *Everyday Problem Solving: Theory and Applications.* New York: Praeger, 1989.

STEVENSON, WILLIAM B., AND GILLY, MARY C. "Information Processing and Problem Solving: The Migration of Problems through Formal Positions and Networks of Ties." *Academy of Management Journal,* December 1991, pp. 918–928.

Chapter 8

ACHIEVING WELLNESS AND MANAGING STRESS

After reading and studying this chapter and doing the exercises, you should be able to

1. Describe and implement strategies for achieving wellness.
2. Explain the symptoms and consequences of stress, including its relationship to job behavior and performance.
3. Explain the general adaptation syndrome model of job stress.
4. Describe how personality factors contribute to job stress.
5. Identify the major sources of stress on the job.
6. Develop a program for managing your own stress.
7. Give examples of what employers can do to help employees to manage stress.

JOB TASKS RELATED TO THIS CHAPTER

A major requirement for being a productive and satisfied worker is to stay well and keep stress under control. Employees who are both not well and continually stressed out are often low producers. Some of this low productivity stems from frequent absenteeism.

The fields of health psychology and behavioral medicine have had a major impact on organizations. In particular, a major thrust in human resource management today is helping employees stay healthy and achieve **wellness,** a formal approach to preventive health care. To be healthy and well is to achieve a state of mental and physical well-being that makes it possible to function at one's highest potential.[1]

A major challenge in achieving wellness is to understand and manage stress. George Vaillant, the Harvard research psychiatrist, contends that effective adaptation to stress permits us to live.[2] As the term is used here, **stress** is the mental and physical condition that results from a perceived threat or demand that cannot be dealt with readily. If you perceive something to be dangerous or challenging, you will experience the bodily response known as stress. A **stressor** is the external or internal force that brings about the stress. The fact that something is dangerous or challenging makes it a stressor.

Stress is often associated with strain, yet the two terms differ in an important way. Stress is your response to a force that upsets your equilibrium. **Strain** is the adverse effects of stress on an individual's mind, body, and actions. Being informed that you have been promoted may create some stress that day, but most people would not experience strain because of the news. To add just one more complexity, stress is also tied in with **burnout,** a state of exhaustion stemming from long-term stress. Burnout is a set of behaviors that result from strain. Keep this relationship in mind to sort out the key terms mentioned so far:

Stressor → Stress → Strain → Burnout

In this chapter we study wellness and the nature of stress, including a new model of stress that helps explain another way in which the brain influences job behavior. In addition, we describe actions the individual and the organization can take to effectively manage stress.

Wellness:
A formal approach to preventive health care.

Stress:
The mental and physical condition that results from a perceived threat or demand that cannot be dealt with readily.

Stressor:
The external or internal force that brings about the stress.

Strain:
The adverse effects of stress on an individual's mind, body, and actions.

Burnout:
A state of exhaustion stemming from long-term stress.

Strategies for Achieving Wellness

Achieving wellness is a desirable life-style to work toward. It helps you become physically and mentally healthy and to develop a positive self-image. Achieving wellness helps a person ward off harmful amounts of stress. Here we describe six strategies and tactics that make a major contribution to achieving wellness:

1. Getting appropriate exercise
2. Maintaining a healthy diet
3. Developing competence
4. Developing resilience
5. Minimizing addictive and physically dangerous behaviors
6. Developing a health-prone personality

Chapter 8 ACHIEVING WELLNESS AND MANAGING STRESS **169**

Getting Appropriate Exercise

The right amount and type of physical exercise contribute substantially to wellness. To achieve wellness, it is important to select an exercise program that is physically challenging but does not lead to overexertion and muscle injury. Competitive sports, if taken too seriously, can actually increase stress. The most beneficial exercises are classified as aerobic, because they make you breathe faster and raise your heart rate.

Most of a person's exercise requirements can be met through everyday techniques such as walking or running upstairs, vigorous housework, yard work, or walking several miles per day. Avoid the remote control for your television or VCR; getting up to change the channel or the commands can burn off a few calories!

The physical benefits of exercise include increased respiratory capacity, increased muscle tone, reduced risk of heart disease, improved circulation, reduced cholesterol level, increased energy, increased rate of metabolism, reduced body weight and improved fat metabolism, and slowed-down aging processes.

The mental effects of exercise are also plentiful. A major benefit stems from morphinelike chemicals produced in a portion of the brain called the thalamus. The endorphins are also associated with a state of euphoria referred to as a "runner's high." Other mental benefits of exercise include increased self-confidence, improved body image and self-esteem, improved mental functioning, alertness and efficiency, release of accumulated tensions, and relief from mild depression.[3]

Diet and Wellness

Eating nutritious foods is valuable for mental as well as physical health. For example, many nutritionists and physicians believe that eating fatty foods, such as red meat, contributes to colon cancer. Improper diet, such as consuming less than 1,300 calories per day, can weaken you physically. In turn, you become more susceptible to stress.

The subject of proper diet has been debated continually. Advice abounds on what to eat and what not to eat. Some of this information is confusing and contradictory, partly because not enough is known about nutrition to identify an ideal diet for each individual. For example, many people can point to an 85-year-old relative who has been eating the wrong food (and perhaps consuming considerable alcohol) most of his or her life. The implication is that, if this person has violated sensible habits of nutrition and lived so long, how important can good diet be?

The food requirements for wellness differ depending on age, sex, body size, physical activity, and other conditions such as pregnancy and illness. A workable dietary strategy is to follow the guidelines for choosing and preparing food developed by the U.S. Department of Agriculture,[4] as shown in Figure 8-1. The pyramid replaces the familiar pie chart used for many years to promote good eating habits. At each successive layer of the pyramid, a food group should be eaten less frequently.

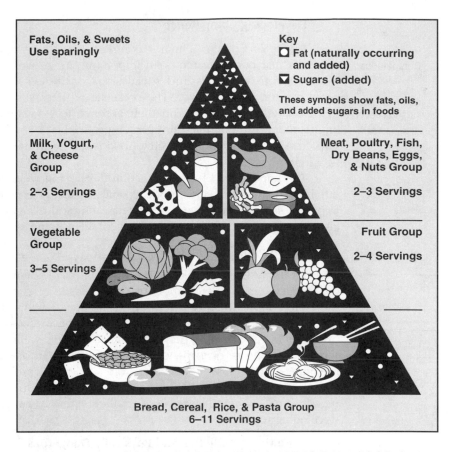

FIGURE 8–1. *THE FOOD GUIDE PYRAMID (A GUIDE TO DAILY FOOD CHOICES).*
Source: U.S. Department of Agriculture, 1992.

At the base of the pyramid are grains (bread, cereal, rice, and pasta), which should comprise six to eleven servings per day. At the next level are fruits and vegetables, of which we should consume from two to five servings per day. As the next narrower level of the pyramid are found two groups of food of which we should eat only about two to three servings per day. One group is milk, yogurt, and cheese; the other is meat, poultry, fish, dry beans, eggs, and nuts. At the top of the pyramid are foods low in nutritional value, such as fats, oils, and sweets. It is recommended that these foods be eaten sparingly.

The U.S. Department of Agriculture guidelines are for people who are already healthy and do not require special diets because of disease or conditions that interfere with normal nutritional requirements. No guidelines can guarantee health and well-being. Health depends on many things, including heredity, life-style, personality traits, mental health, attitudes, and environment, in addition to diet. However, good eating habits based on moderation and variety can keep you healthy and even improve your health.

Developing Competence

Emory L. Cowen, a major contributor to the wellness movement, contends that **competence** is an important part of wellness. Competence refers to both job skills and social skills, including the ability to solve problems and control anger. The presence of these skills has been shown to be related to wellness and their absence to poor adaptation to one's environment. Although acquiring such proficiencies is a lifelong undertaking, Cowen recommends that childhood is the best time to lay the foundation for competency.[5]

The importance of competence in developing wellness illustrates how different wellness strategies produce similar results. Developing competence improves self-confidence and self-esteem. Physical exercise and proper diet also contribute to enhancements in self-confidence and self-esteem.

Developing Resilience

An analysis of extensive case histories has shown that the ability to overcome setback is an important characteristic of successful people.[6] It therefore follows that **resilience,** the ability to withstand pressure and emerge stronger for it, is a strategy for achieving wellness.[7] Most people at one time in their lives experience threats to their wellness. Among these threats are a death of a loved one, having a fire in one's home, a family breakup, or a job loss. Recovering from such major problems helps a person retain wellness and become even more well in the long term. Learning how to manage stress, as described later, is an important part of developing resilience.

Minimizing Addictive and Physically Dangerous Behaviors

To achieve and maintain wellness, it is important to minimize a variety of habits and behaviors that bring on personal defeat. We use the term *minimize* with careful thought. Many people who make occasional use of alcohol or periodically binge on unhealthy foods still lead productive, happy, and healthy lives. Wellness is more likely to be blocked by **addictive behavior,** a compulsion to use substances or engage in activities that lead to psychological dependence and withdrawal symptoms when use is discontinued.

Substance abuse is a common form of addictive behavior. The most frequently abused substances include alcohol, tobacco, coffee, prescription drugs, illegal drugs, soft drinks, and nonnutritious foods. Nutritious foods, however, can become the object of substance abuse for compulsive eaters. Another form of food abuse is severe undereating, as in anorexia.

Many other counterproductive behaviors can prevent wellness. Common forms include physical exercise to the point of injury and illness, sleep deprivation, excessive sleeping, unprotected casual sex, and driving at excessive speeds. Certain sports can interfere with wellness, including skydiving, bungee jumping, and high-risk mountain climbing. However, proponents of these sports contend that with proper supervision they are relatively safe.

Developing a Health-prone Personality

Evidence suggests that people can be taught to develop a personality that helps ward off cancer and heart disease. In one study, people prone to cancer and heart disease were taught to express their emotions more readily and to cope with stress. The training was a step-by-step form of mental healing called behavior therapy. Equally important, the physically ill people were taught to become less emotionally dependent on others and to become more self-reliant.

The results from the behavior training were astonishing. Fifty of the people with cancer-prone personalities received training and fifty did not. Many more people died of cancer and of other causes in the nontherapy group than in the therapy group. Thirteen years later, 45 people who received therapy were still alive. Only 19 in the no-therapy group were still alive. Similar encouraging results were achieved in studies conducted by other psychologists and researchers.[8]

The implication of these studies is that a person might be able to develop a well personality by becoming more emotionally expressive and self-reliant. Even if these behaviors did not prolong life, the person's enjoyment of life would increase. If you are already emotionally expressive and self-reliant, no changes need to be made.

The Symptoms and Consequences of Stress

If you experience stress, you display certain signs or symptoms indicating that you are trying to cope with a stressor. These symptoms can also be considered the consequences of stress. With few exceptions, you experience these symptoms only if you perceive the force to be threatening or challenging. An important exception is the stress associated with physical factors, such as disease. For example, an overdose of radiation will trigger a stress response in your body even if you are not aware of the presence of radiation.

The symptoms and consequences of job stress are organized here into four categories: physiological, psychological, behavioral, and job performance. Changes in job performance accompanying stress are a by-product of the three other sets of symptoms and consequences.

Physiological Symptoms

Fight-or-flight response:
The body's physiological and chemical battle against the stressor in which the person either tries to cope with the adversity head-on or tries to flee the scene.

The body's physiological and chemical battle against the stressor is the **fight-or-flight response.** The person either tries to cope with the adversity in a head-on battle or tries to flee the scene. The physiological changes within the body are virtually identical for different stressors. All types of stressors produce the release of certain enzymes (chemical changes) within the body, which in turn produce certain short-term physiological changes.

Among the most familiar reactions are an increase in heart rate, blood pressure, blood glucose, and blood clotting. To help you recognize these symptoms, try to recall your internal bodily sensations the last time you were almost in an automobile accident or heard some wonderful news. Less familiar changes are a redirection of the blood flow toward the brain and large muscle groups and a release of stored fuels from places throughout the body into the bloodstream.

If stress is continuous and accompanied by these short-term physiological changes, certain annoying or life-threatening conditions can occur. Among them are heart attacks, strokes, hypertension, increased cholesterol level, migraine headaches, skin rashes, ulcers, allergies, and colitis. Prolonged stress can also lead to a weakening of the body's immune system, which makes recuperation from illness difficult. People experiencing emotional stress may have difficulty shaking a common cold or recovering from pneumonia or a sexually transmitted disease. Evidence suggests that some forms of cancer, including leukemia and lymphomas, are related to prolonged stress. In general, any disorder classified as psychosomatic is precipitated by emotional stress. The role of stress in contributing to physical illness can also be viewed from another perspective. More than three-fourths of visits to internal medicine practitioners are stress related.[9]

Stress stemming from overwork is now thought to contribute directly to death, at least among Japanese middle managers. A Health Ministry report indicated that *karoshi* (death from overwork) ranked second behind cancer as a leading cause of death among Japanese workers.[10]

Although most of the physiological consequences of stress described here are negative, the right amount of stress prepares us for meeting difficult challenges that spur us on toward peak performance. This issue is explored in the section on stress and job performance.

Psychological Symptoms

The psychological or emotional symptoms of stress cover a wide range. The major positive psychological consequence is a heightened sense of alertness, perception, and awareness. Among the more frequent negative psychological consequences are **tension, anxiety,** discouragement, boredom, complaints about bodily problems, prolonged fatigue, feelings of hopelessness, and various kinds of defensive thinking and behavior. The defensive behaviors for dealing with sensory information, described in Chapter 2, are also psychological symptoms of stress. People may also experience disturbed inner states as a result of intense or prolonged stress.

Behavioral Symptoms and Consequences

Psychological symptoms of stress indicate how people think and feel when faced with job or personal pressures. These symptoms often lead to actual behavior that is of particular concern to the student of business psychology. Among the more frequently observed behavioral consequences of stress are the following:

- Agitation, restlessness, and other overt signs of tension, including moving legs back and forth while seated at a meeting.
- Drastic changes in eating habits, including decreased or increased food consumption. Under heavy stressors, some people become junk food addicts.

Tension:
A feeling of internal uneasiness that is usually associated with stress or an unsatisfied need.

Anxiety:
Generalized feelings of fear and apprehension that usually result from a perceived threat. Feelings of uneasiness and tension usually accompany anxiety.

- Increased cigarette smoking, coffee drinking, alcohol consumption, and use of illegal drugs.
- Increased use of prescription drugs such as tranquilizers and amphetamines, including diet pills.
- Errors in concentration and judgment.
- Panic-type behavior, such as making impulsive decisions.

A general behavioral symptom of intense stress is for people to exaggerate their weakest tendencies. For instance, a person with a strong temper who usually keeps cool under pressure may throw a tantrum under pressure.

Burnout. An extreme behavioral reaction to stress is **burnout**, a condition of emotional, mental, and physical exhaustion along with cynicism toward work in response to long-term job stressors. Burnout is the final stage of an adverse reaction to job stress and is therefore also associated with some of the physiological and psychological stress symptoms.

Burnout was originally observed primarily among people helpers such as nurses, social workers, and police workers. It then became appar-

ent that people in almost any occupation could develop burnout. Students can also experience burnout. Conscientiousness and perfectionism contribute to burnout: those who strive for perfection stand a good chance of being disappointed about not achieving everything.

A related way of looking at burnout is that it stems from the perception that a person is giving more than he or she is receiving. An antidote to burnout is therefore to develop realistic goals. If the employee knows what he or she wants to achieve each day, he or she will be less concerned with external rewards.[11] Realistic goals are also helpful because the person may become satisfied with "receiving less."

Job burnout has serious consequences for employees and employers. A survey by Northwestern National Life Insurance Co. found that 34 percent of U.S. workers considered seriously leaving their jobs because of long-term stress. Thirty-three percent expected to burn out soon. The survey also found that 14 percent said they had quit or changed jobs because of workplace stress.[12] An example of the type of burnout uncovered in the Northwestern National Life study is illustrated in the statements of a man who attended a burnout workshop:

> I came to this workshop, quite frankly, because I'm frightened. I'm not nearly the hard-driving, hard-charging sales rep I used to be. After 20 years in

The right amount and kind of stress can make you come alive.

the territory, I really don't care too much whether customers buy from us. Our line of office furniture is pretty good, but our competition also has good equipment. I'm also tired of jumping up and down telling people that what we sell is service, when our service really isn't that hot.

I'm sick of facing the same old problems day after day, and I don't know what to do about it.

Job Performance Consequences of Stress

Eustress: Positive stress.

Few people can escape work stress. This is fortunate, because escaping all forms of stress would be undesirable. An optimum amount of stress exists for most people and most tasks. It is referred to as **eustress,** or positive stress. Figure 8-2 depicts this relationship. In most situations, job performance tends to be best under low to moderate amounts of ordinary stress.

Distress: Negative stress.

Too much stress makes people temporarily ineffective because they may become distracted or choke up. This negative type of stress is called **distress.** (As is common practice, we will generally use the term stress to cover both eustress and distress.) Mental health workers estimate that as many as 15 percent of managers suffer from critical levels of job stress that will eventually adversely affect their job performance.[13] Similarly, stress-related disorders now account for 15 percent of all occupational disease claims.[14] Too little stress, on the other hand, tends to make people lethargic and inattentive.

Previously, it was believed that performance improves steadily as stress is increased, until the stress becomes too intense. It is now believed that performance decreases more rapidly as stress increases. The wrong type of stressor can also produce stress that rarely improves job performance, even in small doses. Support for this point was obtained from research conducted with 200 employees in four firms. The study indicated that negative stress was generally associated with lowered productivity. Also, an optimal level of negative stress was not found.[15] Another study also found that negative stress, such as time urgency, interfered with solving complex problems.[16]

FIGURE 8–2. *THE SHORT-TERM RELATIONSHIP BETWEEN STRESS AND JOB PERFORMANCE.*

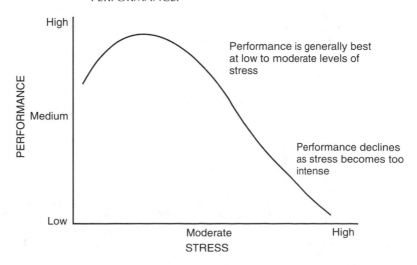

A conclusion to consider is that, for most people, challenge and excitement improve job performance. Irritation and threatening events, such as an intimidating boss, generally lower performance.

The General Adaptation Syndrome Model of Stress

General adaptation syndrome:
The body's response to stress occurs in three stages: alarm, resistance, and exhaustion.

A model of stress developed by the famous physician Hans Selye ties together the consequences of job stress.[17] According to the **general adaptation syndrome,** the body's response to stress occurs in three stages: alarm, resistance, and exhaustion (see Figure 8-3). In the *alarm stage,* the person identifies the threat or stressor. The threat can be physical (such as the presence of a mugger) or psychological (such as a layoff notice). Physiological changes take place such as those described under the fight-or-flight response.

In the *resistance stage,* the person becomes resilient to the pressures created by the stressor. The symptoms that occurred in the alarm stage disappear, even though the stressor is still present. Increased levels of hormones secreted by the pituitary gland and the adrenal cortex mount this resistance.

If exposure to the stressor persists over a long period of time, the person reaches the exhaustion stage in which the resistance fails. The pituitary gland and adrenal cortex no longer provide sufficient hormones to combat the stressor. As a result, the physiological symptoms that took place in the first stage reappear. Severe psychosomatic disorders, such as a heart attack, occur in the exhaustion phase. Burnout is also a distinct possibility.

FIGURE 8–3. *THE GENERAL ADAPTATION SYNDROME.*

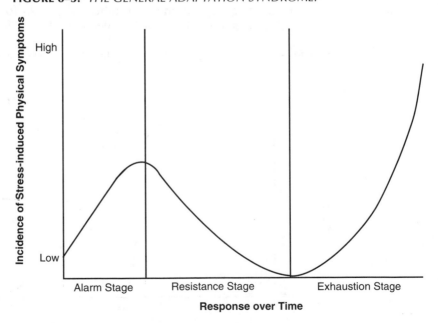

The study of psychology can help you come to grips with the wide range of human problems encountered in any job. *Grant LeDuc/Monkmeyer Press*

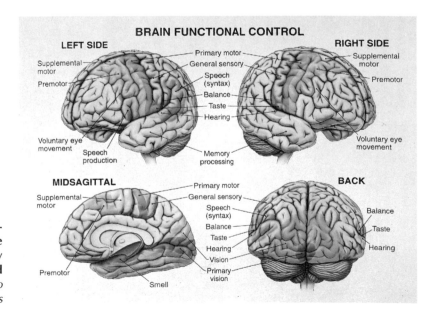

The vast majority of individual difference's among workers can be attributed to factors controlled by the brain, such as intellect and emotion. *MVI/Science Source/Photo Researchers*

BRAIN FUNCTIONAL CONTROL

LEFT SIDE — RIGHT SIDE

Supplemental motor
Premotor
Voluntary eye movement
Speech production
Primary motor
General sensory
Speech (syntax)
Balance
Taste
Hearing
Memory processing
Supplemental motor
Premotor
Voluntary eye movement

MIDSAGITTAL — BACK

Supplemental motor
Premotor
Smell
Primary motor
General sensory
Speech (syntax)
Balance
Taste
Hearing
Vision
Primary vision
Balance
Taste
Hearing

People attending a meeting may interpret the presentation quite differently depending upon their motivation, values, and intelligence.
Randy Matusow

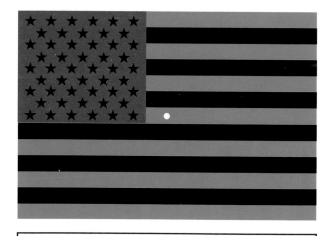

The brain plays an important role in perception. Stare at the dot in the center of the flag for approximately 30 seconds, until the colors begin to shimmer, and then stare at the dot in the center of the white rectangle. You should see a faint image of the U.S. flag as it normally appears - blinking once or twice helps if you do not see it at first. The colors of the afterimage are the complements of the original stimulus colors.

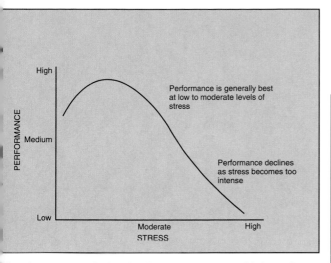

The short-term relationship between stress and job performance.

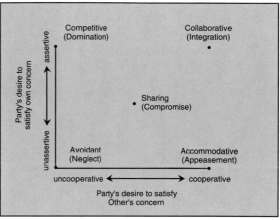

Conflict-handling styles according to degree of cooperation and assertiveness.

Physical fitness is an important part of achieving wellness, including being able to reduce and prevent job stress.
Michael Keller/FPG International

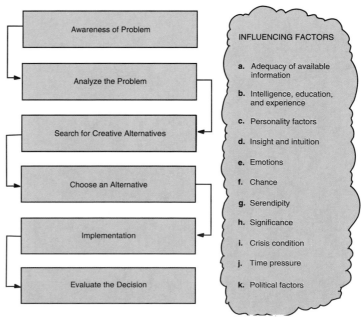

Stages in problem solving and decision making.

Effective decision makers combine careful analysis with intuition when faced with a complex problem. *Dick Luria/FPG International*

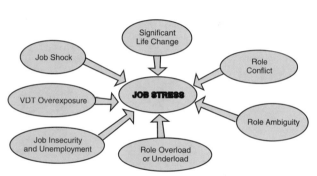

Frequently observed job stressors.

Goal setting is a standard way of increasing work productivity. *Ron Chapple/FPG International*

Conflict inevitably arises in a competitive work environment. *Ed Taylor Studio/FPG International*

People who use a win-win style of conflict resolution believe that both sides should gain something of value. *Ed Taylor Studio/FPG International*

Informal interaction among workers often helps build better relationships that carry over to the job. *L.O.L. Inc./FPG International*

Adhering to the dress code and appearing professional are important parts of adjusting to the organization. *Mike Malyszko/ FPG International*

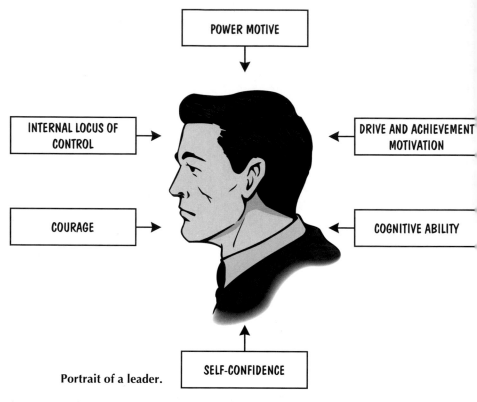

POWER MOTIVE

INTERNAL LOCUS OF CONTROL

DRIVE AND ACHIEVEMENT MOTIVATION

COURAGE

COGNITIVE ABILITY

SELF-CONFIDENCE

Portrait of a leader.

A charismatic and transformational leader can influence large numbers of people to pursue corporate objectives. *Spencer Grant/ Monkmeyer Press*

The vast majority of key decisions in organizations are group decisions. *Roger Dollarhide/Monkmeyer Press*

Communication barriers are likely to surface when the topic is both complex and emotional. *Blair Seiitz/Photo Researchers.*

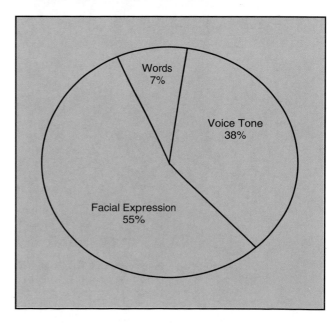

Words
7%

Voice Tone
38%

Facial Expression
55%

The emotional impact of messages.

An important strategy for career advancement is to contribute outstanding job performance. *Arthur Tilley/FPG International*

A cluttered work area often lowers productivity, and creates a poor impression. *Telegraph Colour Library/FPG International*

Workers vary considerably in their susceptibility to job stress based on their personality traits and characteristics. Three characteristics that predispose people to job stress are Type A behavior, negative affectivity, and low perceived control.

Type A Behavior

Type A behavior:
A demanding, impatient, and overstriving pattern of behavior also characterized by free-floating hostility.

A person who exhibits **Type A behavior** is demanding, impatient, and overstriving and is therefore prone to distress. Type A behavior has two main components. One is a tendency to try to accomplish too many things in too little time. This leads the Type A individual to be impatient and demanding. The other component is free-floating hostility. Because of this sense of urgency and hostility, these people are irritated by trivial things. On the job, people with Type A behavior are aggressive and hardworking. Off the job, they keep themselves preoccupied with all kinds of errands to run and things to do. As students, they often take on an unrealistically heavy workload.

Type A personalities frequently have cardiac diseases, such as heart attacks and strokes, at an early age. But not every hard-working and impatient individual is prone to severe stress disorder. Hard chargers who like what they are doing, including many top executives, are remarkably healthy and outlive less competitive people. Type A individuals recover as quickly from heart attacks as Type B individuals.[18] The latter group is relaxed, patient, and usually nonhostile.

Negative Affectivity

Negative affectivity:
A tendency to experience aversive emotional states.

A major contributor to being stress prone is **negative affectivity,** a tendency to experience aversive emotional states. In more detail, negative affectivity is a pervasive disposition to experience emotional stress that includes feelings of nervousness, tension, and worry. The same disposition also includes such emotional states as anger, scorn, revulsion, guilt, self-dissatisfaction, and sadness.[19] Such negative personalities seem to search for important discrepancies between what they would like and what exists.

People with negative affectivity are often distressed even when working under conditions that co-workers perceive as interesting and challenging. In one company, a contest was announced that encouraged company departments to compete against another in terms of improving quality. An employee with a history of negative affectivity said:

> Management is doing it to us again. We're being asked to push ourselves to the limit when we are already overworked. No extra pay, just extra work. The stress level is getting intolerable in this place.

Low Perceived Control

As described in Chapter 3, locus of control refers to whether an individual believes internal or external forces control his or her fate. A special case of locus of control is **perceived control,** the belief that an individual has at his or her disposal a response that can control the aversiveness of an event. A survey of over 100 studies indicated that people with a high level of perceived control had low levels of physical and psychological symptoms of stress. (The same people also had relatively high job satisfaction and performance.)[20] Conversely, people with low perceived control are more likely to experience job stress.

The link between perceived control and job stress works in this manner: If people believe they can control potential adverse forces on the job, they are less prone to the stressor of worrying about them. At the same time, the person who believes that he or she can respond effectively to potential stressors experiences a higher level of job satisfaction. Work is more satisfying and less stressful when you perceive that you can make the right response should a discrepancy arise between the real and the ideal.

Sources of Job Stress

Almost any job situation can act as a stressor for some employees, but not necessarily for others. As just described, personality characteristics can influence job stress. Also, life stress can influence job stress because stress is additive. If a person already has a high stress level from grappling with financial problems, minor job problems may be perceived as insurmountable. For example, a study of 100 professionals showed that stress symptoms thought to originate in the workplace may actually originate in personal life.[21] Here we describe seven frequently encounted job stressors, as shown in Figure 8-4.

FIGURE 8–4. *FREQUENTLY OBSERVED JOB STRESSORS.*

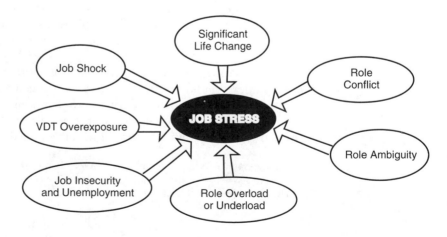

Significant Life Change

A general stressor that encompasses both work and personal life is having to cope with significant change. A pioneering series of studies on stressful life events was conducted by Thomas Holmes and Richard Rahe over a period of 25 years. Their research and updated studies showed repeatedly that being compelled to change one's life pattern created stress.

The research on life changes resulted in the assigning of scale values to the impact of life changes in 42 life events. These values, called **life-change units,** were taken to represent the average amount of social readjustment considered necessary to cope with a given change. The more significant the change a person has to cope with in a short period of time, the greater the probability of experiencing a stress disorder. According to the Holmes–Rahe scale, the maximum negative change (death of a spouse) is assigned 100 points.[22] An example of a life change that would produce modest stress for most people is a minor violation of the law (11 points). The life-change units assigned to a number of events are listed in Table 8-1.

Individual differences are important in understanding the stressful impact of life changes. The mean values listed in Table 8-1 do not hold true for everybody. For example, if a person were on parole, a minor violation of the law might have a considerably higher value than 11.

Life-change unit: A scale value of the impact of a given change in a person's life.

Role Conflict

A major job stressor is **role conflict,** having to choose between competing demands or expectations. If you comply with one aspect of a role (or set of expectations), compliance with the other is difficult. Role conflict has been divided into four types:[23]

Role conflict: Having to choose between competing demands or expectations.

- *Intrasender* conflict occurs when one person asks you to accomplish two objectives that are in apparent conflict. If your boss asked you to hurry up and finish your work but also decrease your mistakes, you would experience this type of conflict.
- *Intersender* conflict occurs when two or more senders give you incompatible directions. Your immediate superior may want you to complete a crash project on time, but company policy temporarily prohibits authorizing overtime payments to support staff.
- *Interrole* conflict results when two different roles that you occupy are in conflict. Your employer may expect you to travel 50 percent of the time, while your spouse threatens a divorce if you travel over 25 percent of the time.
- *Person–role* conflict occurs when the role(s) your employer expects you to occupy are in conflict with your basic values. You might be asked to fire substandard performers, but this could be in conflict with your humanistic values.

Role Ambiguity

Role ambiguity is a condition in which the job holder receives confusing or poorly defined expectations. Workers in all kinds of organizations are placed in a situation where job holders are uncertain of their true

Role ambiguity: A condition in which the job holder receives confusing or poorly defined expectations.

TABLE 8–1. *STRESS IMPACT OF LIFE EVENTS AS MEASURED BY LIFE-CHANGE UNITS*

Life Event	Mean life-change units
Death of spouse	100
Divorce	73
Marital separation	65
Imprisonment	63
Death of close family member	63
Marriage	50
Fired from job	47
Marital reconciliation	45
Pregnancy	45
Retirement	45
Sexual difficulties	39
Gain of new family member	39
Major business readjustment	39
Death of close friend	37
Change to a different career	36
Buying a house	31
Trouble with in-laws	29
Beginning or ending formal schooling	26
Trouble with boss	23
Change in residence	20
Change in eating habits	15
Vacation	13
Minor violation of the law	11

Sources: Rabi S. Bhagat, "Effects of Stressful Life Events on Individual Performance and Work Adjustment Processes within Organizational Settings: A Research Model," *Academy of Management Review,* October 1983, pp. 660–671. The values reported in Bhagat are an updating of Thomas H. Holmes and Richard H. Rahe, "The Social Adjustment Rating Scale," *Journal of Psychosomatic Research,* 15, 1971, pp. 210–223.

responsibilities. Many people become anxious and tense when faced with role ambiguity. A contributing reason is that being out of control is a stressor. If you lack a clear picture of what you should be doing, it is difficult to get your job under control.

Role Overload or Underload

Role overload: Having too much to do.

Having too much or too little to do can create job stress. **Role overload,** having too much to do, can create stress for a person in two ways. First, the person may become fatigued and thus be less able to tolerate annoyances and irritations. Think of how much easier it is to become provoked over a minor incident when you lack proper rest. Second, a person subject to unreasonable work demands may feel perpetually behind schedule, a situation that in itself is a powerful stressor.

Role overload is considered part of an executive's or a professional's work life. Many employees of lesser rank and income are also asked to give up much of their personal freedom and work under continuous pressure.

Gloria, an office supervisor, describes her experience with an overwhelming job:

> I work for a wholesale food distribution company. The profits in this business are thinner than a potato chip. My company made sure everybody has more than enough to do. When new management took over, they tried to squeeze more profits out of the company. This meant that even more was expected from us. Two of the other office supervisors were given early retirement, leaving three of us to do the work of five.
>
> My workload increased about two-thirds for the same pay. This meant working about seven extra hours per week and skipping a lot of important tasks. For example, I now had almost no time to listen to the problems of the support staff reporting to me. In the past I was known for my promptness. Now, I was falling behind on everything. Either I get my job under control soon, or I'll be forced to find a less hectic job.

Role underload:
Having too little to do.

A disruptive amount of distress can also occur when people experience **role underload,** or too little to do. People find role underload frustrating because it is a normal human desire to want to work toward self-fulfillment. Also, making a contribution on the job is one way of gaining self-respect. However, there are exceptions. Some people find it relaxing not to have much to do on the job. One direct benefit is that it preserves their energy for personal life. Role underload has become less frequent because so many organizations today are thinly staffed.

Job Insecurity and Unemployment

People have traditionally worried about losing their jobs because of budget cuts and automation. Two current sources of job insecurity are layoffs caused by mergers and acquisitions and corporate restructuring or downsizing. Layoffs occur when one firm acquires or merges with another for two primary reasons: (1) the merged organization will have duplicate positions, such as two vice-presidents of marketing, and (2) the organization may have to trim the payroll in order to save money. Major expenses involved in purchasing another firm include stock purchases and legal fees. Restructuring or downsizing is a planned method of reducing the number of layers of management, thus laying off many managers and their assistants. Whatever the specific reason for the layoff, worrying about losing one's job is a potential stressor.

Worrying about job loss has become the leading stressor for managers. An American Management Association report found that middle managers continue to experience the most job losses. Although middle managers make up about 7 percent of the work force, 16 percent of job cuts during a three-year period came from their ranks.[24]

Unemployment itself generates more stress than job insecurity. Unemployed people have much higher rates of depression, suicide, homicide, child abuse, and partner abuse. The dramatic increase in workplace violence, such as killing company officials, is related to unemployment stress.

Most of the perpetrators have been laid off and blame their managers or the human resources manager, who then become the murder targets.[25] Not every laid-off worker is a potential murderer. The many instances of workplace violence are usually triggered by an already unstable person being pushed over the edge by the additional stressor of job loss.

Video Display Terminal (VDT) Stress

VDT stress:
An adverse physical and psychological reaction to prolonged work at a video display terminal.

A physical and emotional form of stress associated with computer work is tied specifically to video display terminals. **VDT stress** is an adverse physical and psychological reaction to prolonged work at a video display terminal. Because of continuous work flow and terminal design, some VDT operators may perform as many as 10,000 keyboard strokes per hour. Such a rate places severe strain on hand and wrist muscles, often leading to repetitive motion disorders. Additional symptoms often reported by VDT workers after long hours of operation include headaches, neck aches, fatigue, hot, tired, and watery eyes, and blurred vision.[26]

Adding to the impact of VDT stress is the controversy about whether prolonged exposure to computer monitors can contribute to miscarriages and birth defects. The National Institute of Safety and Health contends that VDTs *do not* emit unsafe levels of electromagnetic radiation (a possible contributor to miscarriages and birth defects).[27]

If ergonomic principles are incorporated into VDT usage, these stress symptoms diminish. Proper use includes frequent rest breaks, the operator having some control over the scheduling of tasks, and using a well-designed combination of work table, chair, and video display terminal. Job rotation to tasks not involving a computer is especially helpful, but not always feasible. Being comfortable while working prevents much physical strain. In Chapter 11, more information is provided about the proper design of equipment to minimize VDT stress.

Individual Methods of Stress Management

Unless stress is managed properly, it may lead to harmful long-term consequences, including disabling physical illnesses and career retardation. Managing stress refers to controlling stress by making it become a constructive force in your life. Managing thus refers to both preventing and reducing stress. However, the distinction between methods of preventing and reducing stress is not clear-cut. For example, meditation not only reduces stress, it also contributes to a relaxed life-style that helps you prevent stress.

Methods of stress management under your control vary from highly specific techniques, such as the relaxation response, to general strategies that reflect a life-style. Included in the latter would be maintaining a diet geared toward wellness, as described earlier. Here we describe six do-it-yourself techniques of stress management. However, should your stress be so overwhelming that self-remedies will not work, seek professional help.

Identify Your Own Stress Signals

An effective program of stress management begins with self-awareness. Learn to identify your own particular reactions to stress. Take note of their intensity as well as the time of the day when the symptoms occur. Often the mere act of keeping a record of stress symptoms lessens their incidence and severity. More than likely, this phenomenon is related to the realization that you are starting to take charge of your health.

Once you have learned to pick up warning signs, the next step is to identify *what* and *how* you were thinking and feeling prior to the onset of the symptoms. For example, if your boss tells you that your report is needed in a hurry, you may begin to fret. What usually triggers stress is your own stream of negative thoughts, such as "I will be criticized if this report isn't finished on time."

It is crucial to learn how to terminate unproductive, worrisome thoughts. A recommended technique is that of thought stopping, or canceling. It works this way: Choose either the term "stop" or "cancel" and quietly but emphatically repeat it whenever you catch yourself engaging in anxiety-provoking thoughts. At first, this may be as many as 50 to 100 times per day.

Eliminate or Modify the Stressor

The most potent method of managing stress is to eliminate or modify the stressor giving you trouble. One value of tranquilizing medication is that it calms down a person enough that he or she can deal constructively with the source of stress. A helpful way to attack the cause of a stressor is to follow the steps in problem solving and decision making. You clarify the problem, identify the alternatives, weigh the alternatives, select one alternative, and so forth. One difficulty, however, is that your evaluation of the real problem could be inaccurate. There is always a limit to self-analysis.

> An inventory specialist thought the source of his job stress was the personal computer he was assigned. He complained that it ran the programs too slowly, forcing him to wait many seconds for important information to appear on screen. Reluctantly, his manager replaced the computer with a faster one from another department. The specialist's stress symptoms continued. In talking the problem over with a human resources specialist, it was concluded that the man's *real* stressor was his boss. A transfer to another department was arranged and the specialist's stress symptoms gradually disappeared.

Build a Support Network

Support network:
A group of people who can listen to your problems and provide emotional support.

A **support network** is a group of people who can listen to your problems and provide emotional support. These people, or even one person, can help you through difficult episodes. Members of your network can provide you with a sense of closeness, warmth, and acceptance that will reduce your stress. Also, the simple expedient of putting your feelings into words can be a healing experience.[28] The way to develop this support network is to become a good listener yourself so that the other person will reciprocate.

Practice Everyday Methods of Relaxation

The simple expedient of learning to relax is an important method of reducing the tension brought about by both positive and negative stress. A sample of everyday suggestions for relaxation is presented in Table 8-2. If you can accomplish these, you may not need formal methods of reducing tension, such as tranquilizing medicine or speaking to a mental health counselor.

Meditate

An old but widely practiced relaxation technique is **transcendental meditation (TM),** a mental technique of establishing a physiological state of deep rest. Transcendental meditation is simple, natural, and easily learned. It consists of getting into a comfortable upright position, closing the eyes, and relaxing for 15 to 20 minutes twice a day. The mind is allowed to

TABLE 8–2. *EVERYDAY SUGGESTIONS FOR RELAXATION* _____

1. Plan to have at least one idle period everyday.
2. Talk over problems with a friend.
3. Take a nap when facing heavy pressures.
4. Have a good laugh; laughter is a potent tension reducer.
5. Concentrate intensely on reading or on a sport or hobby.
6. Avoid becoming stressed about things over which you have no control.
7. Breathe deeply, and tell yourself you can cope with the situation between inhaling and exhaling.
8. Have a quiet place or retreat at home.
9. When feeling stressed, visualize yourself in an unusually pleasant situation.
10. Take a leisurely vacation during which virtually every moment is not programmed.
11. Finish something you have started, however small. Accomplishing almost anything reduces some stress.
12. Stop drinking so much coffee, caffeinated soft drinks, or alcoholic beverages. Try fruit juice or water instead.
13. Stop to smell the flowers, make friends with a preschool child, or play with a kitten or puppy once in awhile.
14. Smile at least five minutes every day.
15. Strive to do a good job, but not a perfect job.
16. Work with your hands, doing a pleasant task.
17. Hug one person you like today.
18. Become well organized and get your work under control.

drift, with no effort or control required. During TM the mind focuses on what is known as a mantra, a sound assigned to the meditator by the teacher. The mantra takes the form of a relaxing sound, such as "om."

During TM, the mind enjoys a settled state of inner wakefulness, while the body achieves a unique state of deep rest. The meditator shows distinct physiological changes, including a decrease in heart and respiratory rate and lower metabolism. Meditators frequently note that they feel more relaxed or less hurried than before they began to meditate.

Transcendatal meditation has become an accepted technique for reducing employee stress-related problems. A dramatic example of the contribution of TM is the experience of a Detroit chemical company. Impressed with his personal experiences with TM, the president encouraged his employees to meditate. During a three-year period, absenteeism among those practicing TM fell by 85 percent, and sick days among those workers dropped by 30 percent.[29] A nonprofit educational organization that sponsors TM provides data showing that transcendental meditation reduces sickness by 50 percent.

Practice the Relaxation Response

The **relaxation response (RR)** is a bodily reaction in which you experience a slower respiration rate and heart rate, lowered blood pressure, and lowered metabolism. The response can be brought about in several ways, including meditation, exercise, or prayer. By practicing the RR, you can counteract the fight-or-flight response associated with stress.

Cardiologist Herbert Benson explains that four things are necessary to practice the relaxation response: a quiet environment, an object to focus on, a passive attitude, and a comfortable position. The RR is practiced 10 to 20 minutes, twice a day. To evoke the relaxation response, "Close your eyes. Relax. Concentrate on one word or prayer. If other thoughts come to mind, be passive, and return to the repetition."[30]

Organizational Methods of Stress Management

Negative stress is disruptive to both productivity and employee well-being. As a consequence, organizations are actively involved in stress management. Here we describe four important ways in which organizations help to prevent and treat job stress: improved job design, emotional support to employees, wellness and physical fitness programs, and employee assistance programs.

Improved Job Design

A major strategy for decreasing job dissatisfaction and stress is to design low-stress jobs. Three key factors that determine satisfaction and stress are task complexity, physical strain, and task meaningfulness. In

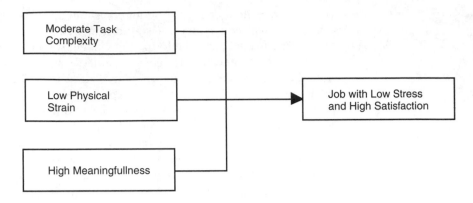

FIGURE 8–5. *THE DESIGN OF A LOW-STRESS JOB.*

general, a low-stress job would be moderately complex, carry moderate physical strain, and be very meaningful,[31] as shown in Figure 8-5.

Task complexity refers to how many different operations there are in a job and how difficult the operations are to learn. Many workers are bored by jobs too low in complexity, but frustrated by those too high in complexity. The complexity of a job is somewhat influenced by an individual's perceptions and abilities. A person with low practical intelligence might find selling real estate to be too complex; a person with high practical intelligence might find the complexity to be just right.

Physical strain is related to how much physical exertion the job requires. In an era of high technology, jobs can still make high physical demands. For example, the job of supermarket cashier carries with it considerable strain despite the presence of optical scanners. Cashiers sometime suffer from back pain and repetitive motion disorders because the new technology pushes them toward working so rapidly. Can you think of any other job where high tech has actually increased the amount of physical strain?

Meaningful jobs are those that workers think have value, such as making a direct contribution to society. Many employees of the Fischer–Price company, for example, think their jobs are meaningful because the company produces toys of recreational and educational value. Managers can help to build meaningfulness into a job by explaining to an employee why the job's output is important to society. A long-distance operator might be told, for example, that he or she is helping keeping families together.

Provide Emotional Support to Employees

Emotional support from their immediate superior can help group members cope better with job stress. One study compared the illness rate between two groups of employees who faced comparable heavy stressors. Those employees who felt they had their bosses' support suffered only half as much illness in 12 months as those who felt they lacked such support. The most helpful boss asks himself or herself this question: "How can I make my subordinates feel as effective as I do?" Supportive behaviors that help employees feel more effective include the following:

Keep Communication Channels Open. Managers can help ward off major stressors by encouraging employees to talk about real or imagined problems. A stress authority suggests to managers, "Go out of your way to communicate with your workers. Acknowledge their fears, their stresses, their worries."

Provide the Right Kind of Backup. Different workers may require different kinds of help. One employee may need a day at home to recover from stress, another employee might need only verbal encouragement, and a third might need additional training.

Act as a Catalyst. When an employee is struggling with a problem, the supervisor should help that employee look at the problem in a new perspective. Helping the employee solve the problem improves the employee's effectiveness more than solving the problem for the employee.

Hold Back on Disseminating Stressful Information. Although being open with group members is usually beneficial, burdening the already stressed employee with additional stressful information may be overwhelming. For example, why discuss a pending cutback that may not come to pass?[32]

Wellness and Physical Fitness Programs

To help combat negative stress, as well as to promote wellness, many employers offer programs that encourage employees to stay in physical and mental shape. A **wellness program** is thus a formal organization-sponsored activity to help employees stay well and avoid illness. The types of physical-fitness and stress-management techniques described in this chapter are included in most wellness programs. Workshops, seminars, activities, and medical procedures offered in wellness programs include:[33]

- Medical examination comprised of life-style questionnaire, blood analysis, flexibility testing, hearing and vision exams, skin inspection, body-fat measurement, blood-pressure screening, and mammograms (screening for breast cancer)
- Stress management
- Weight control (for both overweight and underweight)
- Smoking cessation programs
- Alcohol and illegal drug control
- Substance abuse counseling and referral
- Preventive health care
- Safety on the job and at home

- Hypertension (high blood pressure) control
- Healthy life-style and self-care

All these interventions relate to wellness, or stress management, or both. The directors of these programs are enthusiastic about the contribution of wellness programs to preventing stress-related disorders and reducing medical claims. A comprehensive evaluation was made of the cost-effectiveness of several wellness programs. The risks targeted were hypertension, obesity, cigarette smoking, and lack of regular physical exercise. An important finding was that the most effective programs in terms of helping people and saving money had two things in common: (1) the wellness center personnel aggressively recruited people into the programs and (2) offered follow-up counseling to program participants.[34]

Employee Assistance Programs (EAPs)

The personal problems of some employees create so much stress for them that job performance suffers. In response to this problem, over 6,000 employee assistance programs (EAPs) have been created. An **employee assistance program** is a formal organization unit designed to help employees deal with personal problems that adversely affect job performance. Some of these personal problems, however, are closely related to the job. For example, an employee might overindulge in alcohol because of work stress. Problems typically handled by an employee assistance program include alcoholism, drug abuse, financial difficulties, spouse abuse, child discipline, and personality clashes with superiors.

Most large- and medium-sized organizations have EAPs of their own or belong to an EAP that serves many firms. EAPs are found in both private and public organizations. Employees with performance problems are often referred to the EAP coordinator, who then makes a referral to the on-premises EAP or an outside agency. An increasing number of workers refer themselves to the company EAP. These assistance programs are generally a good investment, because they help employees return to normal levels of productivity and reduce absenteeism and turnover.[35]

Wellness programs and employee assistance programs have many features in common, such as counseling for food abuse. For example, Owens–Corning Fiberglass incorporated a company-wide wellness program into an existing EAP. The company collected data suggesting that the health-promotion campaign (part of the wellness program) improved employee health.[36]

In this section we have emphasized stress reduction. Recognize, however, that it is also part of management's responsibility to create enough stress to keep employees challenged and stimulated. Many workers, for example, feel energized by stress. Such people particularly enjoy the emotional high created by stress-related hormones released by the brain. Bored employees are often both unhappy and unproductive.

Summary of Key Points

❏ A major thrust in human resource management is to help workers stay healthy and achieve wellness. Achieving wellness includes managing stress, the mental and physical condition that results from a perceived threat or demand that cannot be dealt with readily. A stressor is the external or internal force that brings about the stress. Strain is the adverse effect of stress on an individual. And burnout is a state of exhaustion stemming from long-term stress. In short, stressor → stress → strain → burnout.

❏ Six strategies and tactics for achieving wellness are (1) get appropriate exercise, (2) maintain a healthy diet, (3) develop competence, (4) develop resilience, (5) minimize addictive and physically dangerous behaviors, and (6) develop a health-prone personality.

❏ Stress has a variety of physiological, psychological, and behavioral symptoms or consequences. The physiological symptoms are tied in with the fight-or-flight response when faced with a stressor. Psychological symptoms include fear, anxiety, emotional disorder, and defensive attitudes and behavior. Burnout is a long-term consequence of stress.

❏ Changes in job performance are another important consequence of stress. Performance tends to be best under a moderate amount of stress. Stressors that represent challenge and excitement improve job performance. Irritation and threatening events generally lower performance.

❏ Some people are more susceptible to stressors than others because of personality factors. Three such factors predisposing workers to stress are Type A behavior (impatience and hostility), negative affectivity (a "nasty disposition"), and low perceived control over an aversive event.

❏ Job stress has many sources, including life stress, which has a spillover to the job. Significant life changes create both job and personal stress. Specific sources of job stress studied here are role conflict, role ambiguity, role overload or underload, job insecurity and unemployment, and VDT overexposure. Of special note, unemployment stress apparently contributes to workplace violence.

❏ Methods of stress management under an individual's control vary from highly specific techniques to general strategies that reflect a life-style. The individual methods of stress management described here include identify your own stress signals, eliminate or modify the stressor, build a support network, practice everyday methods of relaxation, meditate, and practice the relaxation response.

❏ Organizational methods of reducing and preventing stress include improved job design with an emphasis on moderate task complexity, low physical strain, and high meaningfulness. Other techniques described here are to provide emotional support to employees, to keep communication channels open, and to employ wellness and physical fitness programs and employee assistance programs. Although these programs are important, management sometimes must increase job stress to stimulate people.

GUIDELINES FOR PERSONAL EFFECTIVENESS

1. A major life goal that would benefit anyone would be to achieve wellness. A state of wellness is much more uplifting than merely being free from disease.
2. Discover through trial and error what is the optimum amount of job stress for you. If you avoid virtually all stress, you might become lethargic and complacent. Yet too much stress over a prolonged period of time can have detrimental consequences to your physical and mental health. Your job performance might also suffer.
3. To be successful in today's competitive world, you are strongly urged to maintain an active program of stress management. At a minimum, it is important to eliminate or modify key stressors and to practice relaxation techniques.
4. No one best technique exists for reducing job stress. If you feel tense owing to work or school pressures, experiment with different methods of stress reduction and prevention. Repeat the technique that feels best.

Discussion Questions and Activities

1. Can mentally or physically disabled people achieve a state of wellness if they do not overcome their disability?
2. What is the relationship between wellness and self-actualization?
3. Identify the major stressor where you work or attend school. What can be done to improve the situation?
4. A student told his instructor, "You have to give me a deadline for my paper. Otherwise, I can't handle it." What does this statement tell you about (a) the stressor he was facing, and (b) how pressure influences his work performance?
5. Identify two jobs that you think would be particularly stressful for most workers and explain your reasoning.
6. Identify two jobs that you think would have a minimum of stress for most workers and explain your reasoning.
7. Explain how well the suggestions for individual stress management fit with what you are already doing to manage stress.
8. In some wellness programs, employees are paid a financial bonus for losing weight or stopping smoking. What is your opinion of the ethics of this practice?
9. Suppose you had financial problems serious enough to impair your concentration on the job. Would you volunteer to seek help through the firm's EAP? Why or why not?
10. Interview a person in a high-pressure job in any field. Find out if the person experiences stress and what method he or she uses to cope with it.

The Wellness Buffs

Brett Rodgers, the manager of information systems, left a message on the voice mail of Patti Okata, the director of the corporate fitness program. His message was, "Call me back as soon as possible; this fitness program is leaving me fit to be tied."

After a series of back-and-forth voice mail messages, Brett and Patti finally spoke to each other live. "We have to meet, because your fitness program is getting out of hand," said Brett. Late that afternoon, Patti met with Brett to discuss his concerns about the fitness program. Brett began by explaining that, in his perception, the program was being abused by employees. His observations were that some employees were giving wellness and fitness a higher priority than getting their jobs done.

When asked for specifics, Brett replied, "Here's what I mean. The other day two computer operators refused overtime assignments. The reason they gave was that overtime would place too much emphasis on work at the expense of leading a balanced life.

"Even worse, one of our best systems analysts told me she could not make a 12:20 appointment with a user group because it conflicted with an aerobics class. The class takes place right here in the corporate fitness center."

Patti explained that such instances are probably rare and that Brett should not lose sight of the overall importance of a healthy work force.

Brett said, "I can see we are getting nowhere today. A healthy work force might be OK. But without a healthy balance sheet, we won't have the money to support your feel-good fitness center. I think I'll talk about my concerns with the company president."

1. To what extent do you think Brett has identified a real problem?
2. What policies should the company establish to help employees establish the right priority for wellness?
3. Does this case suggest that Brett is in need of help from the corporate fitness center?

The Stress Epidemic

Wendy Fernandez, human resources manager at Great Western Insurance Company, sifted through her mail and telephone messages on Tuesday morning. She found about 35 requests from supervisors to speak to her about employee health problems. Perplexed about this accumulation of problems, Fernandez conferred with Pete Martin, her assistant.

"What's happening around here that could conceivably be creating so many health problems?" asked Wendy. "Are toxins floating through the air conditioner? Is the LA smog seeping through the building? Are our supervisors putting too much pressure on the work force?"

"Most likely none of the above," responded Pete. "I think we have a classic case of job stress induced by an outside agent. Let me show you this ad that appeared in the Sunday newspapers. I think the ad is putting ideas into the heads of our employees."

Wendy looked intently at the ad, and then said, "What a weekend for me to be out of town on vacation. I didn't catch the paper this weekend. We certainly can't stop this clinic from advertising. Yet we should alert our managers that this ad could be influencing how employees feel about their health. I suspect it could lead employees to exaggerate their symptoms."

Pete reflected, "That's the business these clinics are in. They prey upon the suggestible and the greedy. For instance, who doesn't feel under emotional stress and overworked these days?"

"I agree with your opinion," said Wendy. "Yet we cannot interfere with any employee's right to complain about health problems or contact this clinic.

"What I intend to do is to discuss this problem with top management as soon as possible. My tentative plan is to send out a bulletin to all managers giving them tips on how to handle complaints about stress and health," said Wendy.

"Have you thought of the possibility that all these complaints will subside once the novelty of the ad has worn off? Besides that, a few employees will go to the clinic and find out that a few symptoms of discomfort will not lead to a settlement in their favor. Word will then get back that unless you have a real problem, going through one of these clinics will get you nowhere."

"That could be," said Wendy. "But I still think this problem needs careful consideration by top management."

1. What action, if any, do you think top management should take about the increase in employee complaints?
2. Should this problem even be brought to the attention of top management?
3. Which of the problems mentioned in the ad might be attributed to work stress?
4. Do you think the ad placed by the clinic is an ethical business practice? Explain your reasoning.
5. Do you think that such ads "prey upon the suggestible and the greedy?"

Are You Dealing with Stress Properly?

How well do you cope with stress in your life? Gauge your ability with the following quiz developed by George S. Everly, Jr., for the U.S. Department of Health and Human Services.

1. Do you believe that you have a supportive family? If so, score 10 points.
2. Give yourself 10 points if you actively pursue a hobby.
3. Do you belong to some social activity group that meets at least once a month (other than your family)? If so, score 10 points.
4. Are you within five pounds of your "ideal" body weight, considering your health, age, and bone structure? If so, give yourself 15 points.
5. Do you practice some form of "deep relaxation" at least three times a week? These include meditation, imagery, yoga, etc. If so, score 15 points.
6. Give yourself 5 points for each time you exercise 30 minutes or longer during the course of an average week.
7. Give yourself 5 points for each nutritionally balanced and wholesome meal you consume during an average day.
8. If during the week you do something that you really enjoy and is "just for you," give yourself 5 points.
9. Do you have some place in your home that you can go to relax or be by yourself? If so, score 10 points.
10. Give yourself 10 points if you practice time management techniques in your daily life.
11. Subtract 10 points for each pack of cigarettes you smoke in an average day.
12. Do you use any drugs or alcohol to help you sleep? If so, subtract 5 points for each evening during an average week that you do this to help you to get to sleep.
13. During the day, do you take any drugs or alcohol to reduce anxiety or calm you down? If so, subtract 10 points for each time you do this during the course of an average week.
14. Do you ever bring home work in the evening? Subtract 5 points for each evening during an average week that you bring office work home.

Scoring and Interpretation Calculate your total score. A "perfect" score would be 115 points. The higher the score, the greater the ability to cope with stress. A score of 50 to 60 points indicates an adequate ability to cope with most common stressors. Experts advise against using drugs or alcohol to deal with stress and instead advocate exercising, eating a balanced diet, and using relaxation techniques to minimize the effects of stress.

Source: U.S. Department of Health and Human Services.

References

1. MICHAEL T. MATTESON AND JOHN M. IVANCEVICH, *Controlling Work Stress: Effective Human Resource Management Strategies* (San Francisco: Jossey-Bass, 1987).
2. Quoted in book review appearing in *Academy of Management Review,* October 1989, p. 602.

3. PHILLIP L. RICE, *Stress and Health: Principles and Practice for Coping and Wellness* (Monterey, CA: Brooks/Cole Publishing Company, 1987), pp. 353–354; CYNTHIA M. PAVETT AND GARY G. WHITNEY, "Exercise Makes Employees Work Better," *HRMagazine,* December 1990, p. 83.

4. *Dietary Guidelines for Americans,* 3rd ed., U.S. Department of Agriculture, U.S. Department of Health and Human Services, 1990; updated with food triangle, May 1992.

5. EMORY L. COWEN, "In Pursuit of Wellness," *American Psychologist,* April 1991, p. 406.

6. ANDREW J. DUBRIN, *Bouncing Back: How to Stay in the Game When Your Career Is on the Line* (New York: McGraw-Hill, 1992), p. 1.

7. COWEN, "In Pursuit of Wellness," p. 406.

8. HANS J. EYSENCK, "Health's Character," *Psychology Today,* December 1988, pp. 28–35.

9. DONALD T. DECARLO AND DEBORAH H. GRUENFELD, *Stress in the American Workplace: Alternatives for the Walking Wounded* (Fort Washington, PA: LRP Publications, 1988).

10. "From the Editor," *Academy of Management Executive,* February 1991, p. 4.

11. HUGH F. STALLWORTH, "Realistic Goals Help Avoid Burnout," *HRMagazine,* June 1990, p. 171.

12. *Employee Burnout: America's Newest Epidemic,* Northwestern National Life Insurance Company, 1991.

13. "Stress: The Test Americans Are Failing," *Business Week,* April 1988, p. 74.

14. *Employee Burnout,* 1991; HELEN LAVAN, MARSHA KATZ, AND WAYNE HOCKWARTER, "Employee Stress Swamps Workers' Comp," *Personnel,* May 1990, p. 61.

15. R. DOUGLAS ALLEN, MICHAEL A. HITT, AND CHARLES R. GREER, "Occupational Stress and Perceived Organizational Effectiveness: An Examination of Stress Level and Stress Type," *Personnel Psychology,* Summer 1982, pp. 359–370.

16. KENNETH E. FRIEND, "Stress and Performance Effects of Subjective Work Load and Time Urgency," *Personnel Psychology,* Autumn 1982, pp. 623–633.

17. HANS SELYE, *The Stress of Life* (New York: McGraw-Hill, 1976).

18. JEFFREY R. EDWARDS AND A. J. BAGLIONI, JR., "Relationship between Type A Behavior Pattern and Mental and Physical Symptoms: A Comparison of Global and Component Measures," *Journal of Applied Psychology,* April 1991, p. 276; Study from the *New England Journal of Medicine,* reported in ERIK GUNN, "Type A Life Isn't Harder on Heart, Study Concludes," *Democrat and Chronicle,* Rochester, NY, March 1985, p. 1A.

19. PETER Y. CHEN AND PAUL E. SPECTOR, "Negative Affectivity as the Underlying Cause of Correlations between Stressors and Strains," *Journal of Applied Psychology,* June 1991, p. 398.

20. CYNTHIA LEE, SUSAN J. ASHFORD, AND PHILIP BOBKO, "Interactive Effects of 'Type A' Behavior and Perceived Control on Worker Performance, Job Satisfaction, and Somatic Complaints," *Academy of Management Journal,* December 1990, p. 870.

21. DEBRA L. NELSON AND CHARLOTTE SUTTON, "Chronic Work Stress and Coping: A Longitudinal Study and Suggested New Directions," *Academy of Management Journal,* December 1990, p. 865.

22. RABI S. BHAGAT, "Effects of Stressful Life Events on Individual Performance and Work Adjustment Processes within Organizational Settings: A Research Model," *Academy of Management Review,* October 1983, pp. 660–671.

23. DANIEL KATZ AND ROBERT L. KAHN, *The Social Psychology of Organizations* (New York: Wiley, 1966), p. 184; updated in "Working Smart," *Personal Report for the Executive,* May 15, 1988, p. 3.

24. "Downshifting, Downsizing, Outsourcing—'Power Shifts' That Augur Vast Change," *Human Resources Forum,* December 1991, p. 2.

25. PEGGY STUART, "Murder on the Job," *Personnel Journal,* February 1992, p. 72.

26. LARRY REYNOLDS, "New Illnesses in the Age of Computers," *Management Review,* August 1989, p. 56.

27. "Video Display Terminal Radiation: The Controversy Explored," *Healthy Buildings International Magazine,* March/April 1991, pp. 2–3.

28. DONALD ZAUDERER AND JOSEPH FOX, "Resiliency in the Face of Stress," *Management Solutions,* November 1987, p. 33.

29. NORMA R. FRITZ, "In Focus," *Personnel,* January 1989, p. 5.

30. HERBERT BENSON, *The Relaxation Response* (New York: Morrow, 1975); BENSON (with WILLIAM PROCTOR), *Beyond the Relaxation Response* (New York: Berkely Books, 1985), pp. 96–97.

31. BARRY GERHART, "How Important Are Dispositional Factors as Determinants of Job Satisfaction? Implications for Job Design and Other Personnel Programs," *Journal of Applied Psychology,* August 1987, pp. 366–373.

32. SANDRA L. KIRMEYER AND THOMAS W. DOUGHERTY, "Work Load, Tension, and Coping: Moderating Effects of Supervisor Support," *Personnel Psychology,* Spring 1988, pp. 125–139; "Talking with John Newman about Stress in the Workplace," *Working Smart,* March 1992, p. 7.

33. FRED W. SHOTT AND SANDRA WENDEL, "Wellness with a Track Record," *Personnel Journal,* April 1992, pp. 98–104.

34. JOHN C. ERFURT, ANDREA FOOTE, AND MAX A. HEIRICH, "The Cost Effectiveness of Worksite Wellness Programs for Hypertension Control, Weight Loss, Smoking Cessation, and Exercise," *Personnel Psychology,* Spring 1992, pp. 5–27.

35. "79 percent of Companies Have EAPs: Most use Community Services," *American Society for Personnel Administration/Resource,* April 1989, p. 2.

36. THOMAS L. MOORE, "Build Wellness from an EAP Base," *Personnel Journal,* June 1991, pp. 104–109.

Suggested Reading

ASH, STEPHEN. "Is Job Stress a Pain or a Pleasure?" *Supervisory Management,* April 1990, pp. 10–11.

CAUDRON, SHARI. "The Wellness Payoff." *Personnel Journal,* July 1990, pp. 54–60.

KEITA, GWENDOLYN PURYEAR, AND JONES, JAMES M. "Reducing Adverse Reaction to Stress in the Workplace." *American Psychologist,* October 1990, pp. 1137–1141.

LANDON, LUCIA. "Pump up Your Employees." *HRMagazine,* May 1990, pp. 34–37.

"The Mind Power Diet." *Success,* January/February 1991, pp. 32–34.

MONAT, ALAN, AND LAZARUS, RICHARD S. (eds.) *Stress and Coping: An Anthology,* 3rd ed. New York: Columbia University Press, 1991.

SCHWARTZ, ANDREW E., AND LEVIN, JAY. "Combatting Feelings of Stress." *Supervisory Management,* February 1990, p. 4.

SPELLER, JEFFREY LYNN. *Executives in Crisis: Recognizing and Managing the Alcoholic, Drug-addicted or Mentally Ill Executive.* San Francisco: Jossey Bass, 1989.

THOMPSON, DENNIS. "Wellness Programs Work for Small Employers, Too." *Personnel,* March 1990, pp. 26–28.

WATTS, PATTI. "Are Your Employees Burnout-proof?" *Personnel,* September 1990, pp. 12–14.

Chapter 9

MANAGING CONFLICT AND FRUSTRATION

Learning Objectives

After reading and studying this chapter and doing the exercises, you should be able to

1. Understand how conflict, frustration, and anger relate to each other.
2. Explain how frustration influences job behavior.
3. Identify the major sources of job conflict.
4. Summarize the negative and positive consequences of job conflict.
5. Pinpoint the major conflict management styles.
6. Summarize the major techniques for resolving conflict with others.
7. Be prepared to resolve your next important conflict.

JOB TASKS RELATED TO THIS CHAPTER

Almost any job that includes contact with people inevitably leads to conflict, such as dealing with an angry customer or co-worker. The information in this chapter is designed to help you understand and resolve the conflicts you are likely to encounter in your job. If you supervise the work of others, you will need to use this information extensively.

Our previous study of stress is an important foundation for understanding conflict, because conflict is a major stressor. Conflict is also related to two other strong emotions, frustration and anger. Before proceeding with our study of conflict, we will define a few key terms and explain how they interrelate.

Conflict:
The simultaneous arousal of two or more incompatible motives or demands.

A **conflict** is the simultaneous arousal of two or more incompatible motives or demands. Conflict acts as a stressor and is usually accompanied by unpleasant emotions and feelings such as frustration and anger. It helps to understand conflict by also regarding it as a process in which one or both sides intentionally interfere in the efforts of the other side to achieve an objective. Because one side attempts to prevent the other from attaining an object, the conflict leads to a hostile relationship between individuals or groups.

Frustration:
A blocking of need or motive satisfaction by some kind of obstacle.

Conflict typically leads to **frustration,** a blocking of need or motive satisfaction by some kind of obstacle. You experience a sense of frustration when something stands in the way between you and the goal you want to achieve. It is usually your perception of an event, situation, or thing that determines whether it is an obstacle. For example, if you want to borrow money from a bank to start a business, you will be required to develop a business plan. Some people will regard the business plan as a bureaucratic obstacle making it difficult to borrow money. Others will regard the plan as a sensible way of understanding the success potential of their business.

Anger:
A feeling of extreme hostility, indignation, or exasperation.

Anger is a feeling of extreme hostility, indignation, or exasperation. The feeling of anger creates stress, including the physiological changes described in Chapter 8. One noticeable physical indicator of anger is that eye pupils may enlarge, causing the wide-eyed look of people in a rage. Blood may rush to the face, as indicated by reddening in light-skinned people.

Conflict, frustration, anger, and stress are interrelated. Conflict leads to frustration, which leads to anger, and all three lead to stress. Figure 9-1 summarizes these relationships.

FIGURE 9–1. *THE RELATIONSHIP AMONG CONFLICT, FRUSTRATION, ANGER, AND STRESS.*

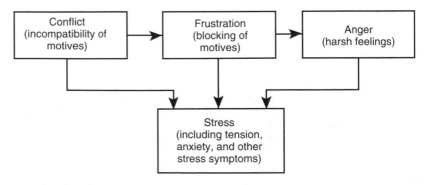

The major purpose of this chapter is to explain the nature of job conflict and how to manage it to your advantage. However, frustration deserves some separate mention because of its association with conflict.

Frustration and Job Behavior

Frustration is most likely to arise when we are ego involved in reaching a particular goal. Suppose that you are sitting in the waiting room of a dentist's office. You begin to solve a crossword puzzle because there is little else to do. You find the puzzle difficult, and you are unable to finish it. However, you do not feel frustrated because you have no personal stake in finishing crossword puzzles.

While seated in the dentist's chair, you learn that you will need extensive root canal work. It will be both painful and expensive. You now experience frustration because you were hoping to purchase a motorcycle for a cross-country trip this upcoming summer. This motorcycle trip is very important to you. The expense of the root canal work blocks your pleasure path, at least for the time being.

As shown in Figure 9-2, job frustrations are many types. Anything that prevents you from reaching a goal that is important to you is a potential source of frustration. If you are discriminated against because of factors beyond your control, such as your age, race, religion, sex, or height,

FIGURE 9–2. *RELATIONSHIP BETWEEN FRUSTRATION AND JOB-RELATED BEHAVIOR.*

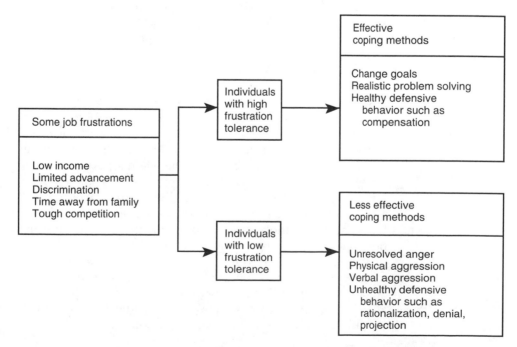

you will probably experience frustration. One woman found employment as a market research assistant in an advertising agency. When asked how she liked her new position, she claimed that she was frustrated: "Oh, the work is fine, and I'm on my way in my career at long last. But it's awfully frustrating being cooped up inside an office building during the day. I'm an outdoors type. I miss the freedom to roam about. Maybe I should try for an outside sales position."

High Frustration Tolerance

If you are a person who can tolerate high frustration, there is a good chance that you will do something constructive about your frustration. In other words, you will use an effective coping method. Among these are changing your goals if you are frustrated. If you cannot become the manager of manufacturing after years of trying, why not be content with the next lower-ranking position? People with high **frustration tolerance** often use a systematic approach to solving the problem that is causing them frustration. A man might be looking for a particular book in the library. He cannot locate it because he does not understand how to use the computer that has replaced the card catalogue. A person with low frustration tolerance might swear at or slam the computer keyboard. A problem solver would ask the librarian for help.

One healthy defensive act in response to frustration is **compensation.** Because you are frustrated in reaching a specific goal, you work overly hard to reach a related goal. One woman who was denied admission to medical school eventually wound up as an owner of a dental hygiene school. One man who couldn't make his high school football team became the team equipment manager.

Low Frustration Tolerance

A person who cannot tolerate much frustration usually responds to frustration with anger, verbal and physical aggression (for instance, kicking a car when it won't start), or counterproductive defensive behavior. Virtually every reader of this book is already somewhat familiar with the human tendency to become defensive when a person receives a threatening blow to the ego. Defense mechanisms are common when people with low frustration tolerance are blocked in reaching their goals. The mechanisms of denial and projection have already been described in Chapter 2.

Rationalization is the most frequently used defense mechanism. A person who rationalizes finds a plausible reason for some event when he or she cannot face up to the real reason. A woman who was passed over for a supervisory position might rationalize, "Who needs the aggravation anyway? In this company a supervisor winds up taking home problems almost every night." Her defense is not particularly constructive, because she still has an unresolved longing to become a supervisor.

Frustration tolerance: The amount of frustration a given individual can handle without suffering adverse consequences.

Compensation: Working overly hard to reach a related goal when you are frustrated in reaching an original goal.

Rationalization: Finding a plausible reason for some event when the person cannot face up to the real reason.

A number of reasons create conflicts in organizational life. We will describe nine important sources of conflict here. All these reasons or *sources* of conflict stem from the same underlying theme of two incompatible motives, demands, or events. You and another person or your department and another department cannot both have what you both want at the same time.

Competition for Limited Resources

A fundamental reason that you might experience conflict with another person is that not everybody can get all the money, material, and human help he or she wants. You might have an important idea you want to present to your boss before he or she leaves for vacation. Upon asking to see the boss before he leaves, he says, "I'm sorry, but I have already agreed to meet with Debbie and Mike. Why don't you catch me first thing after vacation?"

At that moment you will probably feel frustrated because your goal of presenting your idea to the boss is blocked. You might also be in conflict with Debbie and Mike, who have monopolized your boss's time for the balance of the day. The limited resource in this situation is the boss's time.

The Building of Stone Walls

The slow and steady growth of a conflict situation has been likened by Richard J. Mayer to the building of a stone wall. The seed of the conflict is usually a minor incident that is not dealt with openly. The minor incident is called a *pinch*. Next, the person pinched unconsciously gathers data to support his or her view of the situation because of a need to be right. Much of the data are subjected to perceptual distortion. As a result, a wall of minor incidents is built. The incidents eventually become an insurmountable obstacle (or stone wall) for honest and candid interaction with the *pincher*.[1]

A typical pinch is when an employee fails to share credit for a good idea he or she received from a co-worker. The co-worker feels slighted and then looks for other incidents of the first person being dishonest. Communication breaks down between the two, and they are involved in frequent arguments. The employee who failed to share credit may be unaware of how or why the conflict began.

Differences in Goals and Objectives

When two individuals or two groups have major differences in objectives, the potential for conflict is high. Although one might argue that everybody working for the same organization should have the same ultimate goal—the success of the organization—this does not always happen in practice. Frequently, individuals and departments have different aspirations than management.

Conflict between instructors and students sometimes reflects a difference between goals and objectives. An instructor might look on his or her course as a valuable contribution to each student's career. His or her goal is for students to maximize their effort in study and classroom participation. Some of the students may have the goal of receiving the maximum grade for the minimum amount of study and participation. When an examination question is posed based on a minor point made in supplementary reading, conflict occurs. If the students shared the goal of maximizing learning, they would not object to the question. If the instructor shared the goal of maximum grade for minimum effort, he or she might not have asked the obscure question.

Personal Differences and Personality Clashes

Various personality and cultural differences among people contribute to job conflict. Difference in age is one such factor. The generation gap can lead to conflict because members of one generation may not accept the values of another. Cooperation is sometimes difficult to achieve between older and younger members of a department because older employees question the work ethic of the younger employees. Simultaneously, the younger workers may believe that the older workers are resistant to change and blindly loyal to the company.

Personality clash:
An antagonistic relationship between two people based on differences in personal attributes, preferences, interests, values, and style.

Many disagreements on the job arise because some people simply dislike each other. A **personality clash** is thus an antagonistic relationship between two people based on differences in personal attributes, preferences, interests, values, and styles. People involved in a personality clash often have difficulty specifying why they dislike each other. The end result, however, is that they cannot maintain an amiable work relationship. A strange fact about personality clashes is that people who get along well may begin to clash after working together for a number of years. Many business partnerships fold because the two partners eventually clash.

Conflict-prone Jobs

Role:
A set of behaviors a person is supposed to engage in because of his or her job situation or position within a group.

Certain jobs have built-in conflict in the sense that people tend to resent the activities performed by the job holder (his or her role). A **role** is a set of behaviors a person is supposed to engage in because of his or her job situation or position within a group. A "repo man" (a person who repossesses cars when the owner fails to make payments) faces the most conflict of all, including physical retaliation by gun shot. More traditional jobs that invite conflict are tax auditors and customer service representatives who handle complaints full time.

Competing Work and Family Demands

Work–family conflict:
A situation that occurs when an individual has to perform multiple roles: worker, spouse, and, often, parent.

Balancing the demands of career and family life has become a major challenge facing today's work force. The challenge is particularly intense for employees who are part of a two-wage-earner family. **Work–family conflict** occurs when an individual has to perform multiple roles: worker, spouse, and, often, parent.[2] This type of conflict is frequent because the multiple roles are often incompatible. Imagine having planned to attend your child's solo recital and then being ordered at the last minute to attend an after-hours meeting.

The conflict over work versus family demands intensifies when the person is serious about both work and family responsibilities. The average professional employee works about 55 hours per week, including 5 hours on weekends. Adhering to such a schedule almost inevitably results in some incompatible demands from work versus those from family members and friends. Conflict arises because the person wants to work sufficient hours to succeed on the job, yet still have enough time for personal life. In Chapter 11, we describe various approaches to resolving work versus family demands.

Employee Abuse

Employee abuse:
Deliberate and malicious mistreatment that has an adverse effect on the employee's well-being.

When employees are abused by employers in various ways or where they perceive such abuse, the result is often intense conflict. **Employee abuse** is deliberate and malicious mistreatment that has an adverse effect on the employee's well-being.[3] (The next sections deal with two specific forms of abuse, electronic monitoring and sexual harassment.) The abuse results in trauma, similar to an extreme stress disorder. Excessive punishment of employees, such as frequent belittling in front of others, and discharge for no legitimate reason are examples of employee abuse. A clinical psychologist prepared the following illustrative case of employee abuse resulting in workplace trauma:

John worked for a large manufacturer of high-tech products. At age 53, John was earning a high salary along with a pension and other benefits. His work record was superior, as documented by a series of positive work reviews by superiors. During a downsizing, his superior was replaced by a younger manager, who told John, without explanation, that he should start looking for new employment. John was told that if he did not leave voluntarily, the company would find a way to fire him.

Immediately after the discussion, John was moved into a smaller, windowless office. His assistant was reassigned to another manager, his telephone privileges were suspended, and his last seven years of expenses were audited. John began to receive poor employment reviews, and his manager became abusive, including belittling John in the presences of co-workers.

After 11 months of harassment, John was dismissed from the company without severance pay. John had now used up his sick leave and vacation pay attempting to recover from a suddenly irritable bowel and a severe sleep disorder. He was severely depressed, anxious, and despondent. John eventually filed a wrongful discharge (unjust firing) suit against his employer and awaits the outcome.[4]

Overcontrol by Management through Electronics

When some workers are closely supervised, they tend to resent what they perceive to be overcontrol. As a result, they may enter into conflict with management. Rapidly advancing technology has made it possible for management to tightly supervise and control workers. Modern techniques of control include using a computer to calculate keyboarding speed, to flash messages like "work faster" on computer screens, to keep track of the number of packages shipped in a unit of time, and to chart time away from a work station.

An estimated 11 million workers in the United States and Canada receive computer-generated statistical evaluations to judge job performance and increase productivity. For example, TWA airline reservation agents are closely monitored in terms of how much time they actually spend talking to customers and prospective customers.[5] The output of customer service representatives is often monitored electronically with respect to the number of customer complaints handled and the amount of time spent with each complaint.

Critics of electronic monitoring point to data that show that electronic surveillance increases job stress and occupational illness. For example, 83 percent of electronically monitored workers complained of high tension versus 67 percent of those not monitored.[6] Concern is also expressed that electronic devices are used to spy on employees and control their behavior by collecting damaging information.

Whichever side is right, conflict results when workers feel they are being watched too carefully by management. The American Civil Liberties Union has come to the defense of these workers by investigating computerized monitoring in the workplace. If your work were being monitored by computer, would you feel that Big Brother is watching you?

Sexual Harassment

A substantial number of employees find themselves in conflict because they are sexually harassed by a superior, co-worker, or customer. **Sexual harassment** can be generally defined as unwanted sexually oriented behavior in a work setting.[7] It can include something as violent as rape or as subtle as a sexually oriented comment about somebody's body or appearance.

An important Supreme Court decision, *Meritor Savings Bank* v. *Vinson,* reinforced the idea that there are two types of sexual harassment. Both forms are a violation of the Civil Rights Act of 1964. In *quid pro quo* sexual harassment, the individual suffers loss, or threatened loss, of a job

Sexual harassment: Unwanted sexually oriented behavior in a work setting.

benefit as a result of his or her responses to a request for sexual favors. The demands of a harasser can be explicit or implied. A manager promising an employee a promotion in exchange for sexual favors, and then not promoting the employee because the employee refused, is an example of *quid pro quo* harassment.

The other form of sexual harassment is hostile environment harassment. Another person in the workplace creates an intimidating, hostile, or offensive working environment. No tangible loss has to be suffered for this form of sexual harassment. An employee who is continually subjected to sexually suggestive comments, lewd jokes, or advances is a victim of hostile environment harassment. Sexual harassment through creating an intimidating environment received worldwide attention in 1991. The occasion was Congressional hearings to determine if Judge Clarence Thomas, a Supreme Court justice nominee, had sexually harassed a former employee, Professor Anita F. Hill. Although Congress subsequently approved Thomas as a Supreme Court justice, employers became more sensitive to the problem of sexual harassment.

Sexual harassment is also regarded as an expression of power by one individual over another, because the harasser has more formal power than the harassed. The harasser, following this logic, is a power abuser as well as a legal offender.[8]

Sexual harassment is widespread in the U.S. workplace. A study by the U.S. Merit Systems Protection Board found that 42 percent of women and 15 percent of men have experienced some form of sexual harassment on the job within the last two years. According to the U.S. Equal Employment Opportunity Commission, more than 4,800 women filed harassment complaints in one year.[9] More recently, 51 percent of the women surveyed responded yes to the question, "Have you ever experienced an incident of sexual harassment on the job?" The incidents reported included physical contact, off-color jokes, and demeaning comments about women. One manager complained that "filthy" pictures were continually left on her desk.[10]

You be the judge of whether the following two incidents represent sexual harassment. Discuss your opinions with classmates and your instructor.

> *Incident A:* During the lead-in to a speech at a company meeting, the president tells a sexually oriented joke about women politicians. About one-fourth of the people present are women.
>
> *Incident B:* A manager asks one of her subordinates to join her for dinner on Saturday evening. The subordinate responds that he is involved in an exclusive relationship and chooses not to date anybody else. Despite his refusals, the manager asks him out five more times.

Tie-in with Conflict and Frustration. Sexual harassment creates conflict because the harassed person has to make a choice between two incompatible motives. One motive is to get ahead or at least keep the job. But to satisfy this motive, the person is forced to sacrifice the motive of holding on to his or her moral values or preferences. Frustration takes place because the sexual harasser becomes a barrier preventing the individual from reaching his or her goal. The accompanying box provides suggestions for decreasing the problem of sexual harassment.

The Constructive and Destructive Sides of Conflict

Job conflict, like other stressors, has both constructive and destructive consequences. The right amount of conflict may enhance productivity, while too much conflict decreases productivity. Here we describe what happens when conflict is moderate and when it is too high.

Constructive Consequences of Conflict

You can probably recall an incident in your life when conflict proved to be beneficial in the long run. Perhaps you and your manager hammered out a compromise to a problem troubling you only after you complained about working conditions. Properly managed, moderate doses of conflict can produce benefits such as these.

- *Talents and abilities may emerge in response to conflict.* When faced with a conflict, people often become more innovative than they would in a tranquil situation. Assume that your company told you that they would no longer pay for your advanced education unless you used the courses to improve

---

HOW TO HANDLE OR PREVENT SEXUAL HARASSMENT

The potential or actual victim of sexual harassment is advised to use the methods and tactics described below to deal with the problem.

Formal Complaint Procedure

Organizations that have formal policies against sexual harassment typically use a complaint procedure that follows this format:

Whenever an employee believes that he or she has encountered sexual harassment, or if an employee is suspected to be the perpetrator of sexual harassment, the complainant should:

Report the incident to his or her immediate superior (if that person is not the harasser) or to the next highest level of management if the supervisor *is* the harasser. The supervisor contacted is responsible for contacting the Affirmative Action officer immediately regarding each complaint.

The Affirmative Action officer will explain the investigative procedures (both informal and formal inquiries) to the complainant and any supervisor involved. All matters will be kept strictly confidential, including private conversations with all parties.

Dealing with the Problem on Your Own

The easiest way to deal with sexual harassment is to nip it in the bud. The first time it happens, respond with a statement of this type: "I won't tolerate this kind of talk." "I dislike sexually oriented jokes." "Keep your hands off me."

Tell the actual or potential harasser, "You're practicing sexual harassment. If you don't stop I'm going to exercise my right to report you to management." Similarly, "I think I heard you right. Would you like to accompany me to the boss's office and repeat what you said to me?"

---

your job performance. You would probably find ways to accomplish such an end.

- *Conflict can satisfy a variety of psychological needs.* Among them are a desire to express aggressive urges and to be aroused by something in the environment. As a socially acceptable substitute for attacking others, you might be content to argue over work responsibilities.
- *Conflict can lead to worthwhile innovation and change.* Conflict between various functions, such as engineering and manufacturing, have led to the establishment of cross-functional teams. Because these teams contain representatives from the different functions, it has been easier to resolve areas of conflict.
- *Many individuals are bored with their jobs and thus find squabbles with other people and other departments a refreshing pause in their day.* Office conflicts tend to add sparkle to coffee break conversations, even if the discussants are not personally involved in the dispute.
- *Conflict can provide diagnostic information about problem areas in the firm.* When management learns of conflict, an investigation is sometimes initiated that will lead to the prevention of many similar problems. One example would be that many companies have taken a very positive stance against sexual harassment after a conflict of this nature was brought to their attention.
- *As an aftermath of conflict, unity may be reestablished.* The drama of childhood is frequently reenacted in large and small companies. Two adolescents engaged in a fist fight may emerge bloodied but good friends after the battle. Two warring supervisors may also become more cooperative as an aftermath of confrontation.

Destructive Consequences of Conflict

As common sense would suggest, conflict can also have a multitude of harmful consequences to the individual and the organization. It is the harmful consequences of conflict that make it important for people to learn how to resolve conflict. Here are some of the harmful consequences:

- *Conflict consumes considerable managerial time.* Managers report that they spend as much as 20 percent of their time at work dealing with conflict and its consequences. The net result may be lowered managerial productivity, because less time is spent on problems that can increase profits or save money.
- *Conflict often results in extreme demonstrations of self-interest at the expense of the larger organization.* Units of an organization or individuals will place their personal welfare ahead of that of the rest of the firm. For example, a labor union may call a strike or a company may eliminate some jobs primarily to demonstrate power.
- *Prolonged conflict between individuals can be detrimental to some people's emotional and physical well-being.* Many individuals have suffered psychosomatic disorder as a consequence of the intense disputes that take place within their companies. One foreman had a heart attack on the shop floor in the midst of an argument with his boss over the necessity of replacing a machine.
- *Time and energy can be diverted from reaching important goals.* In addition, money and material can be wasted. It is not uncommon for two managers in conflict to spend time writing memos proving each other wrong in a particular dispute.

- *Conflict can lead to costly sabotage by employees.* The computerization of the workplace has increased the consequences of employee sabotage. Angry professional, technical, and clerical employees have been known to destroy databases and shut down company operations. For example, a suspended computer operator entered a number of unauthorized commands, taking 32 tape drives offline. The communications company he worked for was unable to service its customers the next day.[11]
- *Too much conflict is fatiguing, even if it does not cause symptoms of emotional illness.* People who work in high-conflict jobs often feel "spent" when they return home from work. When the battle-worn individual has limited energy left over for family responsibilities, the result is more conflict. (For instance, "What do you mean you are too tired to go to the movies?")

Conflict Management Styles

Before describing specific methods of resolving conflict, it is useful to understand five general styles, or orientations, of handling conflict. As shown in Figure 9-3, Kenneth Thomas identified five major styles of conflict management: competitive, accommodative, sharing, collaborative, and avoidant. Each style is based on a combination of satisfying one's own concerns (assertiveness) and satisfying the concerns of others (cooperativeness).[12]

Competitive. The competitive style is a desire to win one's own concerns at the expense of the other party, or to dominate. A person with a competitive orientation is likely to engage in win–lose power struggles.

FIGURE 9-3. *CONFLICT-HANDLING STYLES ACCORDING TO DEGREE OF COOPERATION AND ASSERTIVENESS.*
Source: Kenneth W. Thomas, "Organizational Conflict," in Steven Kerr, ed., *Organizational Behavior* (Columbus, Ohio: Grid Publishing, 1979), p. 156.

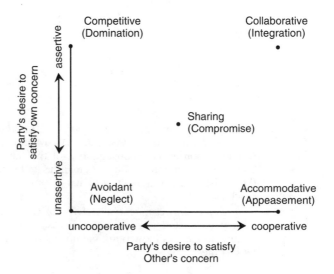

Accommodative. The accommodative style favors appeasement, or satisfying the other's concerns without taking care of one's own. People with this orientation may be generous or self-sacrificing just to maintain a relationship. An irate customer might be accommodated with a full refund, "just to shut him (or her) up." The intent of such accommodation might also be to retain the customer's loyalty.

Sharing. The sharing style is halfway between domination and appeasement. Sharers prefer moderate but incomplete satisfaction for both parties, which result in a compromise. The term "splitting the difference" reflects this orientation and is commonly used in such activities as purchasing a house or car.

Collaborative. In contrast to the other styles, the collaborative style reflects a desire to fully satisfy the desires of both parties. It is based on an underlying philosophy of **win–win,** the belief that after conflict has been resolved both sides should gain something of value. The user of win–win approaches is genuinely concerned about arriving at a settlement that meets the needs of both parties, or at least does not badly damage the welfare of the other side. When collaborative approaches to resolving conflict are used, the relationships among the parties are built on and improved.

Here is an example of a win–win approach to resolving conflict. A manager granted an employee a few hours off on an occasional Friday afternoon if she were willing to be on call for emergency work on an occasional weekend. Both parties were satisfied with the outcome and both accomplished their goals.

Avoidant. The avoider is a combination of uncooperative and unassertive. He or she is indifferent to the concerns of either party. The person may actually be withdrawing from the conflict or be relying on fate. The avoidant style is sometimes used by a manager who stays out of a conflict between two team members who are left to resolve their own differences.

In the following description of specific techniques for resolving conflict, you should be able to relate most of them to these five key styles. For example, you will see that the confrontation and problem-solving technique reflects the collaborative style.

> **Win–win:**
> The belief that after conflict has been resolved both sides should gain something of value.

Techniques for Resolving Conflicts with Others

Because of the inevitability of job conflict, a career-minded person must learn effective ways of resolving conflict. Here we concentrate on methods of conflict resolution that you can use on your own. Most of them emphasize a win–win philosophy. Several of the negotiating and bargaining tactics to be described may be close to the competitive orientation.

Confrontation and Problem Solving

Confrontation and problem solving: A method of identifying the true source of conflict and resolving it systematically.

The most highly recommended way of resolving conflict is **confrontation and problem solving,** a method of identifying the true source of conflict and resolving it systematically. The confrontation in this approach is gentle and tactful rather than combative and abusive. Reasonableness is important because the person who takes the initiative in resolving the conflict wants to maintain a harmonious working relationship with the other party. Confronting and problem solving a conflict involves six steps:

Step 1: Awareness. Party A recognizes that a conflict exists between himself or herself and party B.

Step 2: The decision to confront. Party A decides the conflict is important enough to warrant a confrontation with party B and that such a confrontation is preferable to avoiding the conflict.

Step 3: The confrontation. Party A decides to work cooperatively and confronts party B. At this point, party B may indicate a willingness to accept the confrontation or may decide to gloss over its seriousness. Often the conflict is resolved at this step, particularly if it is not of a serious and complicated nature.

Step 4: Determining the cause of the conflict. The two parties discuss their own opinions, attitudes, and feelings in relation to the conflict and attempt to identify the real issue. For example, the real cause of conflict between two people might be that they have a different concept of what constitutes a fair day's work.

Step 5: Determining the outcome and further steps. In this step the parties attempt to develop specific means of reducing or eliminating the cause of the conflict. If the cause cannot be changed (such as changing one's opinion of a fair day's work), a way of working around the cause is devised. If both parties agree on a solution, then the confrontation has been successful.

Step 6: Follow-through. After the solution has been implemented, both parties should check periodically to ensure that their agreements are being kept.[13]

When the other party has a power advantage over you, it is particularly important to express the confrontation in a tactful manner that does not hint at retaliation. Suppose that you find out that a co-worker is being paid $200 more per month than you, yet he is doing the same job and has the same amount of experience and education. Confronting the issue gently, you would tactfully discuss this problem with your boss and ask if the inequity could be resolved. One statement you might make would be, "I wonder if there has been a mistake in setting my salary. The fellow I work with is being paid $200 dollars more per month than another person doing the same job."

Negotiating and Bargaining

Negotiating and bargaining: Conferring with another person in order to resolve a problem.

Conflicts can be considered situations calling for **negotiating and bargaining,** conferring with another person in order to resolve a problem. When you are trying to negotiate a fair salary for yourself, you are simultaneously trying to resolve a conflict. At first the demands of both parties may seem incompatible, but through negotiation a salary may emerge that satisfies both parties. An example of such a win–win outcome took place between a city school board and a teacher's association.

An agreement was reached to boost teacher's pay an average of 27 percent over a three-year contract. To achieve this substantial gain, certain trade-offs were agreed to by the association. A number of nonteaching positions were eliminated and more administrators were shifted to teaching jobs. The school board could now better afford the 27 percent raise.

Compromise. In compromise, one party agrees to do something if the other party agrees to do something else. "I'll get my reports to you on time if you agree to get them back to me with your suggestions within ten days." Compromise is a realistic approach to resolving conflict and is almost inescapable in our culture. People enter into negotiation and bargaining sessions expecting a compromise solution. Assume, for example, that a company has agreed to have a custom-designed machine built for a certain price. The buyer does not expect to get all the features desired at that price, while the seller anticipates throwing in more features than he or she first offered.

The major problem with compromise is that the two parties may wind up with a solution that pacifies both but does not solve the problem. One example would be buying two department heads half the equipment that each requests. As a result, neither department really shows the productivity gain that would have been possible if the full request had been granted to either side.

Allow Room for Negotiation. The basic strategy of negotiation and compromise is to begin with a demand that allows you room for compromise and concession. Anyone who has ever negotiated for the price of an automobile, house, or used furniture recognizes this vital strategy. If you think your ten-speed bicycle is worth $300, you might put it on sale for $400. A potential buyer makes an initial offer of $250. After negotiation you wind up with an offer of $300, precisely what you anticipated.

Begin with a Plausible Demand or Offer. Most people believe that allowing room for negotiation includes beginning with an extreme demand or offer. The final compromise will therefore be closer to your true demand or offer than if you opened the negotiations more realistically. But a plausible demand is better because it shows you are bargaining in good faith. Also, if a third party has to resolve the conflict, a plausible demand or offer will receive more sympathy than an implausible one.

Focus on Interests, Not Positions. Rather than clinging to specific negotiating points, keep your overall interests in mind and try to satisfy them. Remember that the true object of negotiation is to satisfy the underlying interests of both sides. Here is how this strategy works:

Your manager asks you to submit a proposal for increasing productivity. You see it as an opportunity to acquire an additional staff member. When you submit your ideas, you learn that management is really thinking about additional computerization, not additional staff. Instead of insisting on hiring a new worker, be flexible. Ask to be included in the decision making for acquiring an additional computer. You will reduce your workload (your true interest), and you may enjoy such secondary benefits as having helped the company to increase productivity.[14]

Make Small Concessions Gradually. Making steady concessions leads to more satisfactory agreements in most situations. Gradually, you concede little things to the other side, such as throwing in an air pump and a back pack if the person agrees to move up the offer for the ten-speed bike. The small-concession tactic is described as a soft approach to bargaining. The hard-line approach is to make your total concession early in the negotiation and grant no further concessions. In our example, "My bike is for sale at $300 including an air pump and a back pack. I will keep the bike rather than let it go for less."

Use Deadlines. Giving the other side a deadline is often helpful in winning a negotiation or resolving a conflict. Deadlines often force people into action because they require some type of external control or motivation. Here are two examples of how you might be able to use deadlines to gain advantage in your negotiation:

- "Will I be receiving a promotion to restaurant manager by December 31? If not, I will be forced to accept employment at another restaurant that has offered me such a promotion."
- "I am willing to paint your house for $2,000 if you agree to sign the contract by July 15. After that date my price will go up to $2,500."

Make a Last and Final Offer. In many instances, presenting a final offer will break a deadlock. You might frame your message something like this, "All I am willing to pay for your used refrigerator is $160. Call me when you can let me have it for that price." Sometimes the strategy will be countered by a last and final offer from the other side: "Thanks for your interest. My absolute minimum price for this refrigerator is $190. Call me if that should seem OK to you." One of you will probably give in and accept the other person's last and final offer.

Allow for Face-saving. We have saved one of the most important negotiating strategies for last. Negotiating does not mean that you should try to humiliate the other side, particularly when you believe in the win–win philosophy. You should try to create circumstances that will enable you to continue working with the other side if it is necessary. People prefer to avoid looking weak, foolish, or incompetent during negotiation or when the process is completed. If you do not give your opponent an opportunity to save face, you will probably create a long-term enemy. An example of face-saving took place in a real-estate transaction.

Annette and her brothers were in the business of buying and rehabilitating old buildings and then later renting and/or selling them. They did this on a part-time basis. Annette learned that one of her co-workers at the office was trying to sell a dilapidated building he owned in town for $68,500. After several tries at negotiating the price, Annette's final offer of $54,000 was accepted. She was able to get the property at this low price because the owner was badly in need of cash. To help ease the sting of having obtained the property at such a low price, Annette later told the owner (and co-worker), "Joe, I think you made a smart move unloading your property when you did. The city building codes are so tight they make it just about impossible for landlords to keep their places up to standard. My brothers and I have a big job cut out for us."

Disarm the Opposition

In many instances of interpersonal conflict, the other side has a legitimate complaint about specific aspects of your behavior. If you deny the reality of the complaint, he or she will continue to harp on that point and the issue will remain unresolved. A good alternative is to use **disarm the opposition,** a technique of conflict resolution in which one person disarms another by agreeing with his or her criticism. By agreeing with the criticism, you may set the stage for a true resolution of the problem.

Disarm the opposition:
A technique of conflict resolution in which one person disarms another by agreeing with his or her criticism.

Disarming the opposition has widespread application. It works more effectively than launching a counterattack against the person with whom you are in conflict. Assume that your boss is angry with you because your sales are 25 percent below target. You recognize that your boss might even be angry enough to threaten you with an ultimatum—improve sales or leave the company. Your worst strategy would be to marshal an immediate counterattack during a meeting with your boss. Do not try to dazzle him or her with a long list of reasons why sales have been below forecast.

Instead, disarm your boss with a statement such as, "You are probably upset because my sales are 25 percent below target. I agree that I should not be proud of my performance. Maybe you can help me develop a plan of attack to improve my sales situation."

Exchange Images with Your Antagonist

The essential point to this advanced method of resolving conflict is that you and your antagonist make it clear that you understand the other person's point of view. Empathy of this kind may then lead to a useful and productive compromise. A convenient application of this method is for you to list on a sheet of paper (1) your side of the argument and (2) what you think is his or her side of the argument. Next, he or she does the same for you. Table 9-1 is an example of how images might be exchanged. Each person makes up his or her image sheet without consulting the other person. After the images are exchanged, discussion (and sometimes fireworks) begins.

TABLE 9–1. *AN IMAGE EXCHANGING LIST BETWEEN YOU AND YOUR BOSS BASED ON A CONFLICT ABOUT PUNCTUALITY* _____

You: My Side of the Story	What I Think Is Your Side of the Story
a. I'm usually on time for work.	a. I'm not very dependable.
b. I live on the other side of town.	b. I live too far from the office.
c. Public transportation is unreliable in this city.	c. I take the last possible bus.

Your Boss: My Side of the Story	What I Think Is Your Side of the Story
a. You are late too often.	a. I'm as punctual as most people in the office.
b. If you cared more about your job, you would consider moving closer to the office.	b. I think you don't take my transportation problems seriously.
c. If you got out of bed earlier, you could take an earlier bus.	c. I try hard to get here on time. It's not my fault that I'm late sometimes.

Allow the Other Person to Simmer Down

Watching a professional hockey game, I noticed that the referee and other players did not intervene until a fight between two players had lasted about three minutes. Seated next to me was an avid hockey fan and former player. I asked the gentleman about the delay before the fighting hockey players were separated. He replied, "If you break them up too soon, they'll get right back to fighting. You have to let them blow off most of their steam before you try to separate them."

Similarly, if your conflict with another person in the office is so intense that he or she is verbally violent, play it cool. Let most of the anger dissipate before you return with a counterargument. Until the other party has expressed most of his or her angry feelings, he or she won't listen to your side of the story. Once the person has ventilated his or her feelings, you can begin the process of working out your problem.

Make an Upward Appeal

At times you may be placed in a conflict situation where the other party holds the major share of the power. Perhaps you have tried techniques such as confrontation and problem solving or disarming the opposition, yet he or she still won't budge. In these situations you may have to enlist the help of a third party with power—more power than you or your adversary has. Among such third parties are union stewards, personnel managers, a highly placed relative in the organization, or your boss's boss (when you are convinced that you have been done an injustice).

In some situations, just implying that you will bring in that powerful third party to help resolve the conflict situation is sufficient for you to gain advantage. One woman felt she was repeatedly passed over for promotion because of her sex. She hinted that if she were not given fairer consideration she would speak to the Equal Employment Opportunity Commission (EEOC). She was given a half-step promotion shortly thereafter.

Choosing a Tactic for Resolving a Conflict

How does a person know which of the tactics or strategies presented in this chapter will work best for a given problem? The best answer is to consider both your personality and the situation. With respect to your personality, or personal style, pick a tactic for resolving conflict that you would feel comfortable using. One person might say, "I would like the tactic of using deadlines because I like to control situations." Another person might say, "I prefer confrontation because I'm an open and up-front type of person." Still another person might say, "I'll avoid disarming the opposition for now. I don't yet have enough finesse to carry out this technique."

In fitting the strategy to the situation, it is important to assess the gravity of the topic for negotiation or the conflict between people. A woman might say to herself, "My boss has committed such a blatant act of sexual harassment that I had best take this up with a higher authority immediately." Sizing up your opponent can also help you choose the best strategy. If she or he appears reasonably flexible, you might try to compromise. Or if your adversary is especially upset, give that person a chance to simmer down before trying to solve the problem.

BACK TO THE JOB TASK

The next time you face a conflict on the job, first think through what your goals are in the conflict situation. Are you attempting to be competitive, accommodative, sharing, collaborative, or avoidant? If you intend to be collaborative, you will probably reach a lasting resolution of your conflict. Your next step should be to choose among the specific conflict resolution techniques to find the one best suited to the occasion. For example, if your manager is bombarding you with criticism, allow him or her to simmer down. Then begin to disarm the opposition. The outcome will probably be beneficial.

Summary of Key Points

❑ A conflict is the simultaneous arousal of two or more incompatible motives or demands and is usually accompanied by frustration and anger. Frustration is the blocking of need or motive satisfaction by some obstacle.

❑ People with high frustration tolerance generally use effective coping methods to deal with frustration, including compensation (finding a substitute goal for the one that is blocked). People with low frustration tolerance usually respond to frustration with anger, verbal and physical aggression, or counterproductive defensive behavior.

❑ Job conflict is almost inevitable because so many different factors breed conflict. Nine major reasons for or sources of job conflict are (1) competition for limited resources, (2) the building of "stone walls," (3) differences in goals and objectives, (4) personal differences and personality clashes, (5) conflict-prone jobs, (6) competing work and family demands, (7) employee abuse, (8) overcontrol by management through electronics, and (9) sexual harassment.

❑ Properly managed, moderate amounts of conflict can be beneficial to the organization. Among the benefits of functional conflict are (1) emergence of talents and abilities, (2) need satisfaction, (3) innovation and change, (4) relief of boredom, (5) uncovering of diagnostic information, and (6) reestablishment of unity.

❑ Too much or too intense conflict can be harmful to individuals and the organization. Among the consequences of dysfunctional conflict are (1) consumption of management time, (2) demonstrations of self-interest, (3) emotional and physical damage to people, (4) diversion of efforts away from goals, (5) sabotage, and (6) excessive fatigue.

❑ Five major styles of conflict management have been identified: competitive, accommodative, sharing, collaborative, and avoidant. Each style is based on a combination of satisfying one's own concerns (assertiveness) and satisfying the concerns of others (cooperativeness).

❑ The techniques for resolving conflicts with others described in this chapter are:
1. Confrontation and problem solving.
2. Negotiation and bargaining. (Included here are use compromise; allow room for negotiation; begin with a plausible demand or offer; focus on interests, not positions; make small concession gradually; use deadlines; make a last and final offer; and allow for face saving.
3. Disarm the opposition: agree to the criticism made of you.
4. Exchange images with your antagonist: each side states its and the other side's point of view.
5. Allow the other person to simmer down.
6. Make an upward appeal: take your problem to a higher authority if gentler approaches do not work.

❑ In choosing a tactic for resolving conflict, consider both your personality or style and the nature of the situation facing you. The situation includes such factors as the gravity of the conflict and the type of person you are facing.

GUIDELINES FOR PERSONAL EFFECTIVENESS

1. If your job involves dealing with people, it is almost inevitable that you will experience person-to-person or group-to-group conflict from time to time. Rather than suppress or ignore conflict, it is to your advantage to learn effective techniques to cope or deal with conflict.
2. Underlying most techniques of resolving conflict is being able to face up to (confront) the real issues. Thus, to resolve conflict, you must face your opponent and candidly discuss the problem between the two of you.
3. A general plan for using techniques of conflict resolution is to begin with a tactful, low-key approach and see if that works. If not, try an approach with more power and force. To illustrate, it might be worth your while to begin with a tactful confrontation. If that does not work, appeal to a more powerful third party. As with any strategy for dealing with people, you have to use techniques that you find fit both your personality and the circumstances.

1. Is a price war between two airlines a conflict? Why or why not?

2. How can a person prevent the building of "stone walls" in his or her life?

3. Identify three jobs in which the potential for conflict is very high.

4. What should an employee do who feels he or she is being abused?

5. What is your attitude toward electronic monitoring of employee performance?

6. Which one of the five conflict management styles is supposed to be the most effective? Explain your reasoning.

7. Many lawyers contend that when a case goes to court (is tried before a judge or jury) it represents a negotiation failure. Explain what they mean.

8. Give an example of a conflict in which a compromise solution would probably be ineffective.

9. Assume that your income tax is audited by a government official. The official says to you, "I notice there are many errors in arithmetic on your tax statement. You have done a careless job of preparing your taxes." Respond to the tax auditor, using the technique of disarm the opposition.

10. Assume that you and the instructor of this course exchanged images over the amount of work assigned. Write down (a) what you think would be his or her perception of students about this issue, and (b) your perception of the instructor's stand on this issue.

A Business Psychology Problem

Marketing versus Engineering

Wayne Adams, a product development engineer at an electronics firm, was working on a new product with a tight schedule. The product incorporated a large number of high-tech features. Part of the plan was to release the product in different stages. At the early stage, the product would have some of the new features. The final product would have all the advanced features.

The primary objective of the marketing department was to place the product with suitable customers as soon as possible. Engineering, however, was more concerned about meeting the long-range schedule of a final product that incorporated all the new features.

In the early stages of the project, the marketing team worked closely with the engineering team in trying to evaluate customer needs. The engineering team tried to respond to the requests made by marketing in order to make the product attractive to potential customers. At first the demands were small and changes were fit into the existing schedule. However, as more marketing people were added to the product, the demands for changes escalated. Each representative had potential customers whose needs could be met with different features. The sales representatives depended on such sales in order to earn commissions and thus placed pressure on engineering to add features to the product.

One day Wayne received a telephone call from Terry Lemieux, a sales rep in Los Angeles who had been aggressively seeking new features. "We have a customer who's ready to sign for 200 machines, if you can deliver the ultrasound feature," said Terry.

"The ultrasound feature?" replied Wayne in disbelief. "You guys told us that no one would ever use that feature. The ultrasound is not slated until next year. To incorporate ultrasound, we would have to have an entire new subsystem. There's no way you can get it until next year."

Terry replied, "Look, we already told the customer we could deliver the product with the ultrasound. There could be some legal problems if you can't come through for us."

"Sorry, Terry," replied Wayne. "There's just no way. Even if we dropped everything else from the schedule and started today, we wouldn't finish until late in the year."

Wayne reported the incident about Terry's demands back to the lead engineer. The next day the lead engineer received a phone call from the vice-president of marketing, complaining about the engineers' lack of responsiveness to customer needs.

In the following several months, relations between engineering and marketing became even more strained. So much time was spent arguing about whether or not customer demands could or should be met that the project slipped farther behind.

Marketing claimed that its representatives were losing confidence in engineering's ability to deliver the new product. As a backup plan, the sales representatives began to push other products. Marketing also claimed that customers were losing confidence in the new product because they had not received the features they were promised.

Engineering responded that the sales representatives were only concerned with earning commissions, rather than with the long-term success of the product. As the lead engineer said, "If marketing would wait for the finished product, they would really have something worthwhile to sell."

1. How would you characterize the nature of the conflict being faced by marketing and engineering?
2. What should the company do next about resolving this conflict?
3. How could this conflict have been prevented?

Source: Case researched by Tamara Randall, Rochester Institute of Technology.

A Business Psychology Problem

The Uncomfortable Business Trip

Tammy worked very hard for two years as a marketing assistant at Biotronics, a manufacturer of electronic equipment for the health field. She was then promoted to sales representative, covering the entire state of Indiana. Tammy brought the good news home to her husband, Rick. As she explained the details of the promotion to him, Tammy noticed that Rick developed a glum expression. When asked why he was so unenthusiastic about her promotion, Rick replied:

"You may think that I'm being old-fashioned, but I can see a lot of trouble ahead for you in your new job. You'll be forced into a good deal of overnight travel. In the process, you'll find yourself in some touchy situations with men from your company and also with strangers."

"Rick, I agree with one thing you said. You are being old-fashioned. A woman who isn't looking to get involved with a man on a business trip will have no problem. I just read an article to that effect in *New Woman,* a magazine for career women."

Rick and Tammy continued their discussion for 15 more minutes and then shifted to a talk about plans for the weekend. Two weeks later Tammy's boss arranged a business trip for himself and Tammy to attend a medical conference in Indianapolis. Tammy told Rick that she would be gone for three days on this important trip with "several people from the office."

Duane, Tammy's boss, invited her to have dinner with him the first night of the convention. Tammy mentioned that she was so tired from the day's excitement that she would prefer to have a snack by herself and then retire to her room. But Duane persisted, and not wanting to offend her boss, Tammy met Duane for dinner.

During dinner, Duane shifted quickly from a discussion of business topics to questions about Tammy's hobbies, personal interests, and how well she was getting along with Rick. Toward the end of dinner, Duane extended another invitation to Tammy: "Let's you and I go dancing next.

The evening is young, and we're both adults free to do what we want. Besides that, I feel a lot of good chemistry between us. And if you and I were compatible, I would be more willing to get you assigned to some of our major customers in your territory."

Tammy felt a surge of uneasiness. She thought quickly to herself, "What should I do now? If I turn down Duane, this trip could turn into a disaster. But if I go out with him, I'm sure I'll be facing another kind of disaster—fighting off the advances of my boss. And then if I tell Rick about this fiasco, he'll say 'I told you so' and ask me to quit my job. I've got to say something to Duane right now, but I don't know what."

1. Precisely what conflicts is Tammy facing?
2. What on-the-spot tactic of conflict resolution can you recommend to Tammy?
3. What should Tammy do as a long-range solution to the problem of men trying to convert business occasions into social occasions, when she wants to keep them business occasions?
4. Should Biotronics develop a policy to cover the scenario just described?
5. Can this problem be classified as a case of sexual harassment?

A BUSINESS PSYCHOLOGY ROLE PLAY

The Uncomfortable Business Trip

The case problem just presented lends itself naturally to role playing in order to practice methods of conflict resolution. Reread the scenario presented above and imagine yourself in the role of Tammy, Duane, or Rick. Role plays can then be conducted, of about 15 minutes duration each, for these three situations:

Situation A: Tammy and Duane are in the restaurant trying to work out their differences of opinion about what direction the evening should take next. One person plays Tammy, the other Duane.

Situation B: Tammy agrees to have one dance with Duane and then retire to her room. The first dance is completed, but Duane insists on "just a few more dances." Two people role play the situation as if you were on the dance floor.

Situation C: Tammy and Rick are having a discussion a week later about what took place in the restaurant. Rick wants Tammy to quit, but she wants to continue with her job. One person plays Tammy, the other Rick.

Caution: In each of these situations, do not simply carry out an argument, but use a specific method of resolving conflict.

References

1. RICHARD J. MAYER, *Conflict Management: The Courage to Confront* (Columbus, OH: Batelle Press, 1990).
2. LINDA ELIZABETH DUXBURY AND CHRISTOPHER ALAN HIGGINS, "Gender Differences in Work–Family Conflict," *Journal of Applied Psychology*, February 1991, p. 64.
3. C. BRADY WILSON, "U.S. Businesses Suffer from Workplace Trauma," *Personnel Journal*, July 1991, p. 47.
4. Adapted from WILSON, "U.S. Businesses Suffer," p. 48.

5. SHARON DANANN, "Cracking the Electronic Whip," *Harper's Magazine,* August 1990, p. 58.

6. *VDT News,* November/December 1990, p. 1.

7. STEPHANIE RIGER, "Gender Dilemmas in Sexual Harassment: Policies and Procedures," *American Psychologist,* May 1991, p. 497.

8. "Sex versus Control," *Executive Communications,* September 1988, pp. 1, 4.

9. 1988 Survey by the Merit Systems Protection Board, U.S. Government, Washington, D.C.

10. "Harassment Claimed by Women in Survey," *Working Smart,* January 28, 1991, pp. 1–2.

11. MICHAEL D. CRINO AND TERRY L. LEAP, "What HR Managers Must Know about Employee Sabotage," *Personnel,* May 1989, p. 31.

12. KENNETH THOMAS, "Conflict and Conflict Management," in MARVIN D. DUNNETTE (ed.), *Handbook of Industrial and Organizational Psychology* (Chicago: Rand McNally College Publishing, 1976), pp. 900–902.

13. D. H. STAMATIS, "Conflict: You've Got to Accentuate the Positive," *Personnel,* December 1987, pp. 48–49.

14. "Negotiating without Giving in," *Executive Strategies,* September 19, 1989, p. 6.

Suggested Reading

ALTER, CATHERINE. "An Exploratory Study of Conflict and Coordination in Interorganizational Service Delivery Systems." *Academy of Management Journal,* September 1990, pp. 478–502.

BISNO, HERB. *Managing Conflict.* Newbury Park, CA: 1990.

DENTON, D. KEITH, AND BOYD, CHARLES. *Employee Complaint Handling: Tested Techniques for Human Resource Managers.* Westport, CT: Quorum Books, 1990.

HART, LOIS B. *Learning from Conflict: A Handbook for Trainers and Group Leaders.* Amherst, MA: Human Resource Development Press, 1991.

KABANOFF, BORIS. "Equity, Equality, Power, and Conflict." *Academy of Management Review,* April 1991, pp. 416–441.

LAABS, JENNIFER. "Surveillance: Tool or Trap?" *Personnel Journal,* June 1992, pp. 96–104.

PHILLIPS, DEANNE G., COOKE, JERRY A., AND ANDERSON, AMY E. "A Surefire Resolution to Workplace Conflicts." *Personnel Journal,* May 1992, pp. 111–114.

PINKLEY, ROBIN L. "Dimensions of Conflict Frame: Disputant Interpretations of Conflict." *Journal of Applied Psychology,* April 1990, pp. 117–126.

RAHIM, M. AFZALFUR (ed.). *Theory and Research in Conflict Management.* Westport, CT: Praeger 1990.

SOLOMON, CHARLENE MARMER. "Sexual Harassment after the Thomas Hearings." *Personnel Journal,* December 1991, pp. 32–37.

TERPSTRA, DAVID E. "Outcomes of Federal Court Decisions on Sexual Harassment." *Academy of Management Journal,* March 1992, pp. 181–190.

TJOSVOLD, DEAN. *Managing Conflict: The Key to Making Your Organization Work.* Minneapolis, MN: Team Media, 1988.

part three *Personal Relationships on the Job*

Part three deals with a variety of topics for helping you get along better with others and adjust to the workplace. Chapter 10 describes a variety of useful tactics and approaches to building relationships with people necessary for your success—superiors, co-workers, and customers. Chapter 11 deals with some of the adjustments a success-oriented person has to make. Among these are using proper etiquette, being a team player, balancing the demands of work and personal life, and coping with technology. Chapter 12 explains how to deal with one of the biggest challenges in the workplace, difficult and counterproductive people.

Chapter 10

BUILDING RELATIONSHIPS WITH SUPERIORS, CO-WORKERS, AND CUSTOMERS

Learning Objectives

After reading and studying this chapter and doing the exercises, you should be able to

1. Explain interpersonal attraction in terms of balance theory.
2. Decide on several sensible strategies and tactics for building good relationships with superiors.
3. Decide on several sensible strategies and tactics for building good relationships with co-workers.
4. Decide on several sensible strategies and tactics you might use in building good relationships with customers.
5. Develop an appreciation of cultural diversity in the workplace.

JOB TASKS RELATED TO THIS CHAPTER

Most job tasks require getting along well with others in the workplace. However, let us consider a couple of specific tasks that can be accomplished better if you have built good relationships. First, imagine having to prepare a report that requires input from others. If you have established a good relationship with co-workers, it will be much easier for you to gain the cooperation you need.

Second, imagine that you manage a clothing store. The business is very competitive, and your boss explains that without substantial repeat business the store will probably fold. Any skills you can learn in treating customers well will assist you in getting customers to return.

Anyone who wants to achieve career success must have good working relationships with superiors, co-workers, and lower-ranking employees. Many other workers must also satisfy external or internal customers to achieve success. To receive a decent salary increase, be promoted, or receive a favorable transfer, you almost always need the endorsement of your immediate boss. By having good relationships with your co-workers, you will usually receive the kind of cooperation you need to get your job done. Also, with increasing frequency, the opinion of your peers is asked when you are being considered for promotion.

People of lower rank than yourself have about the same impact on your career and your ability to get your job done as peers. We will therefore not have a separate discussion of downward relationships. A separate discussion on building customer relationships is warranted because of the widespread attention now being paid to customer satisfaction.

Keep in mind that the behaviors that contribute to a good working relationship with one group of workers usually work at other levels. For example, being courteous will hold you in good stead with high-level managers, your immediate manager, your co-workers, those of lower rank, and customers.

Balance Theory: An Explanation of Interpersonal Attraction

Before describing specific tactics for improving personal relationships on the job, it is helpful to seek a systematic explanation of why some people get along with each other.[1] Conventional wisdom says that people of similar interests and backgrounds flock together, and research supports this contention. People with similar attitudes and values are more attracted to each other than those of dissimilar attitudes and values.

Cognitive dissonance:
A mental process by which people try to reduce or eliminate inconsistency in the information they receive.

Why do people tend to like others similar to themselves? A general explanation is based on the idea of cognitive consistency. The concept of **cognitive dissonance** attempts to explain how people reduce internal conflicts when they experience a clash between information they receive and their actions. The same process is used when a person has to resolve two inconsistent sets of information. In both cases, the discrepancy between beliefs and actions, or two different beliefs, creates anxiety, and the person strives to reduce the anxiety.

An example will help explain cognitive dissonance. When informed of research evidence suggesting that over three alcoholic beverages per day can lead to heart disease, an interior designer replied, "That may be true for drinking alone in a bar, but it doesn't mean that having a bottle of wine each evening with friends is harmful." The designer eliminated the inconsistency between her preferences and the research by differentiating between drinking alone (harmful) and drinking with friends (not harmful). According to her logic, the body can differentiate between alcohol consumed alone versus that consumed with friends.

The principle of cognitive consistence has been applied to interper-

Balance theory: An explanation of interpersonal relationships contending that people tend to prefer relationships that are consistent or balanced.

sonal relationships in the form of balance theory. According to **balance theory,** people tend to prefer relationships that are consistent or balanced. If we are very similar to another person, it makes sense (is consistent or balanced) to like that person. Figure 10-1 provides more details about balance theory. Another explanation of why we tend to like similar others is that they reinforce and validate our opinions and values. It is usually reassuring and rewarding to discover that another person agrees with you or has similar values.

FIGURE 10-1. *BALANCED AND UNBALANCED TRIADS.*
Source: John M. Darley, Sam Glucksberg, and Ronald A. Kinchla, *Psychology,* 5th ed. (Englewood Cliffs, NJ: Prentice-Hall, 1992), Reprinted with permission.

So strong is the effect of the balance principle that people often use it as a predictive guide. If I (P) like one person (O), and that person likes another (X), I guess that probably I will like X also (see *a*). If I like O, and O dislikes X, what am I likely to guess about whether I will like or dislike X? Balance theory suggests, and research shows, that I will expect to dislike X (see *b*). Extensions of balance theory are also possible: If I disagree violently with the political opinions of person O, what am I likely to suspect about candidate X's political views? And, therefore, am I likely to vote for candidate X (see *c*)?

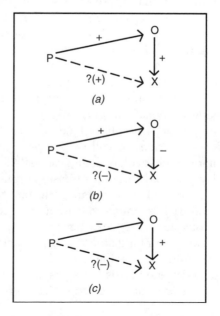

Balance theory has its own limitations as a comprehensive explanation of why people are attracted to each other. Although we generally like people who are similar to ourselves, the belief that opposites attract also has merit. People sometimes get along best with those who possess complementary characteristics. A talkative and domineering manager may prefer a group member who enjoys listening. The explanation is that a dominant person needs someone to dominate and therefore might be favorably disposed toward submissive people.

Building Good Relationships with Superiors

In attempting to build relationships with superiors, as with co-workers and customers, your strategy should be to build satisfying partnerships. The term *partnership* connotes a cooperative relationship in which you and the other person are pursuing compatible goals, such as getting work accomplished or earning a profit.

Good performance refers to not only being able to do your job, but to being well motivated and displaying initiative—looking for problems to work on and getting started working without being told to do so. The 12 strategies and techniques described next must rest on a bedrock of solid job performance. Otherwise, they may backfire by bringing attention to the fact that the individual is more show than substance. Several of the ideas presented will help you to achieve good job performance and assist you in impressing your boss through merit.

Style:
A person's way of doing things.

Understand Your Manager. An important starting point for building a constructive relationship with a superior is to understand that person, including his or her style. A **style** is a person's way of doing things. Walter St. John points out some questions that need to be answered to size up one's manager:[2]

1. What is your supervisor's position in the company pecking order? What are his or her relationships with his or her managers?
2. What are your supervisor's blind spots, prejudices, pet peeves, and sore spots? What are positive and negative words to your manager?
3. Does your manager understand better as a reader (should you send a memo) or as a listener (should you tell him or her in person)?
4. Is your supervisor a morning or an evening person? When is the best time of day to approach your manager?
5. What is your supervisor's preference for getting things done?
6. What is most important to your supervisor?
7. What nonverbal signals does your supervisor communicate to you? (See Chapter 15.)

Finding answers to these questions, including understanding your boss's style, may involve discussions with co-workers. Concentrate on "how" questions, such as "This is my first report for Gwenn. How does she like it done? Does she want a one-page summary on top of the report or at the end?" Speaking to co-workers can also reveal what kinds of attitudes your boss expects you to have. For example, does the boss really believe that the consumer is always right? Your question may also reveal that your boss is jumping to please a demanding superior. If this is true, you may be expected to do the same.[3]

Clarify Expectations. Some people perform poorly on the job simply because they have an incomplete understanding of what their boss expects of them. At times, the individual has to take the initiative to find out what is expected because the boss neglects to do so. One highly regarded manager explains how he clarifies expectations:

> Whenever I get a new boss, I sit down with that person and ask that his or her expectations be made explicit. We try to list not my job activities but the main purposes of my job. To do that, we continue each statement of activity with "In order to...," and try to complete the sentence. By recording my job purposes, we get a clear picture of what I should be accomplishing; and that's what counts—results.[4]

Using this tactic, one department secretary found out that she was supposed to take care of her boss's work first. Once her boss's work was done, she would be free to do work for other professionals in the department. Before the secretary in question asked for clarification, she was trying to give everyone's work equal attention. (Your reaction might be, "The boss should have told her that at the outset." Unfortunately, not all managers are aware of the importance of clarifying work expectations.)

Establish a Relationship of Trust. A fundamental way of impressing superiors is to behave in a trustworthy manner. Trust is established over the long range through such behaviors as meeting deadlines, following through on promises, having good attendance and punctuality, and not passing along confidential information to the wrong people. Five conditions are necessary for trust to develop:[5]

1. *Accessibility.* An accessible subordinate is a person who takes in ideas freely and gives them out freely. A subordinate who does not respect the boss's ideas will not be trusted and will not receive help in developing his or her own ideas.
2. *Availability.* The trusted subordinate is attentive and available physically, mentally, and emotionally when the manager is under pressure and needs support.
3. *Predictability.* This refers to being a predictably good performer and to being dependable about getting things done on time. A subordinate who does not get things done on time quickly loses the trust of his or her boss.
4. *Personal loyalty.* An important way of showing loyalty is to support your boss's ideas. For example, your boss may want to purchase an industrial robot. You could display loyalty by investigating on your own the advantages of robots in factories and then talking about those advantages to oth-

ers. Loyalty can also mean not misusing inside information given to you by the boss. In short, loyalty breeds trust.

5. *Be honest about problems.* Be frank about bringing problems to your manager's attention. (As described later, also bring forth good news.) However, if your manager is already burdened with an overload of problems, soften the impact of the problem without lying. As a sales representative told the sales manager, "One of our biggest accounts has left us, but the news isn't all bad. Our contact said that if the other firm's service proves to be worse than ours, we'll get the account back."

Help Your Manager Succeed. When caught up in the pressures of pursuing your own ambitions, it is easy to forget the primary reason that you were hired. Your boss or the person who hired you originally thought that you could make a positive contribution to helping him or her to accomplish the department's mission. Even if you were hired into the company through nepotism (family relationships), the person who accepted you into the department believed that you would contribute directly or indirectly to his or her success. Most of your job activities should be directed at this vital success strategy of helping your boss to succeed.

Respect Your Manager's Authority. A frequent complaint about modern society is that respect for authority is decreasing. You can capitalize on this problem to help to develop a good relationship with your boss. By showing appropriate respect for your manager's authority, you can enhance your relationship with that person. Here are a few statements that might appeal to a boss's sense of authority without making you appear unduly status conscious:

- "Yes, sir, that sounds like a good idea."
- "Yes, ma'am, that sounds like a good idea."
- "As the head of this department, what do you think we should do about this?"

Bring Forth Solutions as Well as Problems. An advanced tactic for developing a good working relationship with your boss is to bring solutions to your boss's attention, not just problems. Too often group members ask to see their bosses only when they have problems requiring help. A boss under pressure may thus anticipate additional pressure when a subordinate asks for an appointment. The subordinate who comes forth with a solved problem is thus regarded as a welcome relief. In short, you ease your boss's suffering by walking into his or her office and saying, "Here's what I did about that mess that was plaguing us yesterday. Everything is under control now."

Express Constructive Disagreement. At one time the office politician thought an effective way of pleasing the boss was to be a "yes-person." Whatever the boss thought was right, the yes-person agreed with. A more intelligent tactic in the modern business world is to be ready to disagree in a constructive manner when you sincerely believe the boss is wrong. In the long range you will probably earn more respect than if you agree with the boss just to please that person. Constructive disagreement is based on a careful analysis of the situation and is also tactful.

The right way to disagree means not putting your superior in a corner or embarrassing your superior by confronting him or her loudly or in public.[6] If you disagree with your boss, use carefully worded, inoffensive statements. In this way you minimize the chances of a confrontation or hostile reaction. Walter St. John suggests statements of this type:

- "I'm able to agree with you on most things, but on this matter I wonder if you would be willing to reconsider for these reasons."
- "I like your basic idea and wonder if I could make a suggestion that I think would make it work even better."

The reason constructive disagreement helps you build a good relationship with most bosses is that the boss comes to respect your job knowledge and your integrity. However, if you are working with a very insecure boss, he or she may be taken back by disagreement. In that case, you have to be extra tactful in expressing disagreement.

Show Appreciation for Your Manager's Good Deeds. An effective manager is supposed to praise group members for good performance and behavior. Reversing the process can help build a sound superior–subordinate relationship, particularly because your manager may not be receiving positive reinforcement from his or her boss. Appreciation can take such forms as saying thanks when the boss grants you a special favor, or showing your boss what you have been able to achieve because of the new equipment he or she authorized.

Do Not Appear Overly Competitive with Your Manager. Outstanding performers run the risk of appearing to want to displace the boss. The problem is particularly acute when the immediate superior feels insecure about his or her position. Several steps can be taken to overcome the competitive threat yet still maintain good performance, as recommended by Gisele Richardson. The first step is to ask yourself whether you are truly responsible for some of the boss's feelings. For example, in your attempt to perform well, you might be taking over some of your boss's decision-making authority.

Another step is to reassure your boss that you are not after his or her job. Explain to your boss why you appreciate your present position and mention what you still have to learn. Be sure to clarify that you appreciate your manager's strengths as valuable resources. The competitive threat can also be lowered by displaying loyalty through such means as speaking well of your boss to his or her superior.[7]

Talk Big, Shun Trivia. Small talk can keep you placed in a small job. If you have a predilection for talking about the weather, your sinuses, or the food in the company cafeteria, save these comments for the right occasion. The right occasion is when you are spending time with people

Small talk can keep you placed in a small job.

who enjoy small talk. The wrong occasion is when you are trying to impress higher-ups (and also your boss). When you have a chance to talk to an influential person, some trivia may be necessary for an initial warmup. But quickly shift the topic to "big" talk.

Here is an example of the difference between making small talk and big talk over the same issue when meeting a high-ranking official from your organization. The person talking is the manager of a branch motor vehicle department. The visitor is the state commissioner of motor vehicles.

MANAGER (USING SMALL TALK):	Look at that rain outside. It's been like this for three days. This sure is the rainiest place I've ever lived. I guess it's fine if you're a farmer or a plant.
COMMISSIONER:	Did you say something?
MANAGER (USING BIG TALK):	This rain creates an interesting problem for the Motor Vehicle Department at the branch level. Common sense would suggest that our workload would decrease when it rains.

My calculations and those of my staff indicate that we are extra busy on rainy days. I think a good number of people wait for a rainy day to take care of their routine business with us. I wonder if this is a national trend?

COMMISSIONER: You have raised an important issue about our workload. I think the problem warrants further study.

Use Discretion in Socializing with Your Manager. A constant dilemma facing employees is how much and what type of socializing with the boss is appropriate. Advocates of socializing contend that off-the-job friendships with the boss lead to more natural work relationships. Opponents of socializing with the boss say that it leads to **role confusion**—being uncertain about what role you are carrying out. For example, how can your boss make an objective decision about your salary increase on Monday morning when he or she had dinner with you on Sunday? To avoid charges of favoritism, your boss might recommend you for a below-average increase.

Role confusion:
Being uncertain about what role you are carrying out.

One guideline to consider is to have cordial social relationships with the boss of the kind shared by most employees. "Cordial" socializing includes activities such as company-sponsored parties, group invitations to the boss's home, and business lunches. Individual social activities such as

camping with the boss, double-dating, and so forth, are more likely to lead to role confusion.

Sue DeWine recommends that socializing with the boss be kept "professional" if your boss might possibly have a romantic inclination toward you. The more relaxed the setting, the greater the opportunity for misinterpretation of language and behavior. Workers who suspect that their boss's intentions may be romantic or sexual are advised to mention their spouses or "significant others," if the conversation takes such a turn.[8]

In summary, there are no absolute principles about the influence of socializing with the boss on your relationship with that person. A tentative guideline is that you must carefully evaluate the pros and cons of anything more than ceremonial socializing (office parties, company picnics, and so forth) with the boss. It leads to a conflict of roles that can work to your disadvantage. However, many marriages stem from a relationship between the manager and a team member.

Engage in Favorable Interactions with Your Manager. The many techniques described above support the goal of engaging in favorable interactions with your manager. A study of interactions between bank employees and their supervisors showed that purposely trying to create a positive impression on the supervisor led to better performance ratings.[9] Although this finding is not surprising, it is reassuring to know that it is backed by quantitative evidence. Figure 10-2 is a listing of behaviors used by the employees in the study to create positive interactions with their supervisors.

FIGURE 10-2. *SUPERVISOR INTERACTION CHECKLIST.*

Use the following behaviors as a checklist for achieving favorable interactions with your present manager or a future one. The more of these actions you are engaged in, the higher the probability that you are building a favorable relationship with your manager.

1. Agree with your supervisor's major opinions outwardly even when you disagree inwardly. _____
2. Take an immediate interest in your supervisor's personal life. _____
3. Praise your supervisor on his or her accomplishments. _____
4. Do personal favors for your supervisor. _____
5. Do something as a personal favor for your supervisor even though you are not required to do it. _____
6. Volunteer to help your supervisor on a task. _____
7. Compliment your supervisor on his or her dress or appearance. _____
8. Present yourself to your supervisor as being a friendly person. _____
9. Agree with your supervisor's major ideas. _____
10. Present yourself to your supervisor as being a polite person. _____

Source: Adapted from Sandy J. Wayne and Gerald R. Ferris, "Influence Tactics, Affect, and Exchange Quality in Supervisor–Subordinate Interactions: A Laboratory Experiment and Field Study," *Journal of Applied Psychology*, October 1990, p. 494.

Getting along with co-workers is important for several reasons. No matter what your job level, there comes a time when you need the cooperation of people over whom you have no formal authority. By developing these relationships and practicing good human relations, you can get them on your team. Ignore these relationships, and you may fail to get many of your projects completed. Mutual cooperation must also exist for a department to be productive. Furthermore, the chief reason people are fired is not poor technical skill, but inability or unwillingness to form satisfactory interpersonal relationships on the job.

In this section of the chapter, we will describe tactics and strategies designed to help you gain favor or avoid disfavor with peers. As obvious as these suggestions may seem, many people violate them. So many people think they are such experts at human relations that they do not bother to think systematically about their behavior in relation to others.

Group norms:
The unwritten set of expectations or standards of conduct telling group members what each person should do within the group.

Adhere to Group Norms. The basic principle to follow in getting along with co-workers is to pay heed to **group norms.** These refer to the unwritten set of expectations or standards of conduct that tell group members what they ought to do. Norms become a standard of what each person should do within the group. Employees learn about norms both through simple observation and direct instruction from other group members. If you do not deviate too far from these norms, much of your behavior will be accepted by the group. If you deviate too far, you will be subject to much rejection. Here is one example of how group norms influence work output:

> Kathy worked as a receptionist–secretary for the county government. She was one of five women occupying a similar job in the same division of the county. The women had developed the procedure whereby if one receptionist–secretary was overloaded with work, she would ask one of the other women to help her. This was accomplished by calling each of the other receptionist–secretaries in turn to see if one of them had some slack time. It became apparent that Kathy frequently asked for help, but never assisted any of the other women. During a coffee break one day, two of the other receptionist–secretaries confronted Kathy. They told her that if she didn't soon do her share of overload work she would be bad-mouthed to her boss. In addition, they would refuse to have coffee or lunch with her. Within a few days, Kathy was volunteering to help the other women.

Group norms also influence the social aspects of behavior in work settings. Many of these norms relate to such things as the people to have lunch with, getting together with other employees for an after-hours drink on Friday, joining a department team, and the type of clothing you wear to work. If you deviate too far from work or social norms, you run the risk of being ostracized from the group. In some instances you might even be subjected to physical abuse if you make the other employees look bad. The risk of conforming too closely to group norms is that you lose your

Express an interest in their work.

individuality. You become viewed by your superiors as "one of the guys or gals," rather than as a person who aspires to move up in the organization. Getting along too well with peers has its price as well.

Express an Interest in Their Work. Almost everybody is self-centered to some extent. Thus, their favorite topic is themselves or topics closely related to themselves, such as their children, hobbies, or work. Sales representatives rely heavily on this fact in cultivating relationships with established customers. They routinely ask the customer about his or her hobbies, family members, and work activities. You can capitalize on this simple strategy by asking peers questions such as these:

- How is your work going? (highly recommended)
- How did you gain the knowledge necessary for your job?
- What's new on your job?
- How is the output from your department used by the company?

MR. GREMLEN SAID YOU HAD A TALENT FOR LISTENING!

The simplest technique of getting along with co-workers is to be a good listener.

- What's the best part of your job?
- What's the biggest headache on your job?

Be a Good Listener. After you ask questions, you must be prepared to listen to the answers. The simplest technique of getting along with co-workers within and outside your department is to be a good listener. The topics that you should be willing to listen to during working hours include job problems and miscellaneous complaints. Lunch breaks, coffee breaks, and after hours are better suited to listening to people talk about their personal lives, current events, sports, and the like.

Becoming an effective listener takes practice. As you practice your listening skills, try the suggestions offered in Chapter 15. The payoff is that listening builds constructive relationships.

Maintain Honest and Open Relationships. Humanistic psychology attaches considerable importance to maintaining *honest* and *open* relationships with other people. Giving co-workers frank, but tactful, answers to their requests for your opinion is one useful way of developing open relationships. Assume that a co-worker asks your opinion about a memo that he intends to send to his boss. As you read it, you find it somewhat incoherent and filled with spelling and grammatical errors. An honest response to this letter might be:

"I think your idea is a good one. But I think your memo needs more work before that idea comes across clearly."

Display a Helpful, Cooperative, and Courteous Attitude. Many jobs require teamwork. If you display a willingness to help others and work cooperatively with them, you will be regarded as a good team player. Organizations are designed with cooperation in mind. If people do not cooperate with each other, the total system breaks down. Not all your co-workers are concerned about the smooth functioning of the total organization, but they do want cooperation from you.

When evaluating your work performance, many companies include a rating of your cooperativeness. Both management and peers value cooperative behavior on your part. The following question is reproduced from a rating form used by many companies.

COOPERATION AND CONTACTS

Goal: Rating ability to work for and with others.

Criteria: Willing to follow directions? Accept suggestions? Does he or she consider others' viewpoints? Adapt to changing situations? What are his or her attitudes toward others? Does he or she respect them and earn their respect? Successful in dealing with others?

- ❑ Best; upper 10%
- ❑ Next 20%
- ❑ Normal; 40% of group
- ❑ Next 20%
- ❑ Bottom 10%

Keep a Large Balance in the Favor Bank. To maintain good relationships with others, you need to make deposits in the Favor Bank says Robert Dilenschneider, the top executive at a large public relations firm.[10] The strategy is based on the idea that if you make deposits in the Favor Bank other people owe you favors. Ways of making deposits include building good will and looking for favors you can do. You should also take credit discreetly for your favors. For example, if you handled a customer complaint for a co-worker who was on break, let him or her know, but do not inform the manager.

Phrase Demands as a Request for Help. When you need the assistance of a co-worker, express your demand as a request for help rather than a demand. Assume, for example, that you need a co-worker's help in interpreting a spreadsheet. As recommended by Joseph D'O'Brian, say, "I have a problem that I wonder if you could help me with...."[11] This approach is likely to be more effective than saying, "You have to help me interpret this spreadsheet, or I won't get my work done." Requesting help is effective because most people enjoy giving advice and assistance. However, most co-workers resent being given demands or orders from co-workers.

Give Recognition to Others. The least expensive method of cultivating people, in terms of money and time, is to give them attention, kindness, affection, or any appropriate form of recognition. "Show people how important you think they are," contend most books about getting along with people. Similar to warnings about the importance of driving carefully, the number of people who understand the concept far exceed the number who drive carefully. Yet investing a small amount of time in recognizing a co-worker can pay large dividends in terms of cultivating an ally.

Building Good Relationships with Customers

Another important requirement for success is to build good relationships with both external and internal customers. *External customers* fit the traditional definition of customer that includes clients and guests. External customers can be classified as retail or industrial. The latter represents one company buying from another, such as purchasing machinery or a fleet of cars. *Internal customers* are the people you serve within the organization, or those who use the output from your job. For example, if you are a payroll supervisor, your customers include the people whose payroll you process and your manager.

The previous two chapter sections dealt with internal relationships. We therefore emphasize here pleasing the external customer. (Yet some of the techniques described here could also fit elsewhere in the chapter, and vice versa.) Ten representative techniques for building constructive customer relationships are presented next.[12]

1. *Establish customer satisfaction goals.* Decide jointly with your manager how much you intend to help customers. Find answers to questions such as the following: Is your company attempting to satisfy every customer within ten minutes of his or her request? Are you striving to provide the finest customer service in your field? Is your goal zero customer defections to competitors? Your goals will dictate how much and the type of effort you put into pleasing customers.

2. *Understand your customer's needs.* The most basic principle of selling is to identify and satisfy customer needs. Many customers may not be able to express their needs clearly. Also, they may not be certain of their needs. To help identify customer needs, you may have to probe for information. For example, the associate in a camera and video store might ask, "What uses do you have in mind for your video camera?" Knowing such information will help the store associate identify which camcorder will satisfy the customer's needs.

3. *Put customer needs first.* After you have identified customer needs, focus on satisfying them rather than doing what is convenient for you or your firm. Assume, for example, the customer says, "I would like to purchase ten jars of rubber cement." The sales associate should not respond, "Sorry, the rubber cement comes in boxes of twelve, so it is not convenient to sell you ten jars." The associate might, however, offer a discount for a purchase of twelve jars if such action fits company policy.

4. *Show care and concern.* During contacts with your customer, show concern for his or her welfare. Ask questions such as the following: How have you enjoyed the video camera you bought here a while back? How are you feeling today? After asking the question, project a genuine interest in the answer.

5. *Communicate a positive attitude.* A positive attitude is sent by such factors as appearance, friendly gestures, a warm voice tone, and good telephone communication skills. If a customer seems apologetic about making a heavy demand, respond, "No need to apologize. My job is to please you. Without you we wouldn't be in business."

6. *Make the buyer feel good.* A fundamental way of keeping a relationship going is to make the buyer feel good about himself or herself. Also, make the customer feel good because he or she has bought from you. Offer compliments about the customer's healthy glow, or a report that specified his or her vendor requirements (for an industrial customer). An effective feel-good line is, "I enjoy doing business with you."

7. *Smile at every customer.* Smiling is a natural relationship builder and can help you bond with your customer. Smile several times during each customer contact, even if your customer is angry with your product or service. In Chapter 12, we offer suggestions for dealing with abrasive customers who make smiling difficult even for the most patient salesperson.

8. *Follow up on requests.* The simple act of following up to see if your service is satisfactory is a powerful principle of good customer service. A simple telephone call to the requestor of your service is usually sufficient follow-up. A follow-up is effective because it completes the loop in communication between two people.

9. *Find ways to buy from your customers.* A powerful tactic for building customer relationships is to buy as many products or services as possible from the customer's firm. Generally, this tactic applies to industrial customers, yet a store manager might buy from customers who themselves are store owners or managers. Ask your customers for a full listing of the products and services offered by their firm. Make this information available to key managers at your own firm so that perhaps they can find room for a purchase.

10. *Display strong ethics.* Ethical violations receive so much publicity that one can impress customers by being conspicuously ethical. Look for ways to show that you are so ethical that you would welcome making your sales tactics public knowledge. Also, treat the customer the same way you would treat a family member or valued friend. Here is an example of taking positive steps to be ethical:

> Your customer inquires about a late shipment. Instead of claiming that the order will be shipped immediately, you respond, "We've made some mistakes in production scheduling. Your shipment will take another three weeks. Would you like an immediate refund? I can give you the name of a supplier who might have in stock what you need." Your positive steps will defuse your customer's anger, and you will be admired for your high ethics.

Dealing with customers in the manner just prescribed will help you build stronger customer relationships. In addition, you will strengthen your relationship with your manager because customer satisfaction receives such high priority in most organizations.

Appreciating Cultural Diversity

The work force in the United States and Canada is becoming more culturally diverse. A frequent prediction is that by the year 2000, the majority of new workers will be women, African-Americans (and African-Canadians), Hispanics (or Latinos), and immigrants. Only one-third of the projected 140 million person work force is predicted to be native-born white males.[13] The fastest growing segments of the work force are women and people of color.

Succeeding in a diverse environment requires more than avoiding discriminatory behavior. Instead, success is facilitated by working comfortably with people of different sexes, races, religions, ethnicity, values, sexual orientations, and physical capabilities. One viewpoint in appreciating cultural diversity is that white males should be included in the diversity web. Many white males feel that they are being omitted from concerns about appreciating diversity. Members of the same group believe they are excluded from some job opportunities because of their sex and race.[14]

Various groups that have been discriminated against in the past are demanding more equal treatment and greater acceptance. Many gay and lesbian employees, for example, have stepped forward to request the same employee benefits offered married heterosexuals. In response to these demands, some employers, such as U.S. West, Inc., have conducted workshops to address discrimination against gays and lesbians and expanded benefits to the same groups.[15]

The information already presented for dealing with superiors, co-workers, and customers can be applied toward building relationships with diverse groups. In addition, it is important to develop an appreciation of cultural diversity in the workplace. Toward this end, we will discuss recognizing diversity on the job and describe a training program for such purposes.

Recognizing Cultural Differences

As described in Chapter 3, cultural diversity can be better understood if it is recognized that many apparent differences in personality actually arise from culture. For example, white and black North Americans feel that authority should often be challenged. However, Asians and Hispanics tend to respect and obey authority. Another notable difference is that Hispanic culture perceive music, family members, and food as appropriate for the workplace. Americans and Canadians reject these practices and may regard them as unprofessional.

Some forms of discrimination become more explainable, even if still unacceptable, when their cultural origins are recognized. For example, in many Asian countries few women hold key positions in industry. It is therefore difficult for some Asian workers employed in North America to accept women as their administrative superiors.

The accompanying box illustrates how some business organizations are encouraging their employees to welcome differences of all type. Part of being an effective co-worker is to deal comfortably with these differences.

VALUING WORK-FORCE AND CUSTOMER DIVERSITY AT DIGITAL

Memo to Digital Employees

For more than 15 years, Digital [Equipment Corporation] has invested in work that strives to fully utilize our diverse work force. We have learned that employee productivity is linked to company profitability. Profitability is also linked to being sensitive to and responsive to the needs of its diverse customers. It includes leveraging diversity around the world to compete in a global marketplace. It means capitalizing on partnerships with diverse vendors.

Our work-force and customer base is diverse, and is becoming increasingly so. Within the U.S., more than 50 percent of our work force is comprised of employees who are different from the white/Anglo male who traditionally made up the majority of the corporate work force. The majority of our domestic work force is women, people of color, people of different ages and sexual orientation, people with disabilities, single parents, and people over 40.

As the leading worldwide supplier of networked computer systems, Digital's ability to work effectively across cultures is imperative. Customer diversity is also a business imperative within the U.S. It is underscored by the fact that African Americans possess an annual disposable income of $300 billion that is expected to exceed $899 [billion] by the year 2000. Asians currently spend $35 billion annually in this country.

Paying attention to these customers is essential to our business. As an example, a Spanish-speaking customer recently visited our Boston plant. His visit was conducted entirely in Spanish. Our orientation toward understanding and satisfying the customer from a cultural perspective sets us apart from the competition.

Source: Adapted and abridged from an internal memo, Digital, July 1992.

To appreciate cultural diversity, it is also important to fine-tune your perceptions and not lump diverse people under one group. People of one race, as identified by skin color and facial appearance, may have very different ethnic backgrounds. For example, blacks who grew up in New York City, Jamaica, and Central Africa have different sets of cultural values.

A good starting point in applying this information is to recognize that everybody has his or her own ethnic background. Similarly, everybody has an "accent." Identifying your own cultural values is a starting point for becoming flexible in dealing with the ethnicity of superiors, co-workers, and customers.[16]

A Diversity Awareness Training Program

Diversity awareness program: A training activity that provides an opportunity for employees to develop the skills necessary to deal effectively with each other and with customers in a diverse environment.

To help employees relate comfortably to people of different cultures and appreciate diversity, many companies conduct **diversity awareness programs.** These programs provide an opportunity for employees to develop the skills necessary to deal effectively with each other and with customers in a diverse environment.

Lewis Griggs, a diversity consultant, describes the conditions necessary for a diversity awareness program to achieve its goals. Above all, top management must be committed and provide leadership. Every person in the program must start with themselves and recognize that they have a cultural identity that influences their perceptions, values, and style of communication.

The next major step is for workers to realize that they are already making adaptations to different people in different settings. People behave very differently when relating to others at a sporting event, place of worship, or school.

After cultural awareness has been achieved, the workers are ready for employees to speak about their own cultural differences and to perform exercises.[17] Among the exercises designed to promote an appreciation of cultural diversity is the "earliest memory technique." In this exercise, both white and black workers are requested to draw pictures of their earliest memories of black and white people. Latinos and Asians are also included in the exercises. Analyzing these earliest memories helps people realize the origins of their perceptions of different races. Understanding them often leads to changes in behavior.[18] A sampling of these earliest memories is shown the accompanying box.

THE EARLIEST MEMORY TECHNIQUE IN DIVERSITY AWARENESS TRAINING

Participants at a diversity awareness training program were asked to draw pictures of black and white people. Among the images depicted were as follows:

- A black male manager who grew up in an all-black neighborhood in Gary, Indiana, drew white police officers with German shepherds and water hoses.
- A white male manager who grew up in an all-white neighborhood in a New York City suburb drew a black housekeeper serving dinner, dressed in a uniform.
- A black woman professional who grew up in an integrated neighborhood in Chicago drew white children playing hopscotch with black children on a sidewalk.
- A white executive male raised in a mostly white neighborhood in Los Angeles drew a 7-foot black man sending a sky hook (basketball shot) through the basket at a professional sports stadium.
- A black professional woman raised in a multicultural neighborhood in Toronto drew a picture of a smiling white man collecting the rent.

BACK TO THE JOB TASKS

Assume that you are new on the job, or want to make a fresh start in your present job, and that your goal is to build better relationships with others in the workplace. Systematically go through the tactics and strategies in this chapter and identify several that you think might help you the most. For example, maybe you have not been taking the initiative to express an interest in the job activities of co-workers. Or perhaps you have done nothing in particular to make customers feel good. You would then make a conscious effort to implement the tactics of "show an interest in their work" and "make the buyer feel good."

Summary of Key Points

❑ To prosper in your career, it is essential to have good working relationships with superiors, co-workers, lower-ranking employees, and customers. These good working relationships sometimes spring from being attracted to people. Balance theory has been proposed as a way of explaining why some people are attracted to each other. Its key idea is that people tend to prefer relationships that are consistent or balanced. If we are very similar to another person, it makes sense to like that person. People similar to ourselves usually reinforce and validate our opinions and values.

❑ The starting point in building satisfying partnerships with superiors is to perform well in your job. Other important strategies and tactics include:

1. Understand your manager: learn about his or her preferences and style.
2. Clarify expectations: find out what your manager expects of you.
3. Establish a relationship of trust: be accessible, available, predictable, loyal, and honest.
4. Help your manager succeed.
5. Respect your manager's authority.
6. Bring forth solutions as well as problems.
7. Express constructive disagreement: disagree with your boss when necessary, but be tactful.
8. Show appreciation for your manager's good deeds.
9. Do not appear overly competitive with your manager; avoid being perceived as a threat to his or her job.
10. Talk big, shun trivia: keep small talk to a minimum, and engage in some talk about important organizational concerns.
11. Use discretion in socializing with your manager.
12. Engage in favorable interactions with you manager.

❑ Although some of these tactics are helpful in developing constructive relationships at all levels, the following suggestions are particularly geared toward developing good relationships with co-workers.

1. Adhere to group norms (unofficial standards of conduct).
2. Express an interest in their work.
3. Be a good listener.
4. Maintain honest and open relationships.
5. Display a helpful, cooperative, and courteous attitude.
6. Keep a large balance in the Favor Bank (make sure people owe you a favor).
7. Phrase demands as a request for help.
8. Give recognition to others.

❑ Another important success requirement is to build good relationships with both external and internal customers. Representative techniques for building constructive customer relationships include (1) establish customer satisfaction goals, (2) understand your customer's needs, (3) put customer needs first, (4) show care and concern, (5) communicate a positive attitude, (6) make the buyer feel good, (7) smile at every customer, (8) follow up on requests, (9) find ways to buy from your customers, and (10) display strong ethics.

❑ The North American work force is becoming increasingly culturally diverse. Success on the job is facilitated by working comfortably with people of different sexes, races, religions, ethnicity, values, sexual orientations, and physical capabilities. To work comfortably with diverse groups, it is important to appreciate and enjoy cultural diversity. A starting point is to recognize cultural differences by examining your own cultural background. Many companies sponsor diversity awareness training programs to help employees appreciate cultural diversity.

GUIDELINES FOR PERSONAL EFFECTIVENESS

1. Although job knowledge is indispensable for performing well in your job, it is not sufficient to make you a high performer. Another important set of behaviors necessary to perform well

on the job is maintaining constructive relationships with other employees at all levels and with customers. Other important behaviors contributing to job performance (such as high motivation and work habits) are discussed elsewhere in this text.

2. Similarly, if you ignore the strategies presented in this chapter, you do so at great risk of not gaining a wide base of support in your present or future place of work. An important success strategy is to make a deliberate effort to form constructive working relationships with co-workers.

3. To be successful in today's culturally diverse work force, it is necessary to work comfortably and effectively with diverse groups of people. If a person feels, for example, "I would not want an Asian woman for my boss," he or she must attempt to uncover the root of the problem. Next, the person should attempt to bring about an attitude change toward an appreciation of cultural diversity. An attitude shift may occur as the individual engages in frequent positive interactions with Asian people in positions of authority.

Discussion Questions and Activities

1. Based on balance theory, given a choice should a person work for a manager with personal characteristics similar to his or her own? Explain your reasoning.

2. How do personal values enter into choosing among the tactics and strategies described in this chapter?

3. Assume that you have just started a new job. What can you do to "clarify expectations"?

4. What can students do to "engage in favorable interactions" with their instructors?

5. How can a person learn the group norms operating in his or her place of work?

6. One person who read this chapter said, "A lot of ruthless people get ahead in this world. So cultivating co-workers may not really be all that important." What is your opinion?

7. What can you do this week to make deposits in the Favor Bank with important people?

8. Formulate three good questions you might ask the instructor of this course to show that you are interested in his or her work.

9. Have you noticed any age differences in people's ability to appreciate cultural diversity?

10. Ask an experienced manager to identify the best methods a team member (subordinate) might use to form a constructive relationship with him or her. Be prepared to discuss your findings in class.

A BUSINESS PSYCHOLOGY PROBLEM

The Chatty Boss

Suzanne Mendez, a claims adjuster, looked up from her desk as she saw her boss, Aaron Glick, approaching. Suzanne muttered to herself, "I hope Aaron has a brief question related to my job. I just don't have time to chat with him this morning. If I don't get this complicated claim processed this morning, the sales department will be screaming at me."

"Morning, Suzanne," said Aaron. "It looks like another beautiful day here in Monterey. There's not a cloud in the sky. It's criminal to be inside on such a nice day. My family and I would love to be down at the beach."

"How are things going for you today?" continued Aaron.

"Nothing too bad is happening. I'll be caught up with my work soon. I'm on a rush job right now. The sales department is hassling me to get this claim finished by noon today."

"Suzanne, don't let the sales department hassle you. They want everything right away. Somehow the sales department doesn't realize that claims adjusting takes a lot of painful attention to detail. Better late than lousy, I always say."

"I don't disagree with you Aaron. It's just that not getting a claim processed on time gets me a little nervous. We could lose a big customer by being late on paying this claim."

"Don't be so uptight, Suzanne. You're too young for an ulcer or a coronary," replied Aaron.

Aaron proceeded to engage Suzanne in general conversation for another 35 minutes before he was paged by his assistant. "Sorry we didn't have enough time to finish our business," said Aaron as he left Suzanne's work area.

Suzanne then worked through her lunch hour and turned in her report one hour late. Perplexed, she telephoned Laurie, a co-worker in another department, and asked if she would be able to meet for a cup of tea after work.

After their tea was served, Suzanne lamented to Laurie: "I just don't know what to do about Aaron. He's gobbling up my time. At least three days a week he sits in front of my desk chatting for an hour about nothing in particular. If I look like I want him to leave, he becomes annoyed. Once when I tried to politely get Aaron away from my desk, he told me that our conference was not over until he said it was."

"What really worries me is that Aaron sometimes chastises me for being late with my work, when it's he who is making me late. This whole thing has become a ridiculous problem. Any suggestions?"

1. Should Suzanne be so concerned about Aaron taking up her time?
2. What should Suzanne do to preserve her relationship with her boss, yet still get her work accomplished on time?
3. What about Suzanne staying after work to make up for the time she loses in chatting with Aaron?
4. Which specific techniques about boss relationships apply to this case?

A BUSINESS PSYCHOLOGY PROBLEM

The Unpopular Administrative Assistant

While shopping one day, you run into Marlene, a former classmate of yours. Happy to see her, you comment, "Marlene, good to see you. How are things going? Last I heard you were promoted from secretary to administrative assistant. How do you like your new job?"

Marlene answers: "Thanks for asking. That's true. I was promoted to administrative assistant. I work in a different department now. My boss is the director of public relations. The job is exciting. I'm in on a lot of important things and I get to meet a lot of important people. But things in the office aren't going as well as I would like."

Your curiosity aroused, you ask, "What do you mean?"

Marlene continues: "I don't think the other women in the office care too much for me. I feel kind of left out of things. I'm almost never asked to join the 'girls' for lunch or coffee breaks. I don't know what I'm doing wrong. Sometimes I think it could be jealousy over my job. But that isn't such a plausible reason. Being an administrative assistant isn't *that* impressive. Also, I'm a few years older than most of the women in the office. They should be glad to see that experience and hard work pay off.

"Sometimes I feel like the woman in those TV ads who loses out with friends because she needs breath freshener. That certainly isn't the case with me. I don't recall having a problem making friends either at school or in my other jobs.

"If you come up with any ideas that might help me, please let me know. I would feel awkward asking the 'girls' in the office why they don't like me."

1. What should Marlene do (if anything) to discover what she might be doing wrong?
2. Do you have any general suggestions as to how Marlene might become better accepted by the group?

A BUSINESS PSYCHOLOGY ROLE PLAY

Criticizing Your Boss

To prepare for this role play, first review the information presented earlier about expressing disagreement with your boss in a constructive manner. Then get mentally set to assume one of the roles described next. The rest of the class will observe the role play and serve as a source of feedback about how well the tactic was implemented.

Boss: You have a meeting shortly with one of the key employees in your department. You are excited about your ideas for a new product for the company—a coffee pot with a built-in tape device that plays the national anthem when the pot is turned on. You believe there is both a large domestic and international market for your idea. You intend to bounce these ideas off your subordinate before bringing them to higher management.

Subordinate: You like your boss, you value your relationship with that person, but you think the idea for the singing coffee pot is strictly off the wall. You also think it is your duty to save the company from investing in this idea. Tactfully, try to get the boss to bury the idea for a singing coffee pot.

References

1. Most of this section follows closely the presentation in JOHN M. DARLEY, SAM GLUCKSBERG, AND RONALD A. KINCHLA, *Psychology,* 4th ed. (Englewood Cliffs, NJ: Prentice Hall, 1988), pp. 681–82; ROBERT P. VECCHIO, *Organizational Behavior* (Hinsdale, IL: The Dryden Press, 1988), p. 111.

2. WALTER D. ST. JOHN, "Successful Communications between Supervisors and Employees," *Personnel Journal,* January 1983, p. 76.

3. MARILYN MOATS KENNEDY, "How to Manage Your New Boss," *Business Week Careers,* March–April, 1987, p. 93.

4. NORMAN C. HILL AND PAUL H. THOMPSON, "Managing Your Manager: The Effective Subordinate," in J. B. RITCHIE AND PAUL THOMPSON, *Organization and People* (St. Paul, MN: West Publishing, 1980), p. 298.

5. EUGENE E. JENNINGS, *The Mobile Manager* (New York: McGraw-Hill, 1967), pp.

47–50; ROGER FRITZ, "Career Key: How to Influence Your Boss," *Supervisory Management,* August 1980, p. 10.

6. ST. JOHN, "Successful Communications between Supervisors and Employees," p. 77.

7. "Are You a Threat to Your Boss?" *Personal Report for the Executive,* January 1, 1988, pp. 6–7.

8. As quoted in "Socializing with Your Boss," *Personal Report for the Executive,* June 1, 1987, p. 8.

9. SANDY J. WAYNE AND GERALD R. FERRIS, "Influence Tactics, Affect, and Exchange Quality in Supervisor–Subordinate Interactions: A Laboratory Experiment and Field Study," *Journal of Applied Psychology,* October 1990, pp. 487–499.

10. ROBERT L. DILENSCHNEIDER, *Power and Influence: Mastering the Art of Persuasion* (New York: Prentice Hall Press, 1990).

11. JOSEPH D'O'BRIAN, "NEGOTIATING WITH PEERS: CONSENSUS, NOT POWER," *Supervisory Management,* JANUARY 1992, P. 4.

12. ANDREW J. DUBRIN, *Stand Out! How to Gain the Edge with Superiors, Subordinates, Co-workers, and Customers* (Englewood Cliffs, NJ: Prentice Hall, 1993); WILLIAM B. MARTIN, *Quality Customer Service: A Positive Guide to Superior Service,* rev. ed. (Los Altos, CA: Crisp Publications, Inc., 1989).

13. DAVID JAMIESON AND JULIE O' MARA, *Managing Workforce 2000: Gaining the Diversity Advantage* (San Francisco: Jossey-Bass, 1991), p. 1; WILLIAM B. JOHNSTON AND ARNOLD H. PACKER, *Workforce 2000: Work and Workers for the 21st Century* (Indianapolis, IN: Hudson Institute, 1987).

14. CHARLENE MARMER SOLOMON, "Are White Males Being Left Out?" *Personnel Journal,* November 1991, p. 88.

15. BOB SMITH, "Diversity With a Difference," *HRfocus,* December 1991, p. 5.

16. "Different Strokes for Different Folks," *Personnel,* November 1990, p. 19.

17. BILL LEONARD, "Ways to Make Diversity Programs Work," *HRMagazine,* April 1991, p. 38.

18. JANET LIVELY, "Managing Diversity," Rochester *Democrat and Chronicle,* September 2, 1991, p. 2D.

Suggested Reading

BOWER, DAVID E., SIEHL, CAREN, AND SCHNEIDER, BENJAMIN. "A Framework for Analyzing Customer Service Orientations in Manufacturing." *Academy of Management Review,* January 1989, pp. 75–95.

CARNEGIE, DALE. *How to Win Friends and Influence People.* New York: Pocket Books (a classic reprinted every few years).

COX, TAYLOR H., AND BLAKE, STACY. "Managing Cultural Diversity: Implications for Organizational Competitiveness." *Academy of Management Executive,* August 1991, pp. 45–56.

DUBRIN, ANDREW J. *Winning Office Politics: DuBrin's New Guide for the 1990s.* Englewood Cliffs, NJ: Prentice Hall, 1990.

FINKELMAN, DAN, AND GOLAND, TONY. "The Case of the Complaining Customer." *Harvard Business Review,* May–June 1990, pp. 9–25.

GREEN, DAVID. "Learning from Losing a Customer." *Harvard Business Review,* May–June 1989, pp. 54–59.

PUJOL, JUAN L., AND TUDANGER, EDWARD. "A Vision for Excellence." *HRMagazine,* June 1990, pp. 112–116.

RAFAELI, ANAT. "When Cashiers Meet Customers: An Analysis of the Role of Supermarket Cashiers." *Academy of Management Journal,* June 1989, pp. 245–273.

WENDT, ANN C., AND SLONAKER, WILLIAM M. "Discrimination Reflects on You." *HRMagazine,* May 1992, pp. 44–47.

Chapter 11

ADJUSTING TO THE ORGANIZATION

Learning Objectives

After reading and studying this chapter and doing the exercises, you should be able to

1. Recognize the importance of adapting to the informal rules of conduct on the job.
2. Appreciate how dress, appearance, manners, and etiquette can influence career success.
3. Pinpoint tactics for becoming a team player.
4. Select tactics for balancing the demands of work and personal life.
5. Summarize attitudes essential to adjusting well to technology.

JOB TASKS RELATED TO THIS CHAPTER

To be successful in most jobs, a person has to be an effective team player. This chapter describes valuable tactics designed to help you function well as a team member. Knowing how to balance the competing demands of work and personal life is indirectly related to job tasks. Unless a person can achieve such a balance, the ability to perform job tasks may suffer. The description of adjusting to technology will contribute to task accomplishment if working heavily with technology is burdensome.

A challenge faced by workers of all ages is meeting the various demands placed on them by their employer other than direct job responsibilities. Adjusting to the organization includes many activities discussed in this book, such as managing job stress, resolving conflict, getting along with others, and taking the initiative to manage your career. In this chapter we highlight five major challenges in adjusting to organizational life: (1) creating a favorable appearance, (2) following business etiquette and manners, (3) becoming a team player, (4) balancing the demands of work and personal life, and (5) adjusting mentally to technology.

Formal versus Informal Rules in Organizations

Formal organization: The job descriptions, organization charts, procedures, and other written documents that specify how individuals should work with each other.

Organizations are governed by both formal and informal rules. Adjusting to the formal rules is often easier than adjusting to the informal ones. Formal rules are part of the **formal organization**—the job descriptions, organization charts, procedures, and other documents which specify how individuals should work with each other.[1] The formal organization is thus the official, sanctioned way of doing things. By consulting the formal organization you can learn who reports to whom (the organization chart). The formal organization also tells you how various problems should be handled (see the policies and procedures manual).

Informal organization: A pattern of work relationships that develops to satisfy people's social needs and to get work accomplished.

A much more subtle set of rules that govern behavior are part of the **informal organization**—a pattern of work relationships that develops both to satisfy people's social needs and to get work accomplished. The informal organization also includes the customs and traditions that develop in the firm. Informal rules stem from the informal organization. Examples of informal rules governing behavior include these: (1) An office supervisor should never invite the chief executive officer to lunch. (2) A production employee should never wear a three-piece suit to work. Examining codes of dress and appearance is a good starting point in understanding adjustment to the organization.

Standards of Dress and Appearance

Both formal and informal standards of dress and appearance are found on the job. A survey conducted by the Administrative Management Society revealed that 31 percent of companies responding had formal (written) dress codes. Equally significant, 59 percent had an informal (unwritten) set of rules regulating employee dress.[1] A typical formal dress code would be, "Employees must wear conservative and professional attire to the office, and clothing must not violate safety codes." Appearance codes include such matters as restrictions on hair styles and facial hair.

Informal dress codes of dress and appearance can have a larger impact on your career than formal ones. This is true because formal dress codes specify the minimum acceptable standard, while informal codes may point you toward creating a superior professional image. Business and secretarial schools have always emphasized the importance of dress and appearance. A burgeoning of interest in this topic was created by two books written by John T. Molloy, *Dress for Success* and *The Woman's Dress for Success Book*.[2] Since then a number of "wardrobe consultants" have offered similar advice. Some general guidelines can be drawn that will help the career-minded person look successful. However, the advice given by Molloy and other experts should not be taken too literally. If every worker followed these suggestions, they would all look like store associates in an expensive retail store.

Here we will present survey evidence about the movement toward more casual dress on the job and factors influencing the proper choice of clothing.

Research Evidence about the Less Formal Style of Dress

A survey of 200 human resource executives throughout the United States revealed that more companies now permit informal clothing in the workplace. (The survey was conducted by Converse, Inc., a manufacturer of sports shoes.) Similar to the figure presented above, 78 percent of the companies did not have formal dress codes. The survey found that 55 percent of employers allow workers to dress casually on the job. Among the trends in business attire noted were the following:

- Thirty-three percent said less formal suits are being worn by men, with a growing preference toward European-cut garments and sports jacket and slacks combinations.
- Ninety-nine percent reported that more vibrant and colorfully patterned neckties are found on the job, as opposed to flat solids or stripes.
- Seventy-nine percent said women appear to be abandoning the traditional version of the female "power suit" in favor of more stylized combinations.
- Eighty-four percent reported seeing more dresses being worn by women on a regular basis.

Almost half the human resource executives believed that less restrictive dress codes boosted morale. Dress codes of the future may appear even less restrictive because 41 percent of the survey participants believed that corporate policies will become less formal.[3]

Factors Influencing Choice of Clothing

Your choice of clothing should be influenced by general standards of business attire and standards specific to the situation. Five important factors influencing your choice of clothing are described next.[4]

1. *Products or services sold.* The type of product or service heavily influences the choice of appropriate clothing. An office assistant working in a law firm

dresses much more conservatively than his or her counterpart at an automobile dealership.

2. *Type of customer or client served.* Closely related to the preceding is to choose clothing that fits the expectations of the people served by your firm. For example, the manager of an aerobics fitness center usually dresses in athletic, casual attire.

3. *Desired image projected by the firm.* Some firms use dress codes to help project a quality image. For instance, at Cadillac service departments, the automobile technicians wear clean, freshly pressed smocks.

4. *Geography.* Regional differences in dress standards influence the choice of work attire. In southern Florida, for example, executives appear in shirt sleeves more frequently than in Boston, where the traditional, conservative look is more in fashion.

5. *Your comfort and self-image.* Another important consideration is to choose clothing that fits your self-image and is therefore psychologically comfortable. When you are comfortable in your clothing, you project a self-confident image.

In summary, the most helpful guidelines for dress in business center around the idea that you must size up the situation to make appropriate choices. Nevertheless, a number of conclusions can be reached that should prove useful in many situations, as shown in Table 11-1.

TABLE 11–1. *HOW TO DRESS FOR IMPACT* _____

1. Dress to reflect the competent person you are now or expect to be.
2. Resist fads in styles, clothes, and fabrics. (They may become out of date while they are still new.)
3. Dress to look as if you mean business. (Look serious about what you are doing—don't wear running shoes to the office the day you are making a presentation to management.)
4. Dress to make an impression, not to cause a stir about the way you look. (Overdressing is often the sign of an insecure person.)
5. Follow your company's dress code or follow your company's leaders. (Also check out the way the "fast-trackers" dress.)
6. Be aware that you are representing your company through your style of dress. (The public often evaluates companies by the appearance of their employees.)
7. Wear fabrics that travel well and won't make you look rumpled. (A real problem with cheap clothing is that it rumples readily.)
8. Buy clothes from a salesperson whose style you admire. (That individual is likely to show good taste in helping you make clothing selections.)
9. Look and buy for quality. (High-quality clothing can often be purchased at off-price stores that specialize in name brands.)
10. Choose clothes the way you should choose people—for durability and dependability.
11. Dress for comfort. (If you are comfortable, you are likely to feel more confident and be able to concentrate on your work better.)
12. Choose accessories that enhance your image. (Included here are gold pens, solid-color leather briefcase, and a gold watch of simple elegance.)

Sources: Based on information in Caryl Winter, *Present Yourself with Impact: Techniques for Success* (New York: Ballantine Books, 1983), p. 199; John T. Molloy, "Executive Style," *Success!* September 1986, p. 49.

Etiquette and manners are even more strongly linked to informal rules than are dress codes. Like clothing and appearance, you often learn about what is considered correct only after you have committed an error. One management trainee was sharply criticized by his boss for having clipped his nails during a staff meeting. The young man innocently replied, "I didn't know I was doing anything wrong. In my last job, my boss clipped his nails during meetings."

Business etiquette is also important from the standpoint of the employer. The president of a company that provides training programs on etiquette says that customers rarely return to companies that treat them poorly.[5] "Poor treatment" often means that etiquette was not observed. Our discussion of business etiquette will include a sampling of standards of etiquette and the problem of informal socializing on the job.

Standards of Etiquette

Business etiquette:
A code of behavior required in work situations.

Business etiquette is a special code of behavior required in work situations. The term *manners* has an equivalent meaning. Both manners and etiquette generally refer to behaving in an acceptable and refined way. What is considered proper etiquette and manners in the workplace changes over time and may vary with the situation. For example, at one time smoking a cigarette in someone else's office was considered acceptable if an ash tray was available. (Yet good etiquette required asking permission first before smoking a pipe or cigar.) Today, smoking in someone else's office is either banned or considered to be poor etiquette.

When anyone is having trouble carrying something down the hall, when anyone's arms are full and thus can't open the door, when anyone needs help hailing a taxi, women and men should help women and men. Consideration for each other, regardless of gender, is a very important aspect of a person's ability to get along with people, and part of his or her success and rise in the corporate world.[6]

Following are 10 specific suggestions about business etiquette that should be considered in the context of a specific job situation.[7] For example, point 5 about removing coats in the office does not apply in certain divisions of IBM where coats must be kept on at all times.

1. *Greet people assertively.* When you meet another person, stand up, smile, shake hands firmly, make eye contact, and repeat the person's name.

2. *Names should be remembered.* It is both good manners and good human relations to remember the names of work associates, even if you see them only occasionally. If you make a deliberate effort to do so, you can improve your skill in remembering names. Make sure you learn the person's name in the first place.

3. *Respect other people's senses.* Any assault on other people's senses—sight, sound, smell, or touch—should be avoided. Thus, strong cologne and perfume are unwelcome, as are grotesque color combinations in your clothing, pinching co-workers, and making loud noises with chewing gum.

4. *Males and females should receive equal treatment.* Amenities extended to females by males in a social setting are minimized in business settings today. During a meeting, a male is not expected to hold a chair or a door for a woman, nor does he jump to walk on the outside when the two of them are walking down the street. Many women workers resent being treated differently from males with respect to minor social customs.

5. *Coats can be removed in the office.* Today it is considered appropriate to take off your coat, and keep it off, not only in your own work station or office, but when moving to other parts of the building.

6. *The host or hostess pays the bill.* An area of considerable confusion about etiquette surrounds business lunches and who should pay the check, the man or the woman. The new rule of etiquette is that the person who extends the invitation pays the bills. (Do you think this same rule should be extended to social life?)

7. *Address superiors and visitors in their preferred way.* As the modern business world has become more informal, a natural tendency has developed to address people at all levels by their first name. It is safer to first address people by a title and their last name (such as Mr. Baxter or Ms. Leon) and then wait for them to correct you if they desire. If you say, "Ms. Leon, may I call you by your first name," she may feel forced to consent.

8. *Make appointments with high-ranking people rather than dropping in.* Spontaneous visits may be all right with co-workers, but a taboo in most firms is for lower-ranking employees to drop into the office of an executive on a casual basis.

9. *Stand up only for infrequent visitors.* It is still considered polite to stand up when an infrequent visitor of either sex enters the office. However, if another worker enters your work area frequently, such as a file clerk who needs regular access to your files, standing up is not required.

10. *Sexiness in the office should be muted.* Women are strongly advised to avoid looking overly sexy or glamorous in the office. Waist length hair should be avoided and so should dangling jewelry, four-inch heels, and heavy eye makeup. Men too should not appear too sexy; tight pants and shirts are to be avoided.

Frequent violations of etiquette can sometimes set back a person's

career. However, violation of any of the preceding points would not necessarily have a negative impact on one's reputation. It's the overall image that counts most. Therefore, the general principle of being considerate of work associates is much more important than any one act of etiquette or courtesy.

Doing the Right Amount of "Schmoozing"

Few employees devote all their time on the job to direct work activities. Instead, according to a survey of personnel executives, they spend about 30 minutes or more per day socializing with co-workers. Informal socializing is referred to as *schmoozing*. A schmoozer engages in such activities as telling jokes, lingering at the water cooler or photocopying machine, wandering around the work premises, or taking a long lunch break. The general purpose of schmoozing seems to be to relieve boredom or tension. Many personnel executives believe that the time spent in personal chitchat fosters camaraderie and team spirit, which contribute to organizational success.[8]

No company procedure manual will tell you that work breaks of this nature are taboo, but they are certainly not welcomed. On the other hand, if you do not schmooze at all, you may miss out on establishing rapport with co-workers. The adjustment problem relates to finding out how much to schmooze. Too much social interaction, and you are wasting your own time and company resources. Too little, and you may not get the cooperation you need from co-workers to accomplish your job. If you are intent on advancing in your career, I would recommend the minimum amount of social interaction (schmoozing) necessary to keep you on good terms with peers.

Becoming a Team Player

An important part of adjusting to the organization is learning how to work as part of a team. Team skills have gained in importance as organizations face greater change and complexity. At every level of the organization, it is important to work cooperatively and jointly with others. Organizing people into work teams is a common practice with production workers, office support workers, and managers.[9]

A survey of high-level workers about effective tactics for task accomplishment underscores the importance of team play. Forty-nine percent of men and 42 percent of women in the sample agreed that being a team player is an effective method of getting things accomplished on the job.[10] Described next are six related attitudes and methods for becoming an effective team player:

Engage in Organizational Citizenship Behavior. A good team player works for the good of the organization even without the promise of a specific reward. Such activity is called **organizational citizenship behavior.**[11] The aggregate result of organizational citizenship behavior is that the organization functions more effectively.

Organizational citizenship behavior:
Working for the good of the organization even without the promise of a specific reward.

Good citizenship on the job encompasses many specific behaviors, including helping a co-worker with a job task and refraining from complaints or petty grievances. A good organizational citizen would carry out such specific acts as picking up litter in the company parking lot. He or she would also bring a reference to the office that could help a co-worker solve a job problem. Most of the other team player tactics described here are related to organizational citizenship behavior.

Help Co-workers Do Their Jobs Better. Your stature as a team player will increase if you take the initiative to help co-workers to make needed work improvements. Make the suggestions in a constructive spirit, rather than displaying an air of superiority.

> Liz, a software engineer, suggested to the group that they make their overview charts more exciting. She suggested that they add a logo, produce the charts in color, and be more creative. The change dramatically improved the presentation to user groups. People stayed more alert and interested during briefings. Liz received many words of appreciation for her dedication to the group cause.

Share Credit with Co-workers. A direct method of promoting the team concept is to share credit for good deeds with other team members. Instead of focusing on yourself as the person responsible for a work achievement, you point out that the achievement was indeed the product of a team effort. Frank is a good example of the team concept in action:

An important adjustment to organizational life is to become a team player.

"We won, team, we won," said Frank excitedly to his four lunchmates. "The world's largest manufacturer of air conditioners is going to use our new electronic switch in every one of their units. I just received the good news today. Thanks to all of you for giving me so darn many good suggestions for explaining the merits of our switch. I know that the big boss will be thrilled with our sales department."

Touch Base on Important Issues. Team play is also fostered when co-workers are informed about plans you have that could affect them. One example of this concept in action is to inform your peers about a suggestion you are planning to make to management. In this way, if your proposal is accepted, you are more likely to gain the support of your co-workers in implementing your idea than if your suggestion was a big surprise.

Provide Emotional Support to Co-workers. Good team players offer each other emotional support. Such support can take the form of verbal encouragement for ideas expressed, listening to a group member's concerns, or complimenting achievements. An emotionally supportive comment to a co-worker who appears overstressed might be, "This doesn't look like one of your better days. What can I do to help?"

Another form of providing emotional support is to reach out to a group member who is friendless and perhaps lonely. If you engage such individuals in social interaction, your contribution as a team player will be enhanced. However, if the isolated person resists your attempts at friendship, it is best to back off.

Engage in Shared Laughter. Laughter is a natural team builder that enhances understanding and empathy, essential ingredients for team play.[12] The individual can trigger laughter by making humorous comments related to the situation at hand or making in-group jokes.

> Tracy decided to enliven her work area by posting photographs of scantily clad males. (Part of her ploy was to retaliate against the men in the department who had posted photographs of women.) The manager complained about her photographs in a staff meeting, mentioning that such behavior was unprofessional and might be construed as sexual harassment. Tracy blurted out, "I don't understand where your *beef* is coming from." Her one-liner enhanced her reputation as a group member.

The accompanying box describes an activity many employers sponsor to help workers at all levels become better team players. Similar training is also sponsored by some community organizations and business schools to teach teamwork skills.

MANAGERS AND PROFESSIONALS ATTEND OUTWARD BOUND

The chief operating officer of TCI West, Inc., an electronics firm, wanted key company personnel to develop into a smooth team. He chose Outward Bound training because he hoped to break down communication barriers and put all participants on equal footing. The first TCI representatives were sent to a training site in the Nevada desert. Among these people were top managers, marketing directors, and five manager trainees.

The group learned orienteering, first aid, and outdoor activities including rappelling and rock climbing. The TCI men and women hiked through hot desert days and awakened to temperatures around 5 degrees Fahrenheit. Participants cooked meals, pitched tents, rationed water, and taught each other outdoor techniques.

One exercise that incorporates team building, leadership, and communication skills requires participants to intentionally flip the raft over in deep water. Next they return it to the upright position and then help each team member back into the raft.

Developing trust is another critical aspect of Outward Bound. Participants must trust the commands that are shouted from the person leading the raft through swirling rapids. They must trust the lead person's sense of direction while hiking through the desert. Most of all, they must trust the person belaying their rappel that will save them from serious injury or death in case of a fall.

Among the lessons learned are that getting help from others isn't always a sign of weakness, that it's all right not to be perfect, and that most fears can be put into proper perspective.

Source: As reported in Sally Howe, "TCI West Trains Outdoors," *Personnel Journal,* June 1991, pp. 58–59.

Balancing Work and Personal Life

Balancing the demands of work and personal life is a major challenge facing today's work force. (The term *personal life* is used here to encompass family life or life off the job for people who are not part of a family.) Juggling the many activities in work and personal life has been difficult in recent years and promises to continue as a major political and social issue for the future.[13] The challenge is particularly intense for employees who are part of a two-wage-earner family, a group that includes over half the work force in the United States and Canada.

Attempting to meet the demands of work and personal life is a source of role conflict. For example, it is impossible to take an elderly parent for a medical appointment at 11 A.M. and be at your office at the same time. Role conflict leads to stress, which may decrease productivity as workers become preoccupied with unresolved work versus family issues. Here we describe several of the steps individuals can take, including assistance from the organization, to better balance the demands of work and family life. These steps are outlined in Figure 11-1.

Plan Ahead for Family Events. Douglas T. Hall and Judith Richter recommend advanced personal planning as a way of minimizing conflict between work and important family events. This would involve marking on one's office calendar, at the beginning of each year, important family dates (such as birthdays and anniversaries). In this way an attempt could be made to minimize business travel and late meetings on those dates. Similarly, the family could be advised of times when work demands would be at their peak.[14]

Discuss Work Commitments with Your Partner or Prospective Partner. A substantial amount of conflict over work versus family demands can be prevented if each partner has an accurate perception of the prospective mate's work schedule. For example, some career people are prepared to work 60 hours per week to achieve their career objectives, while others prefer to avoid working over 40 hours. A couple that

FIGURE 11–1. *BALANCING WORK AND FAMILY DEMANDS.*

1. Plan ahead for family events.
2. Discuss work commitments with your partner or prospective partner.
3. Get on a parent track (downshifting).
4. Divide household chores equitably.
5. Maintain a buffer time between work and home.
6. Rely on organizational support systems.

cannot agree or compromise on how much time is suitable to invest in a career may not be compatible.

Get on a Parent Tract (Downshifting). Some employers are making it possible for managers and professionals to choose a career track that allows more time for parenting. Investing more time in family and less in career is often referred to as **downshifting.** A person placed on a parent track would avoid positions that interfere heavily with family responsibilities. For instance, if you were on a parent track, you would avoid a position that required frequent overseas travel.

Downshifting:
Investing more time in family and less in career.

The way to get on a parent track would be to first make sure that such an arrangement with your employer is possible. You would then explain to your superiors that you want to perform well, but not be overloaded with career responsibilities at the expense of personal life.

Divide Household Chores Equitably. Many women who work outside the home rightfully complain that they are responsible for too much of the housework. A study was conducted of 131 men and 109 women, all of whom were managers or professionals and has spouses and children. One conclusion reached was that a redistribution of roles within the family did not take place to match to the increased role responsibilities outside the family.[15] In short, few women found they were doing less housework and child rearing.

In the extreme, when women function as both career people and full-time homemakers, conflict at home is highly probable. The recommended solution is for the working couple to divide household tasks in some equitable manner. Equity could mean that tasks are divided according to preference or the amount of effort required. Each couple should negotiate for themselves what constitutes an equitable division of household tasks.

Maintain a Buffer Time between Work and Home. Commuting time between work and home plays an important psychological role in helping people get mentally prepared for work in the morning and to unwind in the afternoon or early evening. The commute serves as a buffer between work life and personal life. People who live too close to work often complain that they are still thinking about the job when they arrive at home. A simple solution to the problem of a too-short commute is to walk around the block before entering the home. Information collected by Hall and Richter suggests a commuting time of about 30 minutes is ideal, because it facilitates "gearing up in the morning and winding down in the evening."[16]

Rely on Organizational Support Systems. Many employers now provide a group of services and programs that supports workers in their quest to manage work and family life successfully. Among the most important of these support systems are flexible work hours and dependent-care options. A **dependent-care option** is any company-sponsored program that helps an employee take care of a family member. Child-care programs, including on-site day-care centers, and parental leave (for mothers *and* fathers) are the most frequently offered. Other company-sponsored pro-

Dependent-care option:
Any company-sponsored program that helps an employee take care of a family member.

grams include eldercare (day care for elderly dependents who cannot take care of themselves entirely) and seminars on work versus family issues.[17]

Job sharing:
An arrangement in which two people share one job by each working half time.

A modified work schedule specifically designed to help people juggle work and family demands is **job sharing,** an arrangement in which two people share one job by each working half-time. Job sharing has its biggest appeal for workers whose family commitments do not allow for full-time work.[18] An advantage to the employer of such an arrangement is that the company gets an output in excess of the equivalent of one full-time person. Two people working half-time will usually produce more than one person working full time, particularly in creative work.

Many human resource professionals contend that work–family programs increase productivity by reducing absenteeism and turnover and enabling parents to concentrate better on their work. Formal research has been conducted to evaluate these claims. A study was conducted at a large electronics and communications firm that had converted idle production space to a child-care center. At the time of the study, approximately 175 children were enrolled, ages six weeks to five years old. Users paid 80 percent of the market cost for the care. Parents are allowed to visit their children during breaks and at lunch time, and mothers are permitted to nurse young children.

The study did not find a significant drop off in work–family conflict in absenteeism because of the child-care center. However, emotionally supportive supervision and satisfaction with child-care arrangements were associated with less work–family conflict. Furthermore, employees who had less work–family conflicts had better attendance records. A major conclusion drawn from the study was that satisfaction with child-care arrangements is related to important work-related outcomes.[19]

Adjusting to Technology

An adjustment faced by many workers is to cope with the human consequences of technology, particularly electronic instruments used in the workplace. In its comprehensive meaning, **technology** refers to all the tools and ideas available for extending the natural physical and mental reach of people.[20] However, few workers have difficulty adjusting to dictionaries and pencil sharpeners. Here we describe four major adjustment problems created by advanced technology in the workplace and also point toward solutions. The four problems are computer shock, cumulative trauma disorders, rudeness and impersonality, and threats of obsolescence.

Technology:
All the tools and ideas available for extending the natural physical and mental reach of people.

Computer Shock

Working intensely with computers can lead to a modern form of job stress called **computer shock** (or computer stress). It is defined as an intense negative reaction to being forced to spend many more hours in front of a computer than one desires. Among its symptoms are a glassy-eyed, detached look, aching neck muscles, and a growing dislike for high technology. The application of human engineering to the design of computer systems may be helpful in minimizing the physical problems that contribute to computer shock. Nevertheless, working closely with computers can still create job dissatisfaction for some people. As told by Ashley, a manufacturing specialist:

> The reason I majored in business was so I could get a job working with people. I never minded doing my share of writing reports and crunching numbers. I put up with it so I could spend most of my time relating to people. After graduation I took an interesting sounding job as an inventory-control specialist. Little did I know I would be sitting in front of a computer almost all day, every day. I hardly talk to anybody. I'm even supposed to communicate with my boss by sending messages on the computer. Now the company is telling me to get more advanced computer training. I'm looking for another job. Especially one that involves working with people.

A possible antidote to computer shock is for affected employees to request the opportunity to spend some work time not working with computers, such as gathering information from customers. Part of making an appropriate adjustment is to take the initiative to confront management about a problem.

Cumulative Trauma Disorder

In Chapter 8 we described the problems created by VDT stress. A closely related problem is **cumulative trauma disorders,** injuries caused by repetitive motions over prolonged periods of time. Cumulative trauma disorders include carpal tunnel syndrome, bricklayer's shoulder, and chicken dresser's wrist. (Carpal tunnel syndrome occurs when frequent bending of the wrist causes tendons or tissue to swell in the tunnel formed by the carpal bones and the ligament. As a consequence, the median nerve that gives feeling to the hand is pinched.) These disorders accounted for 48 percent of all occupational injuries and illnesses in the United States during a one-year period.

Experts attribute the high incidence of cumulative trauma disorders to the use of computers and other high-tech equipment such as price scanners. At U.S. West, for example, almost two-fifths of the company's directory assistance operators in Denver have been diagnosed as having some form of VDT-related repetitive motion disorder. Forty of the 500 operators underwent surgery to relieve the pain and numbness caused by carpal tunnel syndrome.[21]

Fortunately, most cumulative trauma industries are preventable with redesigned equipment and appropriate rest breaks (as described in Chapter 7). Figure 11-2 depicts a workstation based on ergonomic principles, designed to prevent cumulative trauma disorder.

Rudeness and Impersonality

On balance, computerized information probably increases profits and improves the flow of communications. Nevertheless, most readers of

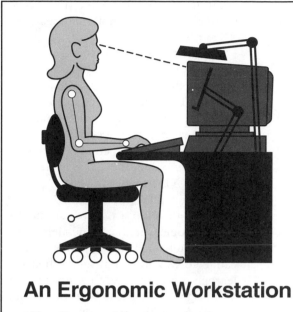

An Ergonomic Workstation

- Keep the screen below your eye level.
- Keep your elbows on the same level with home-key row, with your wrists and lower arms parallel to floor.
- Support your back and thighs with a well constructed chair.
- Position your feet flat on the floor.
- Use a lamp to supplement inadequate room lighting.

FIGURE 11–2. *HOW TO MINIMIZE CUMULATIVE TRAUMA DISORDER.*

this book have heard people poke fun at the rudeness and impersonality of voice mail, call waiting, and electronic mail. An industrial sales representative put it this way: "Voice mail is driving me to look for another job. I can never get to talk to a person in order to set up an appointment. I only deal with voice mail systems and telephone answering machines." Similarly, many people become irritated when they receive a message via electronic mail that a meeting has been canceled or that they will not receive a salary increase this year.

Many companies are already working on the potential rudeness and impersonality of modern communication systems. Most voice mail systems give people an option that will allow them to talk to a person. Other companies are describing guidelines as to which type of information should be transmitted via electronic mail. In general, confidential and sensitive information is best transmitted over the phone (not using voice mail!) and by letter. Electronic mail is reserved for transmitting more routine, less emotional messages.

Threats of Obsolescence

Another adjustment problem to high technology is that employees who are unwilling or unable to learn the new technology may lose their jobs. The majority of people reading this book are probably good technologists. Learning new technology is easy for those people. Yet many other people have virtual mental blocks against technology. These people dread learning new software, and some will not even use an automatic teller machine (ATM).

A sensible way to guard against technological obsolescence is to gradually develop a positive attitude toward new technology. Using electronic gadgets in the home helps one develop a more positive attitude toward high tech in the office or factory. People who operate VCRs or cam-corders and can program their CD record players have little difficulty learning new software to keep track of physical inventory. Reading books and magazine articles about office and factory technology is very helpful, as is taking a high-tech course or attending a technology seminar.

Another antidote is to have available the phone numbers of people who can help you with problems related to technology.[22] Incorporate a few "techies" into your network and keep available the 800 assistance number that accompanies most software.

BACK TO THE JOB TASKS

Assume that you have been assigned to a job that requires teamwork. Even if you have good interpersonal skills, it will help you to carefully review and implement several of the teamwork tactics described in the chapter. For example, it will help your teamwork skills if you purposely engage in organizational citizenship behavior. Should you be having difficulty adjusting to technology, check with your manager to determine if your workstation could be designed better. Or perhaps you need to incorporate technically minded people into your network.

Summary of Key Points

❑ Adjusting to the organization refers to many things that you have to do in order to get along on the job. Several of these major adjustments are described in this chapter. Adjusting to formal rules is often easier than adjusting to informal rules that stem from the informal organization. The latter includes the customs and traditions that develop in the firm.

❑ Standards of dress and appearance are governed by both formal and informal rules, and both may require adjustments by the employee. It is more helpful to use general guidelines for proper dress and appearance than to adhere closely to detailed suggestions about specific items of clothing. Five important factors influencing your choice of clothing are (1) products and services sold, (2) type of customer or client served, (3) desired image projected by the firm, (4) geography, and (5) your comfort and self-image.

❑ Etiquette and manners are even more strongly linked to informal rules than are dress codes. An important generalization about business etiquette is to be considerate of other employees and make them comfortable. Most specific rules stem from this general principle. Knowing how much schmoozing (informal socializing) to engage in is part of adjusting to the etiquette and manners of the firm.

❑ Another part of adjusting to the organization is to learn how to work as part of a team. Strategies and techniques for supporting the team concept include (1) engage in organizational citizenship behavior, (2) help co-workers do their job better, (3) share credit with co-workers, (4) touch base on important issues, (5) provide emotional support to co-workers, and (6) engage in shared laughter.

❑ Balancing the demands of work and personal life is a major challenge facing today's work force, especially in two-income families. Attempting the balance can lead to role conflict and stress. Steps individuals can take to balance work and family life include (1) plan ahead for family events, (2) discuss work commitments with your partner or prospective partner, (3) get on a parent track, (4) divide household chores equitably, (5) maintain a buffer time between work and home, and (6) rely on organizational support systems such as child care and flexible working hours. Research indicates that satisfaction with child care is associated with less work–family conflicts and that less of these conflicts improves attendance.

❑ Coping with the human consequences of technology is another important workplace adjustment. One problem is computer shock, which results in physical problems and a growing dislike for technology. Cumulative trauma disorders are technology related physical injuries that require considerable adjustment, but they can often be prevented with the right workplace design. Technology also breeds its own rudeness and impersonality because machines replace human interaction. Not being willing or able to keep up with job technology (the problem of obsolescence) also creates adjustment problems.

GUIDELINES FOR PERSONAL EFFECTIVENESS

1. An important strategy of adjusting to the organization is to be aware of the informal expectations made of you in such areas as dress codes, socializing on the job, and appropriate business etiquette. To learn of these expectations, both make observations and delicately ask questions.
2. It is important in general to be a good team player if you want to work for an organization. However, do not carry this approach so far that you lose your personal identity or become "one of the gang." Such behavior could decrease your chances for promotion.
3. If you are a family person, it is important to establish a workable plan for balancing career and family demands. If home matters are poorly attended to, it is difficult to concentrate properly on your job.
4. If your job involves extensive keyboarding or other continuous use of the wrist and fingers, investigate if your workstation has the right design to minimize the problem of cumulative trauma disorder.

1. What alternatives are there for people who feel they cannot adjust to organizational life?

2. A wardrobe consultant recommends that people who are serious about getting ahead in business should be willing to invest $10,000 in a business wardrobe. What is your opinion on this issue?

3. What tie-in do you see between the growth of technology in the workplace and the renewed interest in business etiquette?

4. When two or more sales associates in a store are not busy with customers, should they be allowed to engage in general conversation? Why or why not?

5. What evidence do you have that team work is important in business today? (If necessary, use information in this text to help you answer the question.)

6. To what extent do you believe that being a member of an athletic team is good training for becoming a team player on the job?

7. To implement the strategy "engage in shared laughter," do you think it would be advisable to bring a new joke to the office at least once a week?

8. What evidence do you have, including information about friends, that workers actually suffer from computer shock?

9. What is it about a supermarket cashier's job that can lead to cumulative trauma disorder?

10. Ask a small business owner what obligations he or she thinks the employer has to help employees reduce conflicts between work and personal life. Be prepared to discuss your findings in class.

A BUSINESS PSYCHOLOGY PROBLEM

The VDT Uprising

Leisure Time Industries is a well-managed and successful business. The company manufactures such products as bicycles, nautilus equipment, skis, swimming pools, and swing sets. One of their strategies for reducing manufacturing costs is to carefully control production schedules and the amount of parts in inventory. Bud Gavelston is the supervisor of production and inventory control at Leisure Time's North Carolina plant. He recently spoke to his boss, Phil Beechwood, about a problem facing his operation.

"Phil, as you know, I'm not the type to complain about supervisory problems. But this time, I have to make an exception. I'm dealing with a problem so big that it could lead to a special safety investigation by the government."

"I thought we cleared up all the accident hazards in the plant," said Phil.

"We have cleared up the accident hazards. What I'm dealing with is a health hazard that could really exist. Or it could be a problem that only exists in the mind of my employees. As you know, we have three data-entry specialists in our department. Since our production and inventory control system is computerized, we can't get our job done without people keying data into the system.

"The last several months, I've been getting many complaints from all three clerks that they dislike spending so much time working at a display terminal. One of the women joked that she's suffering from 'the VDTs.'"

"What don't they like about being in front of a VDT?" asked Phil. "It's not much different from typing. It's also not much different than watching television. It's simply a matter of sitting in front of a screen."

"You may see it that way," said Bud. "But the three data-entry clerks don't see it that way. They complain that when they go home at night they suffer form from neck aches and headaches. They say that their wrists are very painful. I tell them it's a matter of adjustment, but they still complain."

"Okay, so a little job strain is inevitable. I wouldn't worry too much about a government inspection," said Phil.

"You haven't heard the major problem. Two of the data-entry clerks are pregnant. They visited me together to tell me that they are worried about the health of their unborn children. Somebody has led them to believe that rays from a VDT can create birth defects.

"The other data-entry specialist told me that he is worrying about becoming sterile from radiation."

"Sounds like they are needlessly upset," said Phil. "What have you done so far about the problem?"

"I thought about transferring them to other jobs. The problem is that I don't have any other jobs for them in my department. Besides that, they are all good employees. If they all left at once, our department would fall way behind schedule."

"Bud, have you considered the possibility that both you and the three data-entry specialists are overreacting to the problem? I suggest you write them each a letter of appreciation for all the good work they have done for the department. This should calm them down. They may be just crying out for appreciation from their supervisor. The radiation problem sounds like a bunch of nonsense to me. Also tell them to rest their wrists and fingers on the weekend."

"Thanks for your advice. I'll see what I can do," said Bud. "But I doubt this problem can be solved so easily."

1. How seriously should Gavelston take the complaints of the three data-entry specialists?
2. Should Gavelston go around his boss if the latter does not become more concerned about the employee complaints with regard to working with VDTs?
3. What do you think of notes of appreciation as a solution to the problem?
4. If you were Gavelston, how would you handle the employee complaints about working at the VDTs?

The Lost Job Opportunity

"So long, Skip," said Jason, the branch manager at Cosmopolitan Insurance Company, "you'll be hearing back from me in a few days. The next step in hiring you for this job will be to meet with Mr. William Shields, our regional manager. He's my boss." "Thanks a lot," replied Skip. "I'll wait for your call."

Four days later, Skip did hear from Jason. To his surprise, a three-way luncheon was arranged with Jason, Bill Shields, and Skip. The lunch was held at an attractive Italian restaurant two blocks from where Skip would be working, if hired. At lunch the three men talked about the nature of claims work and how bright the future looked for Cosmopolitan. As Skip finished his spumoni dessert, Mr. Shields commented, "And remember one thing, young man. A claims examiner for Cosmopolitan must be capable of meeting the public in a dignified manner."

Later that afternoon, Bill Shields informed Jason, "I do like your candidate for the open claims examiner spot. But you will have to do better. Skip's manners are just not suited for meeting the public. Did you see how he sucked up his spaghetti? Did you see how he held his fork in his left hand? He just won't do for our company."

"Are you sure you won't change your mind, Bill?" asked Jason. "Skip has a lot of potential. I think we can teach him manners. There must be a charm school we can send him to."

"Sorry, Jason. My decision is final. We have a certain image to uphold at Cosmopolitan Insurance."

The next day Jason wrote Skip a note informing him that the job in question had been filled by a candidate with more appropriate experience. When Skip read the letter, he was stunned.

1. Do you think Shields was justified in refusing to hire Skip because of his table manners?
2. What criticisms might you make of the way Jason informed Skip about his not being hired?

A BUSINESS PSYCHOLOGY ROLE PLAY

The Rejected Job Candidate

As things worked out, Skip did not take his rejection easily. He called Jason and requested an in-person interview to review why he was turned down for the job when it appeared that he was just about hired.

One person plays Skip, who is convinced that he can handle the claims job. Furthermore, he is upset that he was turned down. Another person plays Jason, who decides that, in the interest of decency, he will explain to Skip why he was really turned down. At the same time, Jason does not want the company to appear foolish. Nor does he want the company to be sued.

References

1. ERIC MATUSEWITCH, "Tailor Your Dress Codes," *Personnel Journal,* February 1989, p. 86.
2. JOHN T. MOLLOY, *Dress for Success* (New York: Warner Books, 1976); MOLLOY, *The Woman's Dress for Success Book* (New York: Warner Books, 1978).
3. "Dress for Success Becoming More Casual in Today's Workplace," *HRfocus,* January 1992, p. 18.
4. BARRY L. REECE AND RHONDA BRANDT, *Effective Human Relations in Business,* 2nd ed. (Boston: Houghton Mifflin, 1984), pp. 294–296.
5. JUDITH EVANS, "What's All This Boorish Business?" *Democrat and Chronicle,* Rochester, NY, December 16, 1991, p. 5D.
6. Quoted in RICHARD MICHAELS, "Manners," *Success,* August 1982, p. 43.
7. GEORGE MAZZEI, *The New Office Etiquette* (New York: Simon & Schuster, 1983); MICHAELS, "Manners," pp. 40–43; LETITIA BALDRIGE, "A Guide to Executive Etiquette," *Business Week Careers,* October 1986, pp. 60–63; EVANS, "What's All This Boorish Business?" p. 12D.
8. "Productive Schmoozing," *Personal Report for the Executive,* September 1, 1987, p. 7.
9. JANA SCHILDER, "Work Teams Boost Productivity," *Personnel Journal,* February 1992, pp. 67–71.
10. ANDREW J. DuBRIN, "Sex Differences in the Endorsement of Influence Tactics and Political Behavior Tendencies," *Journal of Business and Psychology,* Fall 1989, pp. 3–14.
11. DENNIS W. ORGAN, *Organizational Citizenship Behavior* (Lexington, MA: Lexington Books, 1988), p. 4.

12. Paul S. George, "Teamwork without Tears," *Personnel Journal,* November 1987, p. 124.

13. Barbara Gutek and Sabrina Searle, "Rational versus Gender Role Explanations for Work–Family Conflict," *Journal of Applied Psychology,* August 1991, p. 560.

14. Douglas T. Hall and Judith Richter, "Balancing Work Life and Home Life: What Can Organizations Do to Help?" *Academy of Management Executive,* August 1988, p. 213.

15. Linda Elizabeth Duxbury and Christopher Alan Higgins, "Gender Differences in Work–Family Conflict," *Journal of Applied Psychology,* February 1991, p. 60.

16. Hall and Richter, "Balancing Work Life and Home Life," p. 218.

17. Julie A. Cohen, "Managing Tomorrow's Workforce Today," *Management Review,* January 1991, p. 17; "New EEOC Ruling Warns against Parental Leave Discrimination," *HRfocus,* June 1991, p. 6.

18. Renee Magid, "The Work and Family Challenge," *AMA Management Briefing,* American Management Association, 1990, p. 43.

19. Stephen J. Goff, Michael K. Mount, and Rosemary L. Jamison, "Employer Supported Child Care, Work/Family Conflict, and Absenteeism: A Field Study," *Personnel Psychology,* Winter 1990, pp. 795–809.

20. Robert Kreitner, *Management,* 5th ed. (Boston: Houghton Mifflin, 1992), p. 94.

21. Robert F. Bettendorf, "Curing the Ills of Technology," *HRMagazine,* March 1990, pp. 35–36, 80.

22. Antoinette K. O'Connell, "Making the New Technology Work," *Supervisory Management,* March 1990, p. 8.

Suggested Reading

Baldrige, Letitia. *Letitia Baldrige's Complete Guide to New Manners for the 1990s.* New York: Rawson Associates, 1992.

Frone, Michael R., Russell, Marcia, and Cooper, M. Lynne. "Antecedents and Outcomes of Work–Family Conflict: Testing a Model of the Work–Family Interface." *Journal of Applied Psychology,* February 1992, pp. 65–78.

Gattiker, Urs E. *Technology Management in Organizations.* Newbury Park, CA: Sage, 1990.

Goodman, Paul S., and Sproull Lee S. and Associates. *Technology and Organizations.* San Francisco: Jossey-Bass, 1990.

Huret, Judy. "Paying for Team Results." *HRMagazine,* May 1991, pp. 39–41.

Jamieson, David, and O'Mara, Julie. *Managing Workforce 2000.* San Francisco: Jossey-Bass, 1991.

Kinlaw, Dennis C. *Developing Superior Work Teams.* San Diego: Lexington Books/University Associates, 1991.

Orsburn, Jack D., and Associates. *Self-directed Work Teams: The New American Challenge.* Homewood, IL: BusinessOne: Irwin, 1991.

Parker, Glenn M. *Team Players and Teamwork: The New Competitive Strategy.* San Francisco: Jossey-Bass, 1991.

Solomom, Charlene Marmer. "Marriott's Family Matters." *Personnel Journal,* October 1991, pp. 40–42.

Chapter 12

MAKING THE MOST OF A VARIETY OF PERSONALITIES

Learning Objectives

After reading and studying this chapter and doing the exercises, you should be able to

1. Take problems professionally rather than personally.
2. Acquire insights into how to confront and criticize counterproductive people.
3. Be aware of the importance of interpreting the games of counterproductive people.
4. Use sympathy to help handle the personality quirks of co-workers.
5. Deal with difficult customers.
6. Be ready to handle a variety of personalities by using tact, diplomacy, and recognition and affection.
7. Recognize that some moodiness may be related to the physical status of the brain.

JOB TASKS RELATED TO THIS CHAPTER

Most workers are forced to invest some of their work time in dealing with difficult or counterproductive people. One specific job task you can accomplish better by studying this chapter is criticizing a co-worker or superior who deserves it. Another task this chapter will help you to do better is dealing with difficult customers.

Counterproductive person:
One whose actions lead him or her away from achieving work goals, often because of a personality quirk.

Most jobs would be much easier if one were not forced to deal with a variety of personalities, some of whom can block your attempts to be productive. Workers can be counterproductive or difficult for many reasons besides intelligence or ability. From the standpoint of a manager, a **counterproductive** (or difficult) **person** can be anybody who turns in substandard performance, yet who could perform well if he or she wanted to. From the standpoint of the individual worker, a peer is classified as counterproductive or difficult if he or she is uncooperative, touchy, defensive, hostile, or even very unfriendly. From the standpoint of any subordinate, a counterproductive or difficult boss is similarly any boss who is uncooperative, insensitive, touchy or defensive, aggressive, hostile, or very unfriendly.

In this chapter we explore some of the psychological techniques that a person might use to deal more effectively with people who are counterproductive or difficult, but not necessarily unintelligent or incompetent. We are dealing primarily with the situation in which the difficult person is a co-worker rather than a subordinate. However, if you have formal authority over another individual (you're the boss), the same techniques can be used to advantage. Also, if the difficult person is your boss, several of the techniques can be used, but with considerable sensitivity and tact.

Many different approaches exist for classifying difficult or counterproductive people.[1] A representative classification of difficult behavior patterns is presented in Figure 12-1. Although not scientifically developed, the categories provide some insight into the nature of counterproductive behavior on the job.

Taking Problems Professionally, Not Personally

A key principle in dealing with a variety of personalities is to take what they do professionally, not personally. Difficult people are not necessarily out to get you. You may just represent an obstacle or a steppingstone for them to get what they want.[2] For example, if a customer insults you because she thinks your prices are too high, she probably has nothing against you personally. She just wants a bargain!

Dru Scott, a human relations trainer, provides an example of the type of thinking one needs in order to take problems with difficult people professionally rather than personally:[3]

> One savvy representative explained how he taught himself to take things professionally when dealing with difficult people. He reminded himself at key moments, "I'm being paid to do this job. This means I'm a professional. Those with whom I deal don't have to like me. I don't have to like them, but I make my living by handling people professionally and will learn something everytime I encounter a difficult situation."

As you learn to take insults, slights, and backstabbing professionally rather than personally, you will experience less stress and harassment on

SEE IF YOU RECOGNIZE THESE PEOPLE...

The Know-It-Alls:
They're experts on everything. They can be arrogant, and they usually have an opinion on any issue. Yet when they're wrong, they pass the buck or become defensive.

The Passives:
You can spot them with their deadpan faces, their weak handshakes, their blank stares. Avoiding controversy at all costs, these people never offer opinions or ideas and never let you know where you stand

The Dictators:
They bully, cajole and intimidate. They're blunt to the point of being insulting. They're constantly demanding and brutally critical. These folks can cause ulcers.

The Yes-People:
They'll agree to any commitment, promise any deadline, yet they rarely deliver. While they're always sorry (and often charming), you can't trust them to do what they say.

The No-People:
Negative and pessimistic, they're quick to point out why something won't work. Worse, they're inflexible; they resist change. They can throw a wet blanket over an entrie organization.

The Complainers:
Is anything ever right with these people? You get the feeling they'd rather complain about things than change them. Even though they're often right, their negativity and nit-picking turn people off.

OF COURSE YOU RECOGNIZE THEM. They're the people you work with, sell to, depend on, live with. Now you can learn to deal with them more effectively, at <u>How To Deal With Difficult People</u>, CareerTrack's one-day seminar.

FIGURE 12-1.
Source: Brochure for CareerTrack Seminars, 3085 Center Green Drive, Boulder, CO 80301–5408

the job. Imagine how short the career of a baseball umpire would be if he or she took every tirade from coaches, players, and fans personally.

Confronting the Difficult Person

A good starting point for overcoming problems created by a difficult person is to confront that individual with his or her annoying or counterproductive behavior. In some instances, simply confronting the problem will make it go away. One co-worker said to another, "Please stop suggesting that we take two-hour lunch breaks every payday. It makes me tense to have to reject you." The requests for the luncheon sojourns stopped immediately.

A fundamental reason why we resist confronting another person, particularly a subordinate, about a sensitive issue is that we recognize how uncomfortable *we* feel when confronted by a boss about a sensitive issue. A manager who is about to confront a subordinate about irregularities on an expense account might say to himself, "I know how bad I would feel if I were told by my boss that I had been overcharging the company on trips. Maybe if I let it pass one more time, Jack [the subordinate] will shape up by himself."

Another reason many people are hesitant to confront another person is fear of reprisal or a quarrel.[4] What specific kind of reprisal might be chosen by the confronted person (should the roles be reversed) is usually unknown, which makes the confrontation seem all the more hazardous. One member of a task force was going to confront another with the opinion that the latter was not carrying her fair share, thus increasing the burden for other members of the task force. The would-be confronter backed off, thinking that the woman confronted might tell lies about her to their mutual boss.

Helpful Confrontation Techniques

Six suggestions are in order to ease the confrontation process.[5] Since confrontation of some sort is a vital step in attempting to influence the behavior of another individual, they are worth giving serious thought.

1. *Attempt to relax during the confrontation session.* If you appear overly tense, you might communicate the message in body language that you are not confident of the position that you are taking about the individual's negative behavior. Sometimes a role playing or rehearsal interview with a friend will be helpful in reducing your tension about the confrontation.

2. *Get to the central purpose of your meeting almost immediately.* Too often when people attempt to confront somebody else about something sensitive, they waste time talking about unrelated topics. Discussions about vacations, professional sports, or business conditions have some value as warm-up material for *other* kinds of interviews.

3. *Avoid being apologetic or defensive about the need for the meeting.* You have a right to demand constructive relationships with other people in your work environment. For instance, there is no need to say, "Perhaps I may be way off base, but it seems like you slam the door shut every time I can't process your request immediately." Let the door-slamming co-worker correct you if you are "way off base."

4. *Confront the other individual in a nonhostile manner.* Confrontations about counterproductive behavior should be conducted with feeling (particularly sincerity), but not with hostility. Confrontations are associated with bitter conflict so frequently that the concept of confrontation connotes hostility. Yet all forms of confrontation need not be conflagrations. Hostility begets hostility. Confrontation mixed with hostility comes across to the person being confronted as an attempt at retribution or punishment.

The suggestion about avoiding hostility does not mean that all emotion should be ruled out of a confrontation session. An appropriate amount of displeasure, annoyance, disappointment, and controlled anger should be conveyed. A confrontation session stripped of legitimate feeling would appear sterile to the person being confronted.

5. *Confront job-related behavior.* The essential skill to be acquired in constructive confrontation is to translate counterproductive behavior into its job-related consequence. Once the counterproductive or difficult behavior is

translated into its consequences in terms of actions, the situation is placed on a problem-solving basis. Instead of confronting a person about feelings, attitudes, or values, discuss their job-related consequences. These consequences are much easier to deal with than internal aspects of people. Two examples follow, designed to illustrate the difference between confrontation related to job behavior and confrontation unrelated to job behavior.

MANAGER TO SUBORDINATE: (*job-related*) I wish you would smile at customers more frequently. They are likely to purchase more goods when they receive a warm smile from the sales associate.

SAME MANAGER TO SUBORDINATE: (*not directly job-related*) I wish you would smile at customers more frequently. If your attitude isn't right, you'll never make a good sales associate.

ONE SUPERVISOR TO ANOTHER: (*job-related*) I can't help but overhear you use all those four-letter words. If you keep that up, you may lose the respect of your employees. Then they won't listen to you when you need something done out of the ordinary.

ONE SUPERVISOR TO ANOTHER: (*not job-related*) I can't help but overhear you use all those four-letter words. There's nothing worse than a foul-mouthed supervisor.

6. *Show that you care.* Human resource consultant Pamela Cole suggests that the word "carefrontation" be substituted for confrontation. She says, "You have to care enough to confront because it's easier not to confront and to avoid the problem. Caring enough to confront increases the likelihood that the situation will be resolved. When I do not confront a situation, I can be pretty much assured that it will go on the way it is or get worse."[6]

Communicating the fact that you care can sometimes be done by the sincerity in your voice and the concerned way you approach the difficult person. Using the words "care" and "concern" can be helpful. To illustrate, "The reason I'm bringing up this problem is that I *care* about our working relationship. And I'm *concerned* that things have been a little rough between us."

The Art of Criticizing Constructively

Confrontation and criticism are closely linked. Confrontation precedes the actual criticism, and both are part of the same process of trying to get other people to change their behavior. It is difficult to criticize productive people in a constructive manner. The challenge multiplies when you try to criticize counterproductive people. One of the problems in criticizing anybody in a job setting is that the person being criticized may have put considerable emotional energy into the job. The person therefore interprets the criticism as an attack on his or her ego.

A second problem is the sense of competitiveness that typically develops among co-workers. If you criticize a peer, your criticism may be interpreted as an attack on his or her work just so your work seems better in comparison. A copywriter in an advertising agency made this comment about the criticisms he was exchanging with a peer:

> Everytime I came up with an idea, Steve managed to find something wrong with it. Of course, we were both playing the same game—every time Steve made a suggestion I found a reason to downgrade and reject it. We were not only competing to see who could come up with the better idea, we were competing to see who could find the most flaws in the other fellow's ideas.[7]

Here are several suggestions for criticizing a difficult person in a constructive manner. Recognize, however, that these suggestions also apply to criticizing anybody on the job.[8] (Several may also be used when making criticisms in personal life.)

Criticized in Private. A primary principle of good human relations is to criticize in private. The counterproductive person will only become more defensive if you confront and criticize him or her in the presence of peers. It also may prove to be less threatening to criticize the person away from the work area. The company cafeteria, parking lot, or vending machine area may prove to be a reasonable place to confront and criticize.

Begin with Mild Criticism. Harsh criticism, however well-intended, hurts the criticized person's ego and triggers defensive behavior. It is therefore helpful to begin with mild criticism and strengthen it later if necessary. Harsh criticism is also a problem because it is difficult to retract.

Base the Criticism on Objective Facts. In criticizing anybody, it is important to base your criticism on objective facts, rather than on subjective perceptions. Much criticism is rejected because it is thought to be invalid. When you use facts to aid your case, you have a better chance of getting through to the counterproductive person. Assume that you are dealing with a superagreeable who has failed to supply you some information that you need to accomplish your job. A criticism based on subjective interpretation would be, "Your unwillingness to cooperate has messed things up for me." An objective—and potentially more effective—criticism would be, "Because I did not get the information you promised me, I was unable to finish my report for our boss."

Express Your Criticism in Terms of a Common Goal. As just implied, if your criticism points toward the accomplishment of a purpose that both of you are trying to achieve, it may get across to the difficult person. Use words that emphasize cooperation rather than competitiveness and blame. For example, "*We* can get the report done quickly if *you'll* firm up the statistical data while I edit the text," will be more effective than "Unless you get moving faster on the statistics I won't be able to finish the report on time."[9]

Avoid Playing Boss. Most employees resent a co-worker assuming the boss's role while criticizing them. Difficult people will resent it all the more because most of them are defensive. "Playing boss" means that you act as if you have formal authority over the other person, when in reality you are a peer or subordinate. One manifestation of playing boss would be to tell a co-worker, "If you don't get that program written for me by this afternoon, you'll have to work overtime to get it done."

When Criticizing Your Boss, Relate It to Your Work Performance. It takes extra tact to do a good job of criticizing your boss, particularly if he or she is a difficult person. An important guideline is to show how your boss's behavior, however well intended, is hampering your job performance. A case in point took place in a retail store chain.

> The loss-prevention managers in each store were supervised by a zone manager, who in many ways behaved in a counterproductive manner. One of his worse practices was to swear at loss-prevention managers (LPMs) when losses were above average at their store. One of the LPMs decided that she could no longer tolerate her boss's tirades. Confronting him after one of his verbal reprimands, she said calmly, "Mr. Gifford, when you swear and scream at me, it interferes with my ability to perform my job well. My records show that I make my biggest mistakes in counting inventory soon after you have screamed at me for something that is not even my fault." Mr. Gifford did temper his criticism in the future.

Interpreting the Games of Counterproductive People

Game:
A repeated series of exchanges between people that appears different on the surface from its true underlying motive.

A considerable amount of game playing takes place on the job. A **game** is a repeated series of exchanges between people that appears different on the surface from its true underlying motive. A game always has a hidden agenda or purpose. The game player acts in a way that is superficially plausible, but there is a concealed motivation.

With a little practice, you can become sensitive to games that a counterproductive person might be playing. Once you think that you have his or her game pegged, you can confront that person with the game. The game player might then stop the game and deal with you more honestly. Dozens of appealing names have been given to games that people play frequently. Following are five games often observed on the job.

Blemish

Blemish is a simple game to play and is often used by superiors to keep subordinates in line. All that is required is for the boss to find some small flaw in every assignment completed by subordinates. The game-playing boss stays one up with comments such as, "Smith, you did a great job on that report except for your conclusion. It just didn't seem to fit the body of the report."

A tactful rejoinder to this Blemish-playing boss might be, "I notice that you usually find one thing wrong with an otherwise acceptable job of mine. Is it your policy to always find at least one fault? Knowing the answer to this question would be very helpful to me in my work."

If It Weren't for That Other Person

A convenient way of avoiding responsibility for our errors is to find somebody else to blame. The person who habitually plays If It Weren't for That Other Person tries to con someone else into being sympathetic. A subordinate of yours might say to you, "I'm sorry to let you down by being one hour late for work. If it weren't for that preposterous rush hour traffic, I would have been here before the office even opened."

One way of stopping such a game player (and a counterproductive individual) in his or her tracks is to retort, "You've been traveling the same route as long as I've known you. Why don't you leave thirty minutes earlier? If you do arrive at the office early, you can read the paper and have a cup of coffee. Why blame the traffic for your lateness? Blame yourself."

The Setup

A very small minority of bosses like to see you fail. A technique they use is to set goals so unrealistically high for you that you are unlikely to reach them. Frustration and discouragement are the predictable results. Your boss can then criticize you both for not reaching your objectives and for having a "poor attitude." Here is a portion of a review session where The Setup is being played:

BOSS: I see that you only cut the cost of cleaning our guest rooms by 8 percent during the last six months. Your goal was to cut costs by 12 percent.

YOU: But without understaffing, it was impossible to cut costs by 12 percent. I think the housekeepers did an enormous job of improving their productivity. I made all the savings I could find without letting service suffer.

BOSS: Nevertheless, you failed to reach your objective. I therefore cannot recommend you for a good salary increase this year.

The best way around this type of game playing is to negotiate any unrealistic goals handed you by your boss. If you think the goal is unrealistically high, carefully explain your position.

Low-balling

Employees play their games too during a performance review. For instance, you might purposely set objectives at an unrealistically low level.

At the time of performance review, you can then "prove" what an outstanding performer you are.

Suppose that you are working as a collection agent for a loan company. You might set a goal of increasing your total amount of dollars collected by 10 percent during the next quarter. In the meantime, you are aware that one of your largest delinquent accounts is ready to settle. That account alone will increase your collections by 9 percent. With very little effort, you can exceed your objective.

Game playing during performance review is generally a destructive process. It is much better for you and your supervisor to be straightforward and honest about the performance review process.

Dr. Jekyll and Mr. (or Ms.) Hyde

The Dr. Jekyll and Mr. (or Ms.) Hyde game refers to managers who have a split personality. When dealing with superiors, customers, or clients, they are pleasant, engaging people—much like Dr. Jekyll. Yet when carrying out the role of a boss they become tyrannical—much like Hyde. Sufferers of this syndrome believe that their need to be liked by subordinates is inconsistent with satisfying their needs for control and self-esteem in their new role.[10] The Jekyll and Hyde manager therefore works extra hard at gaining control of subordinates, hoping to achieve organizational objectives and therefore self-esteem in the process.

Employees who deviate from Mr. or Ms. Hyde's expectations are publicly reprimanded. The basic strategy of these individuals is never to allow superiors or peers to see their Mr. or Ms. Hyde side. Consequently, superiors and peers tend not to believe a subordinate who complains that this manager is being tyrannical.

It is difficult for a subordinate to deal with a Jekyll and Hyde boss because he or she can be vindictive. However, if several group members agree to bring the topic up in a group meetings, the boss might acquire some insight into his or her problem. As a last resort, several group members can agree to discuss the tyrannical behavior with Hyde's boss. Similarly, they might write a letter to the boss explaining the gravity of the problem.

Being Sympathetic toward the Personality Quirks of Co-workers

Personality quirk:
A persistent peculiarity of behavior that annoys or irritates other people.

Both on and off the job, many people have personality quirks that make them difficult to deal with. A **personality quirk** is a persistent peculiarity of behavior that annoys or irritates other people. The manager is usually in the best position to help these people control their quirks so that job performance does not suffer. Often a human resources specialist will assist the manager in dealing with quirks.

Your best defense as a co-worker is to show sympathy for employees with these quirks without submitting to all their demands. Be understanding even if you do not find all their behavior acceptable. By showing sympathy, the co-worker with the quirk may shift to more tolerable behavior. Here are several of the more frequently observed personality quirks.[11]

The Person Who Has a Strong Need Always to Be Correct. Employees with this quirk set up situations so that people who disagree with them are made to look naive or foolish. For example, "All well-educated and intelligent people believe as I do that this is the way we should go on this project. If anybody disagrees, please speak up now." (You can sympathize in this manner: "I recognize, Jennifer, that you research everything before reaching an opinion, and that you are usually right. Nevertheless, I want to point out another perspective on this problem.")

The Person Who Has a Strong Need for Attention, Whether the Attention Be Positive or Negative. Attention seekers may shout louder than others, play the role of the office clown, or tell co-workers all their woes. (You can sympathize in this manner: "We all know, Gus, that you like to be in the limelight. You do deserve our attention, but now it is Amy's turn to speak.")

The Person Who Resents Control, Direction, or Advice from Others. Employees with this quirk are so oversensitive to being controlled that they misinterpret hints as suggestions and orders as direct challenges to their intelligence and self-worth. (You might express sympathy—yet still get through—to a co-worker with this quirk by a statement such as this: "Carlos, I know you like to be your own person. I admire you for it, but I have a teeny suggestion that could strengthen the graphics you just put together.")

The Person Who Views Everything Management Does as Negative and Also Questions Every Action in an Attempt to Uncover the True Reason behind It. Employees with this quirk create doubts in other workers similar to the ones they exhibit, thus contributing to morale problems.[12] (You can sympathize with cynics and perhaps help them achieve insight into their behavior with a comment such as this: "I appreciate your analytical attitude Faye, but did you ever think that management does sometimes do something kind or generous? Is management really always the villain?")

The Jealous Co-worker Who Wants What You Have and Has Feelings of Ill Will toward You. Jealousy can surface when several workers are competing for a promotion, bonus, or recognition from higher ups. Because of his or her emotional turmoil, the jealous worker may attempt to discredit you.[13] If you spot a jealous co-worker, express sympathy toward his or her wanting what you have. Explain that yours is a fair company and good deeds will eventually be rewarded. Also mention that discrediting a co-worker hurts the accuser's reputation.

Passive–aggressive:
A person who
expresses anger and
hostility by not
performing expected
tasks.

The Passive–Aggressive Co-Worker Who Becomes Sulky, Irritable, or Forgetful When Asked to Do Something He or She Does Not Want To Do. A **passive–aggressive** personality expresses anger and hostility by not performing expected tasks.[14] Explain to the sulking person that you realize the task at hand is not something he or she relishes; nevertheless, the project is a joint one that requires the effort of two people.

Handling Difficult Customers

In an era when customer satisfaction is so highly valued, customers are likely to be vocal in their demands. Interviews conducted with 93 employees revealed that interactions with customers can be a major stressor. Stressful events frequently cited were customers losing control, using profanity, badgering employees, harassing employees, and lying. The employees interviewed said that these negative interactions with customers adversely affected the quality of their work environment. Part of the problem is that the sales associate often feels helpless when placed in conflict with a customer.[15] The associate is told "the customer is always right." Furthermore, the store manager usually sides with the customer in a dispute with the sales associate.

When faced with an angry customer or one who is difficult in another way, use one or more of the following techniques, as recommended by Donna Deeprose:[16]

1. *Acknowledge the customer's point of view.* Make statements such as "I understand," "I agree," and "I'm sorry." Assume, for example, that a customer says, "The bank made a $1,000 error in its favor. I want this fixed right away." You might respond, "I understand how difficult this must be for you. Let's work on the problem right away."

2. *Avoid placing blame.* Suggesting that the customer is responsible for the problem intensifies the conflict. With the overdrawn customer, refrain from saying, "People who keep careful checkbooks never have your problem."

3. *Use six magic words to defuse anger:* I understand [that this is a problem]; I agree [that it needs to be solved]; I'm sorry [that this happened to you].

In dealing with a variety of customer personalities, keep in mind also that any of the other techniques in this chapter might apply.

Three Multipurpose Approaches To a Variety of Personalities

Overcoming problems with a variety of personalities always involves selecting a plausible tactic and then hoping for the best. If the first attempt does not work, use a backup tactic. Three multipurpose tactics are described next that will improve your human relations effectiveness with both difficult people and those with more pleasant dispositions. The tactics involve the use of tact and diplomacy, humor, and recognition and affection.

Use Tact and Diplomacy in Dealing with Annoying Behavior

Co-workers who irritate you rarely do annoying things on purpose. Tactful actions on your part can sometimes take care of these annoyances without having to confront the problem. Close your door, for example, if noisy co-workers are gathered outside. When subtlety does not work, it may be necessary to proceed to the confrontation tactics described earlier. Tact and diplomacy can also be incorporated into confrontation. In addition to confronting the person, you might also point out a strength of the individual. For example, "I realize you are creative and filled with good ideas. However, I wish you would give me an opportunity to express my opinion."

Use Humor in Dealing with Difficult People

Nonhostile humor can often be used to help a difficult person understand how his or her behavior is blocking others.[17] Also, the humor will help you to defuse conflict between you and that person. The humor should point to the person's unacceptable behavior, yet not belittle him or her. Assume that you and a co-worker are working jointly on a report. Whenever you turn over a portion of your work for her to review, she finds some fault. You suspect she is playing Blemish. An example of nonhostile humor that might change her behavior here is:

> Judy, I know that you believe in zero defects and doing things right the first time. But aren't you worried about my mental health? I've read that striving for absolute perfection can create loads of stress.

Your humor may help Judy realize that she is placing unrealistic standards on her review of your work. By pointing to your own weaknesses, you are being self-effacing and thus drawing criticism away from her. In addition, self-effacement is a proven humor tactic.

Give Recognition and Affection

Counterproductive or difficult people, like misbehaving children, are sometimes crying out for attention. By giving them recognition and affection, their counterproductive behavior will *sometimes* cease. If their negative behavior is a product of a deeper-rooted problem, recognition and affection alone will not work. Other actions will need to be taken. The most direct strategy is to give the misbehaving individual attention and affection. If the negative behavior stops, you have found the proper antidote. The successful resolution of such a problem took place in a photo studio:

> Rich, one of the commercial photographers, had an annoying habit of interrupting the conversation of other people during staff meetings or with customers. In one instance during negotiations with an important customer, Rich blurted out, "I'm the local expert on nature photographs. If you want

anything done along those lines, your best bet would be for me to shoot the job."

Mandy, Rich's boss, then tried spending a few minutes each week telling Rich how great a photographer he was and how much the studio needed him (not a lie because Rich was talented and valuable). In addition, Mandy arranged for Rich to have some of his work put on display at a local photo show.

Rich changed his behavior toward that of a more subdued and contented individual. In the words of one of his colleagues, "I can't understand what happened to Rich. He's become much easier to live with."

Brain Sturcture and Unusual Job Behavior

Most counterproductive job behavior is attributable to a combination of personality factors and situational pressures. For example, if an employee has high negative affectivity, he or she will be hostile toward others during a peak workload. It has been speculated that mood swings among people may also be related to the brain structure. In Chapter 7 we described how the two brain halves are related to differences in intellectual functioning. It is also possible that the brain hemispheres are specialized for different emotional experiences.[18]

Depression and Brain Waves. An example of research attempting to link emotional experiences with brain hemispheres was conducted with college students. The students were given a test measuring emotional depression, and their brain waves were measured by EEGs. The more depressed students had more electrical activity in the brain's right frontal region, suggesting that the right hemisphere plays a special role in depressed feelings.

Brain Injury and Emotional Brakes. Another tie-in may exist between the status of the brain and negative emotions. A neuropsychologist has speculated that, under normal circumstances, mood fluctuations are consistent with what is happening in our lives. However, anything that jars the neural system, such as brain injury or a severe emotional loss, is likely to release negative emotions. According to this theory, the depressed person lacks the "brakes" to stop the flood of negative emotion. The counterproductive behavior of a worker could then in some instances be attributed to a brain injury caused by physical or emotional trauma.

The Role of Both Hemispheres. Another theory of how the brain is linked to emotion suggests that either hemisphere can be involved in pleasant or unpleasant emotions. Yet each hemisphere has its special linkages. The left hemisphere is involved in emotional states characterized by alert expectation—positive ones such as happy anticipation and negative ones such as anxious worry. In contrast, the right hemisphere is involved with more reflexive emotional states—positive ones such as relaxed awareness and negative ones such as depression.

Assume that some moodiness among workers can be traced to differences in brain structure. Dealing with their behavior becomes more difficult but not impossible. Behavior that is related to brain structure can still be modified or controlled, just as people who are left brain dominant can learn to become more creative.

BACK TO THE JOB TASKS

Assume that you are faced with the problem of criticizing a co-worker or boss. Review the suggestions for confrontation and constructive criticism, and follow the guidelines. Similarly, if you have to deal with a difficult customer, follow the suggestions outlined for dealing with difficult customers. Before using the tactics, rehearse them first using a tape recorder or camcorder.

Summary of Key Points

❑ Counterproductive or difficult people are found in most places of work and also include customers. Such people include those who are uncooperative, touchy, defensive, hostile, unfriendly, and substandard performers. The difficult employee is not necessarily of low intelligence or ability.

❑ A key principle for dealing with a variety of personalities is to take what they do professionally, not personally. This is true because for a difficult person you may just represent an obstacle or a steppingstone for them to get what they want.

❑ A major aspect of dealing with counterproductive people is to confront them with the job-related consequences of their behavior. Confrontation is difficult for most people because it makes them feel uncomfortable. Suggestions for effective confrontation include these: (1) Attempt to relax during the session; (2) quickly get to the core topic; (3) avoid being apologetic or defensive; (4) be nonhostile in your confrontation; (5) confront job-related behavior, not personal traits, characteristics, and motives; and (6) show that you care.

❑ Criticism and confrontation are both part of the same process of trying to get other people to change their behavior. Criticizing difficult people is especially difficult because they are usually defensive. Suggestions for constructive criticism include (1) be sensitive to the setting; (2) begin with mild criticism; (3) base the criticism on objective facts; (4) express criticism in terms of a common goal; (5) avoid playing boss; and (6) when criticizing your boss, show how the behavior is interfering with your work performance.

❑ Another approach to dealing with counterproductive people is to interpret their games. A game is a repeated series of transactions between people with a concealed motive. The five described here are Blemish (finding flaws in another's work); If It Weren't for That Other Person (blaming somebody else); The Setup (setting somebody else up to fail); Low-balling (underpredicting your performance in order to look good when you perform well); and Dr. Jekyll and Mr. (or Ms.) Hyde (a person who is polite to superiors and co-workers but tyrannical as a boss).

❑ Being sympathetic toward the personality quirks of co-workers without submitting to all their demands is another approach to dealing with a variety of personalities. A personality quirk is a persistent peculiarity of behavior that annoys or irritates others, such as resenting control, direction, or advice.

❑ Three tactics are suggested here for dealing with difficult customers: (1) Acknowledge the customer's point of view. (2) Avoid placing blame on the customer. (3) Say, "I understand," "I agree," and "I'm sorry."

❑ A multipurpose approach to dealing with difficult people and improving your human relations skills in general is to use tact and diplomacy, humor, and recognition and affection.

❑ Most counterproductive behavior is attributable to a combination of personality factors and situational pressures. However, mood swings and other emotional states might also be related to brain structure. Among these speculative findings are the following: (1) The right hemisphere of the brain is linked to depressed feelings. (2) When the brain is physically or psychologically traumatized, it loses its capacity to brake negative emotions. (3) The left hemisphere is involved with emotional states of alert expectation, and the right hemisphere with more reflexive emotional states.

GUIDELINES FOR PERSONAL EFFECTIVENESS

Corporate training director Donald H. Weiss advises that after you identify the problem with a difficult person, engage the person in a discussion that follows these four steps:

First, set the other person at ease by talking in private. State the meeting's purpose in nonthreatening terms, and show that you want to work with the person on the problem by using "we" rather than "you" statements.

Second, exchange viewpoints by first listening to the other person's proposed solution to the problem.

Third, if you don't agree, state your opinion concisely and clearly. Attempt to resolve the disagreement by exchanging viewpoints again.

Fourth, design an action plan for ending the difficulty. Set deadlines and dates for reviewing progress in overcoming the difficulty the person has created for you.[19]

Discussion Questions and Activities

1. Identify three personality traits described in previous chapters that could predispose an employee toward being a difficult person.

2. Why shouldn't as many counterproductive people as possible be fired?

3. Should difficult employees still be held responsible for their actions, even if their problem might be related to a brain condition?

4. How does the idea of jobs with built-in conflict relate to the suggestion of "learn to take problems professionally, not personally"?

5. Some managers take a team member out for lunch when they want to confront that person. What do you think are the advantages and disadvantages of this practice?

6. Suppose a co-worker is rude toward you. How can you relate this rudeness to objective facts, rather than to a subjective interpretation?

7. Suppose a student annoys classmates by monopolizing class discussion. What common goal might you bring to that student's attention?

8. How might a student play Low-ball with an instructor?

9. What is the purpose of showing sympathy toward a co-worker with a personality quirk?

10. Obtain the opinion of an experienced worker about what he or she perceives to be the most difficult type of people in the workplace. Relate this perception to the categories of difficult people described in this chapter.

A BUSINESS PSYCHOLOGY PROBLEM

The Brilliant But Impossible Proposal Writer

Rodney Webb has worked for several years as a research proposal writer for a firm in Alexandria, Virginia. The firm's primary business is to conduct research for governmental agencies, private foundations, and business corporations. Webb recently was promoted to senior proposal writer because of his outstanding success rate in writing proposals that result in actual contracts for the firm.

Despite his promotion, several managers in the firm and most of his co-workers have expressed objections to Webb's work habits. Two of the managers think Webb should be terminated despite his high productivity. Charlotte Mendez, vice-president of government contracts, expresses it this way:

"Rodney Webb has gone beyond the edge of what I think we should have to put up with. He sets a poor example for the rest of the workers. Rodney strolls into work whenever he pleases. Once on the job, he begins reading the newspaper or taking care of personal phone calls. He rarely shows up for staff meetings, and his clothing is abominable. His sense of humor leaves me flat. He had the nerve to ask the president in a group meeting whether he thought our firm had any socially redeeming value.

"Despite our reservations that he might behave inappropriately, we once invited him to a client presentation. Our reservations proved to be correct. During the presentation he reached into his attaché case, took out a beanie with a propeller attached, and wore the thing. Do you see what I mean about Rodney having gone over the edge?"

Alan Penfield, a senior research analyst with the firm, has this to say about Webb: "I don't know what hold Rodney has over management. But he sure has alienated the rest of us. We don't think he puts in a fair day's work. He snubs the rest of us, acting as if we were peons and he's the king. The guy is bad for morale."

Barbara Goldman, the president, has this to say about Webb: "I can understand that Rodney is not the most popular employee in our firm. But from my perspective he's a bargain. There are very few really good proposal writers in this business. Rodney Webb is the best I've ever seen. Sure he behaves immaturely most of the time and isn't always around the office. What most other workers don't understand is that Rodney puts in a lot of time at night and on weekends grinding out the proposals. When he's preparing a proposal, he devotes his total energy to the task."

"I see no reason to upset Rodney," concluded Goldman. "He gives us a tenfold return on his compensation."

1. What should those other workers who are disturbed by Rodney's behavior do?
2. Is Goldman being shortsighted in her analysis of Webb?
3. Might Webb be damaging his own career?
4. What is Webb's problem? Or does he have one?

The Borrowed Dresses

Michelle Platt considered herself fortunate to have obtained a job as assistant manager at Kathy's, an upscale dress store in downtown Chicago. Kathy's offers an expensive line of dresses for evening wear and the office. Some of the dresses have price tags as high as $2,100. The typical age range of customers is from the late thirties to late fifties.

Although Michelle held the title of assistant manager, she spent about one-half of her time dealing directly with customers. On Monday of her sixth week on the job, Kathy sold an evening dress for $2,000 to an attorney. The attorney said she was so pleased to find exactly what she was looking for and paid for the dress with a personal check. Michelle followed strictly the store procedures for check approval and then wrapped the dress for the customer.

One week later the attorney returned to the store and asked to exchange the dress. The customer said, "Unfortunately, this dress does not fit me right. It tugs in the waist and rises in the back. This problem was not apparent when I tried the dress on in the store."

Michelle recalled vividly that the dress fit the customer beautifully. With a skeptical look on her face, she said to the customer, "Perhaps there is another dress you would like in exchange." The customer replied, "Most definitely yes. I see another model here for only fifty dollars more. I will take this one and pay your the difference."

Michelle had the vague feeling that the woman was ripping off the store, but obliged the customer and thanked her for the purchase.

Next Monday morning the customer returned. She told Michelle, "I'm sorry, but this dress is quite uncomfortable. It's also unflattering to my figure. I am returning this dress, and I would like you to give me a check now, or mail me one within ten days."

"Wait a minute," said Michelle. "My gut reaction is that you bought these dresses just to wear them once and get your money back. What you've done is borrow them for free. I don't see why we should accept the dress back. Look, it's obviously wrinkled."

The customer said angrily, "Young lady, I don't like your attitude. Furthermore, do you realize that I'm an attorney? I'll sue you for defamation of character, and I'll sue the store for refusing to accept back merchandise."

"I'm not going to stand here and let you rip off the store. Let me talk to my manager before I do any thing else. Will you please wait for fifteen minutes? The store manager should be back by then."

The customer replied, "Who do you think you are talking to? If I don't have my check by this afternoon, you'll have no job."

1. What is your opinion of how Michelle handled the customer?
2. In this situation, is the customer right?
3. If you were Michelle's manager, how would you handle this situation?

The Irate Customer

The case just presented serves as the necessary background information and setting for this role play. The information about handling difficult customers should be consulted before assuming the following roles. The goal in these role plays is to resolve the problem and retain customer goodwill. One person plays Michelle when the customer returns with the second dress, asking for a return. Another person plays the attorney, who insists on the return.

Another role play assumes that Michelle and the customer have not come to an agreement. We then add a third person, the store manager, who gets together with Michelle and the customer.

References

1. A representative scheme is presented in MURIEL SOLOMON, *Working with Difficult People*. (Englewood Cliffs, NJ: Prentice Hall, 1991).
2. Cited in "Help! I'm Surrounded by Difficult People," *Working Smart,* March 25, 1991, p. 2.
3. DRU SCOTT, *Customer Satisfaction: The Other Half of Your Job* (Los Altos, CA: Crisp Publications, 1991), p. 16.
4. "Face-to-Face," *Personal Report for the Executive,* February 15, 1988, p. 4.
5. GARY G. WHITNEY, "When the News Is Bad: Leveling with Employees," *Personnel,* January–February 1983, pp. 37–45.
6. Quoted in PRISCILLA PETTY, "Shortest Route to Good Communication Is Often a Straight Question," Gannett News Service, October 18, 1983.
7. HENDRIE WEISINGER AND NORMA M. LOBSENZ, *Nobody's Perfect: How to Give Criticism and Get Results* (New York: Warner Books, 1981), p. 204.
8. WEISINGER AND LOBSENZ, *Nobody's Perfect,* pp. 198–230.
9. WEISINGER AND LOBSENZ, *Nobody's Perfect,* p. 214.
10. ERIC FLAMHOLTZ, "The Dr. Jekyll and Mr. Hyde Game Managers Play," *Management Solutions,* November 1987, pp. 4–9.
11. The first three quirks are from MICHAEL E. CAVANAGH, "Personalities at Work," *Personnel Journal,* March 1985, pp. 55–64.
12. SHANE R. PREMAUX AND R. WAYNE MONDY, "Problem Employees: The Cynic," *Management Solutions,* October 1986, pp. 14–16.
13. TERESA BRADY, "When a Jealous Co-worker Is Giving You a Hard Time," *Supervisory Management,* June 1991, p. 5.
14. JEFFREY C. CONNOR, "Managing Passive–Aggressive People," *HRMagazine,* November 1991, p. 76.
15. JAMES D. BRODZINSKI, ROBERT P. SCHERER, AND KAREN A. GOYER, "Workplace Stress: A Study of Internal and External Pressures Placed on Employees," *Personnel Administrator,* July 1989, pp. 77–78.
16. DONNA DEEPROSE, "Helping Employees Handle Difficult Customers," *Supervisory Management,* September 1991, p. 6. Point three is quoted from DEEPROSE, p. 6.
17. KAYE LORAINE, "Dealing with the Difficult Personality," *Supervision,* April 1989, pp. 6–8.
18. This discussion is based on LAURENCE MILLER, "The Emotional Brain," *Psychology Today,* February 1988, pp. 34–42.
19. DONALD H. WEISS, "How to Deal with Unpleasant People Problems," *Supervisory Management,* March 1992, pp. 1–2.

Suggested Reading

BERNE, ERIC. *Games People Play.* New York: Grove Press, 1964.

BERNSTEIN, ALBERT J., AND CRAFT ROZEN, SYDNEY. *Dinosaur Brains: Dealing with All Those Impossible People at Work.* New York: Wiley, 1989.

BING, STANLEY. *Crazy Bosses: Spotting Them, Serving Them, Surviving Them.* New York: William Morrow, 1992.

COX, CHARLES E. "18 Ways to Improve Customer Service." *HRMagazine,* March 1992, pp. 69–72.

DUBRIN, ANDREW J. *Your Own Worst Enemy: How to Prevent Career Self-sabotage.* New York: AMACOM, 1992.

FRIED, N. ELIZABETH. *Outrageous Conduct: Bizarre Behavior at Work.* Dublin, Ohio: Intermediaries Press, 1990.

———. "Bizarre Behavior at Work." *HRMagazine,* June 1991, pp. 86–91.

KLAREICH, SAMUEL H. *It Can't Happen to Me: How to Overcome 99 of Life's Most Distressing Problems.* New York: Brunner/Mazel, 1992.

KRUPAR, KAREN R. "Jerks at Work." *Personnel Journal,* June 1988, pp. 68–75.

part four   *Dealing with Small Groups*

Part four of the book is about a major segment of life on the job, dealing with small groups. Chapter 13 provides useful information for understanding how groups operate, along with details about group decision making. Chapter 14 describes the nature of leadership and influence, along with the traits and behaviors you need to lead others effectively. Chapter 15 describes the universal topic of how to improve communication with others in the workplace.

Chapter 13

WORKING EFFECTIVELY WITHIN A GROUP

Learning Objectives

After reading and studying this chapter and doing the exercises, you should be able to

1. Explain the difference between a formal and an informal group.
2. Understand how decisions are made by a group.
3. Conduct a brainstorming session about a problem facing you.
4. Explain the nominal group technique and the problem-solving method used by quality-improvement teams.
5. Conduct yourself more effectively in a meeting.
6. Summarize some of the advantages and disadvantages of group effort, including group decision making.

JOB TASKS RELATED TO THIS CHAPTER

Most employers emphasize group problem solving for workers at all levels. It is therefore likely that you are currently engaging in group problem solving or will be in the future. For example, you might be asked to join forces with co-workers in making suggestions for improving quality or decreasing costs. This chapter offers you tools to accomplish these tasks.

Groups are vital to the understanding of business psychology because they are the building blocks of the larger organization. The department you are assigned to, the people you share a rest break with, and the special meeting you are asked to attend are among the many groups found within a firm. Because so much of organizational life involves group effort, much of your time on the job will be spent working with a small group of people. Another important reason for studying groups is that most of the achievements of modern organizations are really the product of team effort, rather than the accomplishments of individual superstars.[1]

If you understand the nature of work groups, you will be better able to capitalize on the benefits of belonging to a group. Also, you will be better able to avoid some of the problems a group might create for you.

Group:
A collection of individuals who regularly interact with each other, who are psychologically aware of each other, and who perceive themselves to be a group.

A **group** is a collection of people who interact with each other, are aware of each other, are working toward some common purpose, and perceive themselves to be a group. Two state troopers seated in a patrol car, watching for speeders and accidents, would thus be a group. So would the head of a company copy center and her staff. In contrast, 12 people in an airport waiting for the same plane would not be a group in the technical sense. Although they might talk to each other, their interaction would not be on a planned or recurring basis. Nor would they be engaged in collective effort, a fundamental justification for forming a group.

An important consideration for understanding groups is that people often behave and perform differently as a group member than they would individually. A group of people may laugh at a comment that its members individually would not find humorous. A group can accomplish a task, such as building a house, that could not be accomplished by combining the individual contributions of its members. And, unfortunately, a group of people will sometimes commit acts of vandalism and physical violence that the individual members would never do.

Aspects of working effectively within a group are studied at various places in this text. For example, Chapter 12 included a description of how to be an effective team player, and Chapter 14 will include a description of how leaders develop teamwork. In this chapter we discuss the nature of work groups in more detail and emphasize group decision making. Our perspective is from the viewpoint of the group member, but the same information is useful to group leaders.

Formal versus Informal Groups

Different schemes have been developed to classify the many types of groups found in work organizations. One particularly useful distinction is that drawn between formal and informal groups. Unless you understand the difference in functioning between formal and informal groups, you will have a difficult time adjusting to almost any place of work.

Formal Groups

Formal group: A collection of people deliberately formed by the organization to accomplish specific tasks and achieve objectives.

A **formal group** is one deliberately formed by the organization to accomplish specific tasks and achieve objectives. The most common type of formal group is a work unit or department such as accounting, quality control, or young women's apparel. Formal groups can also be committees or task forces (a special-purpose group with a time limit).

Formal groups are frequently designated by the organization chart. At other times they are indicated on the bulletin board or through office memos. For example, "The undernamed people are hereby assigned to the safety committee." Several different types of formal groups are defined in Figure 13-1. The work unit meeting (also referred to as a staff meeting or department meeting) deserves special attention because of its increasing popularity. Formal, regularly scheduled meetings of higher-ranking managers have been common for years. Small group meetings of a work unit, conducted by the unit manager, are a more recent development. The general purpose of these meetings is to keep employees informed and to improve their productivity and morale. Specific agenda items include work performance, employee complaints, progress reports, new work procedures, and cost-reduction ideas.[2]

FIGURE 13–1.

A Sampling of Formal Work Groups

Because organizations are composed of work groups, many types of work groups can be found in an organization. Quite often an employee belongs to both a permanent work group (such as a department) and a temporary work group (such as a labor-management participation team). The following is a sampling of six important types of formal work groups.

Department. A basic unit within the firm that carries out a specific task over an indefinite period of time. For example, it is the job of the maintenance department to keep company equipment running smoothly and to keep the building and grounds in good shape.

Committee. A group of people from different parts of the organization who are asked to study a particular problem and then make recommendations to management. Standing committees are permanent, while ad hoc committees are temporary groups set up to study a nonrecurring problem.

Work unit (or staff meeting). A meeting composed of a department head and key department members (the staff). Its purposes include solving a particular problem and communicating information from the manager to the staff members, or in the opposite direction.

Project team. A group of people called together by the firm to accomplish a particular purpose or mission (such as building a space station or launching a new product). It involves a temporary group of specialists from diverse disciplines working together under the same project leader.

Quality circles. Teams of workers, including supervisors and employees, who meet regularly to solve production and quality problems and sometimes to think of new ways to improve productivity. QCs are a form of participative management developed and popularized by Japanese industry, but originated by an American quality-control expert.

Labor–management teams. Groups composed of management and labor (usually union members) who jointly try to solve production and morale problems. They represent a high level of cooperation between management and labor and are based on a belief in group decision making and employee participation.

Informal Groups

An organization cannot be understood by studying its formal groups alone. A large number of groups evolve naturally in an organization to take care of the desire for friendship and companionship. Such entities are referred to as **informal groups.** Although these groups are often thought of in relation to production and clerical workers, informal groups can be formed at any level in the organization. Here are three examples of informal groups:

Informal group:
A natural grouping of people in a work situation that evolves to take care of people's desires for friendship and companionship.

1. Five assistants from the marketing department meet once a month for lunch to discuss mutual concerns and to seek relief from the tedious aspects of their job.
2. Four computer operators form a jogging club that meets three days per week at lunch time to run two miles.
3. Three managers from different parts of the company commute to work together every business day when they are all in town. They often discuss current events and the stock market, but they also discuss company business while commuting to work.

As illustrations 1 and 3 suggest, informal groups are often work related. One function of the informal organization is to fill in the gaps left by the formal organization. Few organizations have a job description written for the "coffee pot tender," yet such a person arises on a rotating basis in many offices. Similarly, when somebody in your department is absent for legitimate reasons, you might take care of his or her emergency work, even though it is not a formal part of your job. Jill, an advertising copywriter, describes an apt example of the potential contribution of an informal group:

> I work in a very creative "shop." We are paid to be creative idea people. We don't dare bring an idea forward to one of the agency heads unless it's a good one. Before submitting an idea to management, we try it out on each other. We use the simple code of "thumbs up" or "thumbs down" to give candid feedback to each other on creative ideas.
>
> Once I was doing work for an Australian Trade Association. I was supposed to come up with a slogan that would help promote Australian merchandise in the United States and Canada. I went to three of my colleagues with the slogan, "Why not bring a little kangaroo spirit into your life?" I received three down-turned thumbs. I came back with "Up from Australia." That received three thumbs up from my colleagues and an accolade from my boss. Best of all, the client was sold on the idea.

Group Decision Making and Problem Solving

Most big decisions in organizations are made by groups, rather than individuals. Even if a group of people does not sit together to thrash out a decision, several people provide their input to any major decision. In general, decision making by groups has proved superior to individual decision making.[3] Yet this generalization is not overwhelmingly true. Many talented and imaginative individuals do not require group discussion to make an effective decision.

Our description of group decision and problem solving is divided into five parts: (1) group decision-making styles, (2) general problem-solving groups, (3) brainstorming, (4) the nominal group technique, and (5) quality-improvement teams.

Group Decision-making Styles

The term *group decision making* refers to the fact that the group plays a role in making the decision. The opposite would be individual decision making in which the group leader makes a decision without consulting anybody. Group decision making itself takes place in different degrees. One extreme is *consultative* in which the group leader consults with members before making a decision. The other extreme is *democratic* decision making in which the problem at hand is turned over to the group, and they are delegated the authority to arrive at a decision themselves.

Midway between the two is *consensus decision making* in which the manager shares the problem with group members. Together they generate and evaluate alternatives and attempt to reach agreement on a solution. Consensus is achieved when every member can say, "I have had an opportunity to express my views fully, and they have been thoughtfully considered by the group. Even though this solution is not the one I believe is optimal, it is acceptable and I will support it. I endorse the validity of the process we have undertaken."[4]

The balance of our discussion of group decision making involves a description of brainstorming and the nominal group technique. A description of the advantages and disadvantages of group decision making are included in a discussion of the pros and cons of group effort that appears toward the end of the chapter.

General Problem-solving Groups

When a group of workers at any level gathers to solve a problem, they typically hold a discussion, rather than rely on a formal method of group decision making. These general problem-solving groups are likely to produce the best results when they follow the decision-making steps outlined in Chapter 7. Equally important, the group members should follow the suggestions for conducting themselves in a meeting, described later in this chapter. Table 13-1 describes recommended steps for conducting group decision making; these are similar to the decision-making steps outlined in Figure 7-1.

Brainstorming

One of the best methods of understanding how a group can contribute to problem solving is to observe group **brainstorming.** This

Brainstorming:
A conference technique of solving specific problems, amassing information, and stimulating creative thinking. The basic technique is to encourage unrestrained and spontaneous participation by group members.

TABLE 13–1. *STEPS FOR EFFECTIVE GROUP DECISION MAKING* _____

1. *Identify the problem.* Describe specifically what the problem is and how it manifests itself.
2. *Clarify the problem.* If group members do not perceive the problem the same way, they will offer divergent solutions to their own individual perceptions of the problem.
3. *Analyze the cause.* To convert "what is" into "what we want," the group must understand the causes of the specific problems and find ways to overcome those causes.
4. *Search for alternative solutions.* Remember that multiple alternative solutions can be found to most problems.
5. *Select alternatives.* Identify the criteria that solutions must meet; then discuss the pros and cons of the proposed alternatives. No solution should be laughed at or scorned.
6. *Plan for implementation.* Decide what actions are necessary to carry out the chosen solution to the problem.
7. *Clarify the contract.* The contract is a restatement of what group members have agreed to do and deadlines for accomplishment.
8. *Develop an action plan.* Specify who does what and when to carry out the contract.
9. *Provide for evaluation and accountability.* After the plan is implemented, reconvene to discuss progress and to hold people accountable for results that have not been achieved.

Source: Derived from Andrew E. Schwartz and Joy Levin, "Better Group Decision Making," *Supervisory Management,* June 1990, p. 4.

method has become a standard way of generating multiple alternatives for solving a problem. (In Chapter 7 we described *brainwriting,* which is *brainstorming* by yourself.)

Brainstorm:
A clever idea.

The term **brainstorm** has become synonymous with a clever idea. It really means to "storm the brain" in order to search for alternatives. Brainstorming is best suited to finding lists of alternatives to problems. Later, the technical details of how to achieve and implement these alternatives can be worked out. Brainstorming was developed for use in creating advertising campaigns.[5] It is now put to such diverse uses as thinking of new products, making recommendations for new employee benefits, finding ways of raising money for a cause, and improving software. Brainstorming is not well suited to arriving at complex solutions to problems or working out the details of a plan (for example, how to arrange the equipment in an office).

Rules for Brainstorming. To conduct an effective brainstorming session, keep in mind these straightforward rules:

1. Group size should be about five to seven people. Too few people and not enough suggestions are generated. If too many people participate, the session becomes uncontrolled.

2. No criticism allowed. All suggestions should be welcome, and it is particularly important not to use derisive laughter. As the old saying goes, "They laughed at Thomas Edison."

3. Freewheeling is encouraged. The more outlandish the idea, the better. It's always easier to tame down an idea than to think it up.

4. Quantity and variety are very important. The greater the number of ideas put forth, the greater the likelihood of a breakthrough idea.

5. Combinations and improvements are encouraged. Building on the ideas of others, including combining them, is very productive. "Hitchhiking" is an essential part of brainstorming.

6. Notes must be taken during the sessions either manually or with an electronic recording device. One person serves as a recording secretary.

7. The alternatives generated during the first part of the session should later be edited for duplication and refinement. At some point the best ideas can be set aside for possible implementation.

8. Do not overstructure by following any of the preceding seven rules too rigidly. Brainstorming is a spontaneous small-group process.

Electronic brainstorming:
A problem-solving method in which group members simultaneously enter their suggestions into a computer, and the ideas are distributed to the screens of other group members.

A recent development in brainstorming is **electronic brainstorming.** Using this method, group members simultaneously enter their suggestions into a computer, and the ideas are distributed to the screens of other group members. Although the group members do not talk to each other, they are still able to build on each other's ideas and combine ideas. Electronic brainstorming is much like the nominal group technique, to be described shortly. An experiment with electronic brainstorming indicated that, with large groups, the method produces more useful ideas than does verbal (the usual type) of brainstorming.[6]

Brainstorming Applied to Quality Improvement. Brainstorming is now used extensively to help to improve the quality of products and services. For example, Pacific Bell includes a chapter on brainstorming in its quality handbook for employees. The purpose of using brainstorming and other quality-improvement techniques is to make employees aware of how things need to be different in order to satisfy customers.[7]

At another telephone company, members of top management and marketing personnel were assigned to a brainstorming group. The agenda was to suggest new ways for improving the quality of service to customers. Improving the quality of service has become important to telephone companies because competition exists for some services, such as long distance. Among the many suggestions derived by the group was to improve the quality of service by expanding the capability of the telephone. A specific product stemming from this brainstorm was Unitel. This service enables customers to use the telephone to send voice and data over one line, using a modem.

The Nominal Group Technique

At times a leader is faced with a major problem that would benefit from the input of group members. Because of the magnitude of the problem, it would be helpful to know what each member thought of the others' positions on the problem. Brainstorming is not advisable because the problem is still in the exploration phase and requires more than a list of alternative solutions. A problem-solving technique developed to fit this situation is the **nominal group technique (NGT).** It calls people together in a structured meeting with limited interaction. The group is called "nominal" because people present their ideas initially without interacting with each other, as they would in a "real" group. George P. Huber provides a general description that will help you gain insight into the process.[8]

Nominal group technique (NGT): A group problem-solving method that calls people together in a structured meeting with limited interaction.

> Imagine a meeting room in which seven to ten individuals are sitting around a table in full view of each other. At the beginning of the meeting they are not speaking to one another. Instead, each individual is writing ideas on their pads of paper. At the end of five to ten minutes, a structured sharing of ideas takes place. Each individual, in round-robin fashion, presents one idea from his or her private list. A recorder or leader writes that idea on a flip chart in full view of other members. There is still no discussion at this point of the meeting—only the recording. Round-robin listing continues until all members indicate they have no further ideas to share.

The output from this phase is a list of ideas. For example, a school system faced with a declining student population arrived at these alternatives, using the nominal group technique: "Why not sell three small schools and replace them with one large, central building?" or "I wonder if we should be talking about consolidation until we first obtain more information about population trends in this district?"

Next, a very structured discussion takes place; this is called the *interactive phase* of the meeting. Questions and comments are solicited for each idea posted on the flip chart. ("What do you folks think about this idea of selling the smaller buildings and constructing one new, large building?") When the process of asking for reactions to the ideas is complete, *independent evaluation* of the ideas takes place. Each group member, acting alone, indicates his or her preference by ranking the various ideas. Again, these ideas may be alternative solutions to the problem or factors the group should take into consideration in trying to solve the problem. At this stage, we know the average rank the group has attached to each idea. The idea with the highest average rank becomes the alternative chosen—and therefore the decision made—by the group.

The Nominal Group Technique Applied to a Work Schedule Problem. A division of Baxter Healthcare Corporation faced a surge in demand for blood therapy products from human plasma. To meet this demand, the departments had to change from a 24-hour operation five days a week to seven days per week. A variation of the nominal group technique called multiattribute decision making (MAD) was used to arrive at new work schedules. An employee advisory committee of supervisors and technicians was appointed to form the decision-making team.

After 16 meetings, the committee proposed a new work schedule for a select group of volunteers that was accepted by management. The schedule consisted of a three-day work week totaling 34.7 hours of actual work, but pay for 40 hours. Employees on the full-time weekend shift were scheduled to work every Saturday and Sunday for 12 hours and a third day of 10.7 hours between Monday and Friday. The same employees were scheduled to work eight designated company holidays at premium pay.[9] How would you like the work schedule the Baxter group derived through group decision making?

Quality-improvement Teams

Quality improvement teams:
Groups of workers who use problem-solving techniques to enhance customer satisfaction.

To improve customer satisfaction, many companies turn to **quality improvement teams,** groups of workers who use problem-solving techniques to enhance customer satisfaction. Because quality is usually defined in terms of meeting customer needs, any change that increases customer satisfaction results in quality improvement. Quality improvement teams are also referred to as *kaizen* groups. (*Kaizen* is the Japanese word for gradual, continuous improvement.)

Cause-and-effect diagram:
A decision-making technique widely used by quality-improvement teams.

Cause-and-Effect Diagrams. A **cause-and-effect diagram** is a decision-making technique widely used by quality-improvement teams. The diagram is also known as the *Ishikawa* (after its originator Karou Ishikawa) or the *fishbone* (because of its shape) diagram. According to this technique, any manufacturing process can be divided into four major categories or causes, as shown in Figure 13-2. The causes have an impact on a quality characteristic, or effect. The four causes are person, machine, method, and material.

In the cause-and effect diagram, the four causes are usually subdivided. For example, the person category might be divided into selection of employee, education, training, motivation, and job satisfaction. Being more

FIGURE 13–2. *BASIC CAUSE AND EFFECT DIAGRAM.*

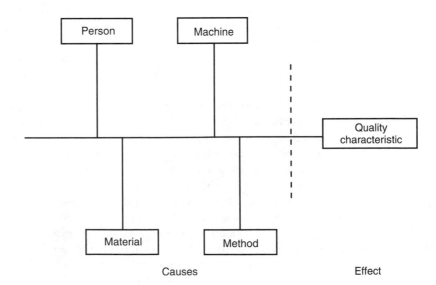

Causes · Effect

specific, a quality defect might be traced to the low job satisfaction of employees who are disgruntled about physical working conditions. The job of the quality improvement team would be to investigate such a possibility.

Many people will have the opportunity to use the four problem-solving techniques described above. We turn next to a small-group activity that virtually every member of this book will experience.

How To Conduct Yourself in a Meeting

A substantial part of work life takes place in meetings. In a study of 200 top and middle-level managers, senior managers spent an average of 23 hours a week in meetings and middle managers spend 11.[10] Another analysis concluded that managers spend as much as 60 percent of their time in meetings.[11] With the increased emphasis on teamwork, professional, technical, and support workers are also required to attend many meetings. Work groups that require meetings include committees, task forces, quality circles, and quality-improvement teams.

It is fashionable to put down meetings with such statements as "Ugh, not another meeting!" or "I wish I didn't have to attend today's meeting. I'd much prefer to work." Along the same lines, the effectiveness of committees is often questioned with jokes such as "A committee is a place where minutes are taken and hours are lost."

Despite these criticisms, collective effort would be very difficult without formal meetings. A constructive viewpoint about meetings is not to try to avoid them, but to learn how to be an effective contributor to them. The task at hand could possibly serve some worthwhile purpose. Also of significance, meetings represent an exceptional opportunity to be observed by important people in your firm. If you observe the guidelines presented in the following paragraphs, you will most likely perform well in meetings.

Be Qualified to Serve. People perform the best in meetings when they have the necessary background of knowledge and interest to do a good job. If you know the topic of the meeting in advance, do your homework. Carefully read some relevant information about the topic and/or speak to some knowledgeable people. In this way you will be prepared to make intelligent comments and suggestions.

The study mentioned above found that the main factor in unproductive business meetings is having the wrong people present. Meetings often include people who are "dead weight"—people who are not directly involved in the matter under discussion.[12] Preparing in advance for a meeting and knowing how the meeting applies to you or your work unit can help you to avoid being classified as dead weight.

Be Punctual and Stay to the End. Arriving late at a meeting is taboo unless you are a high-ranking executive who has called the meeting. Leaving early creates an equally negative impression. Why irritate the influential people who might be present at the meeting?

Take Notes on Key Points during the Meeting. By so doing you will be able to refer back to useful ideas when you want to formulate a suggestion of your own. The notes can also be used when you are studying the problem at a later time. Taking notes will also serve to impress the meeting chairperson.

Do Not Dominate or Contribute Too Little. An effective attendee at a meeting participates neither too much nor too little. The dominator quickly irritates others and tends to subvert a major purpose of the meeting—gathering ideas from several people. The person who contributes too little may be perceived as uninterested in the meeting or as too shy to become a leader. The idea of not dominating meetings is supported by the study of 200 managers. It was also found that one of the most destructive forces in a group can be the participant who is trying harder than everybody else.

Stick with the Agenda. Other people present at the meeting, including the leader, will become annoyed if you digress to irrelevant topics. If somebody else is going off on a tangent, perhaps you can salvage the situation by asking "Excuse me, but how do your comments relate to the agenda?"

Ask Intelligent Questions. If you do not have relevant ideas to contribute to the meeting, you can at least ask intelligent questions. The ability to ask intelligent questions is characteristic of competent people in all fields. An example of a multipurpose intelligent question to ask at most meeting is, "If we follow your suggestion, what would be the impact on other departments in our organization?"

Focus Your Attention on Surmountable Problems. Many problem-solving groups make the mistake of spending time discussing "who is to blame for the problem" or "what should have been done to avoid the problem." Rather than try to change the past, an impossible task, it is better for you to focus on how things can be improved in the future.

Use Gestures, Posture, and Facial Expressions to Show That You Are Interested. In Chapter 15, we present details about the use of nonverbal communication. For now, keep in mind the importance of looking interested during a meeting. Use gestures, posture, and facial expressions to communicate an intense interest in the topic under discussion. Smile frequently, sit erect, lean toward a member who makes a useful comment, and so forth.

Display Good Manners and Meeting Etiquette. Your manners, good, bad, or mediocre, are always on display in a meeting. It is therefore important to display good manners such as being polite and encouraging others. Bad manners often displayed in meetings include side conversations, reading information other than handouts for the meeting, and eating food during the meeting when it is not served to all participants.

Advantages and Disadvantages of Group Effort and Group Decision Making

Group effort, including group decision making, is essential for collective activity, yet still has many well-known disadvantages. A description of these major advantages and disadvantages is helpful in recognizing when a group approach to problem solving is advisable. The box entitled Guidelines for Personal Effectiveness provides additional insight into choosing between individual and collective effort.

Advantages of Group Activity

Group decision making offers several advantages over individual decision making. First, a greater variety of alternative solutions is considered. If several knowledgeable people are brought into the process, a number of worthwhile possibilities may be uncovered. Second, group decision making is helpful in gaining acceptance and commitment. If you and your friends were planning a vacation together, you would probably have less bickering after the decision is made if it is a joint decision. If one person arbitrarily chose a lakeside cottage, the other members of the group would probably complain heatedly about the mosquitoes. If you all agreed to the lakeside, the mosquitoes would probably be less bothersome. People tend to accept a decision when they have contributed to its making.

Third, groups can help people overcome blocks in their thinking, leading to more creative solutions to problems. Also, groups are less likely than individuals to get into ruts in their thinking. Another group member can step in and help the blocked person pursue another path by gentle prodding.

Fourth, group members evaluate each other's thinking, so major errors are likely to be avoided. The information systems manager in one company was formulating plans to have a computer network installed that would make electronic mail feasible. Shortly before a contract was signed with a vendor, one of the committee members asked, "Are you sure the PCs we have throughout the company have sufficient memory to run that system?" A quick review of equipment revealed that the PCs on premises lacked sufficient memory to handle the network. The electronic mail system had to be postponed until the PCs were upgraded.

Fifth, groups are willing to take greater risks than are individuals, leading to more aggressive solutions to problems. (This advantage illustrates the point that some of the advantages to group decision making can readily become disadvantages.)

Sixth, working in a group enhances the job satisfaction of many members. Being a member of a work group makes it possible to satisfy more needs than if one worked alone. Among these are needs for affiliation, security, self-esteem, and self-fulfillment. For example, many people prefer working in groups to individual effort because of the opportunity the former provides for socializing with others and being part of the office gang. In this way, the need for affiliation can be satisfied.

Disadvantages of Group Activity

Group activity, including group decision making, has some potential disadvantages for both organizations and individuals. We will first discuss four potential disadvantages of group membership, followed by two potential disadvantages of group decision making.

Pressures toward Conformity. A major problem that you face as a group member is that pressure will be placed on you to act in the same manner as the other members of your group. Harmless types of conformity include such things as adhering to a dress code or joining the other members of your work group for an after-work drink on Friday. In some situations, conformity can be detrimental. For instance, one design engineer in a group of five may believe that a car-braking mechanism is unsafe. After learning that his co-workers think that the braking mechanism is safe, he may say to himself, "If the other members of the group disagree with me, I'm probably wrong. Why be an odd ball? I'll call the mechanism safe."

These comments should not be interpreted to mean that conformity is either harmless or detrimental. In many situations, conformity can be beneficial to the group and the people served by the group. A case in point is conformity to regulations in accepting blood from potential donors.

Pressures toward Mediocre Performance. A special case of conformity to group standards is that groups sometimes exert pressures on members to engage in mediocre performance, as illustrated by the following case history.

> A woman took a position as a claims examiner in a casualty insurance company. Filled with enthusiasm to satisfy customer needs, she worked diligently, often taking work home. Her rate of productivity was so high that her co-workers told her to "cool it" because she was making them look bad. The woman slowed down her output temporarily. Feeling guilty about restricting her productivity, she shortly reverted to her preferred speed of processing claims. The woman said, "My judgment proved right. I was appointed to supervisor much sooner than my office mates who preferred to work at a more leisurely pace."

Shirking of Individual Responsibility. Unless assignments are given out carefully to each member of the group, an undermotivated person can often squeeze by without contributing his or her fair share to a group effort. **Social loafing** is the psychological term for shirking individual responsibility in a group setting. The social loafer risks being ostracized by the group, but may be willing to pay the price rather than work hard. Loafing of this type is sometimes found in groups such as commit-

Social loafing: Shirking of individual responsibility in a group setting.

Groups can sometimes foster mediocre performance.

OBVIOUSLY ANOTHER INSPIRED DECISION, MR. BULLSEY.

The "big boss" often dominates the group because people are hesitant to criticize him or her.

tees and project teams. For example, when the committee head asks for volunteers to serve on a subcommittee, some people turn their head or look down at the conference table.

Breeding of Conflict. At their worst, groups foster conflict on the job. People within the work group often bicker about matters such as doing a fair share of the undesirable tasks within the department. They also argue about who is dominating the boss's time. Your co-workers may accuse you of playing politics when you go out of your way to please the boss.

Conflict often takes place between groups as well as within the work group. Such intergroup conflict occurs when group members develop the attitude that their work group is more important than the organization as a whole. Rivalries develop, and "beating the opposition" becomes more important than trying to reach goals important to the organization. It is folly to try to outwit the opposition, rather than solving bigger problems. This observation is illustrated by the comments of a manager of an in-plant printing department to one of his supervisors:

> We're being taken advantage of by management. The next time somebody busts into our department demanding a rush job, give him the runaround. Tell him we've got too many rush orders or that we're experiencing machine failure. If that doesn't work, tell him he has to go through me to order printing. If we don't shake them up a little bit, they're going to continue to treat us like servants.

Individual dominance:
A problem in group decision making that occurs when one individual dominates the group, thus negating the potential benefit of group input.

Individual Dominance. A problem frequently encountered in group decision making is **individual dominance**—one individual dominates the group, thus negating the potential benefits of input from all the members. Dominance by one member tends to take place more frequently when people in the group are of unequal rank. The "big boss" often dominates the group because people are hesitant to criticize him or her. David Hampton suggests that, if you are the head of a group or a high-status participant, you should do four things to circumvent the problem of individual dominance.[13]

- Refrain from announcing your preferred solution while the group is working through the problem.
- Listen carefully to suggestions from every group member.
- Encourage every group member to participate.
- Demonstrate concern for achieving a high-quality solution.

Groupthink:
A deterioration of mental efficiency, reality testing, and moral judgment in the interest of group solidarity.

Groupthink. A potential disadvantage of group decision making is **groupthink,** a deterioration of mental efficiency, reality testing, and moral judgment in the interest of group solidarity. Simply put, group-think is an extreme form of consensus. The group atmosphere values getting along more than getting things done.[14] The group thinks as a unit, believes it is impervious to outside criticism, and begins to have illusions about its own invincibility. As a consequence, the group loses its powers of critical analysis.

A new perspective on groupthink has been developed by Glen Whyte. He believes that many instances of groupthink can be explained by decision makers seeing themselves as choosing between inevitable losses. The group believes that a sure loss will occur unless action is taken. Caught up in the turmoil of trying to make the best of a bad situation, the group takes a bigger risk than would any individual member. The arms-for-hostage deal (Iran–Contra) was perceived by those who made it as a choice between losses. The status quo of U.S. citizens held hostage by terrorist groups was a certain loss. Making an arms deal with Iran created some hope of averting that loss, although the deal would most likely fail and create more humiliation.[15]

Examples of Groupthink. Groupthink was first observed by Irving L. Janis in his research on governmental policy groups faced with difficult problems in a complex and changing environment. A widely cited example of groupthink relates to the U.S. invasion of Cuba in 1961. President John F. Kennedy and his staff decided to invade Cuba at the Bay of Pigs, despite information that the invasion would fail and damage our relations with other countries. Arthur Schlesinger, Jr., one of Kennedy's closest advisors, stated that he had strong reservations about the invasion proposal, yet he failed to present his opposing views. He believed his dissenting opinions were unlikely to sway the group from the invasion plan and would probably have made him appear to be a nuisance.[16]

Another historically important example of groupthink took place in relation to the explosion of the space shuttle Challenger. According to several analyses of the incident, NASA managers were so committed to reaching space program objectives that they ignored safety warnings from people both within and outside the agency. As reported in the internal NASA briefing paper dated July 20, 1986, both astronauts and engineers expressed concern that the agency's management had a groupthink mentality.

Of related significance, the management style of NASA managers is characterized by a tendency not to reverse decisions and not to heed the advice of people outside the management group. The analysis of their styles was conducted by a series of management-style tests administered several years prior to the Challenger explosion.[17]

A business example of groupthink was the decision of Chrysler Corporation executives to sell as new cars they had personally sampled. The illusion of newness was created by dolling up the cars and turning back the odometer. The top management of Chrysler later apologized for the decision and offered generous trade-ins and rebates on the executive cars sold as new.

How to Prevent Groupthink. The team leader can take certain steps to guard against groupthink occurring, as described next. However, team members can take similar steps if they observe groupthink happening.[18]

- Encourage all members of the group to express doubts and criticism of proposed solutions to the problem.
- Do not mistake silence for consensus. Risk takers often dominate meetings, and silent members may not come forth and express dissent.
- Show by example that you are willing to accept criticism.
- Divide the group into subgroups to develop ideas. Then have the subgroups confront one another to examine why they differ.
- Periodically invite qualified outsiders to meet with the group and provide suggestions.
- If groupthink seems to be emerging, bring it to the attention of the group. For instance, you might say, "I get the impression we are too eager to think as one. What is your reaction to this problem?"

BACK TO THE JOB TASKS

Assume that it is your responsibility to coordinate the efforts of a team to arrive at a group decision. Before beginning the actual decision making, select the decision-making technique described in this chapter that seems to fit your situation best. For example, if you want a carefully worked through alternative, try the nominal group technique. If you are looking for some quick, rough ideas, use brainstorming. Do not neglect the cause-and-effect diagram if you are wondering what caused the problem.

Summary of Key Points

❑ A group is a collection of people who interact with each other, are aware of each other, are working toward some common purpose, and perceive themselves to be a group. Groups are the building blocks of the larger organization. A formal group is one deliberately formed by the organization to accomplish specific tasks and achieve objectives. An informal group is one that evolves naturally in an organization to take care of people's desires for friendship and companionship.

❑ Most major decisions in organizations are made by groups. Group input into decisions varies from merely being consulted to having full authority for making the decision.

❑ General problem-solving groups are widely used for decision making. They are likely to produce the best results when they follow the recommended decision-making steps.

❑ Brainstorming is a method by which a group arrives at a wide range of potential solutions to a problem. Each group member basically contributes as many ideas as his or her imagination will allow. After a while, the ideas are sorted out and refined.

❑ The nominal group technique (NGT) is a method of exploring the nature of a problem and generating alternative solutions. It involves a group of seven to ten individuals contributing their written thoughts about the problem and then all other members responding to their ideas. Members rank or rate the ideas, and the final group decision is the pooled outcome of the individual votes.

❑ A cause-and-effect diagram is a decision-making technique widely used by quality-improvement teams. According to this technique, any manufacturing process can be divided into four major categories or causes: person, machine, method, and material. The causes have an impact on a quality characteristic (or effect).

❑ If you advance in your career, it is almost inevitable that you will be required to attend meetings. A number of suggestions for performing well in them are offered in this chapter. Among the major suggestions are these: (1) be qualified to serve, (2) do not dominate or contribute too little, (3) stick with the agenda, (4) ask intelligent questions, and (5) display good manners.

❑ Group decision making offers several advantages. A greater variety of alternative solutions are considered, acceptance and commitment increases, members are helped in overcoming blocks to their thinking, major errors are avoided, groups take bigger risks than individuals, and job satisfaction may increase.

❑ Group activity, including group decision making, has some potential disadvantages, including (1) pressures toward conformity, (2) pressures toward mediocre performance, (3) shirking of individual responsibility, (4) breeding of conflict, (5) individual dominance, and (6) groupthink. The latter is an extreme form of consensus in which the group loses its power for critical analysis.

GUIDELINES FOR PERSONAL EFFECTIVENESS

1. Being able to function well in a group is a requirement for effectiveness in virtually any organization. However, from the standpoint of long-term career growth, be willing to loosen your ties with your work group. Identifying too closely with a work group narrows your perspective and may lead to overconformity.

2. Group decision making is an important contribution to improving the quality of decisions. However, it is time consuming and is best reserved for major decisions.

3. When faced with an important problem for which an out of the ordinary solution is required, it could be to your advantage to utilize brainstorming or the nominal group technique. As with other skills, both techniques require practice to perfect.

4. An important skill for advancing your career is to handle yourself well in meetings. They are good vehicles for making suggestions to the organization. In addition, many judgments are made about you on the basis of your actions in meetings. To improve your skills as a participant in a meeting, follow the suggestions presented in the chapter.

Discussion Questions and Activities

1. Is a family a group? Why or why not?

2. Are the people in a company who run the employee physical fitness center a formal group? Explain your reasoning.

3. What informal groups have you observed in a school setting? What are their purposes?

4. If a team leader uses the democratic decision-making style, does it imply that he or she is indecisive?

5. To what extent do you think most managers go through the steps for effective decision making when faced with a major decision?

6. Identify two problems you have observed in any job that might be tackled with brainstorming.

7. Why is the nominal group technique considered to be a more refined method than brainstorming?

8. How does the cause-and-effect diagram fit in with the general approach for group decision making summarized in Table 13-1?

9. What can a person do to improve his or her chances of appearing alert and interested at a meeting?

10. Ask an experienced manager or professional to provide an example of groupthink he or she has witnessed or heard about. (It may be necessary to first define and explain groupthink to the person you interview.) Report your findings.

A Business Psychology Problem

The Torpedoed Submarine Rolls

Chad Davis is the sales manager for Guarino's Bakery, a supplier of bread products, cakes, and pastries to local restaurants and stores. He enjoys the challenge of his job and welcomes the opportunity to practice the skills and techniques of a professional manager. Chad has acquired some of these techniques through experience and many others through reading business books and through course work.

During the last three months, five accounts have stopped ordering the Italian bread from Guarino's that they use for submarine sandwiches. The president and owner, Angelo Guarino, told Chad, "Our submarine bread sales are being torpedoed. Our reputation is getting so bad that we'll soon be out of business. Find out by next week what has gone wrong with our line of bread. Max (the head baker) swears the bread hasn't changed."

"Angelo, I've been trying hard to find the answer," responded Chad. "So far, the only clue I have is that our submarine rolls just don't taste right. Something is wrong, but our customers don't know what it is. Several of them have complained that their customers say the bread is just not as good as in the past."

Angelo retorted, "Then go back and investigate some more. We've got to know what's wrong."

Chad said to himself, "Now is the time for action. But I'm not sure which action. Should I take a survey of dissatisfied customers? Should I increase the advertising budget?"

1. Why is this case included in a chapter about groups and group decision making?

2. Which technique should Chad use to solve the problem of customer resistance to the submarine roles?

3. What is the underlying, or true, problem facing Guarino's Bakery?

The Uneasy Metric Conversion

Diane Turtino, director of County Social Services, looked forward to her Monday afternoon staff meeting. Eager to receive acceptance for her new program, she opened the meeting with these words: "I'm not one for lengthy introductions to important topics. I have a major program for your approval that could make us pacesetters in the social services field. By following my basic program, we will demonstrate that the county government means business about moving into the modern age.

"I'm proposing that, effective July 1 of this year, our agency make the switch from the decimal to the metric system. No more hesitation; no more blocking the inevitable. From July 1 forward, we think metric around here. When I read client files, I want to see their height and weight expressed in centimeters and kilograms. When you tell me they need heating fuel, I want to know how many liters, not how many gallons.

"As most of you know, the federal government is required to use the metric system in its procurements, grants, and other business activities. Congress has officially designated metric as our preferred measurement system for trade and commerce."

Carlos Alvarez, director of housing, was the first to react: "Diane, I hear what you're saying, but I'm not in total agreement. I think you would need ten levels of approval to make the switch you're talking about. We still receive a big chunk of our funding from state and federal sources. The federal government is in the metric age, but our state isn't. If we fall out of line with the state's official procedures, we could get penalized, and maybe even lose some of our funding."

Jean LaMont, director of administrative services, spoke next: "Diane, I wish you and I had thrashed this out before you made up your mind on the topic. Are you aware of the administrative nightmare you would be creating by converting to the metric system? We'd have to calculate metric equivalents for all the data in our files. Whenever we sent files to out-of-county agencies, we'd get a barrage of complaints."

Diane replied: "I hear some resistance from the group surfacing. But any worthwhile change will have its critics. So I won't be dissuaded by a few negative comments."

Gilbert Chen, director of income maintenance, commented: "Diane, you're dealing with more than a few negative comments. So far the metric conversion program has had its biggest impact on the federal government and diary and calendar makers. Engagement calendars and the like now all contain metric conversion tables. So why bother with a program that has not really caught hold? In Canada, it's a different story. But we're in the United States."

Helen Moore, director of child services, spoke next: "I make a motion that we postpone the idea of a metric conversion program at this time. Perhaps we should set up a task force to study the issue more carefully."

Reluctantly, Diane said, "Okay, who seconds the motion to postpone further discussion on the metric conversion program? After we vote on this motion, we will introduce the motion of setting up the necessary task force."

As the group considered the motion, Diane thought to herself: "What did I do wrong? Maybe I should have just issued an edict to convert to the metric system."

1. Explain why Diane should or should not have used group decision making on the metric conversion project.
2. What does this case illustrate about the advantages and disadvantages of group decision making?
3. What is your evaluation of Diane's group decision-making technique?

Brainstorming

Divide the class into groups of about seven people. Each group will then brainstorm one of the following problems, using the guidelines for brainstorming presented in the chapter. If preferred, the groups can substitute a general problem of their own instead of one of those suggested here. Be careful to choose a generic problem, one that does not require a specific background to handle well.

1. How might we effectively utilize the senior citizens in our community?
2. How can we earn extra money, aside from holding a regular job?
3. How do you find new people to date?
4. How can we save money on food costs?
5. How can we save money on gasoline?

References

1. ROBERT B. REICH, "Entrepreneurship Reconsidered: The Team as Hero," *Harvard Business Review,* May–June 1987, p. 78.
2. JACK J. PHILLIPS, "We've Got to Keep Meeting Like This!" *Personnel,* January 1988, pp. 42–45.
3. LARRY K. MICHAELSEN, WARREN E. WATSON, AND ROBERT H. BLACK, "A Realistic Test of Individual versus Group Decision Making," *Journal of Applied Psychology,* October 1989, pp. 834–839.
4. WILLIAM B. EDDY, *The Manager and the Working Group* (New York: Praeger, 1985), pp. 150–151.
5. OSBURN's ideas were first published in 1941. The key reference on this topic is ALEX F. OSBURN, *Applied Imagination* (New York: Scribner's, 1963).
6. R. BRENT GALLUPE AND ASSOCIATES, "Electronic Brainstorming and Group Size," *Academy of Management Journal,* June 1992, p. 352.
7. JOYCE E. SANTORA, "Pacific Bell Primes the Quality Pump," *Personnel Journal,* October 1991, p. 64.
8. GEORGE P. HUBER, *Managerial Decision Making* (Glenview, IL: Scott, Foresman, 1980), p. 199.
9. LARRY BLAKE, "Group Decision Making at Baxter," *Personnel Journal,* January 1991, pp. 76–82.
10. DANIEL GOLEMAN, "New Research Is Changing Old Concepts of How Groups Function," *The New York Times,* June 12, 1988.
11. DAVE DAY, "Making the Most of Meetings," *Personnel Journal,* March 1990, p. 34.
12. GOLEMAN, "New Research Is Changing Old Concepts."
13. DAVID R. HAMPTON, *Contemporary Management* (New York: McGraw-Hill 1977), p. 397.
14. MICHAEL J. WOODRUFF, "Understanding—and Combatting—Groupthink," *Supervisory Management,* October 1991, p. 8.
15. GLEN WHYTE, "Groupthink Reconsidered," *Academy of Management Review,* January 1989, p. 47.

16. I<small>RVING</small> L. J<small>ANIS</small>, *Victims of Groupthink: A Psychological Study of Foreign Policy Decisions and Fiascos* (Boston: Houghton Mifflin, 1972), pp. 39–40; Janis, *Crucial Decisions: Leadership in Policy Making and Crisis Management* (New York: Free Press, 1989), p. 200.

17. K<small>ENNETH</small> A. K<small>OVACH</small> and B<small>ARRY</small> R<small>ENDER</small>, "NASA Managers and Challenger: A Profile of Possible Explanations," *Personnel,* April 1987, p. 40.

18. H<small>AMPTON</small>, *Contemporary Management,* pp. 184–195; Woodruff, "Understanding—and Combatting—Groupthink," p. 8.

Suggested Reading

B<small>UCH</small>, K<small>IMBERLY</small>. "Quality Circles in a Unionized Setting: Their Effect on Grievance Rates." *Journal of Business and Psychology,* Fall 1991, pp. 147–154.

C<small>IAMPA</small>, D<small>AN</small>. *Total Quality: A User's Guide for Implementation.* Reading, MA: Addison-Wesley, 1992.

D<small>RISKELL</small>, J<small>AMES</small> E., <small>AND</small> S<small>ALAS</small>, E<small>DUARDO</small>. "Group Decision Making under Stress." *Journal of Applied Psychology,* June 1991, pp. 473–478.

G<small>ALLUPE</small>, R. B<small>RENT</small>, B<small>ASTIANUTTI</small>, L<small>ANA</small> M., <small>AND</small> C<small>OOPER</small>, W<small>ILLIAM</small> H. "Unlocking Brainstorms." *Journal of Applied Psychology,* February 1991, pp. 137–142.

G<small>EORGE</small>, J<small>ENNIFER</small> M. "Personality, Affect, and Behavior in Groups." *Journal of Applied Psychology,* April 1990, pp. 107–116.

G<small>OODMAN</small>, P<small>AUL</small> S., <small>AND</small> L<small>EYDEN</small>, D<small>ENNIS</small> P<small>ATRICK</small>. "Familiarity and Group Productivity." *Journal of Applied Psychology,* August 1991, pp. 578–586.

H<small>ACKMAN</small>, R<small>ICHARD</small>. *Groups That Work and Those That Don't.* San Francisco: Jossey-Bass, 1991.

M<small>ICHAELSEN</small>, L<small>ARRY</small> K., <small>AND</small> A<small>SSOCIATES</small>. "Group Decision Making: How You Frame the Question Determines What You Find." *Journal of Applied Psychology,* February 1992, pp. 106–108.

W<small>ATSON</small>, W<small>ARREN</small>, M<small>ICHAELSEN</small>, L<small>ARRY</small> K., <small>AND</small> S<small>HARP</small>, W<small>ALT</small>. "Member Competence, Group Interaction, and Group Decision Making: A Longitudinal Study." *Journal of Applied Psychology,* December 1991, pp. 803–809.

Chapter 14

LEADING AND INFLUENCING OTHERS

Learning Objectives

After reading and studying this chapter and doing the exercises, you should be able to

1. Describe how leaders use power to achieve goals.
2. Identify influence tactics used by leaders.
3. Identify important traits and behaviors of leaders.
4. Describe three key leadership styles.
5. Explain the transformational and charismatic type of leader.
6. Describe the importance of self-leadership.
7. Overview the leader's role in developing teamwork.

JOB TASKS RELATED TO THIS CHAPTER

Many jobs require exercising leadership or influence. If your job title is supervisor, manager, or team leader, you are obviously required to lead others. However, many other professional and technical jobs entail influencing others. The information in this chapter can be applied directly to doing a more effective job of leading and influencing others.

Leadership has been rated as the most important topic in business psychology.[1] Of greater significance, effective leadership has been evaluated as the most important ingredient for moving organizations forward in a complex and competitive world. To achieve such ends, effective leadership is needed at all levels, from supervisor to top executive.

The reason leadership is so important is revealed in its definition: **Leadership** is the process of influencing others to achieve certain objectives. Leadership involves influencing the activities of an individual or a group in efforts toward reaching a goal in a given situation. However, unduly coercive tactics such as gun threats are not part of leadership. If influence is not exerted, leadership, strictly speaking, has not been performed. An employee who performs satisfactorily with almost no boss contact is not being led.

Leadership:
The process of influencing other people to achieve certain objectives.

To understand leadership, it is important to know the differences among the terms *leadership, management,* and *supervision.* Leadership is but one component of **management,** working with and through individuals and groups to accomplish organizational goals. Management includes the major activities of planning, organizing, controlling, and leading. The nonleadership aspects of a manager's job are sometimes referred to as administrative work, while the interpersonal aspects involve leadership.

Management:
Working with and through individuals and groups to accomplish organizational goals.

Leadership is regarded as a force that inspires and energizes people and brings about change.[2] The other aspects of management deal more with the status quo. Among the leadership aspects of a manager's job described in this text are motivation, communication, and conflict resolution. Both good management and effective leadership are important for an organization to run well.

Supervision is first-level management. Supervisors plan, organize, control, and lead as do other managers. However, supervisors spend more time in direct leadership activities than do higher-level managers.

Supervision
First-level management, or the overseeing of workers.

Our study of leadership encompasses an understanding of leaders themselves, influence tactics, leadership styles, inspirational leadership, leading oneself, and how leaders develop teamwork.

How Leaders Use Power To Achieve Goals

Leaders influence others to achieve goals through the use of **power**—the ability to get others to do things and to influence decisions. When power stems from the formal position you occupy, it is referred to as **position power.** When it stems from your personal characteristics and skills, it is referred to as **personal power.** Here we will examine subtypes of power in detail and point out some guidelines for their proper use.[3] The message for your career is that, if you want to be an effective leader, you must be able to use power in an intelligent and sensitive manner.

Power:
The ability to control resources, to influence important decisions, and to get other people to do things.

Position power:
The ability to
influence others
based on the formal
position you occupy
(legitimate power).

Personal power:
The ability to
influence others
based on personal
characteristics and
skills.

Legitimate power:
The ability to
influence others that
stems directly from
the leader's position.

Reward power:
The leader's control
over valuable
rewards.

Coercive power:
The leader's control
over punishments.

Position Power

Position power can be divided into three subtypes: legitimate, reward, and coercive. **Legitimate power** is the ability to influence others that stems directly from the leader's position. It is the easiest type of power to understand and accept. People at higher levels in an organization have more power than the people below them. However, the culture of an organization helps decide the limits to anybody's power. A store manager in Los Angeles, for example, does not have the right to demand that a sales associate converse with customers only in Spanish (or English).

Although employees generally accept their boss's right to make requests, they do not like to be given orders in a way that implies they are not as good as the leader. Effective leaders therefore exercise authority by making polite requests, rather than arrogant demands.[4]

Reward power refers to the leader's control over rewards valued by the subordinate. For example, if a sales manager can directly reward sales representatives with cash bonuses for good performance, that manager will exert considerable power. Effective leaders do not use rewards as bribes for getting employees to do what they want. Instead, rewards are used to reinforce desirable behavior after it has already taken place.

Coercive power refers to the leader's control over punishments. It is based on fear and thus may create anxiety and defensiveness. Effective leaders generally avoid the use of coercive power except when absolutely necessary because coercion is likely to create resentment and undermine their personal power. Yet, if skillfully used, coercion can get some people to comply with rules, regulations, and orders.

Personal Power

Expert power:
The ability to control
others through
knowledge relevant to
the job as perceived
by subordinates.

Personal power has two subtypes: expert power and referent power. **Expert power** is the ability to control others through knowledge relevant to the job as perceived by subordinates. You can also exercise expert power when you do not have a formal leadership position. An example is the engineering technician who is talented at getting industrial robots to work properly. The company becomes dependent on that individual, giving him or her some power with respect to receiving special privileges. To accumulate expert power, a leader should cultivate an image of experience and competence. Credibility must be preserved by avoiding careless statements and rash decisions. It is also important to remain cool. A leader who appears confused, vacillates, or is obviously panicked will quickly lose expert power.[5]

Referent power:
The ability to control
based on loyalty to
the leader and the
subordinates' desire
to please that person.

Referent power refers to the ability to control based on loyalty to the leader and subordinates' desire to please that person. The charisma (roughly personal charm and magnetism) of the person is the basis of referent power. Some of the loyalty to the leader is based on an identification with the leader's personality traits and personal characteristics.

Charisma, and therefore referent power, are both based on the subjective perception of the leader's traits and characteristics. Much more will be said about referent power in the discussion of transformational and charismatic leadership. (Referent power stems from charisma.)

Although both position and personal power are important, effective leaders rely more heavily on personal power to get work done through others.

Specific Influence Tactics Used by Leaders

The judicious use of the various types of power is an important way of influencing group members. Leaders also rely on many other influence tactics, as described next.

Leading by example:
Influencing group members by serving as a positive model.

Leading by example is a simple but effective way of influencing group members. The ideal approach to leading by example is to be a "Do as I Say and Do" manager. This type of manager shows consistency between actions and words. Also, actions and words confirm, support, and often clarify each other. For example, if the firm has a dress code and the supervisor explains the code and dresses accordingly, a role model has been provided that is consistent in words and actions. The action of following the dress code provides an example that supports and clarifies the words used to describe the dress code.[6]

Assertiveness:
Being forthright with one's demands, expressing both the specifics of what one wants done and the feelings surrounding the demands.

Assertiveness refers to being forthright with your demands, expressing both the specifics of what you want done and the feelings surrounding the demands. An assertive leader might say, "I'm worried about the backlog of customer inquiries on your desk. I want the inquiries answered by Thursday at 4:30." A leader might also be assertive by checking frequently on subordinates.

Ingratiation:
Getting somebody else to like you, often using political behaviors.

Ingratiation refers to getting somebody else to like you, often using political behaviors. Two specific ingratiating behaviors in the study under consideration were "Acted in a friendly manner prior to asking for what I wanted" and "Praised the subordinate just before asking for what I wanted." Strong leaders tend not to rely heavily on ingratiating tactics.

Rationality:
Appealing to reason and logic.

Rationality is appealing to reason and logic. It is an influence tactic used frequently by effective leaders. Pointing out the facts of a situation to a group member in order to prompt that person to act is an example of rationality. One manager convinced an employee to take on a field assignment by informing her that every member of top management had field experience. The group member in question was ambitious, which made her receptive to a course of action that could help her achieve her goals.

Exchange:
The use of reciprocal favors in order to influence others.

Exchange is the use of reciprocal favors in order to influence others. Leaders with limited personal and position power tend to emphasize exchanging favors with group members. An example of exchange would be promising to endorse an employee's request for a two-week leave of absence if the subordinate takes on an unpleasant short-term assignment.

Upward appeal means asking for help from a higher authority. Here the leader exerts influence by getting a more powerful person to carry out the influence act. A specific example: "I sent the guy to my superior when he wouldn't listen to me. That fixed him." More than occasional use of upward appeal weakens the manager's stature in the eyes of subordinates and superiors and erodes effectiveness as a leader.

Blocking refers to work slowdowns or the threat thereof, thus being used primarily to exert upward rather than downward influence. However, a leader will sometimes use blocking in ways such as these: "I ignored him until he came around to my way of thinking" or "I stopped being friendly until she started listening to me."

Joking and Kidding. A survey has documented that joking and kidding are widely used to influence others on the job. Good-natured ribbing is especially effective when a straightforward statement might be interpreted as harsh criticism. In an effort to get an employee to use the electronic mail system, one manager said, "We don't want you to suffer from technostress. Yet you're the only supervisor here who can only be reached by telephone, paper memo, or carrier pigeon." The supervisor smiled and proceeded to ask for help in learning how to use electronic mail.

Charm and Appearance. A leader can sometimes influence others by being charming and creating a positive appearance. A survey showed that both men and women rely on charm to accomplish tasks.[7]

Traits, Motives, and Characteristics of Effective Leaders

Early attempts at studying leadership focused on the traits, motives, and characteristics of leaders themselves. For many years, the trait approach to understanding leadership was downplayed. Substantial research has shown that leadership is best understood when the leader, the group members, and situation in which they are placed are analyzed. In recent years, new emphasis has been placed on understanding leaders themselves. Both widely quoted consultants and prominent researchers have emphasized the traits, motives, and characteristics of leaders.[8] The study of transformational and visionary leaders is but one example.

A realistic view is that certain traits and behaviors contribute to effective leadership in a wide variety of situations. Correspondingly, similar situations require similar leadership traits and behaviors. A case in point is the leadership experiences of Susan Bennett King. Before being appointed as the president of Steuben Glass, King was chairperson of the U.S. Consumer Safety Commission. Her understanding of the consumer point of view helped her shift smoothly from a high-level leadership position in government to one in business.

In this section we describe a sampling of key leadership traits, motives, and characteristics. However, traits alone are not sufficient to lead effectively.

The leader also has to possess key skills and take certain actions, as described in the following section. The traits and motives described in this section illustrate ways in which leaders differ from nonleaders. Figure 14-1 summarizes these differences. Our choice of these particular traits, motives, and characteristics does not imply that others are unimportant.

Power Motive. Effective executive leaders have a strong need to control resources. Leaders with high power drives have three dominant characteristics: (1) they act with vigor and determination to exert their power, (2) they invest much time in thinking about ways to alter the behavior and thinking of others, and (3) they care about their personal standing with those around them.[9] The strong need for power is important because it means that the leader is interested in influencing others. The power needed to satisfy the power motive can be obtained through acquiring the right position or through developing personal power. Although Donald Trump has lost some power in recent years, he remains an executive with an extraordinary power motive. A tipoff is his penchant for naming buildings, a yacht, and an airline after himself.

Drive and Achievement Motive. Leaders are noted for the high level of effort they invest in achieving work goals. *Drive* refers to such aspects of behavior as ambition, energy, tenacity, initiative, and, above all, achievement motivation.[10] The **achievement motive** is reflected in finding joy in accomplishment for its own sake. High achievers find satisfaction in completing challenging tasks, attaining high standards, and

Achievement motive:
Finding joy in accomplishment for its own sake.

FIGURE 14–1. *PORTRAIT OF A LEADER.*

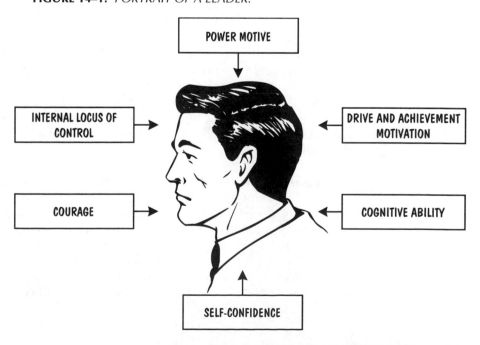

developing better ways of doing things. Achievement motivation contributes to the leadership effectiveness of both entrepreneurial and hired managers. William Stoltz, a man who has founded several businesses, said at age 67, "I don't need the money, but I would rather get a new business going than lie in the sand."

Cognitive Ability. A current theory of leadership supports what has been known for many years: effective leaders have good problem-solving ability. According to **cognitive resource theory,** "intelligent and competent leaders make more effective plans, decisions, and action strategies than do leaders with less intelligence or competence."[11] Despite the importance of intelligence for leadership, an advanced capacity for solving abstract problems can be disadvantageous. John D. Geary, a company president makes this comment about intelligence and leadership success:

> Sometimes a less than top IQ is an advantage because that person doesn't see all the problems. He or she sees the big problem and gets on and gets it solved. But the extremely bright person can see so many problems that he or she never gets around to solving any of them.

Self-confidence. In virtually every setting, it is important for the leader to be realistically self-confident. A leader who is self-assured without being bombastic or overbearing instills confidence in subordinates. Aside from being a psychological trait, self-confidence or self-assurance refers to the behavior exhibited by a person in a number of situations. It is like being cool under pressure. We can conclude that a given leader is self-confident if the leader exhibits such behavior as deftly handling an unrealistic demand by a key employee.

Courage. A study of 200 U.S. and Japanese managers indicates that courage is an important leadership attribute for revitalizing an organization. Managerial courage involves a manager giving voice to ideas that deviate from current thinking because the manager believes they will produce improved benefits for the organization. Sometimes the ideas recommend change; at other times the ideas advocate maintaining the status quo.[12]

Internal Locus of Control. Effective leaders believe they are the primary causes of events happening to them. A study has shown that supervisory leaders with an internal locus of control are favored by group members.[13] Part of the reason is than an "internal" person is perceived as more powerful than an "external," because that person takes responsibility for things happening. In contrast, the leader with an external locus of control might lament, "Sorry this is all the money we have to work with; those tightwads upstairs wouldn't give us a decent budget."

Leadership effectiveness includes the inner qualities of a leader combined with the right behaviors, or actions, and skills. Next we describe an illustrative group of behaviors and skills associated with effective managerial leadership. Scanning this list will enable you to see the link between traits and behaviors. For example, a self-confident and courageous leader will usually be stable under pressure.

Technical Competence. Knowledge of the business, or technical competence, is a very important leadership skill. An effective leader has to be technically competent in some discipline, particularly when leading a group of specialists. It is difficult to establish rapport with group members when the leader does not understand their work. Group members also have to respect the leader's technical skill. At a minimum, the manager of specialists has to be *snowproof* (not readily bluffed about technical matters by group members).

Knowledge of the business is also important for top-level executives. Executives hired to turn around an ailing company are usually hired for their business knowledge, along with leadership and administrative abilities. For example, when the U.S. divisions of Campeau's retailing operations were facing bankruptcy, Allen I. Questrom was hired as chairman and chief executive officer. Questrom had established his reputation as a merchandising expert who had revitalized other retailing chains.

Credibility and Integrity. Data from 7,500 managers indicate that honesty is the most sought after leadership trait. Group members, however, measure honesty by the deeds (behavior) of leaders. Leaders are considered honest by their constituents when they follow through on promises. In a related study, it was found that of all behaviors describing leadership the most essential was the leader's display of trust of others.[14]

Insight into People and Situations. **Insight** is a depth of understanding that requires intuition and common sense. It is thus a skill closely associated with cognitive ability and could be classified as a trait *or* behavior. A leader with good insight is able to make better work assignments, do a better job of training team members, and be sensitive to peoples' feelings. The reason is that such a leader makes a careful assessment of the strengths and weaknesses of group members.

Another major advantage of being insightful is that the leader can size up the situation and adapt his or her leadership approach accordingly. For instance, in a crisis situation, group members would welcome a decisive leadership style.

Maintaining High Standards. Effective leaders consistently hold group members to high standards of performance, which raises productiv-

> **Insight:**
> A depth of understanding that requires intuition and common sense.

ity. Setting high expectations for others becomes a self-fulfilling prophecy. Workers tend to live up to the expectations set for them by superiors (the Pygmalion effect). Setting high expectations might take the form of encouraging team members to establish difficult goals.

Stability under Pressure. Effective leaders are steady performers, even under heavy workloads and uncertain conditions. Remaining steady under conditions of uncertainty contributes to effectiveness because it helps subordinates cope with the situation. When the leader remains calm, group members are reassured that things will work out satisfactorily.

Recover Quickly from Setbacks. Effective managerial leaders are resilient; they bounce back quickly from setbacks such as budget cuts, demotions, and being fired.[15] An intensive study of executives revealed that they don't even think about failure and don't even use the word. Instead, they rely on synonyms such as "mistake," "glitch," "bungle," and "setback."[16] In practice, this means that the leader sets an example for subordinates by not crumbling when something big goes wrong. Instead, the leader tries to conduct business as usual.

Supportiveness. Supportive behavior toward subordinates is frequently associated with leadership effectiveness. A **supportive leader,** one who gives praise and encouragement to subordinates, usually increases morale and productivity. Supportive supervisors also make an important contribution to preventing burnout among group members, as revealed by a study of working adults in a variety of organizations.[17]

Supportive leader: A person in charge who gives praise and encouragement to subordinates.

Power Sharing. A dominant trend in the workplace is for managers to share authority and power with team members. Power sharing is the basis of **empowerment,** a manager sharing power with team members to help them achieve greater confidence in their abilities. Production work teams and quality circles are examples of empowerment techniques. By sharing power, the leader multiplies his or her own effectiveness. As the team members engage in more significant work, the leader can move on to additional responsibilities.

Empowerment: A manager sharing power with team members to help them achieve greater confidence in their abilities.

FIGURE 14–2. *THE LEADERSHIP CONTINUUM.*

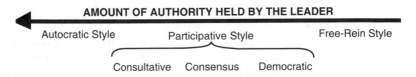

AMOUNT OF AUTHORITY HELD BY THE LEADER

Autocratic Style   Participative Style   Free-Rein Style

Consultative   Consensus   Democratic

AMOUNT OF AUTHORITY HELD BY GROUP MEMBERS

So far we have described the traits, motives, characteristics, behaviors, and skills of leaders. Another way of understanding leaders is to draw some stereotypes of their behavior called **leadership style.** A leadership style is a leader's characteristic way of behaving in most situations. The leadership continuum, or classical approach to understanding leaders, classifies leaders according to how much authority they retain for themselves versus how much is turned over to the group. Three points on the continuum are autocratic, participative, and free-rein leaders, as shown in Figure 14-1. Most other explanations of leadership stem from this classical approach, as will be illustrated later in the situational theory of leadership.

> **Leadership style:**
> A leader's characteristic way of directing people in most situations.

Autocratic Leadership (Boss-centered)

An **autocratic leader** attempts to retain most of the authority granted to the group. Autocratic leaders make all the major decisions and assume subordinates will comply without question. Leaders who use this style give minimum consideration to what group members are likely to think about an order or decision. An autocrat is sometimes seen as rigid and demanding by group members.

> **Autocratic leader:**
> One who attempts to retain most of the authority granted to the group.

Although the authoritarian (a synonym for autocratic) style of leadership is not in vogue, many successful leaders are autocratic. Among them are **crisis managers**—those who specialize in turning around failing organizations or rescuing them from crisis. Other situations calling for crisis management include earthquakes, product recalls, and workplace violence. Several years ago at the Chevy Chase Federal Savings Bank, an employee returned from lunch with a gun. He killed three co-workers, wounded another, and then committed suicide. A. L. Weide, the human resources manager, moved swiftly to manage the crisis. A major task was to comfort some employees and deal with others who were thinking of litigation. Weide observes that when a crisis strikes the response has to be immediate: "Your thought process has to be so clear and so absolutely correct. You just cannot make a mistake."[18]

> **Crisis managers:**
> Those who specialize in turning failing organizations around or rescuing them from a crisis.

The autocratic style generally works best in situations where decisions have to be made rapidly or when group opinion is not needed. One situation calling for autocratic leadership would be extinguishing an oil rig fire at sea. Another would be when a company is undergoing liquidation.

Participative Style

A **participative leader** is one who shares decision-making authority with the group. Although the participative approach is usually associated with a strong people orientation, one analysis observes that the participative leader can be tough minded. Such a leader motivates group members to work as a team toward high-level goals.[19] The participative style encompasses so much of the leadership continuum that it is useful to divide it into three subtypes: consultative, consensual, and democratic.

> **Participative leader:**
> A person in charge who shares decision-making authority with the group.

Consultative leader:
One who solicits opinions from the group before making a decision, yet does not feel obliged to accept the group's thinking.

Consultative Leaders. A **consultative leader** solicits opinions from the group before making a decision, yet does not feel obliged to accept the group's thinking. Leaders of this type make it clear they alone have authority to make the final decisions. A standard way to practice consultative leadership would be to call a group meeting and discuss an issue before making a decision.

Consensual leader:
One who encourages group discussion about an issue and then makes a decision that reflects the consensus of group members.

Consensual Leaders. A **consensual leader** encourages group discussion about an issue and then makes a decision that reflects the consensus of group members. Consensus-style leaders thus turn over more authority to the group than do consultative leaders. The consensus style results in long delays in decision making, because every party involved has to agree.

Democratic leader:
See free-rein leader.

Democratic Leaders. A **democratic leader** confers final authority on the group. He or she functions as a collector of opinion and takes a vote before making a decision. Democratic leaders turn over so much authority to the group that they are sometimes referred to as *free-rein leaders*. The group usually achieves its goals when working under a democratic leader. Democratic leadership has more relevance for community activities than for most work settings.

Evaluation of the Participative Style. Although participative management in the form of empowerment and employee involvement is widespread today, the results of participation have been mixed. The three participative styles are suited to managing competent and well-motivated people who want to get involved in making decisions and giving feedback to the leader. For example, Proctor & Gamble claims to have achieved a 30 to 40 percent improvement in productivity from its employee participation program.[20] A participative style is also useful when the leader wants the group members to commit to a course of action. A supervisor might ask a group, "What should we do with group members who stay outside the building too long during their smoking breaks?" If the group agreed on a fitting punishment, they would tend to accept the punishment if it were administered.

Participative management and leadership often fail when trust is low between workers and upper management. In an era of constant downsizing of organizations and wage freezes, many lower-level managers and workers distrust top management. Employees lack faith in participative management because they do not believe top management has their best interests in mind.

If procedures or alternative solutions to a problem have already been agreed on, participative management is superfluous. For instance, in highly repetitive, machine-paced operations, little room is left for employee problem solving. Very few bank employees are asked to participate in making decisions about setting interest rates on loans; such decisions are made in the executive suite.

Another problem is that participative decision making is often re[...]
ed by first-level and middle managers because they worry about losing
power and having to do extra work. One consequence of companies trim-
ming down is that many of them have concentrated power at the top.
Middle managers and supervisors are then reluctant to surrender the little
power they have left.

Free-rein Leadership (The Subordinate-centered Style)

A **free-rein leader** is one who turns over virtually all authority to
the group. The free-rein leadership style is also referred to as *laissez-faire*
("allow them to do"). Free-rein leaders are the most casual of all. They
issue general goals and guidelines to the group and then do not get
involved again unless requested. The only limits directly imposed on the
group are those specified by the leader's boss. "So long as it doesn't violate company policy, do what you want." Such extreme degree of group
freedom is rarely encountered in a work organization. One exception
might be a research group in which scientists, engineers, and technicians
are granted the freedom to solve problems as they see fit.

A real problem with free-rein leadership in practice is that it frus-
trates many subordinates. Most people feel a leader is paid to give direction and advice. People often characterize a free-rein leader as weak and
ineffective. In one business school an instructor ran a seminar using the
free-rein style of teaching. Student evaluations of the course emphasized
the fact that the instructor was "undynamic," "lazy," or, worse, "did nothing to prepare for the course."

Sex Differences in Leadership Style

Controversy rages as to whether men and women have different
leadership styles. Several researchers and writers argue that women have
certain acquired traits and behaviors that suit them for a people-oriented
leadership style. Consequently, women leaders frequently exhibit a cooperative, empowering style that includes nurturing team members. According to this same perspective, men are inclined toward a
command-and-control, somewhat militaristic leadership style. Women find
participative management more natural than do men because they feel
more comfortable interacting with people. Furthermore, it is argued that
women's natural sensitivity to people gives them an edge over men in
encouraging group members to participate in decision making.

A prominent example of an executive emphasizing the relationship
aspects of leadership is Paula Forman. As the executive management director
at Saatchi & Saatchi Advertising Worldwide, she has faced many tough decisions about laying off people because of business downturns. She notes:

> Women learn the importance of relationships early on. But putting a value
> on intimacy isn't a luxury I give up when times get tough. I don't think com-

mand-and-control management is ever effective in business. It's about creativity, and I can't command creativity.[21]

Assume that these differences in the preferred leadership style between men and women were generally true. Women managers would therefore be better suited for organizations that have shifted to participation and empowerment. It may be true that more women than men gravitate naturally toward the consultative, consensus, and democratic leadership styles, and men toward the autocratic. Nevertheless, there are many male leaders who find the participative style to be a good fit, and many women who are autocratic.

Transformational and Charismatic Leadership

Transformational leader:
One who helps organizations and people make positive changes.

An important development in understanding leaders and leadership is the emphasis on the type of leader who, through charm and talent, captivates the imagination of others. The **transformational leader** is one who helps organizations and people make positive changes. Transformational leadership is a combination of charisma, inspirational leadership, and intellectual stimulation.[22] The transformational leader exerts more influence on people than a *transactional leader,* who mainly conducts transactions with group members.

The transformational leader is adept at turning around failing situations (much like a crisis manager), but can also move a firm performing adequately to much higher levels of achievement. Here we describe how these transformations take place, the role of charisma, and the downside of transformational and charismatic leadership.

How Transformations Take Place

Although the concept of the transformational leader is abstract, it appears that transformations take place in one or more of three ways.[23] First, the transformational leader raises people's awareness of the importance and value of certain rewards and how to achieve them. The leader might point out the pride workers would experience if the firm became number one in its field and the financial rewards associated with such success.

Second, the transformational leader gets people to look beyond their self-interests for the sake of the work group and the firm. The leader might say, "I know you would like more support workers, but if we don't cut expenses, we'll all be out of a job." Third, the transformational leader helps people go beyond a focus on minor satisfactions to a quest for self-fulfillment. In this way, people are urged to move to a higher point on the need hierarchy. He or she might explain, "I know that a long lunch break is nice, but just think if we get this project done on time, we'll be the envy of the industry."

The Link between Charisma and Transformational Leadership

Transformational leaders have **charisma,** the ability to lead others based on personal charm, magnetism, inspiration, and emotion. Charisma is the basis for referent power. To label a leader as charismatic does not mean that everybody grants him or her referent power. The best a charismatic leader can hope for is that the majority of people in the organization grant him or her referent power. Following are some significant qualities and actions of charismatic leaders.[24]

1. *Charismatic leaders have vision.* A major requirement of a charismatic leader is that the person offer the organization an exciting image of where the organization is headed and how to get there. A vision is more than a forecast. It describes an ideal version of the future of an organization or an organizational unit. A sense of vision inspires an organization to perform well, such as Sam Walton's early vision of Wal-Mart becoming the nation's largest retailer.

2. *Charismatic leaders are masterful communicators.* To inspire people, the charismatic leader uses colorful language and exciting metaphors and analogics. The founder of Rollex watches once told his employees, "We are not merely in the watch business, we are in the luxury business."

3. *Charismatic leaders inspire trust.* People believe so strongly in the integrity of charismatic leaders that they will risk their careers to pursue the chief's vision. For example, many people left high-paying, relatively secure positions with other computer companies to join Steve Jobs at NeXT Computer.

4. *Charismatic leaders help group members feel capable.* The charismatic leader recognizes the importance of effort-to-performance expectancies. One technique used to help people feel more competent is to let them achieve success on relatively easy projects. The group members are then praised and given more demanding assignments.

5. *Charismatic leaders have energy and an action-oriented leadership style.* Most charismatic leaders are energetic and serve as a model for getting things done on time. Key people at Domino's Pizza marvel at the energy of Tom Monahan, the company founder and top executive.

Although the characteristics of the charismatic leader are the basis for referent power, maintaining such power requires continuing effort. Referent power varies with the amount of favorable interaction between the leader and group members. Referent power can be increased by being considerate to subordinates, treating them fairly, and responding to their interests. A leader can lose referent power quickly if he or she expresses hostility, distrust, and suspicion, rejects employees, or is indifferent toward them. Not defending subordinates' interests to outsiders also erodes referent power. A recommended way of using referent power is to make a personal appeal that evokes feelings of loyalty, such as "It is very important to me that we enhance our reputation for quality."

The Downside of Transformational and Charismatic Leadership

Charismatic business leaders are seen as corporate heroes because of their great deeds. Among these contributions are turning around failing businesses, launching new enterprises, revitalizing organizations, and inspiring employees toward peak performance. Nevertheless, there is also a dark side. Some charismatic leaders are unethical and lead their organizations toward illegal and immoral ends.[25] People are willing to follow the charismatic leader down a quasi-legal path because of his or her referent power. For example, several financial deal makers who were found guilty of illegal financial transactions inspired hundreds of people.

An in-depth study of 25 charismatic business leaders concluded that the constructive and destructive leaders among them can be differentiated in terms of their ethics. The specifics of these ethical versus unethical practices are outlined in Table 14-1.

TABLE 14–1. *QUALITIES AND PRACTICES OF ETHICAL VERSUS UNETHICAL CHARISMATIC LEADERS*

Unethical Charismatic Leader	Ethical Charismatic Leader
• Uses power only for personal gain or impact	• Uses power to serve others
• Promotes own personal vision	• Aligns vision with follower's needs and aspirations
• Censures critical or opposing views	• Considers and learns from criticism
• Demands own decisions be accepted without question	• Stimulates followers to think independently and to question the leader's view
• One-way communication	• Open, two-way communication
• Insensitive to followers' needs	• Coaches, develops, and supports followers; shares recognition with others
• Relies on convenient external moral standards to satisfy self-interests	• Relies on internal moral standards to satisfy organizational and societal interests

Source: Jane M. Howell and Bruce J. Avolio, "The Ethics of Charismatic Leadership: Submission or Liberation? *The Executive,* May 1992, p. 45. Reprinted with permission.

Superleadership: Leading Others To Lead Themselves

SuperLeader:
One who leads others to lead themselves.

An important goal for leaders is to become a **SuperLeader,** one who leads others to lead themselves.[26] When people are self-directing, they require a minimum of external control. A SuperLeader leads others to lead themselves by acting as a teacher and a coach, not a director. The idea of being self-directing is akin to intrinsic motivation. People structure their work in such a way that it becomes self-rewarding. Another approach is for workers to learn to how to reward themselves. This approach follows the behavior modification techniques for self-motivation described in Chapter 5.

The key aspect of SuperLeadership deals with learning the right thought patterns. Charles Manz and Henry Sims, who formulated the Super-Leadership theory, contend that the leader must teach team members how to develop productive thinking. The purpose of productive, or constructive, thinking is to enable workers to gain control over their own behavior. A central part of SuperLeadership is the leader serving as a model of constructive thought patterns. For example, the leader should minimize expressing pessimistic, self-critical thoughts to team members. He or she should also reward people when they engage in constructive thought.

Charles Manz recommends several specific methods of establishing and altering thought patterns in desirable ways. Managers and nonmanagers alike who adapt these methods should be able to practice self-leadership.[27]

1. *Identify destructive beliefs and assumptions.* After identifying these negative thoughts, replace them with more accurate and constructive ones. For example, an employee might regard the boss's criticism as an indicator of personal dislike. A more productive thought is that the boss is just trying to help him or her perform at a higher level.

2. *Make a habit of talking to yourself positively and constructively.* At the same time, minimize negative self-assertions such as "I don't have good enough math skills to tackle this assignment." A more positive thought on the same issue would be, "In order to do this job well, I will need to improve my math skills. I'll get started brushing up on math tonight."

3. *Visualize methods for effective performance.* Imagine yourself moving effortlessly through a challenging assignment, using methods that have served you well in the past. For example, if you have been successful in making unsolicited sales calls in the past, imagine using them in introducing a new product. In addition to visualizing the positive, avoid picturing yourself failing an assignment.

In summary, the SuperLeader helps create conditions whereby workers require very little leadership. Achieving such a goal is important because organizations have reduced the number of managers available to lead people. Also, work arrangements such as quality-improvement teams require a high degree of self-management.

The Leader's Role in Encouraging Teamwork

Synergy:
A condition when the group output is higher than what would be expected from the combined output of individuals.

As emphasized throughout this text, teamwork is an important requirement in the modern workplace. A key role for the leader is therefore to encourage teamwork. To meet this expectation, there are many actions a leader can take.[28] The most effective way to encourage the emergence of teamwork is by example. If the leader is a good team player, members will follow. Part of being a model of teamwork is for the leader to be honest and candid. A consultant observed that, for a group to achieve **syner-**

gy, honesty among members is required.[29] (Synergy refers to the group output being higher than what would be expected from the combined output of individuals.)

An overall strategy the team leader should use is to cultivate the attitude among members that working together effectively is the norm. A major requirement for encouraging teamwork is for the leader to assign the team a complete task. Teams given only part of a job, such as analyzing data for a report to be written by somebody else, may lose interest. Team spirit thus does not develop. Teamwork and pride increase when the team can point to a whole project as an end product of their work.[30]

An obvious but often overlooked method of team building is to encourage cooperation, rather than intense competition, within the group. One such method would be for the leader to praise employees for having collaborated on joint projects. Perhaps the best-known way to encourage teamwork is to rally the support of the group against a real or imagined threat from the outside. Beating the competition makes more sense when the competition is from outside your own organization.

Good teamwork includes emotional support to members. Such support can take the form of spoken encouragement for ideas, listening to group member's problems, or even providing help with a difficult technical problem. Laughter is a natural team builder that enhances understanding and empathy, which are essential to group cohesiveness. Simple techniques that work are daily calendars with humorous stories and ingroup jokes at meetings.

Teamwork on the athletic field is enhanced by team symbols, such as uniforms and nicknames (Hoosiers, Bearcats, Orangemen, Lady Wildcats, and so forth). Symbols are also a potentially effective team builder in the work site. Company jackets, caps, T-shirts, mugs, and business cards can be modified to symbolize a unit of the organization.[31] It is important to avoid the common mistake of creating ingroups and outgroups within the work group. The team members who are "in" may cooperate with each other, but the "outs" probably will not cooperate with the "ins." Furthermore, this type of favoritism tends to breed dissension instead of teamwork.[32]

As in SuperLeadership, team members should be helped to develop shared leadership skills. Instead of the manager having all the leadership responsibility, he or she should rotate some of the leadership tasks. For example, one person might be given primary responsibility for hiring a new group member.

Finally, a key strategy in encouraging teamwork is to reward the group as a whole when such rewards are deserved. A popular form of group incentive is to reward good group performance with a company-paid banquet. Scheduling the banquet on a weekend and inviting spouses and guests is even a bigger morale booster. This is important because teamwork depends on high morale.

Summary of Key Points

❑ Leadership is the process of influencing others to achieve certain objectives. Management includes leadership, but leadership is regarded as a force that inspires and energizes people and brings about change.

❑ Leaders influence people through the use of power. The three subtypes of position power are legitimate power (formal authority), reward power (the ability to control rewards), and coercive power (the ability to control punishments). The two types of personal power are expert power and referent power (loyalty stemming from an identification with the leader). Charisma is the basis of referent power.

❑ Other influence tactics of leaders include leading by example, assertiveness, ingratiation, rationality, exchange, upward appeal, blocking, joking and kidding, and charm and appearance.

❑ Certain traits, motives, and personal characteristics contribute to leadership effectiveness in a wide variety of situations. Among them are the power motive, drive and achievement motive, cognitive ability, self-confidence, courage, and internal locus of control. The behaviors and skills of effective leaders include technical competence, credibility and integrity, insight, high standards, stability under pressure, resiliency, supportiveness, and power sharing.

❑ A leadership style is a leader's characteristic way of behaving in most situations. The leadership continuum classifies leaders according to how much authority they retain for themselves. An autocratic leader retains almost all authority. Participative leaders are divided into three types: consultative, consensual, and democratic. The participative style works best with people who are competent and well motivated. A free-rein leader turns over virtually all authority to the group.

❑ Sex differences in leadership style have been observed. Women tend toward a cooperative, empowering style that includes nurturing team members. It is argued than men lean toward a command—and—control, autocratic style.

❑ Transformational and charismatic leadership is of considerable current interest. The transformational leader helps organizations and people make positive changes. He or she is a combination of charisma, inspirational leadership, and intellectual stimulation. Transformations take place through such means as pointing to relevant rewards, getting people to look beyond self-interest, and encouraging people toward self-fulfillment.

❑ Qualities and actions of charismatic leaders include vision, masterful communication, inspiring of trust, helping people feel capable, and an action orientation. To maintain their referent power, charismatic leaders must continue to engage in favorable interactions with the people they are attempting to influence. A problem noted with charismatic leaders is that some of them are unethical and use their power to accomplish illegal and immoral ends.

❑ An important goal for leaders is to become a SuperLeader, one who leads others to lead themselves. Teaching team members to develop productive thought patterns helps develop self-leadership. For example, the leader encourages people to talk to themselves positively and constructively.

❑ A key role for the leader is to encourage teamwork. Many actions taken by the leader foster this result. They include setting the right example, encouraging cooperation, maintaining open communication channels, giving emotional support, sharing laughter, using team symbols, minimizing the creation of ingroups and outgroups, and encouraging shared leadership. Group incentives also foster teamwork.

GUIDELINES FOR PERSONAL EFFECTIVENESS

1. Most of the traits, motives, characteristics, and behaviors associated with effective leadership can be improved with education, training, or experience. Thus you do not have to be a "born leader" to improve your leadership potential or skill. For example, if your self-confidence is moderate, you might be able to increase your self-confidence by following the suggestions in Chapter 4.
2. In the present leadership environment, expert power is more important at every level of responsibility. In addition to having good managerial and leadership skills, you also should possess a thorough knowledge of the business, or technical competence.
3. Almost all leadership experience is helpful in developing your long-range leadership potential. A difficult leadership assignment can prove to be valuable experience because it requires more leadership skill to lead poorly motivated, rather than highly motivated, people.

Discussion Questions and Activities

1. Explain whether a person who does not have a formal leadership title can exercise leadership.
2. Give an example from your own experience of how joking and kidding can be a successful influence tactic on the job.
3. Why are drive and the achievement motive such important qualifications for leadership?
4. Many companies that have bought other companies in the past have sold some of these acquisitions and returned to their core business. How does this fact relate to the discussion of leadership behaviors and skills?
5. What is the relationship between power sharing and participative management?
6. Explain which style of leadership would be best suited to leading a group of untrained, unskilled, and poorly motivated workers being paid the minimum wage.
7. Although women may tend toward power sharing, there are plenty of autocratic leaders who are women. Provide an example from business, government, or fiction.

8. Identify a charismatic leader, and explain why you think he or she is charismatic.

9. How does SuperLeadership tie in with self-defeating behavior?

10. What might be a disadvantage of a leader encouraging too much teamwork?

What Kind of Leader Is Sue Wong?

Sue Wong, an office manager at Great Western Mutual, recently took a leadership development course sponsored by her company. The major thrust of the course was to teach supervisors how to implement participative management. In the words of the course leader, "Today, almost all employees want to get involved. They want a say in all important decisions affecting them. The era of the industrial dictator is over."

Wong was mildly skeptical about the course leader's universal endorsement of participative management. Yet she decided that if this is what the company wanted, she would adopt a more participative style. Wong took extensive notes on how to implement participative decision making.

Six months after the leadership development program was completed, the human resources department attempted to evaluate its impact. One part of the evaluation consisted of interviews with managers who had attended the program. Managers were asked how they liked the program and how it had helped them. Another part of the program evaluation was to speak to employees about how the course influenced their boss's approach to supervision.

Rick Alutto, the company training director, conducted several of the interviews with employees. He spoke first with Amy Green, a claims processor who reported to Sue Wong. Alutto told Green her answers would be confidential. He said that the purpose of these interviews was to evaluate the leadership effectiveness training program, not to evaluate the manager.

Green responded, "It would be okay with me if Sue did hear my comments. I have nothing very critical to say. I think the leadership training program was very useful. Sue is a much better manager now than in the past. She's much more aware that the people in her group have something useful to contribute. Sue asks our opinion on everything.

"I'll give you an example," Green continued. "Sue was going to order a new office copier. In the past she might have just ordered a new copier and told us when it was going to be delivered. Instead, we held three meetings deciding on which copier to purchase. Three of us formed a committee to study the problem. We finally chose a copier that everybody in the office agreed would be okay. We even obtained approval from the new office assistant. It sure made him feel good."

Green concluded, "I think that every manager at Great Western should learn how to be a participative manager."

Alutto then spoke to Kent Nelson, another claims analyst reporting to Sue Wong. Nelson said he appreciated the fact that the interviews would be confidential. However, he hoped that the drift of his comments would get back to Wong so long as he was not identified. Nelson offered this evaluation:

"Sue has gone downhill as a manager ever since she took your training program. She has become lazier than ever. Sue always did have a tendency to pass off too much work to employees. Now she's gone overboard. The recent purchase of a photocopying machine is a good example. Too many people spent too much time deciding on which machine to purchase. To make matters worse, a committee of three people was formed to research the matter. It seems to me we can make better use of working time.

"If Sue keeps up her approach to supervision much longer, she won't have a job. We will be doing all her work. How can you justify a supervisor's salary if other people are doing her work?"

Alutto thought to himself, "I wonder if Amy and Kent are talking about the same supervisor. Their comments make it difficult for me to know whether the development program is getting the job done."

1. How do you explain the different perceptions of Green and Nelson?
2. What might be wrong with the leadership development program?
3. Can you offer Sue Wong any suggestions for making better use of consensus decision making?
4. What is the counterargument to Nelson's point about Wong not justifying her pay?

A BUSINESS PSYCHOLOGY ROLE PLAY

Contrasting Leadership Styles

In each of the three following role plays, a subordinate is given the assignment of estimating the cost of insulating a basement of an old factory. The subordinate later informs the supervisor that he or she doesn't have enough experience to make the right estimate. One person plays the role of the subordinate asking for help from the boss in making the estimate. Three pairs of people are thus required. In situation A, the subordinate makes the request to an autocratic boss. In situation B, the request is made to a participative boss; in situation C, the request is made to a free-rein boss. If you are playing the role of the boss, think through how each style of leader would react to the request.

BUSINESS PSYCHOLOGY

What Is Your Leadership Style?

The following quiz will help you to assess your leadership style whether you are currently a boss or might be in the future. Answer "agree" or "disagree" to the left of each item.

_____ 1. Ambition is essential in leadership.
_____ 2. Outdated methods in industry must be eliminated in spite of people's feelings.
_____ 3. Knowhow and initiative are two of the most important qualities a person can have.
_____ 4. What gets done is more important than how pleasant it is to perform the task.
_____ 5. A supervisor's job is more important than that of a social worker.
_____ 6. Newspapers don't give enough space to people who complete worthwhile projects.
_____ 7. My primary goal in life is to reach the top of the heap.
_____ 8. The greatest satisfaction for me is the feeling of a job well done.
_____ 9. Friends are more important than career ambition.
_____ 10. Schools should put less emphasis on competition and more on getting along with others.

Scoring and Interpretation. Autocratic bosses would answer "agree" to items 1 through 8 and "disagree" to items 9 and 10. Participative bosses would answer "disagree" to items 1 through 8 and "agree" to items 9 and 10. Give yourself 1 point for each answer that follows these patterns, and consider a score of 3 to 5 in either category as average. Any score above 6 is high and indicates that you would be (or are) either strongly autocratic or participative as a boss.

Source: Excerpted and adapted with permission from Salvatore Didato, "Do Your Employees Like You or Respect You? It's Hard to Have Both," *Rochester Democrat and Chronicle,* January 19, 1985, p. 14B.

References

1. JAMES R. MEINDL AND SANFORD B. EHRLICH, "The Romance of Leadership and the Evaluation of Organizational Performance," *Academy of Management Journal,* March 1987, p. 92.

2. JOHN P. KOTTER, *A Force for Change: How Leadership Differs from Management* (New York: The Free Press, 1990).

3. JOHN R. P. FRENCH, JR., AND BERTRAM RAVEN, "The Bases of Social Power," in Dorwin Cartwright and Alvin Zander (eds.). *Group Dynamics: Research and Theory* (New York: Harper & Row, 1960), pp. 607–623; Timothy R. Hinkin and Chester A. Schriesheim, "Power and Influence: The Vision from Below," *Personnel,* May 1988, pp. 47–50.

4. The suggestions for using each of the five types of power are based on Gary Yukl and Tom Taber, "The Effective Use of Managerial Power," *Personnel,* March–April 1983, pp. 37–44.

5. YUKL AND TABER, "The Effective Use of Managerial Power," p. 42.

6. R. BRUCE MCAFEE AND BETTY J. RICKS, "Leadership by Example: Do as I Do!" *Management Solutions,* August 1986, p. 10.

7. DAVID KIPNIS, STUART M. SCHMIDT, AND IAN WILKINSON, "Intraorganizational Influence Tactics: Explorations in Getting One's Way," *Journal of Applied Psychology,* August 1980, pp. 440–452; Chester A. Schriesheim and Timothy R. Hinkin, "Influence Tactics Used by Subordinates: A Theoretical and Empirical Analysis and Refinement of the Kipnis, Schmidt, and Wilkinson Subscales," *Journal of Applied Psychology,* June 1990, pp. 246–257; Andrew J. DuBrin, "Sex and Gender Differences in Tactics of Influence," *Psychological Reports,* 1991, 68, pp. 635–646.

8. SHELLY A. KIRKPATRICK and EDWIN A. LOCKE, "Leadership: Do Traits Matter?" *The Executive,* May 1991, pp. 48–60.

9. DAVID C. MCCLELLAND AND RICHARD BOYATZIS, "Leadership Motive Pattern and Long-term Success in Management," *Journal of Applied Psychology,* December 1982, p. 737.

10. KIRKPATRICK AND LOCKE, "Leadership," p. 49.

11. FRED E. FIEDLER AND JOSEPH E. GARCIA, *New Approaches to Leadership: Cognitive Resources and Organizational Performance* (New York: Wiley, 1988).

12. HARVEY A. HORNSTEIN, "Managerial Courage: Individual Initiative and Organizational Innovation," *Personnel,* July 1986, p. 16.

13. AVIS L. JOHNSON, FRED LUTHANS, AND HARRY W. HENNESSEY, "The Role of Locus of Control in Leader Influence Behavior," *Personnel Psychology,* Spring 1984, p. 70.

14. JAMES M. KOUZES AND BARRY Z. POSNER, "The Credibility Factor: What Followers Expect from Their Leaders," *Management Review,* January 1990, p. 30.

15. ANDREW J. DUBRIN, *Bouncing Back: How to Get Back in the Game When Your Career Is on the Line* (New York: McGraw-Hill, 1992).

16. WARREN BENNIS and BURT NANUS, "The Leadership Tightrope," *Success,* March 1985, p. 62.

17. JOSEPH SELTZER AND RITA E. NUMEROF, "Supervisory Leadership and Subordinate Burnout," *Academy of Management Journal,* June 1988, pp. 439–446.

18. STEPHENIE OVERMAN, "After the Smoke Clears," *HRMagazine,* November 1991, p. 44.

19. CHARLES W. JOINER, *Leadership for Change* (Cambridge, MA: Ballinger, 1987).

20. DONNA BROWN, "Why Participative Management Won't Work Here," *Management Review,* June 1992, p. 42.

21. MARY BILLARD, "Do Women Make Better Managers Than Men?" *Working Women,* March 1992, pp. 68–71, 106; Judy B. Rosener, "Ways Women Lead," *Harvard Business Review,* November–December 1990, pp. 119–125.

22. KENNETH E. CLARK AND MIRIAM B. CLARKE, (eds.), *Measures of Leadership* (West Organge, NJ: Leadership Library of America, A Center for Creative Leadership Book, 1990).

23. JOHN J. HATER AND BERNARD M. BASS, "Superiors' Evaluations and Subordinates' Perceptions of Transformational and Transactional Leadership," *Journal of Applied Psychology,* November 1988, p. 695.

24. JAY A. CONGER, The Charismatic Leader: Beyond the Mystique of Exceptional Leadership *(San Francisco: Jossey-Bass, 1989);* Jane M. Howell and Bruce Avolio, *"The Ethics of Charismatic Leadership: Submission or Liberation,"* The Executive, *May 1992, pp. 43–52.*

25. HOWELL AND AVOLIO, "The Ethics of Charismatic Leadership," pp. 52–53.

26. CHARLES C. MANZ AND HENRY P. SIMS, JR., "SuperLeadership: Beyond the Myth of Heroic Leadership." *Organizational Dynamics,* Spring 1991, p. 18.

27. CHARLES C. MANZ, "Helping Yourself and Others to Master Self-leadership," *Supervisory Management,* November 1991, p. 9.

28. J. RICHARD HACKMAN (ed.), *Groups That Work (and Those That Don't): Creating Conditions for Effective Teamwork* (San Francisco: Jossey-Bass, 1990); "Team Builders," *Executive Strategies,* April 1992, pp. 10–11.

29. ROBERT E. LEFTON, "The Eight Barriers to Teamwork," *Personnel Journal,* January 1988, p. 18.

30. "Team Builders," p. 10.

31. PAUL S. GEORGE, "Teamwork without Tears," *Personnel Journal,* November 1987, pp. 126.

32. DAVE DAY, "Beating the In-Group–Out-Group Problem," *Supervisory Management,* August 1989, pp. 17–21.

Suggested Reading

ASTIN, HELEN, AND LELAND, CAROLE. *Women of Influence, Women of Vision.* San Francisco: Jossey-Bass, 1991.

AUTRY, JAMES A. *Love and Profit: The Art of Caring Leadership.* New York: William Morrow, 1990.

Barry, David. "Managing the Bossless Team: Lessons in Distributed Leadership." *Organizational Dynamics,* Summer 1991, pp. 31–49.

CONGER, JAY A. "The Dark Side of Leadership." *Organizational Dynamics,* Autumn 1990, pp. 44–55.

———. "Inspiring Others: The Language of Leadership." *The Executive,* February 1991, pp. 31–45.

"Debate: Ways Men and Women Lead." *Harvard Business Review,* January–February 1991, pp. 150–160.

GATTO, REX P. *Teamwork through Flexible Leadership.* Pittsburgh, PA: GTA Press, 1992.

KOTTER, JOHN P. "What Leaders Really Do." *Harvard Business Review,* May–June 1990, pp. 103–111.

PHILLIPS, DONALD T. *Lincoln on Leadership.* New York: Warner Books, 1991.

WHITMIRE, MARSHALL, AND NIENSTEDT, PHILIP R. "Lead Leaders into the '90s." *Personnel Journal,* May 1991, pp. 80–85.

Chapter 15

COMMUNICATING WITH PEOPLE

Learning Objectives _____

After reading and studying this chapter and doing the exercises, you should be able to

1. Describe the steps in the communication process.
2. Understand the difference between formal and informal communication pathways.
3. Identify the major types of nonverbal communication.
4. Develop tactics for overcoming communication barriers.
5. Explain what needs to be done to become a more persuasive communicator.
6. Know how to improve your listening and telephone communication skills.

JOB TASKS RELATED TO THIS CHAPTER

All managerial, professional, and technical positions, including those related to customer service, are based on communication with people. The information in this chapter will help you send and receive messages in such situations as meetings, interviews, writing memos, and communicating by telephone.

The New York State Department of Taxation and Finance recently mailed self-employed taxpayers a new form. A line at the top of the form read, "As of the above date, our records indicate that the balance in your 19___ estimated income tax account is:_____." The tax department received hundreds of phone calls from confused taxpayers wondering why they owed money, when they had dutifully paid their estimated taxes. The tax officials patiently explained that the form indicated how much the taxpayers had already paid (the balance *in the account*), not the *balance due*.

The well-intended message sent by the tax department thus cased considerable confusion and worry. Similarly, almost every organization is plagued by communication problems. A thorough understanding of communications on the job can improve productivity by helping to reduce wasted time and effort. Understanding how to communicate effectively is also important for advancing your career.

Communication:
The sending,
receiving, and
understanding of
messages.

Communication is the sending, receiving, and understanding of messages. It is also the basic process by which managers and professionals accomplish their work. The purpose of communication is to gather, process, and disseminate information.

Steps in the Communication Process

A convenient starting point in understanding how people communicate is to examine the steps involved in the transmission and reception of a message. The process involves the following sequence of events: ideation, encoding, transmission over a medium, receiving, decoding, understanding, and, finally, taking action. The clouds above and below the diagram in Figure 15-1 symbolize barriers to communication (noise, roadblocks, and so forth) that can take place at any stage in communication. Later in the chapter we will deal with the challenge of overcoming major barriers to communication.

The communication process is cyclical. Upon decoding a message, understanding it, and then taking action, the receiver sends out his or her own message. The cycle is thus repeated at least once. Assume that Conrad wishes to communicate to his boss, Barbara, that he wants a salary increase.

Step 1: Ideation. Conrad organizes his thoughts about this sensitive problem. This stage is both the origin and the framing of the idea or message in the sender's mind. Conrad says to himself, "I think I'll ask for a raise."

Step 2: Encoding. Here the ideas are organized into a series of symbols such as words, hand gestures, body movements, or drawings. The symbols are designed to communicate to the intended receiver. Conrad says, "Barbara, there is something I would like to talk to you about if you have the time."

Step 3: Transmission. The message is transmitted orally, in writing, or nonverbally. In this situation, the sender chose the oral mode.

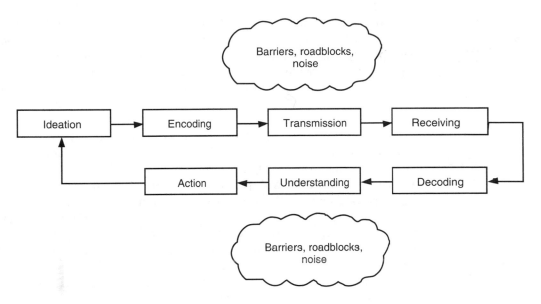

FIGURE 15–1. *STEPS IN THE COMMUNICATION PROCESS.*

Step 4: Receiving. The message is received by the other party. Barbara can receive the message only if she pays attention to Conrad.

Step 5: Decoding. The symbols sent by the sender to the receiver are decoded. In this case, decoding is not complete until Barbara hears the whole message. The opening comment, "Barbara, there is something I would like to talk to you about..." is the type of statement often used by employees to broach a sensitive topic, such as discussing a resignation or salary increase. Barbara therefore listens attentively for more information.

Step 6: Understanding. Decoding should lead to understanding. Barbara has no trouble understanding that Conrad wants a salary increase. When communication barriers exist, understanding may be limited.

Step 7: Action. Understanding *sometimes* leads to action. Barbara understands Conrad's request, but does not agree. She acts by telling Conrad that he will have to wait three more months until his salary will be reviewed. Action is also a form of feedback, because it results in a message being sent back to the original sender from the receiver.

The Importance of Follow-up. The action step in communication has an important practical implication. After sending a message, you will often have to follow up to see if action has been taken. Following up your message measures whether your message has been understood. The follow-up also serves as a prompt or motivator to achieve the action. Effective communication involves much more than delivering a message and waiting for the desired action to take place.

Communication Directions. The conversation between Conrad and Barbara illustrated two directions of communication: upward (from subordinate to superior) and downward (from superior to subordinate).

Upward communication usually does not flow as readily as management would like. One way to encourage upward communication is the **open-door policy.** According to this policy, any employee can bring a gripe to higher management's attention without checking with his or her immediate manager. Another approach to upward communication is the suggestion box for voicing complaints (in addition to making creative suggestions).

The third common form of communication is **lateral,** or from one co-worker to another. Ample lateral communication is characteristic of an effective organization, because it means that co-workers are sharing ideas and helping each other with problems.[1] A form of communication becoming more frequent in the modern organization is diagonal. This occurs when a manager from one department communicates with a lower-ranking employee from another department. In very formal organizations of the past, most communications were sent from a manager outside the department through one's superior.

People who are adept at sending messages in one direction are not necessarily adept at communicating in other directions. For example, some people are comfortable in communicating with co-workers, but they are too shy to communicate effectively with superiors. And some bosses are good at sending messages down the organization, but they are not good at listening to messages sent to them from employees.

Formal and Informal Communication Pathways

In addition to traveling in more than one direction, messages are sent over more than one pathway. Organizational communication takes place over both formal and informal channels or pathways.

Formal Communication Pathways

Formal communication pathways are easy for most employees to understand. They represent the official, sanctioned path over which messages are supposed to travel. Assume that an admitting specialist in a hospital formulates an idea he thinks would improve the productivity of his department—computerizing all patient information. The formal pathway for his suggestion might be as follows: admitting specialist → admitting office supervisor → manager of administrative services → chief hospital administrator → hospital board of directors. His message would have to follow the formal chain of command, or the path dictated by the organization structure.

Work flow is another important factor that shapes the formal path for sending and receiving messages. A sales representative might initiate work for a credit analyst. The "rep" makes a tentative sale on a big piece of equipment. Before the customer is approved for receiving the equipment prior to paying for it in full, the credit analyst must approve the customer's credit rating.

Informal Communication Pathways

Informal communication pathway:
An unofficial network of communications used to supplement a formal pathway.

The paths by which messages travel from person to person are more numerous than those designated by the organization chart or those prompted by the work flow. An **informal communication pathway** is an unofficial network of communications used to supplement a formal pathway. Many of these pathways arise out of necessity. For example, employees may consult with someone outside their department to solve a technical problem. Another important fact about informal pathways is that they account for some of the most baffling communication problems. A good way of gaining insight into these pathways is to study the grapevine, the rumors it carries, and gossip (everybody's favorite topic).

Grapevine:
The major informal communication channel or pathway in an organization.

The Grapevine. The **grapevine** is the major informal communication channel in an organization. The term refers to the tangled branches or wires that can distort information. Yet there are times when information transmitted along the grapevine is accurate. The speed with which messages travel along the grapevine is legendary, as indicated by the comments of Alan Zaremba:[2]

> Many messages travel along the grapevine at an extremely rapid pace. This innate speed can pose some serious organizational problems. Rumors spread quickly and inaccurate information can move throughout a large organization in a matter of hours. Incorrect information is tough to stall once it begins to travel. As a British politician once said, "A lie can be half-way around the world before the truth has its boots on."

The grapevine is sometimes used deliberately by management to transmit information that it may not wish to transmit formally. One example would be to feed the grapevine with the news that salary increases will be very small this year. When increases turn out to be average, most employees will be satisfied. A related use of the grapevine is to measure the reaction of employees to an announcement before it is transmitted through formal channels. If the reaction is too bad, management can sometimes modify its plans, such as not going ahead with a program of shortening vacations.

Rumor:
A message transmitted over the grapevine, although not based on official word.

Rumors. A **rumor** is a message transmitted over the grapevine, although not based on official word. The message can be true or false. An important problem with rumors is that they are capable of disrupting work and lowering morale. A dress company in Brooklyn found itself the victim of an untrue rumor that created morale problems during its peak season. A disgruntled employee started the rumor that the company had formalized plans to subcontract its dressmaking to a company in Pakistan. Consequently, most of the work force would be laid off after this season. When the owner learned of the problem, he held a companywide meeting to dispel the rumor.

Preventive measures are the most effective strategy for managing rumors. Walter St. John advises management to be alert to situations that promote rumors. Among them are when employees are confused about what is happening and information is unclear, incomplete, or lacking, and when there is excessive anxiety and conflict present in the workplace.[3] Despite these preventive measures, there may be times when management or an individual has to combat a potentially harmful rumor. Here are several things that can be done:

- First, try to wait it out. The rumor may run its course before doing too much damage.
- To cut the rumor short, communicate the information that people want. Do so promptly, clearly, accurately, and factually. At the same time, keep open formal channels of communication and encourage employees to use them. ("Call my assistant for an appointment any time you want to see me, about anything you think is important.")
- As a countermeasure, feed the grapevine with actual information to get the facts through informal communication channels. If the rumor is of grave enough consequences, have members of top management meet with small groups of employees to place matters in proper perspective.[4]

Gossip. A special form of rumor is **gossip,** the idle talk or tidbits of information about people that are passed along informal communication channels. We all know that gossip can hurt reputation and wastes time (it is often the raw material for schmoozing). Yet gossip also serves a number of useful purposes on the job. Among them are the fact that gossip can be a morale booster, a socializing force, a guidebook to group norms, and an expression of employee concerns.

Gossip can improve morale by adding spice and variety to the job. It may even make some highly repetitive jobs bearable. In an increasingly technological and depersonalized workplace, gossip may be an important humanizing factor. At the same time it is a deep-well source of team spirit.[5]

Gossip serves as a socializing force because it is a mode of intimate relationship for many employees. People get close to each other through the vehicle of gossip. It also serves as the lifeblood of personal relationships on the job. Gossip acts as a guidebook because it informs employees of the *real* customs, values, and ethics of the work environment. For instance, a company might state formally that no employee can accept a gift of over $20 from a supplier. Gossip may reveal, however, that some employees are receiving expensive gifts from suppliers. Furthermore, the company makes no serious attempts to stop the practice.

Another perspective on gossip is that it is an important barometer of employee concerns. Gossip is an important way for employees to express anger or fear. As one human resources specialist notes, "In the case of organizational changes such as mergers and acquisitions, gossip can dilute the shock factor." Employees mutually support each other and share the experience, thus reducing some stress.[6]

Our discussion so far has emphasized the use of words, or verbal communication. However, a substantial amount of communication between people takes place at the nonverbal level. **Nonverbal communication** refers to the transmission of messages through means other than words. A nonverbal communication can be regarded as a *silent message*. These messages accompany verbal messages and sometimes stand alone. The general purpose of nonverbal communication is to convey the feeling behind a message. For instance, you can say "no" with a clenched fist or with a smile to communicate the intensity of your negative feelings.

A widely quoted study by Albert Merhabian dramatizes the relevance of nonverbal communication. He calculated the relative weights of three elements of overall communication. The words we choose account for only about 7 percent of the emotional impact on others; our voice tone accounts for 38 percent; our facial expression for 55 percent. Nonverbal communication therefore accounts for 93 percent of the emotional meaning of a message,[7] as shown in Figure 15-2. This famous study should not be interpreted to mean that 93 percent of communication is nonverbal. It deals with the emotional force of your message and does not mean that the content of your message is unimportant.

The three aspects of nonverbal communication covered here are modes of transmission, problems revealed by body language, and cross-cultural differences.

Modes of Transmission of Nonverbal Communication

Nonverbal messages can be transmitted in many modes, as described in the following paragraphs. We will also describe mirroring, because it is an interesting application of nonverbal messages.

FIGURE 15–2. *THE EMOTIONAL IMPACT OF MESSAGES.*

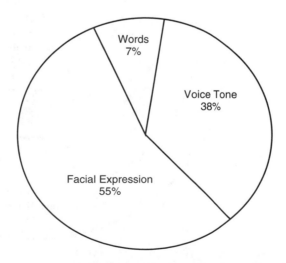

Environment. The environment or setting in which you send a message can influence the receiving of that message. Assume that your manager invites you out to lunch to discuss a problem. You will think it is a more important topic than if the manager had lunch with you in the company cafeteria. Other important environmental silent messages include room color, temperature, lighting, and furniture arrangement. A person who sits behind a large, uncluttered desk, for example, appears more powerful than a person who sits behind a small, messy desk.

Interpersonal Distance. The placement of one's body in relation to someone else (**proxemics**) is widely used to transmit messages. In general, getting physically close to another person conveys a positive attitude toward him or her. Putting your arm around someone is generally interpreted as a friendly act. (Some people, however, recoil when touched by someone other than a close friend.) Practical guidelines for judging how close to stand to another person in the United States and Canada, or in a similar culture, are shown in Figure 15-3.

Proxemics:
The placement of
one's body in relation
to someone else.

FIGURE 15–3. *FOUR CIRCLES OF INTIMACY.*

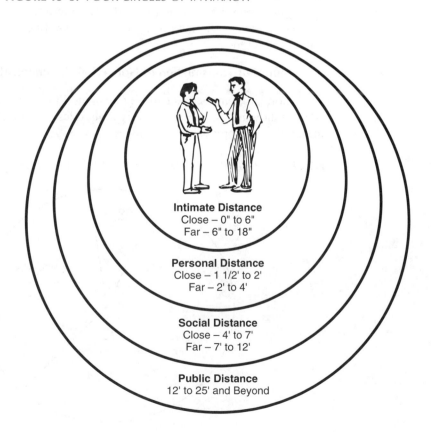

Intimate Distance
Close – 0" to 6"
Far – 6" to 18"

Personal Distance
Close – 1 1/2' to 2'
Far – 2' to 4'

Social Distance
Close – 4' to 7'
Far – 7' to 12'

Public Distance
12' to 25' and Beyond

Posture. Your posture communicates a variety of meanings. If you stand erect, it usually conveys the message that you are self-confident and experiencing positive emotion. If you slump, you will appear to be lacking in self-confidence or down in the dumps.

Another interpersonal meaning of posture involves the direction of leaning. Leaning toward another individual suggests that you are favorably disposed toward his or her message; leaning backward communicates the opposite message. Openness of the arms or legs serves as an indicator of liking or caring. In general, people establish closed postures (arms folded and legs crossed) when speaking to people they dislike.

Can you think of an aspect of your posture that conveys a specific message?

Gestures. Your hand and body movements convey specific information to others. Positive attitudes toward another person are shown by frequent gesturing. In contrast, dislike or disinterest usually produces few gestures. An important exception here is that some people wave their hands while in an argument, sometimes to the point of making threatening gestures. The type of gesture displayed also communicates a specific message.

Gestures are also said to provide clues to levels of dominance and submission. The gestures of dominant people are typically directed outward toward the other person. Examples include the steady, unwavering gaze and the touching of one's partner. Submissive gestures are usually protective, such as touching oneself or shrugging the shoulders.[8]

Facial Expressions. Using your head, face, and eyes in combination provides the clearest indications of interpersonal attitudes. Looking at the ceiling—without tilting your head—combined with a serious expression almost always communicates the message, "I doubt what you are saying is true." As is well known, maintaining eye contact with another person improves communication with that person. To maintain eye contact, it is usually necessary to correspondingly move your head and face. Moving your head, face, and eyes away from another individual is often interpreted as defensiveness or a lack of self-confidence.

The astute salesperson learns to know how well his or her sales presentation is going by watching the customer's facial expressions. If the potential customer is frowning or looking bored, it is a signal to modify the presentation. Similarly, if the potential customer looks interested, it may be the signal to take the order!

Voice Tone. The tone of voice deals with aspects such as pitch, volume, quality, and the rate of the spoken word. As with most nonverbal messages, there is a danger in overinterpreting a single voice quality. A team member might speak to you about the status of a project in a high-pitched voice, not out of fear but because of laryngitis. Three emotions frequently experienced on the job—anger, boredom, and joy—can often be interpreted from voice quality.

TABLE 15–1. *USING TONE OF VOICE TO STRESS THE ELEMENTS IN A MESSAGE*

Consider the following statement: "The boss is giving Sheila a promotion." By emphasizing a particular word in this message through tone of voice, we can obtain different interpretations of the statement:

The *boss* is giving Sheila a promotion.
THE BOSS is the one giving the promotion, not the president of the company, not the boss's supervisor, but the boss.
The boss is *giving* Sheila a promotion
The boss is GIVING the promotion, implying that perhaps Sheila is not qualified.
The boss is giving *Sheila* a promotion.
The person getting the promotion is SHEILA, not Art, not Betty, not Ken, but Sheila.
The boss is giving Sheila a *promotion.*
Sheila is receiving a PROMOTION, not a raise, not a demotion, not "the sack."

Source: Lyle Sussman and Paul D. Krivnos, *Communication for Supervisors and Managers* (Sherman Oaks, CA: Alfred Publishing Co., 1979), p. 83.

Anger is best perceived when the source speaks loudly, at a fast rate, in a high pitch, with irregular inflection and clipped enunciation. Boredom is often indicated by moderate volume, pitch, and rate and a monotone inflection. Joy is often indicated by loud volume, high pitch, fast rate, upward inflection, and regular rhythm.[9] The exercise presented in Table 15-1 will help you to recognize the importance of voice tone in communicating a message.

> **Mirroring**
> **(posturing):**
> A form of nonverbal
> communication used
> to establish rapport
> with another
> individual by imitating
> that person's physical
> behavior.

Mirroring to Establish Rapport. One form of nonverbal communication used to achieve rapport with another is **mirroring** (or **posturing**). To mirror someone is subtly to imitate that individual. It is one small aspect of *neurolinguistic programming,* a method of communication that combines features of hypnosis, linguistics, and nonverbal behavior. "Neuro" refers to the way the human nervous system processes communication. "Linguistic" refers to the way that words, tone, timing, gestures, and inflection can be used in communication. "Programming" refers to using a systematic technique to communicate with others.[10]

The most successful mirroring technique for establishing rapport is to imitate another's breathing pattern. If you adjust your own breathing rate to match someone else's, you will soon establish rapport with that individual. Mirroring sometimes takes the form of imitating a boss in order to curry favor. Many subordinates show a relentless tendency to copy the boss's mannerisms, gestures, way of speaking, and dress.[11]

Problems Revealed by Body Language

Nonverbal messages sometimes signal the existence of problems. For example, if a vendor promises you a delivery date while looking away

TABLE 15–2. *NONVERBAL SIGNALS OF JOB PROBLEMS*

1. *Stress:* A blank expression or phony smile; tight posture, with arms held stiffly at person's side; abrupt motion, such as suddenly shifting the eyes, a quick turn of the head, nervous tapping of a leg; sudden mood shifts in speech, from toneless and soft answers to animated and loud ones.

2. *Depression:* Sagging shoulders; sad facial expression; slower than usual speech; decrease in gesturing; slow breathing rate; frequent sighing.

3. *Lack of comprehension:* Knitted brows; a deadpan expression; tentative, weak nodding or smiling; one slightly raised eyebrow; "Yes" or "I see" in a strained voice; "I understand," accompanied by looking away.

4. *Hesitation to speak about sensitive topic:* A slight raising of the head and eyebrows; licking the lips; deep breathing with eye contact.

5. *Disagreement in the form of hostile submission:* Downward movement of the body or eyes, or both, resembling bowing to authority; closed eyes and a hand put over the nose, as saying, "Oh no!"

6. *Fraud and deception:* Inappropriate finger or foot tapping; body shifting or some other movement that suddenly appears. Inability to maintain eye contact is less reliable indicator.

Source: Compiled from information in "Body Language," *Executive Strategies,* June 5, 1990; "Use Your Body Language," *Executive Strategies* April 17, 1990; Pauline E. Henderson, "Communication without Words," *Personnel Journal,* January 1989, p. 27.

from you and blushing, you might suspect that the deal is unrealistic. Table 15-2 describes nonverbal cues that could be indicative of significant problems.

Cross-cultural Differences in Nonverbal Communication

People from different cultures obviously speak and write different languages. Cultural differences in language can also be found within the same country, such as some groups using "go" to mean "say." A variety of cross-cultural differences are also found with respect to nonverbal communication. Being aware of the existence of these differences in silent messages will alert you to look for them when dealing with people from another culture. A sampling of these differences follows:

- A Japanese person smiling and nodding connotes understanding, not necessarily agreement.
- In many Asian cultures it is considered improper to look a superior in the eye too often. A bowed head is therefore a sign of deference, not an indicator of low self-confidence.
- Asians may smile to avoid conflict, rather than to show approval.
- British, Scandinavians, and other Northern Europeans prefer plenty of space between themselves and another person. They seldom touch when talking. In contrast, French, Italians, Latin Americans, and Eastern Europeans tend to stand close together, and they touch one another, indicating closeness or agreement.
- A German manager appearing in short sleeves at a business meeting would

be displaying substantial indifference, while an American or Canadian would just be behaving informally.

- For Americans, forming a circle with one's thumb and forefinger and extending the remaining three fingers signifies, "OK." To the Japanese the same signal means money, to the French it means zero, in some Arab countries it's viewed as a curse. In Germany, Brazil, and the Commonwealth of Independent States, the American OK gesture is obscene.[12]

Overcoming Barriers To Communication

Communication problems in the workplace are ever-present. Some interference usually takes place between ideation and action, as suggested by the "clouds" in Figure 15-1. The type of message influences the amount of interference. Routine or neutral messages are the easiest to communicate. Interference is most likely to occur when a message is complex, emotionally arousing, or clashes with a receiver's mental set.

An emotionally arousing message deals with such topics as a relationship between two people or money. A message that clashes with a receiver's mental set requires the person to change his or her typical pattern of receiving messages. The reader is invited to try this experiment. The next time you visit a restaurant, order dessert first and the entree second. The waiter or waitress will probably not receive your dessert order because it deviates from the normal sequence.

Here we will describe strategies and tactics for overcoming some of the more frequently observed communication problems in organizations. The following section deals with overcoming cross-cultural communication barriers. We then deal with general approaches to overcoming barriers—being more persuasive and improving listening and telephone skills.

Understand the Receiver

Understanding the person who you are trying to reach is a fundamental principle of overcoming communication barriers. The more you know about your receiver, the better able you are to deliver your message in an effective manner. Three important aspects of understanding the receiver are (1) developing empathy, (2) recognizing that person's motivational state, and (3) understanding the other person's frame of reference.

To develop empathy, you are required to figuratively put yourself in the receiver's shoes. To accomplish this, you have to imagine yourself in the other person's role and assume the viewpoints and emotions of that individual. Assume a 25-year-old customer representative works at a public utility. She is responsible for helping a group of older employees to understand the importance of becoming customer oriented. The customer representative must ask herself, "If I had been working in a monopoly for twenty years, how difficult would it be for me to understand that we now have competition? And that we must therefore please the customer?"

The receiver's **motivational state** could include any active needs

Motivational state: An inner state of arousal directed toward a goal. Work motivation is essentially motivation directed toward the attainment of organizational goals.

Communication rarely proceeds as smoothly as we would like.

and interest at the time. People tend to listen attentively to messages that show promise of satisfying an active need. The hungry person who ordinarily does not hear low tones readily hears a whispered message, "How would you like to eat dinner?" And management usually listens attentively to a suggestion framed in terms of cost savings or increased profits.

Frame of reference: A perspective or vantage point for receiving information.

People perceive words and concepts differently because their vantage points and perspectives differ. Such differences in **frame of reference** create barriers to communication. To reduce this barrier, you have to understand where the receiver "is coming from." An example of different frames of reference creating a communication barrier took place in a financial services agency.

Jeb, a second-year agent, showed his sales figures for the month to his boss, Gary. Proud of his good results, Jeb said, "Well, what do you think of this kind of production for a man of my age?" Gary replied, "That's fine if you want to make $35,000 a year for the rest of your life." Jeb responded, "Sounds fine to me."

Gary looked at him quizzically and said, "You mean you'd be happy making $35,000 a year for the rest of your life? I made that comment to shake you up a bit." Jeb answered, "No disrespect, Gary, but where I come from $35,000 is one big lump of money. My parents never came close to that."

Engage in Two-way Communication

Effective face-to-face communication proceeds in two directions. An exchange of information or a transaction takes place between people. Person A may send messages to person B to initiate communication, but B must react to A to complete the communication loop. One reason written messages frequently fail to achieve their purpose is that the sender of the message cannot be sure what meanings are attached to its content. Face-to-face transactions help to clarify meanings because they communicate feelings as well as facts.

Use Appropriate Timing

Many messages do not get through to the receiver because they are sent at the wrong time. It is a waste of time to send a message when the receiver is distracted with another issue or is rushing to get somewhere. The best time to deliver a message depends on the uniqueness of a situation. Many sales representatives and consultants have found that Tuesday morning is a good time to get a message across to a busy manager. On Mondays many managers are preoccupied with meetings and getting the week started with a burst of productivity. By Tuesday morning they are more willing to attend to new business. Later in the week, the managers may be absorbed in attempting to complete the goals for the week.

Another aspect of timing is to postpone delivering an important message when the intended receiver is angry or upset. The best time to ask for a major commitment is when your intended receiver is in a good mood. Thinking about good news, such as record profits or a tri-

umph in personal life, can be distracting. Nevertheless, thinking about good news is less distracting than thinking about bad news.

Use Multiple Channels

Repetition usually enhances learning. Repetition also enhances communication, particularly when different channels are used to convey the same message. Effective communicators at many job levels follow up spoken agreements with written documentation. Since most communication is subject to at least some distortion, the chances of a message being received as intended increase when two or more channels are used.

It has become standard practice in many large companies for managers to use a multiple-channel approach to communicating the results of a performance appraisal. The subordinate receives a verbal explanation from his or her superior of the results of the review. He or she is also required to read the form and indicate by signature that he or she has read and understands the meaning of the review.

Avoid Mixed Signals

A major reason many communicators do not get their message across is that they have lied or communicated half-truths in the past. A related but less obvious reason for communication failure is sending **mixed signals**—the sending of different messages about the same topic to different audiences.[13] For example, a company might brag about the high quality of its products in its public statements. Yet on the shop floor and in the office the company tells its employees to cut corners wherever possible to lower costs.

Another type of mixed signal occurs when you send one message to a person about desired behavior, yet behave in another way yourself. Such behavior is the opposite of leading by example, as described in Chapter 14. A mixed signal of this type would occur when an executive preaches the importance of social responsibility, yet practices blatant job discrimination.

Mixed signals: The sending of different messages about the same topic to different audiences. Also, sending one message to an individual about desired behavior, yet behaving in another way yourself.

Use Verbal and Nonverbal Feedback

To be able to conclude that your message has been received as intended, it is helpful to ask for feedback. A frequent managerial practice is to conclude a conference with a question such as, "Okay, what have we agreed on today?" Unless feedback of this nature is obtained, you will not know if your message has been received until the receiver later carries out (or fails to carry out) your request. After speaking to a group you are trying to influence, it would be helpful to ask them to state what message they thought you were trying to convey. Nonverbal cues are sometimes more revealing than verbal cues. Here is an example of nonverbal behavior (or body language) that could help you to interpret whether or not your comments were being accepted:

> You ask your boss when you will be eligible for a promotion and he looks out the window, cups his mouth to cover a yawn, and says, "Probably not too far away. I would say your chances aren't too bad." Keep trying. He is not yet sold on the idea of promoting you in the near future.

Decrease Physical Barriers

Do you ever try to communicate with somebody while standing in the doorway of their office or room? Do you ever try to communicate with somebody with a huge desk separating the two of you? In both situations your communications effectiveness would probably increase if you reduced the barriers. In the first instance, it would be helpful to enter the room and stand closer to the person. In the second situation, it would be preferable to move around the table to a point where you are both seated at two adjacent corners of the desk.

In a conference setting, a major way of increasing and improving person-to-person communication is to seat people in a circle without a table separating them. (Student chairs with an arm big enough for notetaking are particularly useful in this regard.) Another way of decreasing physical barriers is to provide employees with ample opportunity to chat with each other about work-related topics. Informal interaction of this type is particularly important for employees involved in creative or complex work. "Batting around" ideas with a co-worker can help clarify thinking on a challenging problem.

Use Appropriately Difficult Language

"From this point forward you folks are going to have to interface with a CAD/CAM, robotics configuration in our operations environment," said the production engineering manager to the manufacturing specialists. Seeing mostly blank stares on the faces of his intended receivers, the manager rephrased his message, "In the future, a lot of our production work is going to be computerized." At first the manager was falling prey to a common communications barrier, speaking at too high a level of complexity for the intended receiver. The manager recovered by rephrasing his message in a form that was (1) simpler and (2) less filled with jargon.

It is not always advisable to avoid complexity and jargon. People may feel patronized when you send messages that are too easy to understand. Jargon may also play an important psychological role because it communicates the message that the sender believes the receiver is part of his or her ingroup. In an effort to reduce complexity, some people create communication barriers. One way to alienate your intended receivers, for example, is to say, "I'm going to explain this to you in such a way that even a layperson can understand it."

Jargon is sometimes used deliberately to soften the impact of a harsh word or phrase. For example, the U.S. Defense Department uses euphemisms such as "servicing the target" for bombing, "force packages" for warplanes, "soft targets" for people, and "hard targets" for buildings.

Use Bias-free Language

An important implication of semantics is that certain words are interpreted by some people as a sign of bias. When people perceive a statement to be biased, or discriminatory, an emotional barrier may be erected

TABLE 15–3. *BIASED TERMS AND BIAS-FREE SUBSTITUTES*

	Biased	*Bias free*
Sex-related	Girl (for adult)	Woman
	Boy (for adult)	Man
	Salesman, saleswoman	Sales representative
	Female engineer	Engineer
	Cleaning woman, maid	Housekeeper, cleaner
	Cleaning man	Custodian, cleaner
	Stewardess	Flight attendant
	Mailman	Mail carrier
Disabilities	Handicapped	Physically challenged, physically disabled
	Blind[†]	Visually impaired
	Confined to a wheelchair	Uses a wheelchair
Race	Nonwhite, colored person	Person of color, black, African-American; Asian
	Indian	Native American; Native Canadian
	Eskimo	Native American; Native Canadian
	Newfie	Newfoundlander
	Whitey, honkey	White, white person, Caucasian
	"Scottish in me"	"My frugality"
	Ethnic jokes	Jokes with nationality unspecified

Note: Many people who cannot hear prefer the term "deaf" as a matter of deaf pride. "Hearing-impaired" may soon be considered biased.
[†]From a technical standpoint, visually impaired refers to some seeing ability rather than total blindness.

that interferes with the message being received. The use of bias-free language therefore avoids one type of discrimination and helps to overcome one more communication barrier. An example of a biased statement would be for a supervisor to say, "I need a real man for this job." The bias-free expression would be, "I need a courageous person for this job."

Table 15–3 presents a list of biased words and terms, along with their bias-free equivalents. Recognize, however, that your choice of words can never please everybody. For example, many women prefer to be addressed as "Miss" or "Mrs." rather than "Ms." Furthermore, a term that is bias free (or *politically correct*) today may become a biased term tomorrow. For example, the deaf community used to regard the term "deaf" as biased and "hearing impaired" as bias free. The same people have virtually reversed their position. As a computer scientist who is deaf explains it, "We have deaf pride." How far one needs to go to be politically correct has become the subject of humor, as suggested by the accompanying cartoon.

Avoid Communication Overload

A major communication barrier facing today's managers and specialists is communication overload. So much information comes across the desk that it is often difficult to figure out which information should receive attention and which should be discarded. A flood of information reaching a person acts as a communication barrier because people have a tendency to block out new information when their capacity to absorb information becomes taxed. Literally, their "circuits become overloaded," and they no longer respond to messages.

To help overcome this problem, it is advisable for firms to be selective in the amount of information they send to employees. Toward this end, it is now becoming common practice for managers to be sent only summaries of general information, while critical information is sent in fuller form. Some executives subscribe to executive abstract services. Their function is to provide brief summaries of business and general news.

You can decrease the chances of suffering from information overload by such measures as carefully organizing and sorting through information before plunging ahead with reading. Speed reading may also help, provided you stop to read carefully the most relevant information.

Minimize Defensive Communication

Defensive communication: The tendency to receive messages in such a way that one's self-esteem is protected.

An important general communication barrier is **defensive communication,** the tendency to receive messages in such a way that our self-esteem is protected. Defensive communication is also responsible for people sending messages to make themselves look good.[14] For example, when criticized for achieving below-average sales, a store manager might shift the blame to the sales associates in her store.

WHICH OF THE FOLLOWING PHRASES ARE "OFFENSIVE" AND THUS NOT **POLITICALLY CORRECT?**

☐ A. PET
☐ B. ANIMAL COMPANION

☐ A. SHORT
☐ B. VERTICALLY CHALLENGED

☐ A. WOMAN
☐ B. PERSON OF GENDER

Courtesy Gannett Rochester Newspapers, 1991.

Overcoming the barrier of defensive communication requires two steps. First, people have to recognize the existence of defensive communication; second, they have to try not to be defensive when questioned or criticized. Such behavior is not easy because of the unconscious or semiconscious process of **denial,** the suppression of information we find uncomfortable. For example, the store manager just cited would find it uncomfortable to think of herself as being responsible for below-average performance.

Denial:
A defense mechanism in which the person blocks out or denies that a particular event has taken place.

Overcoming Cross-cultural Communication Barriers

We have already discussed the importance of understanding culturally based differences among people. In Chapter 3, we described how cultural differences can create individual differences. Earlier in this chapter we described how culture can influence nonverbal behavior. Understanding how to react to cultural differences is important because the work force has become more culturally diverse in two major ways. More subgroups from within our own culture have been assimilated into the work force. In addition, there is increasing interaction with people from other countries.

Because of this diversity, many workers face the challenge of preventing and overcoming communication barriers created by differences in language and customs. Here we describe several strategies and specific tactics to help overcome cross-cultural communication barriers.

Be Sensitive to the Fact That Cross-cultural Communication Barriers Exist. If you are aware of these potential barriers, you will be ready to deal with them. When you are dealing with a person in the workplace with a different cultural background than yours, solicit feedback in order to minimize cross-cultural barriers to communication.

Use Straightforward Language and Speak Slowly and Clearly. When working with people who do not speak your language fluently, speak in an easy-to-understand manner. Minimize the use of idioms and analogies specific to your language. An accountant from Taiwan left confused after a performance review with her manager. The manager said, "I will be giving you more assignments because I notice some *good chemistry between us.*" (He was referring to good work rapport.) The woman did not ask for clarification because she did not want to appear uninformed.

Speaking slowly is also important because even people who read and write a second language at an expert level may have difficulty catching the nuances of conversation. Facing the person from another culture directly also improves communication because your facial expressions and lips contribute to comprehension.

Observe Cultural Differences in Etiquette. Violating rules of etiquette without explanation can erect immediate communication barriers. A major rule of etiquette is that in many countries people address each other by last name, unless they have worked together for a long time. Letitia Baldrige recommends that you explain the difference in custom to prevent misunderstanding. Imagine this scenario in which you are working with a man from Germany, and you are speaking:

> Herr Schultz, in my country by now I would be calling you Heinrich and you would be calling me Charlie. Would you be comfortable with that? Because if you wouldn't, I would be glad to call you Herr Schultz until you tell me it's time to call you Heinrich.[15]

Be Sensitive to Differences in Nonverbal Communication. Stay alert to the possibility that your nonverbal signal may be misinterpreted by a person from another culture. You will recall the problem with the OK sign described earlier. An engineer for a New Jersey company was asked a question by a German co-worker. He responded OK by making a circle with his thumb and forefinger. The German worker stormed away because in his native country the same gesture is a personal insult.[16]

Do Not Be Diverted by Style, Accent, Grammar, or Personal Appearance. Although these superficial factors are all related to business success, they are difficult to interpret when judging a person from another culture. It is therefore better to judge the merits of the statement or behavior.[17] A brilliant individual from another culture may still be learning your language and thus make basic mistakes in speaking your language. He or she might also not yet have developed a sensitivity to dress style in your culture.

Becoming a More Persuasive Communicator

An elegant tactic for overcoming communication barriers is to communicate so persuasively that obstacles disappear. Persuasiveness refers to the sender convincing the receiver to accept his or her message. Persuasion thus involves selling ideas to others. One analysis defines persuasiveness as "that hard to pin down quality made up of an effective mix of commitment, eloquence, honesty, enthusiasm, and humor."[18]

Hundreds of articles, books, tapes, and videos have been developed to help people become more persuasive. As part of the quality-improvement movement in the workplace, many organizations now offer employees training in oral and written communications. Following are some representative suggestions for becoming a more persuasive communicator both in speaking and in writing.[19]

1. *Know exactly what you want.* Your chances of selling an idea increase to the extent that you have clarified the idea in your own mind. The clearer and more committed you are at the outset of a selling or negotiating session, the stronger you are as a persuader.

2. *Develop fallback positions.* Keep in mind what you might do if you cannot convince the other side to accept your first proposal. If plan A does not work, shift to plan B, then to plan C.

3. *Never suggest an action without telling its end benefit.* In asking for a raise, you might say, "If I get this raise, I'll be able to afford to stay with this job as long as the company likes."

4. *Phrase your proposition in terms of their interests.* This basic rule of selling is an extension of the communication strategy "understand the receiver." People are far more likely to accept your idea if it is clear how they will benefit. Almost every receiver wants to know, "What's in it for me?"

5. *Explore the reasons for people's objections.* Assume a potential customer says, "I like this model but I don't want it in my living room." An effective response would be, "What is it that you don't like about it?" Another would be, "What features do you like in this product?"

6. *Say why you are asking whenever you ask a question.* The sales representative above might say, "The reason I asked you about features is that maybe we have another model with similar features."

7. *Get a "yes" response early on.* It is helpful to give the selling session a positive tone by establishing a "yes pattern" at the outset. Assume that an employee wanted to convince his boss to allow him to perform some of his work at home, during normal working hours. The employee might begin the idea-selling session with the question, "Is it important for the company to obtain maximum productivity from all its employees?"

8. *Use power words.* An expert tactic for being persuasive is to sprinkle your speech with power (meaning powerful) words. Power words stir emotion and bring forth images of exciting events. Examples of the use of power words include *decimating* the competition, *bonding* with customers, *surpassing* previous profits, *capturing* customer loyalty, and *rebounding* from a downturn.

9. *Avoid or minimize common language errors.* You will enhance your persuasiveness if you minimize common language errors because you will appear more articulate and informed. Here are several common language errors: (a) "Just between you and I" is wrong. "Just between you and me" is correct. (b) "Irregardless" is a nonword; "regardless" is correct. (c) "Imply" means to hint or suggest, while "infer" means to assume something. It would therefore be correct to say, "I infer from your report," and "Your report implies...." (d) "We are customer oriented" is correct. "We are customer orientated" is wrong.[20]

Persuasion and negotiation are closely related. Additional suggestions for improving persuasiveness can be obtained by reviewing the negotiating techniques described in Chapter 9.

Improving Your Listening Skills

Persuasion deals primarily with sending messages. Improving one's receiving of messages is another important aspect of developing better communication skills. Unless you receive messages as they are intended, you cannot perform your job properly or be a good companion. Listening has even been described as our primary communication activity. Studies demonstrate that we spend about 80 percent of our waking hours communicating. And 45 percent of that time is spent in listening.[21] Listening is a particularly important skill for anybody whose job involves troubleshooting, since one needs to gather information in order to solve problems.

Another reason that improving the listening skills of employees is important is that insufficient listening is extraordinarily costly. Listening mistakes lead to word processing letters a second time, rescheduling of appointments, reshipping of orders, and recalling of defective products. Lee Iacocca, the former CEO of Chrysler Corporation, once said that listening can make the difference between a mediocre and a great company. The suggestions presented next[22] will help improve listening if practiced regularly. They apply to listening both in face-to-face situations and when listening to a speaker.

1. *Concentrate and avoid distractions.* Improved concentration leads to improved listening. If you concentrate intently on the sender, you will receive much more information than if you pay superficial attention. While listening, attempt to leave distracting problems and concerns behind. External distractions and concerns, such as the weather or another person in the room, also have to be resisted. In short, a good listener fights distractions.

2. *Listen empathically.* Listen with compassion and understanding, even if you are not aware why the person is bothering to tell you something. An important part of empathic listening is to accept what is being said, even if you disagree. People frequently choose to communicate for emotional release, even during working hours.

3. *Listen for total meaning.* Look closely to discover the feeling behind the facts. Nonverbal cues will often be a tipoff as to how the sender really feels about his or her message. At times it will be necessary to ask for clarification to obtain the true meaning. Suppose your boss says to you, "I wonder if we're putting you under too much pressure." Asking, "What do you mean by that?" could reveal at least two different meanings. Your boss could mean that you look like you're faltering under the pressure. Or he or she could mean that you have been carrying an unfair burden.

4. *Capitalize on the fact that thought is faster than speech.* The average rate of speech is 125 words a minute for English. We think, and therefore listen, at almost four times that speed. A poor listener tends to daydream when encountering all but the most rapid speakers. A better approach is to challenge, anticipate, mentally summarize, weigh the evidence, and listen for the tone of voice to gauge feeling.

5. *Judge content not delivery.* Poor speakers as well as good speakers may have something important to say. One of the most noted scientists in his field is considered to be one of the poorest teachers at his university. Therefore, be careful not to tune out a speaker whose delivery is poor. Judge the content and be less concerned about errors in delivery.

6. *Work at listening.* Listening is hard work, as most psychotherapists will tell you. The bad listener shows no energy output, but instead fakes attention. In contrast, the good listener works hard at receiving messages and exhibits an active body state.

7. *Observe the nonverbal aspects of the message.* An astute supplement to listening is to observe the nonverbal behavior of the person delivering the message. The description of nonverbal behavior presented previously should be helpful in making some inferences about the speaker's true meaning. One example might be that you can judge the sincerity of a message by the sender's voice tone and whether he or she has a serious facial expression.

8. *Offer encouragement to the sender.* Good listeners encourage speakers by asking questions, giving nods and words of approval, and finding points of agreement.

Telephone communication skills are important for several reasons. Many private organizations lose money and many public organizations irritate the public because their employees have poor telephone communication skills. Also, a substantial amount of work among employees is conducted via telephone. Most of the previous comments about overcoming communication barriers apply to telephone communications. A number of suggestions related specifically to improving telephone communications are also worth considering. The general goal of these suggestions is to help the telephone communicators sound courteous, cheerful, cooperative, and competent.[23]

1. When answering the telephone, give your name and department. Also give the company name if the call is not a transfer from a main switching center.
2. When talking to customers or clients, address them by name, but not to the point of irritation.
3. Vary your voice tone and inflection in order to avoid sounding bored or uninterested in your job and the company.
4. Speak at a moderate pace of approximately 150 to 160 words per minute. A rapid pace conveys the impression of impatience, while a slow rate might suggest disinterest.
5. Smile while speaking on the phone—somehow a smile gets transmitted over the telephone wires!
6. Exercise good listening skills, and take notes while listening. Be alert to both verbal statements and nonverbal cues, such as voice hesitancy or sighs of exasperation.
7. Keep a telephone note pad and a writing instrument near the phone so that you can avoid saying, "Hold on while I get a pen."
8. If the caller does not identify himself or herself, ask "Who is calling please?" Knowing the caller's name helps give a human touch to the conversation.
9. Use *fast and friendly* language that builds cooperation. Certain phrases in response to telephone callers are perceived as friendly and helpful while others come across as irritating and not so helpful. Here are some examples: "I'll try" versus "I will." "Your problem" versus "This situation." "As soon as I can get to it" versus "Before ___ o'clock."[24]
10. Do not hang up until the caller has finished speaking. One widely used tactic is to be the last to hang up. However, if too many people try to be last, phone calls will consume enormous amounts of time.

BACK TO THE JOB TASKS

Before giving your next presentation on the job or writing a memo, carefully review the section on persuasive communication. Follow the suggestions to make your message more persuasive. If you have an assignment that involves considerable listening, such as handling a supervisory role, review the suggestions for effective listening.

❑ Communication is the transmission of a message from a sender to a receiver. Its purpose is to gather, process, and disseminate information, making it a vital work activity. The seven steps in the communication process are ideation, encoding, transmission, receiving, decoding, understanding, and action. Interference, or barriers to communication, can take place at any of these steps.

❑ Organizational communication takes place in several different directions and over both formal and informal pathways. Formal pathways are the official, sanctioned path over which messages are supposed to travel. The chain of command and the actual flow of work both help shape formal communication channels. Informal pathways are more numerous than formal pathways. The grapevine is the major informal communication network in an organization.

❑ A rumor is a message transmitted over the grapevine, although not based on official word. Rumors are capable of disrupting work and lowering morale. Providing people with timely and accurate information is a good way of both preventing and stopping rumors. Gossip is a special form of rumor that does waste time, but also serves a few useful purposes. Gossip can be a morale booster, a socializing force, and a guidebook to group norms.

❑ Nonverbal communication refers to the transmission of messages through means other than words. It is used to communicate the feeling behind your message. Six common forms of nonverbal communication are the environment or setting of the message, interpersonal distance, posture, gestures, facial expression, and voice tone. Mirroring is a form of nonverbal communication that involves imitating some aspect of a person, such as breathing pattern, to establish rapport. Nonverbal messages sometimes reveal the existence of problems, such as lack of comprehension or deception. Cross-cultural differences in nonverbal communication are worth observing because, if not observed, they can lead to misunderstanding.

❑ Communication problems are ever-present in the workplace. Interference is most likely to occur when a message is complex, is emotionally arousing, or clashes with a receiver's mental set. Specific methods of overcoming communication barriers include (1) understand the receiver, (2) engage in two-way communication, (3) use appropriate timing, (4) use multiple channels, (5) avoid mixed signals or messages, (6) use verbal and nonverbal feedback, (7) decrease physical barriers, (8) use appropriately difficult language, (9) use bias-free language, (10) avoid communication overload, and (11) minimize defensive communication.

❑ Strategies and tactics have been proposed to help overcome cross-cultural communication barriers: be sensitive to their existence, use straightforward language and speak slowly and clearly, observe differences in etiquette, be aware of nonverbal differences, and do not be diverted by superficial factors.

❑ Communication problems can also be overcome through persuasive communication. Persuasiveness can be increased through such techniques as knowing exactly what you want, stating the benefits of your proposition, and appealing to the interests of the other party. Improving listening skills can also improve communication. A major improvement in listening can be achieved through better concentration. Improving telephone communication skills should receive special attention.

GUIDELINES FOR PERSONAL EFFECTIVENESS

1. Practice two-way rather than one-way communication if you are concerned about getting

your message across. While delivering your message, ask for verbal feedback and be sensitive to nonverbal cues about how your message is getting across.

2. Becoming a persuasive communicator is an important part of achieving success in a wide range of jobs. To be persuasive, you need to both make an effective presentation and understand the needs and interests of the person you are trying to persuade.

3. A requirement of the modern workplace is to deal effectively with people from different cultures from both within your own country and from other countries. Learning more about their customs and etiquette is very helpful. In addition, if you want to develop exceptional skills in an international environment, learn to speak, read, and write in another language. In the near future, some of the best jobs for business graduates will be reserved for those who are bilingual.

Discussion Questions and Activities

1. Most employers say that one of the most important attributes they look for in a new hire from business school is good communication skills. Why so much emphasis on communication skills?

2. What steps can a person take to follow up an important message?

3. Why do rumors about negative news travel so fast?

4. To what extent do actors and actresses make use of nonverbal communication?

5. Should the sex (or gender) of the receiver influence how close you stand to that person on the job?

6. How can you tell from nonverbal behavior that your boss likes you?

7. What physical barriers to communication exist in a classroom? In what way do instructors sometimes decrease these barriers?

8. What is the bias-free title for waiters and waitresses?

9. After reading about cross-cultural communication barriers, one manager said, "Enough about Americans always bending over backward. What about foreigners adapting to our way of doing things when they are working in the United States?" How would you respond to this manager?

10. Ask a few people what they think are the most frequent acts of telephone discourtesy. Report back to class.

A BUSINESS PSYCHOLOGY PROBLEM

Professionalism at Abilene Health Center

Joan McKenzie, the health care administrator at Abilene Health Center (AHC), had become concerned about the casual behavior of nurses at the center. McKenzie observed that some of the RNs (registered nurses) and LPNs (licensed practical nurses) were dressing and acting in a manner that detracted from the professional image of the health center. McKenzie set up a meeting to deal with what she perceived to be a problem of professionalism. At the outset of the meeting, McKenzie distributed an agenda that described the goals and objectives for the nursing staff. She instructed the people present to read the memo and then said, "After you have digested the information, we will have a full group discussion of the issues raised." A copy of her memo follows:

To: All members of the AHC nursing staff
From: Joan McKenzie, health care administrator
Re: Professionalism

We are *professional* adults and must behave accordingly. Professionalism can be achieved by keeping the following goals and objectives in mind.

1. Provide comprehensive health care of high quality in a cost-effective manner that provides satisfaction to those who receive and those who deliver services.
2. Assist, guide, and direct each nurse to her or his highest potential. Help each nurse be the best she or he can be.
3. Maintain and improve respect, pride, and dignity for co-workers.

In order to resolve existing problems, please observe the following rules:

1. Cursing will not be tolerated.
2. Screaming, yelling, or raising your voice is not acceptable.
3. Calling others names is not acceptable.
4. Everybody is to be at work from 8 A.M. to noon, and 1 to 5 P.M. If you have a problem with leaving at noon or 5 P.M., please call your supervisor one hour before that time.
5. If you are sick, you should call AHC before 8 A.M. at 442-0483. Lori Fanuco will answer the telephone and take your message. If there is no answer, please keep trying.
6. When you are asked to float to an area, please stay in that area and work appropriately.
7. There will be no nail-polishing in nurses' stations. Reading should be confined to nursing journals. Breaks must be taken in the break room.
8. As of May 1, the nursing staff is to wear white dresses or white pants or skirts with white or colored uniform-type tops. White nurses' shoes and sheer hose are also required. Name tags are to be worn by all employees at all times while at AHC.
9. A policies and procedures manual will be available in each nurses' station in the future.

As the nursing staff finished reading the memo, Joan McKenzie looked around the room to see if she could gauge their reaction.

1. How effective is the above memo from a communication standpoint?
2. What communication barriers might McKenzie be erecting?
3. What improvement in nonverbal communication is McKenzie seeking, as revealed by her memo?
4. How effective are the goals set forth in the memo (review Chapter 6)?

A BUSINESS PSYCHOLOGY ROLE PLAY

Discussing a Controversial Memo

The role play is a follow-up to McKenzie's memo and meeting. One of the nurses at the meeting initiates a discussion of his or her reaction to the memo and its implications. The nurse feels that McKenzie is putting the nursing staff on the defensive by using accusatory and hostile language.

McKenzie believes that her memo is a useful communication vehicle and that the nurse is being too sensitive. One person plays the role of McKenzie, another person plays the role of the dissenting nurse. Several other people can play the roles of other meeting participants who want to express how they feel about McKenzie's written message.

A Business Psychology Exercise

Rate Your Communication Skills

The following questionnaire is designed to help you evaluate the effectiveness of your communication skills. The developer of the questionnaire advises you to be fair in making your ratings: "You are probably a better communicator than you think." (Score 3 for excellent, 2 for good, and 1 for fair.)

In speaking:

____ My attitude is positive.

____ I analyze the situation and listener and adapt to these.

____ I plan my purpose related to listener interest and attitude.

____ I try to get on common ground.

____ My prejudices are submerged.

My message:

____ Is organized clearly

____ Has a definite and clear purpose

____ Adapts opening remarks to listener(s)

____ Presents points (not too many) in clear order

____ Goes clearly from one point to another (transitions)

____ Has sufficient proof and support

____ Holds interest and attention

____ Uses appropriate language

____ Shows clear thinking

In presenting the message:

____ My manner is enthusiastic.

____ I look directly at listener(s).

____ My posture and gestures are appropriate.

____ I project my voice with emphasis and variety.

____ I speak clearly and distinctly.

____ I adapt to listener reactions.

As a listener:

____ I pay full attention to the speaker

____ I look at the speaker.

____ I am openminded and empathetic.

____ I help establish a pleasant climate.

____ I try to understand speaker's purpose.

____ I separate facts from opinion.

____ I evaluate, not jumping to conclusions.

____ I avoid daydreaming.

____ I listen fully before trying to talk back or refute the speaker.

____ I apply the message to my needs.

____ **Total score**

Evaluating your communication rating:

80–90: Excellent

70–80: Good

60–70: Fair

1. What are the possible sources of distortion in the above evaluation of your communication skills?
2. Which questions in the test relate to nonverbal aspects of communication?

Source: Harold P. Zelco, "Communication: Rate Your Communication Skills," *Personnel Journal,* November 1987, p. 133.

1. VALORIE A. MCCLELLAND AND RICHARD E. WILMOT, "Improve Lateral Communication," *Personnel Journal,* August 1990, p. 32.

2. ALAN ZAREMBA, "Working with the Organizational Grapevine," *Personnel Journal,* July 1988, p. 39.

3. WALTER ST. JOHN, "In-house Communication Guidelines," *Personnel Journal,* November 1981, p. 877.

4. DONALD D. SIMMONS, "The Nature of the Organizational Grapevine," *Supervisory Management,* November 1985, p. 42.

5. ROBERT S. WIEDER, "Psst! Here's the Latest on Office Gossip," *Success,* January 1984, pp. 22–25.

6. "Gossip Can Convey the Awful Truth," *Personal Report for the Executive,* October 1, 1985, p. 5.

7. ALBERT MEHRABIAN AND M. WIENER, "Decoding of Inconsistent Communications," *Journal of Personality and Social Psychology,* 6, 1967, pp. 109–114.

8. Research cited in Salvatore Didato, "Our Body Movements Reveal Whether We're Dominant or Submissive," Rochester *Democrat and Chronicle,* December 20, 1983, p. 1C.

9. JOHN BAIRD, JR., AND GRETCHEN WIETING, "Nonverbal Communication Can Be a Valuable Tool," *Personnel Journal,* September 1979, p. 609.

10. ERIC H. MARCUS, "Neurolinguistic Programming," *Personnel Journal,* December 1983, p. 972.

11. LARRY REIBSTEIN, "Mimic Your Way to the Top," *Newsweek,* August 8, 1988, p. 50.

12. ROGER E. AXTELL, *Gestures: The Do's and Taboos of Body Language around the World* (New York: Wiley, 1991).

13. VALORIE MCCLELLAND, "Mixed Signals Breed Distrust," *Personnel Journal,* March 1987, pp. 24–29.

14. ROBERT A. GIACOLONE AND STEPHEN B. KNOUSE, "Reducing the Need for Defensive Communication," *Management Solutions,* September 1987, pp. 20–25.

15. The etiquette suggestion is from "Letitia Baldrige: Arbiter of Business Manners and Mores," *Management Review,* April 1992, p. 50.

16. AXTELL, *Gestures.*

17. DAVID P. TULIN, "Enhance Your Multi-Cultural Communication Skills," *Managing Diversity,* Volume 1, 1992, p. 5.

18. JIMMY CALANO AND JEFF SALZMAN, "Persuasiveness: Make It Your Power Booster," *Working Woman,* October 1988, p. 124.

19. CALANO AND SALZMAN, "Persuasiveness," pp. 124–125.

20. Several of these examples are from "Avoid These Top Ten Language Errors," *Working Smart,* October 1991, p. 8.

21. JOHN W. RICHTER, "Listening: An Art Essential to Success," *Success,* September 1980, p. 26.

22. ROBERT A. LUKE, "Improving Your Listening Ability," *Supervisory Management,* June 1992, p. 7; CYNTHIA HAMILTON AND BRIAN H. KLEINER, "Steps to Better Listening," *Personnel Journal,* February 1987, p. 21; G. Michael Barton, "Manage Words Effectively," *Personnel Journal,* January 1990, p. 38.

23. JANICE ALESSANDRA AND TONY ALLESSANDRA, "14 Telephone Tips for Ernestine," *Management Solutions,* February 1988, pp. 17–20; FRANKLIN J. STEIN, "Telephone Techniques That Help You Make a Good Impression," *Management Solutions,* July 1988, pp. 35–36.

24. DRU SCOTT, *Time Management and the Telephone: Making It a Tool and Not a Tyrant* (Los Altos, CA: Crisp Publications, 1991).

Suggested Reading

BUSH, JOHN B., JR., AND FROHMAN, ALAN L. "Communication in a 'Network' Organization." *Organizational Dynamics,* Autumn 1991, pp. 23–36.

DAVIDSON, ELEANOR. "Communicating with a Diverse Workforce." *Supervisory Management,* December 1991, pp. 1–2.

JOANETTE, YVES, GOULET, PIERRE, AND HANNEQUIN, DIDIER. *Right Hemisphere and Verbal Communication.* New York: Springer-Verlag, 1990.

LAABS, JENNIFER J. "Oliver: A Twist on Communication." *Personnel Journal,* September 1991, pp. 79–81.

MCTAGUE, MICHAEL. "Six Rules to Get Your Messages Across." *Supervisory Management,* August 1991, p. 9.

OVERMAN, STEPHENIE. "Managing the Diverse Workforce." *IIRMagazine,* April 1991, pp. 32–36.

ROGERS, CARL R., AND ROETHLISBERGER, F. J. "Barriers and Gateways to Communication." *Harvard Business Review,* July–August, 1952 (*HBR* classic reprinted, November–December 1991), pp. 105–111.

SCHWEIGER, DAVID M., AND DENISI, ANGELO S. "Communication with Employees Following a Merger: A Longitudinal Field Experiment." *Academy of Management Journal,* March 1991, pp. 110–135.

TRUITT, JOHN. *Phone Tactics for Instant Influence.* (New York: Dember Books/W. W. Norton, 1990.)

WHALEN, JOHN. "Winning Presentations: Less Talk Is More Convincing." *Supervisory Management,* October 1990, pp. 1–2.

part five   *Realizing Your Potential*

The final part of the text contains information to help you make good use of your potential. Chapter 16 provides essential information for being a productive individual whose work is of high quality. To achieve these ends one must develop effective work habits and time management. Chapter 17 is about developing your career including conducting a job search, using career-advancement tactics, and preventing career self-sabotage.

Chapter 16

ACHIEVING HIGH PERSONAL PRODUCTIVITY AND QUALITY

Learning Objectives

After reading and studying this chapter and doing the exercises, you should be able to

1. Become a more productive and quality-oriented worker.
2. Reduce any tendencies you might have toward procrastination.
3. Identify attitudes and values that contribute to personal productivity and quality.
4. Identify skills and practices that could improve your personal productivity.
5. Recognize which steps can be taken to reduce time wasting.
6. Understand how individual differences influence the development of good work habits and time management.

JOB TASKS RELATED TO THIS CHAPTER

Every job task can be accomplished more quickly and with higher quality through principles of work habits and time management. Among the specific tasks performed better by using the information in this chapter are beginning and finishing a major project, getting started on an assignment that seems overwhelming, and completing a project on time.

Assume that the instructor for this course announced that a term project will be due December 31, 1999, the absolute latest. Close to that date a handful of people would ask for an extension into the year 2000. Among the excuses offered would be, "I just didn't have time to do the paper with all those celebrations going on." "I would have been ready, but my word processor broke down December 30th." "Just my luck. My brother-in-law is getting married the same day that the project is due."

One reason for improving your work habits and time management is to avoid the trap faced by people who are always late with projects, even if the lead time is five years! Several other reasons are also important. People who use good work habits and manage time well eliminate a major potential stressor—a feeling of being out of control of one's job. Well-organized people also tend to be more successful in their careers than poorly organized people. Another reason for having good work habits is that it allows you more time to spend on personal life. In addition, personal life is more enjoyable when you are not preoccupied with unfinished job assignments.

Personal productivity:
An individual's level of efficiency and effectiveness.

Personal productivity refers to your level of efficiency and effectiveness. Efficiency means that you accomplish tasks with a minimum of wasted time, material, and fanfare. If you are a collection agent and it costs you $900 to collect $950 in past due accounts, you are not being very efficient. Effectiveness refers to accomplishing important results, while at the same time maintaining high quality. Efficiency and effectiveness are related. Being efficient often clears the way for being effective. If you are on top of your job, it gives you the time to work on important tasks and to strive for quality.

We have organized information about becoming more productive into four categories that show some overlap. One is overcoming procrastination, a problem that plagues everybody to some extent. The second is developing the attitudes and values that foster efficiency and effectiveness. The third category is developing the proper skills and techniques that lead to productivity and quality. The fourth is overcoming time wasters. We also describe individual differences that can influence a person's ability to develop good work habits and time management.

Dealing with Procrastination

Procrastination:
The delaying of action for no good reason.

Procrastination is the delaying of action for no good reason. Unproductive people waste considerable time, but even productive people are not immune from procrastination. If these people did not procrastinate, they would be even more productive.

The enormity of the problem makes it worthwhile to examine the most probable underlying causes of procrastination and the tactics for minimizing it. Only a charlatan would propose that procrastination can be *eliminated*. Before reading ahead, see Figure 16-1 to obtain further insight into the signs of procrastination.

FIGURE 16–1. *HOW DO YOU KNOW WHEN YOU ARE PROCRASTINATING?*

When you have no valid excuse for not getting things accomplished, you are probably procrastinating. The signs of procrastination can also be much more subtle. You might be procrastinating if one or more of the following symptoms apply to you:

- You overorganize a project by such rituals as sharpening every pencil, meticulously straightening out your desk, and discarding bent paper clips.
- You keep waiting for the "right time" to do something such as getting started on an important report.
- You underestimate the time needed to do a project, and say to yourself, "This won't take much time, so I can do it next week."
- You trivialize a task by saying it's not worth doing.

Source: Based on information in "Procrastination Can Get in Your Way." *Research Institute Personal Report for the Executive.* December 24, 1985, pp. 3–4.

Why People Procrastinate

People procrastinate for many different reasons. One major cause is fear of failure, including a negative evaluation of one's work. For example, if you delay preparing a report for your boss, that person cannot criticize its quality. The fear of bad news is another contributor to procrastination. If you think the brake system on your car needs overhauling, delaying a trip to the service station will postpone the diagnosis: "You're right. Your brake system is unsafe. We can fix it for $350." Another major cause of procrastination is to avoid a task that is overwhelming, unpleasant, or both.

Fear of success is another cause of procrastination. People who fear success share the conviction that success will bring with it some unwelcome outcomes, such as isolation or abandonment.[1] Some people procrastinate because they fear independence. These people put things off so long that they bring on a real crisis and hope or arrange for someone to rescue them. Or some may simply prefer to avoid the responsibility that success will bring. And a quick way to avoid success is to procrastinate over something important, such as completing a key assignment.

A deep-rooted reason for procrastination is **self-defeating behavior,** a conscious or unconscious attempt to bring about personal failure. For example, a person might be recommended for an almost ideal job opportunity. Yet the person delays sending along a résumé for so long that the potential employer loses interest. Self-defeating behavior and fear of success are closely related: the person who fears success may often engage in self-defeating behavior.

Procrastination may also stem from a desire to avoid uncomfortable, overwhelming, or tedious tasks. A business owner might delay preparing an employee pension report for the government for all these reasons. Perfectionism can also lead to procrastination. Because the worker does not

Fear of success:
A conviction that success will bring with it some unwelcome outcomes, such as isolation or abandonment.

Self-defeating behavior:
A conscious or unconscious attempt to bring about personal failure.

want to consider a project complete until it is perfect, the project is seriously delayed or never completed.

People frequently put off tasks that do not appear to offer a meaningful reward. Suppose you decided that your computer files need a thorough updating, including deleting inactive files. Even if you know it should be done, the accomplishment of updated files might not be a particularly meaningful reward.

Finally, people often procrastinate as a way of rebelling at being controlled. Procrastination, used this way, is a means of defying unwanted authority.[2] Rather than submit to authority, the person might say silently, "Nobody is going to tell me when I should get a report done. I'll do it when I'm ready."

Ways of Reducing Procrastination

A general method of coping with procrastination is to raise your level of awareness about the problem. When you are not accomplishing enough to meet your schoolwork, job, or personal goals, ask yourself if the problem could be one of procrastination. Then, through self-discipline, try to overcome that incident of inaction. You might also consider trying one or more of the seven techniques described next.

1. *Calculate the cost of procrastination.* You can reduce procrastination by calculating its cost. One example is that you might lose out on obtaining a high-paying job you really want by not having your résumé and cover letter ready on time. Your cost of procrastination would include the difference in salary between the job you do find and the one you really wanted. Another cost would be the loss of potential job satisfaction.

2. *Create some momentum to get you moving.* One way to get momentum going on an unpleasant or overwhelming task is to set aside a specific time to work on it. Another way to create some momentum is to find a **leading task** to perform. A leading task is an easy, warmup activity.[3] If you were procrastinating about conducting an audit, you might begin by starting a file for the project.

3. *Apply behavior modification to yourself.* Give yourself a pleasant reward soon after accomplishing an unpleasant task, rather than having procrastinated. The second part of the tactic is to punish yourself with something you despise immediately after you procrastinate.

4. *Make a commitment to other people.* Try to make it imperative that you get something done on time by making it a commitment to one or more other people. You might announce to co-workers that you are going to get something accomplished by a certain date. If you fail to meet this date, you are likely to feel embarrassed.

5. *Break the task into manageable chunks.* To reduce procrastination, cut down a project that seems overwhelming into smaller projects that seem less formidable. If your job calls for inspecting 20 locations within 30 days, begin by making dates to inspect the two closest to home. It also helps ease the pain by planning the job before executing it. In this situation, you would plan an itinerary before starting the inspection. The planning would probably be less painful than actually getting started at making all the arrangements.

6. *Use subliminal messages about overcoming procrastination.* Software, called *MindSet,* flashes reinforcing messages across the menu bar on your com-

---

Leading task:
An easy warmup activity used to help avoid procrastination.

puter. You can adjust the frequency and duration of the suggestions. The message can flash by subliminally (below the level of conscious awareness) or remain on screen for a few seconds. The procrastination message is: "My goals are obtainable. I am confident in my abilities. I make and keep deadlines."[4]

7. *Integrate your brain functions to stop procrastinating.* Another proposed method is to work directly with your brain to overcome procrastination by consciously integrating your right-brain and left-brain functions. Teri E. Belf contends that the integration will take place by such means as starting in the middle of a project and doodling and sketching while listening to music. You can also program the brain during its sleeping state by going to sleep with positively stated questions.[5] For example, "How can I get this project completed on time and in a high-quality manner?"

Developing the Proper Attitudes and Values

Developing good work habits and time-management practices is often a matter of developing the right attitudes toward your work and toward time. If, for example, you think that your schoolwork or job is important and that time is a precious resource, you will be on your way toward developing good work habits. In this section we describe a group of attitudes, values, and beliefs that can help a person become more productive through better use of time and improved work habits.

Total quality management:
A system of management in which all activities are directed toward satisfying external and internal customers.

Develop a Total Quality Management (TQM) Philosophy. **Total quality management** is a system of management in which all activities are directed toward satisfying external and internal customers. TQM involves painstaking attention to detail to ensure that all work activities are done right the first time.[6] If your mental set is that of totally satisfying your customer, you will produce work of high quality based on pride. Knowing that getting things done on time pleases customers, you will also be prompt. Yet, again, you must avoid the trap of perfectionism. You should strive for continuous improvement. However, if you never pass along your portion of a project until you are convinced no error can be found, your productivity will be low.

Establish Goals and Develop a Strong Work Ethic. Being committed to a goal propels you toward good use of time. Imagine how efficient most employees would be if they were told, "Here is five days of work facing you. If you get it finished in less than five days, you can have all that saved time to yourself." One negative side effect, however, is that the employees might sacrifice quality for speed.

Work ethic:
A firm belief in the value and dignity of work.

Closely related to establishing goals is developing a strong **work ethic**—a firm belief in the dignity and value of work. Developing a strong work ethic may lead to even higher productivity than goal setting alone. For example, one might set the goal of earning a high income. It would lead to some good work habits, but not necessarily a high commitment to quality. A person with a strong work ethic believes in quality, is highly motivated, and minimizes time-wasting activities.

Work Smarter, Not Harder. People caught up in trying to accomplish a job often wind up working hard, but not in an imaginative way that leads to good results. Much time and energy are therefore wasted. An executive report provides a case example of working harder versus working smarter:[7]

> *Working harder:* In a manufacturing company, profits are down despite higher sales. To compensate, the sales manager is pushing salespeople for larger volume, using richer commissions to spur them on.
> *Working smarter:* In one company with a similar problem, the sales manager saw that profit, not volume, was the problem. She designed a sales compensation system that deducts the costs of sales from each order, thus rewarding salespeople for keeping costs low. They started to go after accounts that provided longer, more profitable production runs. Volume did not change, but profits increased 12 percent in six months.

Value Your Time. People who place a high value on their time are propelled into making good use of time. If a person believes that his or her time is valuable, it will be difficult to engage that person in idle conversation during working hours. Valuing your time can also apply to personal life. The yield from clipping grocery coupons is an average of $8 per hour. Would a busy professional person therefore be better off clipping coupons or engaging in self-development for the same amount of time? Being committed to a goal, as described previously, is an automatic way of making good use of time.

Avoid Attempting Too Much. Many workers become disorganized and fall behind schedule because they assume more responsibility than they can handle. Especially significant is when the stressed out person has voluntarily attempted too much. A worker already overloaded with responsibility, for example, might accept an invitation to join yet another community activity. His or her work schedule becomes all the more cramped, and the list of unfinished tasks mounts.

To avoid attempting too much, you must learn to say no to additional demands on your time. You cannot take care of your own priorities unless you learn to tactfully decline requests from other people that interfere with your work. If your boss interrupts you with an added assignment, point out how the new tasks will conflict with higher-priority ones and suggest alternatives. However, do not turn down your manager too frequently. Much discretion and tact are needed to use this approach to increasing personal productivity. Knowing *when* to say no is also very important.

Avoid Workaholism. A valid attitude to maintain is that overwork can be counterproductive, leading to negative stress and burnout. Proper physical rest contributes to mental alertness. **Workaholics,** people who are obsessed with work, often approach their jobs in a mechanical, unimaginative manner.[8] (A small number of workaholics, however, are creative people at the top of their fields. But to these people, work is truly relaxing.)

Workaholic: Person addicted to work to the extent that it has adverse consequences for family and personal life.

Constant attention to work or study is often inefficient. It is a normal human requirement to take enough rest breaks to allow oneself to approach work or study with a fresh perspective. Each person has to establish for himself or herself the right balance between work and leisure, within the bounds of freedom granted by the situation. A young middle manager painted this picture of working conditions at his company: "Sure, I believe in leading a balanced life. But at my company you can't if you want to climb the ladder. Management expects us to work about 60 hours per week. You dare not be caught entering the building after 8 in the morning or leaving before 6:30 at night."

Value Cleanliness and Orderliness. An orderly desk, set of computer files, or attaché case does not inevitably indicate an orderly mind, but it does help most people to become more productive. Less time is wasted, and less energy is expended if you do not have to hunt for information that you thought you had on hand. Knowing where information is and what information you have available is a way of being in control of your job. When your job gets out of control, you are probably working at less than peak efficiency.

Valuing cleanliness helps in two other ways. According to the Japanese system, cleanliness is the bedrock of quality. Also, after you have thoroughly cleaned your work area, you will usually attain a fresh outlook.

Value Good Attendance and Punctuality. Good attendance and punctuality are expected of both experienced and inexperienced employees. You cannot be productive if you are not physically present in your work area. The same principle applies whether you work on company premises or at home. One exception is that some people can work through solutions to job problems while engaged in recreation. Keep in mind, too, that being late for or absent from meetings sends out the silent message that you do not regard the meeting as important.

Developing the Proper Skills and Techniques

So far we have discussed two important strategies for improving productivity and quality. One is to minimize procrastination, while the other is to develop the appropriate values and beliefs. You also need the right skills and techniques to become productive and achieve high quality. Later we devote separate attention to a subset of skills and techniques—minimizing time wasting. Next we summarize well-known skills and techniques of good time management, along with a few new ones.

Make Good Use of Office Technology. Only in recent years have companies begun to derive productivity increases from office automation. One reason office automation has not been as successful as hoped is that many office workers do not make extensive use of the technology available. Used properly, most high-tech devices in the office can improve productivity and quality. Among the most productivity-enhancing devices are word processors, spreadsheets, computer graphics, fax machines, voice mail, telephone answering machines, and photocopiers. How you use these devices is the key to increased productivity. Two examples follow:[9]

- A laptop computer can help you be much more productive during periods of potential downtime. While waiting in someone's office or in an airport or on the plane, you can spend your time answering correspondence.
- A fax machine has many productivity-enhancing applications. One manager frequently visits clients in the late afternoon. If there are important papers she must see before she leaves, she has them faxed to her office at home. Using this method, she saves a trip back to the office, but she can review the work in ten minutes during the evening.

The accompanying box provides several more examples of how computers are being used to help people worker smarter, not harder. To best understand any computer application, one needs to study carefully the manual accompanying the software. Careful study also allows a person to capitalize on the productivity-enhancing advantages of the software.

USING THE COMPUTER TO WORK SMARTER, NOT HARDER

Managers, professionals, sales representatives, and business owners use personal computers regularly to manager time more productively. Two such applications are for writing form letters and for sorting out contacts.

Writing Sales Letters

SALES *LetterWorks* enables you to prepare a customized form letter. Just pick the appropriate letter or form from the program's manual, call it up on your PC, and tailor it to your specific requirements. Print out the finished document, and you have accomplished the job in a minimum amount of time. SALES *LetterWorks* contains over 300 letters, including proposals, customer follow-ups, direct-mail solicitations, and price conformations. All the letters are designed to enhance sales.

Managing Names, Addresses, and Phone Numbers

INtouch is a desk accessory that stores an unlimited number of contracts in a single file and sorts through them instantly. You prompt it with a few letters from someone's name and up comes his or her card. Each card is scrollable and can hold 32 Kbytes of information. This allows you to take detailed notes on each conversation. *INtouch* also prints envelopes, including your return address and postal bar code, and dials the phone. It quickly imports data from other programs and contains a "snapshot" feature that will transfer a name and address in a letter or other document.

Source: Jenny C. McCune, "Take a Letter, Please," *Success,* June 1992, p. 56; Michael Maren, "Put Your Mac to Work," *Success* April 1991, p. 48.

Clarify Your Own Objectives. A basic starting point in improving work habits and time management is to know what it is you are supposed to accomplish. A careful review of your job description and objectives with your boss is fundamental. Some people are accused of being ineffective simply because they do not know what is really expected of them. Unsure of what to do, they waste time on projects of limited value to the organization.

Prepare a "To Do" List and Set Priorities. At the heart of every time-management system is list making. We described this technique in relation to setting daily goals (refer to Figure 6-2). Almost every successful person in any field composes a list of important and less-important tasks that need to be done. Some executives and professional people delegate their list making and errand running to a subordinate. Before you can compose a useful list, you need to set aside a few minutes of quiet time a day to sort out the tasks at hand. Such activity is the most basic aspect of planning. As implied in Figure 16-2, many people find it helpful to set up "to do" lists for both work and personal life.

FIGURE 16–2. *A COMBINED ACTIVITY CALENDAR AND "TO DO" LIST*
Source: Reprinted with permission from Desk-Day Timer Inc., Allentown, PA 18001.

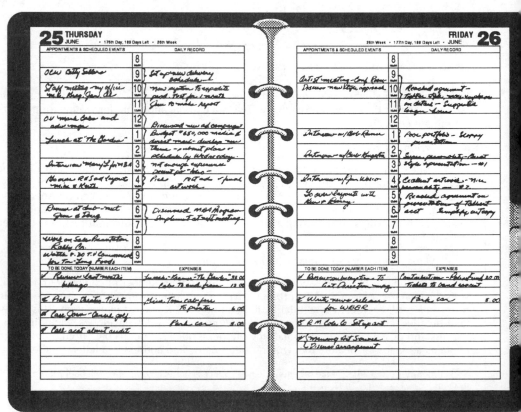

Where Do You Put Your Lists? Some people dislike having small "to do" lists stuck in different places. One reason is that these lists are readily lost among other papers. Instead you use a notebook, either looseleaf or spiral bound, that is small enough to carry around with you. The notebook becomes your master list to keep track of errands, things to do or buy, and general notes to yourself about anything requiring action. A desk calendar or planner can serve the same purpose, as shown in Figure 16-2.

Setting Priorities. Everything on a person's "to do" list is not of equal importance; therefore, priorities should be attached to each item on the list. A typical system is to use A to signify critical or essential items, B to signify important items, and C for the least important ones. Although an item might be regarded as a C (for example, refilling the cellophane-tape dispenser), it still has a contribution to make to your management of time and sense of well-being. Many people report that they obtain a sense of satisfaction from crossing off an item on their list, however trivial. Second, if you are at all conscientious, small, undone items will come back to interfere with your concentration.

Carefully Schedule Activities. The use of a "to do" list and a desk planner enables a person to schedule activities in a productive manner. Six other important scheduling suggestions are described next:

Allow Time for Emergencies. Because many managerial and professional jobs require handling emergencies, enough slack has to be built into the schedule for handling unpredictable problems. In essence, the careful scheduler creates room for unscheduled events. Similarly, a household budget must allow enough room for the inevitable "miscellaneous" category.

Minimize Unscheduled Interruptions. Although legitimate emergencies must be handled quickly, most other types of unscheduled interruptions should be minimized in order to maintain productivity.

One solution to the problem of interruptions is for you to schedule a period of time during the day in which you have uninterrupted work time. You give co-workers a definite time during which you want to be disturbed with emergencies only. It is also helpful to inform co-workers of the nature of the important work you ordinarily conduct during your quiet period. You might say, for example, "I have to tally the sales figures every Friday afternoon."

Schedule Your Most Demanding Tasks for When Your Energy Is Highest. Tasks that require the most energy, such as creative decision making and confrontations with difficult people, are best performed during energy peaks. Most people have their highest energy at the start of their workday,

Tackle your intellectually most demanding assignment during your energy peaks.

but others gain energy as the day progresses. The most routine items should be handled during energy lows.

Schedule Similar Tasks Together. An efficient method of accomplishing small tasks is to group them together and perform them in one block of time. To illustrate, you might make most of your telephone calls in relation to your job from 11 to 11:30 A.M. each workday morning. Or you might reserve the last hour of every workday for correspondence. By using this method you develop the necessary pace and mental set to knock off chores in short order. In contrast, when you flit from one type of task to another, your efficiency may suffer.

Schedule Yourself by Computer. Software is available that can turn your personal computer into an electronic calendar to help you keep track of appointments and lists of chores. The first step, of course, would be to enter into your computer's memory your appointments, tasks, and errands. For instance, a person might enter the following:

3/1 Meet with Ms. Godwin to discuss term project.
3/6 Get inventory audit started.
3/7 Lunch with Liz to discuss St. Patrick's Day party.
6/10 Start shopping for gift for parents' Silver Anniversary.

From this point forward, the computer's information-processing capabilities could be tapped. Suppose you couldn't remember the date of your upcoming luncheon date with Liz. You would command the computer to "Find lunch date with Liz." Or, if you were an extremely busy person, you might have reason to ask the computer to tell you when you had the next opening for lunch. Another use of this type of software is to command the computer to flag key appointments and chores.

Concentrate on One Task at a Time. Effective executives have a well-developed capacity to concentrate on the problem or person facing them, however surrounded they are with other obligations. The best results from concentration are achieved when you are so absorbed in your work that you achieve the *flow* experience (see Chapter 5). Intense concentration leads to crisper judgment and analysis and also minimizes major errors. Another useful by-product of concentration is that it helps reduce absentmindedness. If you really concentrate on what you are doing, the chances diminish that you will forget what you intended to do.

Concentrate on High-output Tasks. To become more effective on the job or in school, you have to concentrate on tasks in which superior performance could have a large payoff. No matter how quickly a restaurant manager pays the utility bill, this effort will not make the restaurant a success. However, looking for a new special that customers will appreciate is an example of a high-output item. Looking for high-output items for your effort is akin to looking for a good return on investment for your money.

In following the A–B–C system, you should devote ample time to the essential tasks. You should not pay more attention than absolutely necessary to the C (least important) items. However, if you find that working on C items is tension reducing, then do so, but recognize that you must return to A items as soon as you feel relaxed. When the suggestion of working on high-output items is offered, many people respond, "I don't think concentrating on important tasks applies to me. My job is so filled with routine, I have no chance to work on breakthrough ideas." True, most jobs are filled with routine requirements. What a person can do is spend some time, perhaps just one hour per week, concentrating on tasks that may prove to have high output.

Work at a Steady Pace. In most jobs and programs of study, working at a steady pace pays dividends in efficiency. The spurt worker creates many problems for management, while the spurt student is in turmoil at exam time or when papers are due. Some employees take pride in working rapidly, even when the result is a high error rate. An important advantage of the steady-pace approach is that you accomplish much more than someone who puts out extra effort just once in a while.

The completely steady worker would accomplish just as much the day before a holiday as on a given Monday. That extra hour or so of productivity adds up substantially by the end of the year. Despite the advantages of maintaining a steady pace, some peaks and valleys in your work may be inevitable. The seasonal demands placed on public accountants and related workers are a prime example.

Stay in Control of Paper Work and Electronic Work. Although it is fashionable to complain about paper work in responsible jobs, the effective career person does not neglect paper work. (Paper work includes electronic work such as electronic mail and voice mail.) Paper work involves taking care of administrative details such as correspondence, personnel reports, and inventory forms. Unless paper work and electronic work are attended to, a person's job may get out of control. An out-of-control job leads to lowered productivity and employee stress.

A small amount of time should be invested in paper work every day. Nonprime time (when you are at less than your peak of efficiency, but not overfatigued) is the best time to take care of paper work.

A simple system for categorizing the inflow of papers follows this format:[10]

- Action (A): for immediate follow-up.
- File (F): required for doing business.
- Information (I): useful, worth reading or scanning.
- Discard (D): obviously dispensable.

Stand up for Certain Tasks. According to Merrill E. Douglass, standing rather than sitting is one of the most overlooked secrets for getting more done during working hours. People tend to take longer to accomplish things when they sit down. If forced to stand, they will answer you more quickly rather than become engaged in a long conversation. Because of this fact, many managers schedule stand-up meetings when an agenda is not too long or complicated. Also, some companies have experimented successfully with stand-up conference tables.[11]

Standing is perceived by most people as more formal than sitting. Because people tend to respect time more in formal than informal settings, they make better use of standing time. Also, they waste less time than when slouched in chairs. A physical reason for people getting things done more quickly while standing is that they find it less comfortable than sitting. To avoid discomfort, they get to the point quickly.

Do you think that stand-up meetings have pushed comfort and courtesy too far in the quest for high productivity?

Telecommuter:
An employee who performs regular work duties from home or at another location.

Become a Telecommuter. A **telecommuter** is an employee who performs regular work duties from home or at another location. Approximately 16 million employees spend most of their working hours in their homes. Another 10 million employees who work at home are self-employed. Many employees persuaded to take early retirement from large employers have established small businesses operating out of their homes. Furthermore, companies that do not offer an office-at-home option, at least part time, are losing workers to employers that do.[12] Telecommuters stay in touch with the office through telecommunications devices such as phones, computers, and fax machines. They also have regularly scheduled time on company premises, typically about one day per week.

The link to personal productivity is that being a telecommuter will ordinarily increase your output about 20 percent, assuming you do not squander the opportunity.[13] Productivity increases are possible because commuting time is eliminated, there are fewer office-created interruptions, and you do not have to spend time socializing with co-workers. Considerable self-discipline and emotional maturity are required to make productive use of the freedom afforded by telecommuting. Many telecommuters lose productivity by engaging in such activities as raiding the refrigerator, watching television, running household errands, and jogging during normal working hours.

Overcoming Time Wasters

Another basic thrust to improved personal productivity is to minimize wasting time. Many of the techniques already described in this chapter help to save time. The tactics and strategies described next, however, are directly aimed at overcoming the problem of wasted time.

Minimize Daydreaming. "Taking a field trip" while on the job is a major productivity drain. Daydreaming is triggered when the individual perceives the task at hand to be boring, such as reviewing another person's work for errors. Brain research suggests that younger people are more predisposed to daydreaming than older people. Apparently, older people use neurons better to focus on tasks. In one study, people aged 24 to 71 were asked questions about their tendency to daydream when working at some task. The researchers asked the same people the same questions six to eight years later.

According to the self-reports of the subjects, mind wandering decreased. The conclusion reached was that minds wander less as people get older.[14]

Unresolved personal problems are an important source of daydreaming, thus blocking your productivity. This is especially true because effective time utilization requires good concentration. When you are preoccupied with a personal or business problem, it is difficult to give your full efforts to the task at hand. The solution is to do something constructive about whatever problem is sapping your ability to concentrate (as discussed in Chapter 8 under stress and burnout). Sometimes a relatively minor problem, such as driving with an expired operator's license, can impair your work concentration. At other times, a major problem, such as how to best take care of a parent who has suffered a stroke, interferes with work. In either situation, your concentration will suffer until you take appropriate action.

Use a Time Log to Track Time Wasters. An advanced tool for managing time efficiently is to prepare a time log of how you are currently investing time. For five full workdays, write down everything you do, including such activities as answering mail and taking rest breaks. An activity calendar is ideally suited to preparing a time log. One of the most important outputs of a time log is uncovering **time leaks,** anything you

Time leaks:
Anything you are doing or not doing that allows time to get away from you.

are doing or not doing that allows time to get away from you. An example would be shutting down your work 15 minutes before you leave the office. Another important output from a time log is to uncover scraps of time that are being squandered. For example, while waiting for an elevator, you might be able to read a 100-word report. And if you have finished your day's work 10 minutes before quitting time, use that time to clean out a drawer in your desk. By the end of the year, your productivity will have increased much more than if you had squandered these bits of time. A man from Nebraska, who was transferred to New York City, explains how this strategy helped his personal life:

> When I lived in Nebraska, I could never find a good time to get my reading done. I'm talking about both the daily newspaper and office correspondence. When I did this type of reading at home, it seemed to interfere with my relationship with my wife and child. After I was transferred to the Big Apple, I became a subway commuter. Despite being jostled by the crowd, I could get all my reading done on workdays. The result was more relaxed time with my family.

Avoid Being a Computer "Goof-off." We are all aware of the productivity improvements possible when computers are used in the office. An unproductive use of computers, however, is to tinker with them to the exclusion of useful work. Many people have become intrigued with computers to the point of diversion. They become almost addicted to creating new reports, exquisite graphics, and even playing computer games on company time. Some managers spend so much time involved with computers that they neglect leadership responsibilities, thus lowering their productivity. In short, avoid becoming a computer goof-off.

Keep Track of Important Names, Places, and Things. How much time have you wasted lately searching for such items as a telephone number you jotted down somewhere, your keys, or an appointment book? A manager suddenly realized he had forgotten to show up for a luncheon appointment. He wanted to call and apologize but was unable to locate the person's name and phone number! Standard solutions to overcoming these problems are to keep a wheel file (such as a Rolodex) of people's names and companies. It is difficult to misplace such a file. Many other managers and professionals store such information in a database or even in a word-processing file. Such files are more difficult to misplace than a pocket directory.

Two steps are recommended for remembering where you put things. First, have a parking place for everything. This would include putting your keys and appointment book back in the same place after each use. Second, make visual associations. In order to have something register in your mind at the moment you are doing it, make up a visual association about that act.[15] Thus you might say, "Here I am putting my résumé in the back section of my attaché case."

Set a Time Limit for Certain Tasks. Spending too much time on a task or project wastes time. As a person becomes experienced with certain projects, he or she is able to make accurate estimates of how long a project will take to complete. A paralegal assistant might say, for example, "Getting this will drawn up for the lawyer's approval should take two hours." A good work habit to develop is to estimate how long a job should take and then proceed with a strong determination to get that job completed within the estimated period of time.

A productive variation of this technique is to decide that some low- and medium-priority items are only worth so much of your time. Invest that much time in the project, but no more. Preparing a file on advertisements that cross your desk is one example.

Be Decisive and Finish Things

An often overlooked way of improving your personal productivity is to be decisive. Move quickly, but not impulsively, through the problem-solving and decision-making steps outlined in Chapter 7 when you are faced with a nonroutine decision. Once you have evaluated the alternatives to the problem, choose and implement one of them. By acting quickly, time is saved.

Superintelligent and highly educated people are sometimes poor decision makers because they keep on collecting facts. The result is that they procrastinate instead of acting. Some people of more modest intelligence waste time when faced with a decision not because they want more facts, but because they are fearful of committing themselves. In short, if you agonize too long over too many decisions, your personal productivity will suffer.

Ziegarnik effect:
The phenomenon of uncompleted tasks creating a disturbing level of tension.

A specific productivity drain stemming from not finishing things is the **Ziegarnik effect**—the phenomenon of uncompleted tasks creating a disturbing level of tension. Not finishing a task can thus serve as a distraction that interferes with productivity on future tasks.

Individual Differences Related To Work Habits and Time Management

Individual differences influence a person's ability to make use of the suggestions for productivity and quality improvement described in this chapter. Of particular significance are skill in diagnosing underlying problems, personal characteristics, and personal style.

Diagnostic Skill. Many people are unable to identify the reasons behind their poor work habits, including the cause of their procrastination. Often it is necessary to identify the true problem before much progress can be made. For example, some people want to remain disorganized because they are self-defeating. Yet they deny having self-defeating tendencies.

Personal Characteristics. A person needs the right talents, such as planning ability and motivation, to make much improvement in work habits and time management. Personality traits are also significant. At the top of the list is **compulsiveness,** a tendency to pay careful attention to detail and to be meticulous. An individual with a compulsive personality takes naturally to being well organized and neat. If you are less concerned about detail and meticulousness by nature, it will be more difficult for you to develop exceptional work habits.

Compulsiveness:
A tendency to pay careful attention to detail and to be meticulous.

People who are highly spontaneous and emotional also tend to be naturally inclined toward casual work habits. Being overly compulsive can also be a detriment to personal productivity. The compulsive person may have a difficult time concentrating on important tasks. He or she may tend to get hung up on details and become the unproductive type of workaholic. The truly productive person finds an optimum balance between concern for detail and time, on the one hand, and being able to look at the "big picture" on the other.

Personal Style. People vary somewhat in which set of time-management principles and work habits are best suited to their personal style. Some people work best when their activities are preplanned and tightly scheduled. They would benefit from a rigid adherence to lists and calendars. In contrast, John Kotter has observed that the best executives do not necessarily map out their daily schedules in advance. Instead, they respond to important situations as they crop up.[16] In essence, these successful executives allow considerable slack time in their schedule within the framework of pursuing a major goal.

Differences in personal style about organizing work are partially traced to brain dominance. Left-brain-dominant people (preference for logical and analytical thinking) take readily to "To Do" lists and scheduling by a daily planner. Right-brain-dominant workers (preference for creative and intuitive thinking) manage their time best by paying little attention to the clock, schedules, and constraints. What works best for right-brain-dominant workers is knowing how to spend their time most productively.[17] For example, right-brain-dominant workers might develop imaginative solutions to a work problem while stalled in traffic. Or they might choose to jog around the office building instead of taking a coffee break.

BACK TO THE JOB TASKS

Whatever job or school task is facing you today, you can probably perform it more efficiently and effectively if you apply one or more of the techniques and principles described in this chapter. For example, before getting started on your next workday, spend a few minutes planning what you hope to accomplish. Incorporate this planning into your "To Do" list.

Summary of Key Points

❑ By improving your work habits and time management, you can improve your job productivity and quality and enhance your personal life. Personal productivity refers to your level of efficiency and effectiveness and thus includes performing high-quality work.

❑ Procrastination is the major time waster for most employees and students. People procrastinate for many reasons, including their perception that the task is either unpleasant or overwhelming and a fear of the consequences of their actions. The feared consequences can be positive or negative. Awareness of procrastination may lead to its control. Seven other techniques recommended for reducing procrastination are (1) calculate the cost of procrastination, (2) create some momentum to get you going, (3) apply behavior modification to yourself, (4) make a commitment to other people, (5) break the task down into manageable chunks, (6) use subliminal messages about overcoming procrastination, and (7) integrate your brain functions to stop procrastinating.

❑ Developing good work habits and time-management practices is often a matter of developing the right attitudes toward your work and toward time. Eight such attitudes, values, and beliefs are as follows:

1. Develop a total quality management philosophy.
2. Establish goals and develop a strong work ethic.
3. Work smarter, not harder.
4. Value your time.
5. Avoid attempting too much.
6. Avoid workaholism.
7. Value cleanliness and orderliness.
8. Value good attendance and punctuality.

❑ Ten skills and techniques to help you become more productive, including producing high-quality work, are as follows:

1. Make good use of office technology.
2. Clarify your own objectives.
3. Prepare a "To Do" list and set priorities.
4. Carefully schedule activities. (This includes allowing time for emergencies, minimizing interruptions, using energy peaks, scheduling similar tasks together, and computerized scheduling.)
5. Concentrate on one task at a time.
6. Concentrate on high-output tasks.
7. Work at a steady pace.
8. Stay in control of paper work and electronic work.
9. Stand up for certain tasks.
10. Become a telecommuter.

❑ Another way of achieving high productivity is to minimize wasting time. Six such techniques are as follows:

1. Minimize daydreaming.
2. Use a time log to track time wasters.
3. Avoid being a computer goof off.
4. Keep track of important names, places, and things.
5. Set a time limit for certain tasks.
6. Be decisive and finish things.

❑ Individual differences influence a person's ability to use the suggestions for productivity and quality improvement described in this chapter. Of particular significance are skill in diagnosing your mental blocks, personal characteristics such as compulsiveness, and personal style, such as a preference for reacting immediately to demands.

GUIDELINES FOR PERSONAL EFFECTIVENESS

Reading about these methods of improving your work habits alone will not lead to permanent changes in behavior. You must select one or two areas in which you are particularly weak and then begin to implement a remedial plan of action.

Suppose that you recognize that your day is filled with time leaks because you rarely accomplish what you set out to. Try these steps:

1. Identify the two most obvious time leaks. Perhaps (a) time wasted in gathering your friends for lunch and (b) stopping work 15 minutes before quitting time.
2. For the next five workdays force yourself to plug these time leaks. You might have to say to your friends, "I'm only taking 30 minutes for lunch today. I want to avoid bringing home work tonight. So I'll meet you in the cafeteria at 11:45 sharp."
3. If this approach works, move on to subtle and difficult leaks, such as a tendency to daydream when work pressures lessen.
4. Now try another time-management method of improving your work habits that you think applies to one of your areas for needed improvement.

Discussion Questions and Activities

1. The book *Your Own Worst Enemy: How to Prevent Career Self-sabotage* (AMACOM, 1992) states that procrastination is the leading cause of self-defeating behavior on the job. Why might this be true?

2. Give several examples of punishments a person might self-administer in order to overcome procrastination.

3. It has been argued that well-organized people are so rigid that they lack spontaneity and creativity. What is your opinion on this issue?

4. How does being well organized contribute to total quality management?

5. When you meet a stranger, how can you tell if he or she is well organized?

6. Many successful scientists, artists, and professors have cluttered work areas. How does this fit with the suggestion to "value cleanliness and orderliness"?

7. How can voice mail or a telephone answering machine contribute to an individual's productivity?

8. How would a customer service representative whose job it is to listen to customer complaints make use of the suggestion to "minimize unscheduled interruptions"?

9. Many time-management experts recommend that you handle a piece of paper only once. How might this technique be counterproductive?

10. Ask an experienced high-level worker for his or her most effective method of time management. Be prepared to report your findings to the class.

How to Cure Pilomania

Jeffrey J. Mayer claims to have developed a cure for *pilomania,* the piling up of papers on the desk. He says that you are suffering from pilomania if your desk is buried under piles of papers. It doesn't matter if the papers are in neat orderly piles, in stackable trays, or totally disorganized.

Many people suspect that out of sight is out of mind and therefore hesitate to put things away for fear of misplacing them. Ultimately, you are working less efficiently because your desk area is being improperly used. Mayer claims that if you eliminate the clutter you will save at least 30 minutes a day because you will be able to find all the unfinished work hidden in the piles.

To cure pilomania, Mayer recommends creating a *master list.* Begin by making a two-hour appointment with yourself. Use that time to go through every piece of paper on your desk. Keep papers calling for work yet to be done or an action not yet taken. Throw out the rest. Next, go through your keeper file and create a master list, an inventory of all your unfinished work and ongoing projects.

For each paper on your list, ask: Is there any work that needs to be done, such as a phone call to make, an electronic message to send, a letter to write? Record the action to be taken on the master list. After you have made your entry, either throw out the paper or place it in a properly labeled file.

The master list is modeled after the directory on a computer that lists all the filed located within its memory. With the master list you have a directory of your unfinished work stored in hard copy. Mayer proposes that you use your master list all day long. It should be the first thing you look at when you start work and the last thing you look at before leaving.

Part of the master list system is to develop an efficient filing system. Place all papers that deal with a customer, client, or project in a manila folder. Label your files by hand according to whatever categories fit best, such as by project or customer.

New items are added to the master list as the day progresses, and old items are crossed off when they are done. To get the biggest productivity gain from your master list, follow these additional suggestions:

- Use a lined legal or letter-size pad. Avoid small pieces of paper because you will end up in piles of lists.
- Write on every line, but do not number the items.
- When you have filled up a page, continue on the next one. After half the items on a page are completed, transfer the unfinished items to the next page.
- Date your lists so you know how long some unfinished items have been there.
- Keep your master list on top of your desk where it can be readily located. Do not put it inside a file folder.
- Each evening before going home, scan your list and ask yourself, "What is the most important thing I must do tomorrow?"

1. How effective do you think this system would be for most office workers?
2. What other suggestions for improved work habits and time management does the master list replace?
3. What problems might the master list method create?

Source: Jeffrey J. Mayer, *If Your Haven't Got the Time to Do It Right, When Will You Find the Time to Do It over?* (New York: Simon & Schuster, 1990); "Curing Pilomania," *The Pryor Report,* July 1990, p. 4.

The Overwhelmed Administrative Assistant

Mary looked into the storeroom mirror and thought to herself, "You're looking bad, kid. Somehow you've got to get your life straightened out. You're on a treadmill, and you don't know how to get off. But it's a bad time to be thinking about myself right now. It's time to meet with my boss, Beatrice. I wonder what she wants?"

Beatrice Reynolds began the meeting with Mary in her usual open manner: "Mary, I'm concerned about you. For a long time you were one of the best administrative assistants in our firm. You received compliments from me and the other department heads who had contact with your department. Now you're hardly making it. You've become so irritable, so lacking in enthusiasm. And a lot of your work contains glaring errors and is also late. The reason I'm bringing the subject up again is that things have gotten worse. What's your problem?"

"I wish it were only one problem, Beatrice. I feel like the world is caving in on me. I work here about 40 hours a week. I'm trying to upgrade myself in life. As you know I'm taking two courses in a business administration program. If I can keep up the pace, I'll have an associate's degree by next spring. But it's getting to be a grind."

"How are things at home, Mary?"

"Much worse than they are here. My husband works, too, and he's getting fed up with never seeing me when he comes home. It seems that when he's home, I'm either working late at the office, in class, or studying at the library. Thursday is the one weekday night I'm home for sure. And that's Tony's bowling night."

"Our son, Steve isn't too happy either. He's only five but the other day he asked me if Daddy and I were getting divorced. Steve doesn't see us together much. When he does see us, he can feel the tension between us."

"So, you're under pressure at the office and at home," said Beatrice.

"Add school to that list. I'm having a devil of a time getting through my business statistics course. If I flunk, my chances of getting a degree are set back considerably."

"Do the best you can, Mary. I'm sympathetic, but I need better performance from you."

As Mary left Beatrice Reynold's office she said, "Thanks for being candid with me. My problem is that my boss, my husband, my child, and my professors all want better performance from me. I wish I knew how to give it."

1. What suggestions can you offer Mary for working her way out of her problems?
2. Why is this case included in a chapter about improving your personal productivity?
3. How well do you think Beatrice Reynolds handled the interview?

Improving Your Personal Productivity

Studying this chapter will rarely lead to improvements in efficiency and effectiveness. You need to back up studying these ideas with a specific plan of action for improvement as described in the chapter section "Guidelines for Personal Effectiveness." A useful mechanical aid toward achieving this end is to study the checklist presented next, which covers the techniques mentioned in this chapter. Pick out the five or six items on the checklist in which you need the most help. For each item you select, write a one- or two-sentence action plan. Suppose you checked the item "Be Decisive and Finish Things." Your action plan might take this form:

- Next time I'm faced with an important decision, I'll make up my mind within two days, instead of the usual entire week.
- I'll make note of the date on which the problem faced me and the date on which I finally made up my mind.

THE PERSONAL PRODUCTIVITY AND QUALITY CHECKLIST

Procrastination

1. Calculate the cost of procrastination. ____
2. Create some momentum to get you going. ____
3. Apply behavior modification to yourself. ____
4. Make a commitment to other people. ____
5. Break the task into manageable chunks. ____
6. Use subliminal messages. ____
7. Integrate your brain functions. ____

Attitude, Value, or Belief

1. Develop a total quality management philosophy. ____
2. Establish goals and develop a strong work ethic. ____
3. Work smarter, not harder. ____
4. Value your time. ____
5. Avoid attempting too much. ____
6. Avoid workaholism. ____
7. Value cleanliness and orderliness. ____
8. Value good attendance and punctuality. ____

Skills and Techniques

1. Make good use of office technology. ____
2. Clarify your own objectives. ____
3. Prepare a "To Do" list and set priorities. ____
4. Carefully schedule activities.
   a. Allow time for emergencies. ____
   b. Minimize interruptions. ____
   c. Use energy peaks. ____
   d. Schedule similar tasks together. ____
   e. Use computerized scheduling. ____
5. Concentrate on one task at a time. ____
6. Concentrate on high-output tasks. ____
7. Work at a steady pace. ____
8. Stay in control of paper work and electronic work. ____

9. Stand up for certain tasks. ——
10. Become a telecommuter. ——

Time Wasting

1. Minimize daydreaming. ——
2. Use a time log to track time wasters. ——
3. Avoid being a computer goof off. ——
4. Keep track of important names, places, and things. ——
5. Set a time limit for certain tasks. ——
6. Be decisive and finish things. ——

References

1. DONNAH CANAVAN, "Fear of Success," in REBECCA C. CURTIS, *Self-defeating Behaviors: Experimental Research, Clinical Impressions, and Practical Implications* (New York: Plenum Press, 1989), pp. 159–188.
2. THEODORE KURTZ, "Ten Reasons Why People Procrastinate," *Supervisory Management,* April 1990, pp. 1–2.
3. MICHAEL LE BOEUF, quoted in Priscilla Petty, "Saying No to Unproductive Jobs Frees Time for High Priority Goals," Rochester *Democrat and Chronicle,* June 23, 1983, p. 10D.
4. MICHAEL MAREN, "Program Yourself: Software for the Right Side of Your Brain," *Success,* October 1991, p. 58. (Software produced by Visionary Software, Portland, Oregon.)
5. "Program Yourself for Success," *Executive Strategies,* January 1992, p. 8.
6. LINDA A. JERRIS, "Quality Shines in Small Details," *Personnel Journal,* January 1990, pp. 26–30.
7. "Working Harder vs. Working Smarter," *Personal Report for the Executive,* October 15, 1988, p. 1.
8. DIANE FASSEL, *Working Ourselves to Death: The High Cost of Workaholism and the Rewards of Recovery* (San Francisco: Harper, 1990).
9. "Save Time by Doing Two Things at Once," *Working Smart,* October 1991, p. 5.
10. "Clear Your Desk for Action!" *Personal Report for the Executive,* January 1, 1987, p. 5.
11. MERRIL E. DOUGLASS, "Standing Saves Time," *Executive Forum,* July 1989, p. 4.
12. "The Future Is No Office," *Infoworld,* July 8, 1991, p. 40.
13. ANDREW J. DUBRIN, "Comparison of the Job Satisfaction and Productivity of Telecommuters versus In-house Employees: A Research Note on Work in Progress," *Psychological Reports,* 1991, 68, pp. 1223–1234.
14. PAUL CHANCE, "The Wandering Mind of Youth," *Psychology Today,* December 1988, p. 22.
15. PETER A. TURLA AND KATHLEEN L. HAWKINS, "Remembering to Remember," *Success,* May 1983, p. 60.
16. "Time Management Techniques—A Rundown," *Personal Report for the Executive,* August 1, 1987, p. 4.
17. "From the Right," *Executive Strategies,* November 1991, p. 10.

BITTEL, LESTER R. *Right on Time*. New York: McGraw-Hill, 1990.

BOWLES, JERRY. "Is American Management Really Committed to Quality?" *Management Review,* April 1992, pp. 42–46.

DRUCKER, PETER F. "The New Productivity Challenge." *Harvard Business Review,* November–December 1991, pp. 69–79.

FRAM, EUGENE H. "Time Pressed Consumer." *Marketing Insights,* Summer 1991, pp. 34–39.

KIECHEL, WALTER, III. "Overscheduled and Not Loving It." *Fortune,* April 8, 1991, pp. 105–107.

MACKENZIE, ALEC. *The Time Trap*. New York: AMACOM, 1990.

McCORMACK, MARK H. *The 110% Solution: Using Good Old American Know-how to Manage Your Time, Talent, and Ideas*. New York: Villard Books, 1991.

PETERS, TOM. "Time-obsessed Competition." *Management Review,* September 1990, pp. 16–20.

STIASEN, SARAH. "Making Time: How Tracking the Hours Yields Hidden Benefits." *Success,* April 1990, p. 198.

YOUNG, J. A. "The Advantages of Telecommuting." *Management Review,* July 1991, pp. 19–21.

Chapter 17

ACHIEVING A REWARDING AND SATISFYING CAREER

Learning Objectives

After reading and studying this chapter and doing the exercises, you should be able to

1. Recognize that you must take responsibility for managing your own career.
2. Be familiar with various measures of career success.
3. Pinpoint how people select fields and occupations for themselves.
4. Conduct an effective job campaign.
5. Describe at least ten career advancement strategies and tactics.
6. Understand why and how people switch careers.

JOB TASKS RELATED TO THIS CHAPTER

This chapter is about the most important job task of all—managing your career in such a way as to capitalize on your education and talent. Among the assignments related to this chapter are to conduct an effective job campaign and have a rewarding and successful career.

Although many companies have career-development programs, you must still assume the major responsibility for managing your career. One reason is that employers freely adjust the number of employees to meet their financial condition. Layoffs and early retirements have become standard business practice. Another reason managing your career is so important is that the competition for good positions is intense. The baby boomers (the large number of people born between 1946 and 1964) are still in the work force competing with each other for available promotions. Promotions are also scarce because so many employers strive to operate with the minimum feasible number of employees.

As you reflect on the information presented in this chapter, keep an optimistic observation in mind. A marketing manager reminds us that good people will still have successful careers in the upcoming decade.[1] Effective career management will help you make his prediction come true.

The major purpose of this chapter is to present information that will help you manage, or develop, your own career. A **career** is a lifelong series of experiences that form some kind of coherent pattern. We ordinarily think of a career as involving progressive achievement over most of its course. The information in this chapter is organized according to the logical flow of events a person faces in building a career. Arriving at a personal definition of career success → finding a field → finding a job → selecting relevant career-advancement tactics and strategies → switching careers if the need arises.

Career:
A lifelong series of experiences that form some kind of a coherent pattern.

The Meaning of Career Success

Career success:
Being able to live out the subjective and personal values one really believes in and to make contributions to the world of work.

A major part of achieving a rewarding and satisfying career is achieving career *success*. Many people argue that if you are satisfied you are successful. Following this logic of an internal definition of success, C. Brooklyn Derr defines **career success** as "being able both to live out the subjective and personal values one really believes in and to make contributions to the world of work."[2] Another point of view is that career success should be defined in terms of both internal (such as satisfaction) and external (such as income) standards. The criteria of success specified and defined in Table 17-1 reflect both internal and external measures.

Finding a Field and an Occupation

A starting point in establishing a rewarding and satisfying—and therefore successful—career is to find a field compatible with one's interests. Many readers of this book may have already identified a field they wish to enter or are already working in that field. But many other readers are probably still in the process of identifying a field of work and an occupation within that field to their liking. Here we identify seven of the most likely ways of identifying a field and occupation to pursue.

TABLE 17–1. *RESEARCH MEASURES OF CAREER SUCCESS* _____

Variable Name	Definition
Earnings	Considering all sources of personal income, how much would you say you earned last year?
Job satisfaction	In general, how satisfied are you with your job?
Life satisfaction	How do you feel about your life as a whole?
Self-assessed success	Compared to other people your age who are involved in the same occupation, how successful do you feel you are?
Prestige	Prestige rating of job according to a scale.
Budget responsibilities	What is the largest budget (work or personal) you have ever been responsible for?
Career identification	Do you feel that you have identified or been involved in a career for yourself?
Problem-solving effectiveness	How effective do you perceive yourself to be in dealing with the problems that confront you?
Job effectiveness	How effective do you perceive yourself to be in the job in which you are presently involved?
Number supervised	What is the greatest number of people you have ever supervised?
Peer rate	How successful would the people you work with say you are?
Progress	How well do you feel your career is progressing, compared to your peers?

Source: Adapted from Auralee Childs and Richard J. Klimoski, "Successfully Predicting Career Success: An Application of the Biographical Inventory," *Journal of Applied Psychology,* February 1986, p. 5.

1. *Influence of parent, relative, or friend:* "My uncle owned a pharmacy, so I became interested in pharmacy at an early age."
2. *Reading and study:* "While in high school I read about astronomy, and decided that I wanted to be an astronomer."
3. *Natural opportunity:* "I was born into the business. Who would give up a chance to be a vice-president by the time I was 25? Our family has always been in the retail business."
4. *Forced opportunity:* "I had never heard about electronics until I joined the army. They told me I had aptitude for the field. I enjoyed working as an electronics technician. After the army I applied for a job with IBM as a field service engineer. It has worked out well."
5. *Discovery through counseling and/or testing:* "I took an interest test in high school. My guidance counselor told me that I had interests similar to those of a social worker. Not knowing what else to do, I decided to become a social worker." (This is the most systematic of the six methods mentioned here.)
6. *Matching yourself with a compatible person:* An indirect way of finding a field and occupation within that field is first to locate a person with whom you have similar interests. You then choose that person's field of work for yourself, using this reasoning, "I seem to like what that person likes in most things. All things being equal, I would probably like the kind of work that person does."
7. *Making use of occupational information:* Acquiring valid information about career fields can often lead to sensible career choices. Such information can

be found in reference books about careers such as the *Occupational Outlook Handbook,* computer-assisted career guidance (available in most counseling centers), newspapers and trade periodicals, and by speaking to people working in fields of interest to you. When speaking directly to career people, it is helpful to get the perspective of people at different stages in their field.

Conducting the Job Campaign

Some people who have identified a career field never have to look for a job. Some of them enter into family businesses. Others are in such high-demand occupations that employers come looking for them (two current examples are paralegal assistant and environmental technician). And some people capitalize on chance opportunity, with small effort on their part, such as being offered a job by a neighbor. Most other people have to conduct a **job campaign** to find employment at various times in their career. Included in the job campaign are job-hunting tactics and preparing a job résumé and cover letter.

Job campaign:
All the activities involved in finding a job.

Job-hunting Tactics

Most people already have some knowledge about how to find a job. Some of the ideas discussed next will therefore be familiar to you; some will be unfamiliar. We recommend using this list of tactics and methods as a checklist to ensure that you have not neglected something important. It is easy to overlook the obvious when job hunting because your emotions may cloud your sense of logic. This list should be supplemented with the advice offered by placement offices, job-finding books, and software.[3]

Identify Your Position Objective(s). A proper job search begins with a clear perception of what kind of job or jobs you want. Your chances for finding employment are directly proportional to the number of positions that will satisfy your job objective. One person with a background in writing might be willing to accept only a job as a newspaper reporter (always a difficult position to find). Another person with the same background is seeking a job as (1) a newspaper reporter, (2) a magazine staff writer, (3) a copywriter in an advertising agency, (4) communications specialist in a company, or (5) copywriter in a public relations firm. The second person has a better chance than the first of finding a job.

Identify Your Skills and Potential Contribution. Today's job market is skill based. Employers typically seek out job candidates with tangible skills that can be put to immediate use in accomplishing work. Skills as an important source of individual differences were described in Chapter 3. Job-relevant skills you might identify include computer skills, written communication skills, oral communication skills, foreign language skills, sales skills, problem-solving skills, math skills, and listening skills. A successful job candidate for a customer representative position told the interviewer at NYSEG (a gas and electric utility), "I know I can help you resolve customer complaints. In college I worked as a dorm counselor and had to listen to problems as part of my job. Give me a chance to listen to your customers."

Develop a Comprehensive Marketing Strategy. A vital job-finding strategy is to use multiple approaches to reach the right prospective employer. Among the possible sources of job leads are placement offices, private employment agencies, government employment services, classified ads in local and national newspapers and trade magazines, employment booths at trade associations, and inquiries through acquaintances. One recently developed approach is to have your résumé entered into a computerized database. Subscribers to the system across the country would then have access to your résumé.

If you qualify, consider making contact with an employment agency specializing in placing minority group members. An example is HispanData, a Santa Barbara, California, human resources recruiting service. The firm assists employers identify and hire entry-level and experienced Hispanic professionals and sales workers nationwide.

Yet another standard approach is to place a situation-wanted ad in a newspaper. The following ad helped one graduate find a job: "Productivity-minded problem solver wants to become a member of your first-line management team. Give me a chance to give you a big return on your investment. Write Box 8592 this newspaper."

Networking:
Seeking friends and acquaintances and building systematically on these relationships to create a still wider set of contacts who might lead to employment.

Insider system:
A job-hunting technique in which a person searches for nonadvertised jobs that are usually offered to company insiders, friends, and relatives of insiders or applicants who write unsolicited letters to the firm.

Internal job market:
The jobs that have not been advertised and that are usually filled by word of mouth or through friends and acquaintances of employees.

Use Networking to Reach the Internal Job Market. It has been estimated that up to 95 percent of successful job campaigns stem from personal contacts. **Networking** is seeking friends and acquaintances and building systematically on these relationships to create a still wider set of contacts who might lead to employment. A key advantage of networking is that it taps you into the **insider system** or internal job market. The **internal job market** is the large array of jobs that have not been advertised and that are usually filled by word of mouth or through friends and acquaintances of employees.

About 85 percent of job openings are found in the internal job market; the other 15 percent are advertised or registered with employment agencies and placement offices. The best way to reach these jobs is by getting someone to recommend you for one. When looking for a job, it is important to tell every potential contact of your job search. The more influential the person, the better. Be specific about the job you are seeking.

To use networking effectively, it may be necessary to create contacts aside from those you already have. Potential sources of contacts include almost anybody you know, as summarized in Table 17-2. The networking technique is so well known today that it suffers from overuse. It is therefore important to use a tactful, low-key approach with a contact. For example, instead of asking a person in your network to furnish you a job lead, ask that person how a person with qualifications similar to yours might find a job.

TABLE 17–2. *POTENTIAL SOURCES OF NETWORK CONTACTS* _____

Co-workers and previous employers
Friends and neighbors
Faculty and staff
Graduates of any school you have attended
Former employers
Present employer (assuming you hold a temporary position)
Professionals such as bankers, brokers, and clergy
Political leaders at the local level
Members of your club or athletic team
Community groups, churches, temples, and mosques
Trade and professional associations
Student professional associations
Career fairs
People met in airports and on airplanes
People met at aerobics classes and Nautilus

Another way of reaching the internal job market is to write dozens of letters to potential employers. A surprisingly large number of people find jobs by contacting employers directly. Prepare a prospective employer list, including the names of executives to contact in each firm. The people who receive your letters become part of your network. A variation of this approach is to develop a 30-second telephone presentation of your background. After you have researched organizations that may have opportunities for you, call them and make your pitch.

Be Persistent. Finding a job is a tedious and time-consuming activity for many people. Persistence is vital in turning up good leads, and may help you find a job even after you have had some rejection. Marilyn Moats Kennedy explains that even in a recession about 10 percent of the people who take a job fail after three months. Sometimes they are fired at the end of the probationary period, or they leave because of low interest or inability to perform on the job. Therefore, check with the firms who said you were their second choice.[4] Another reason for being persistent is that it keeps pressure on you. Without this self-pressure, some people become too lethargic about conducting a job campaign. Remember that finding a job is frequently one of the most challenging "jobs" in a person's career.

Take Rejection in Stride. Finding a job you really want is fraught with rejection. It is not uncommon for a recent graduate or an experienced career person to send out 150 letters of inquiry to find one job. When your job search is confined to places that are trying to fill a position that matches your speciality, you still may have to be interviewed many times in order to land a suitable job. Often you will be rejected when it appears to you that your qualifications match perfectly those required for the opening. The hiring manager may have interviewed another applicant he or she thinks is even better qualified than you. Or the same person may have felt a stronger "chemistry" between himself or herself and another candidate. In short, do not take rejection personally. It is an inevitable part of job hunting.

Smile at Network Members and Interviewers. James Challenger recommends that you smile because happy people get jobs. "People would rather work with people who have pleasant dispositions. If you have been looking for a job for three months with no success, it may be hard to smile, but make yourself do it. It works."[5]

Avoid Common Mistakes. A good way of summarizing and integrating information about job hunting is to be aware of mistakes to avoid. Several of these mistakes cover the points mentioned above.[6]

- Not knowing the type of work you want to do.
- Not taking the initiative to generate job leads.
- Meeting with too few prospects.
- Not viewing the job from the employer's perspective. (Employers are more interested in knowing what you can do for them, rather than vice versa.)
- Asking too directly for a job. (It is considered preferable to discuss job opportunities in an "informational interview.")
- Not making contact with the people with whom you would be working.
- Approaching prospects in an impersonal way. (Never address a letter "To Whom It May Concern." Instead, write to a specific person whose name can be found through a directory or a phone call.)
- Overlooking your selling points. (For example, you might have exceptional computer skills or writing skills.)
- Not making follow-up contacts after you have generated a lead.
- Having a poor résumé or cover letter.

The Job Résumé and Cover Letter

No matter what method of job hunting you choose, inevitably somebody will ask you for a résumé. The author is aware that many job-hunting books are adamant about not handing out a résumé, but instead insisting on a personal interview. The reality is that virtually every company requires a résumé before seriously considering a job candidate from the outside. Sometimes you will be asked to complete a job application form instead of, or in addition to, a résumé. Résumés are also important for job hunting within your own firm. You may need one to be considered for a transfer within a large firm.

Résumé Purpose. Regard your résumé as a marketing tool for selling your skills and potential to handle new responsibilities. The most specific purpose of a résumé is to help you obtain a job interview that can lead to a job. Your résumé must therefore attract enough attention for an employer to invite you for an interview. Recognize that you are competing against many carefully prepared résumés. Should the demand for your skills be high enough, it is conceivable to be hired without an interview.

Résumé Length and Format. Opinions vary about the desirable length for a résumé. For a recent graduate with limited work experience, a one-page résumé may be acceptable. For more experienced people, it would seem too short. Employers today demand considerable detail in résumés, particularly about the candidate's skills, accomplishments, and leadership experience. Nevertheless, a four-page or longer résumé may irritate an impatient reader. Two or three pages is therefore recommended for most purposes.

To attract attention, some job seekers print résumés on tinted paper, in a menulike folder, or on an unusual-sized paper. Still others do not print them. Instead, they dictate the résumé onto a tape cassette or present a video of themselves. If done in a way to attract positive attention to yourself, the nonconventional résumé formats have merit. The menulike folder has worked well for a number of job seekers. It should therefore be given consideration if it is not being overused in your community. But do not (as one joker did) label your job objective "the appetizer," your work experience "the entree," and your education "the dessert."

Three Different Types of Résumés. The three most commonly used formats are the chronological, functional, and target.[5] You might consider using one of these types, or a blend of them, based on the information about yourself that you are trying to highlight. Whichever format you choose, you must include essential information.

The **chronological résumé** presents your work experience, education, and interests, along with accomplishments in reverse chronological order. A chronological résumé resembles the traditional résumé, with the addition of accomplishments and skills. Some people say the chronological résumé is too bland. However, it contains precisely the information most employers demand, and it is easy to prepare. A sample chronological résumé is presented in Figure 17-1. Note the emphasis on skills.

The **functional résumé** organizes your skills and accomplishments into the functions or tasks that support the job you are seeking. A section of the functional résumé might read:

SUPERVISION: Organized the work of ten employees as a restaurant manager, resulting in two years of high profits and customer satisfaction. Trained and supervised five data-entry specialists to produce a smooth-running data-entry operation.

The functional résumé is useful because it highlights the things you have accomplished and the skills you have developed. An ordinary work experience might seem more impressive following this format. For instance, the tasks listed under "supervision" may appear more impressive than listing the jobs of "assistant restaurant manager" and "data-entry supervisor." One problem with the functional résumé is that it omits the factual information many employers demand.

Chronological résumé: A presentation of work experience, education, interests, and accomplishments, in reverse chronological order.

Functional résumé: One that organizes skills and accomplishments into the functions or tasks that support the job sought.

FIGURE 17-1. GENERAL-PURPOSE JOB RÉSUMÉ

Scott Wayland
170 Glenview Drive
Dallas, Texas 75243
(312) 385-3986

JOB OBJECTIVE

Industrial sales, handling large, complex machinery. Willing to work largely on commission basis.

CAPABILITIES AND SKILLS

Professional sales representative. Able to size up customer manufacturing problem and make recommendation for appropriate machinery. Precise in preparing call reports and expense accounts.

MAJOR ACCOMPLISHMENT

In one year sold at a profit $250,000 worth of excess machine inventory. Received letter of commendation from company president.

WORK HISTORY
1991–present

Industrial account representative, Bainbridge Corporation, Dallas. Sell line of tool and die equipment to companies in Southwest. Duties include servicing established accounts and canvasing new ones.

1989–1991

Inside sales representative, Bainbridge Corporation. Answered customer inquiries. Filled orders for replacement parts. Trained for outside sales position.

1985–1989

Tool and die maker apprentice, Texas Metals, Inc., Dallas. Assisted senior tool and die makers during four-year training program. Worked on milling machines, jigs, punch presses, computer-assisted manufacturing, computer-assisted design (CAD/CAM).

FORMAL EDUCATION
1985–1989

Madagascar College, Dallas, Texas. Associate Degree in Business Administration; graduated with 3.16 grade point average. Courses in marketing, sales techniques, consumer behavior, accounting, and statistics. President of Commuter's Club.

1981–1985

Big Horn High, Dallas. Honors student; academic major with vocational elective. Played varsity football and basketball. Earned part of living expenses by selling magazine subscriptions.

PERSONAL INTERESTS
AND HOBBIES

Personal computer enthusiast (write programs for own computer), scuba diving, recreational golf player, read trade and business magazines.

References on request.

The **targeted résumé** focuses on a specific job target, or position, and presents only information that supports the target. Using a targeted résumé, an applicant for a sales position would list only sales positions. Under education, the applicant would focus on sales-related courses, such as marketing and communication skills. A targeted résumé is helpful in dramatizing your suitability for the position you are seeking. Yet this type of résumé omits other relevant information about you. Also, a new résumé must be prepared for each target position.

Common Mistakes in Résumés. Abundant useful information is available about résumé preparation. Nevertheless, many job seekers continue to prepare résumés that virtually disqualify them from further consideration in the eyes of employers. Do your best to avoid most of the following errors by editing your own résumé and asking at least two other people to do the same.

- Too lengthy, containing much useless information. Or written in narrative, rather than short, punchy statements.
- Disorganized, including the same type of information presented under different headings.
- Poorly word processed, including narrow margins and writing in the margins, using a faded ribbon, excessive spacing.
- Skimpy or insufficient information (only dates, titles, and incomplete addresses).
- Excessive information, including general information (such as a listing of the product line of an employer like IBM).
- No listing of accomplishments or skills.
- Misspellings, input errors, input errors corrected by pen, poor grammar, and frequent abbreviations.
- Starting sentences with phrases such as "I did," "I was," "I am," instead of verbs like initiated, created, supervised, and so on.
- Overly elaborate résumé, such as calligraphy, fancy typesetting, or plastic binder.
- So much emphasis on nontraditional résumé that basic facts are missing (for example, work experience and addresses of schools attended). Since the company official cannot verify facts or assess qualifications, he or she places résumé in circular file.
- Lying or inflating facts about yourself that prove to be untrue when references are checked. These types of résumé errors usually lead to immediate disqualification. If the error is discovered after the candidate is hired, he or she is liable for dismissal.

The Cover Letter. A résumé should be accompanied by a cover letter explaining who you are and why you are applying for this particular job. The cover letter customizes your approach to a particular employer, while the résumé is a more general approach. Most job applicants use the conventional approach of writing a letter attempting to impress the prospective employer with their background. An alternate approach is to capture the reader's attention with a punchy statement of what you might be able to do for them. Later in the letter you might present a one-para-

Capture the letter reader's attention with a punchy statement of what you might be able to do for them.

graph summary of your education and the highlights of your job and educational experience. Here are two examples of opening lines geared to two different types of jobs:

1. Person seeking employment as customer service manager in a large automobile dealership: "Do you want your old customers to return to your dealership when it's time to purchase a new car? Then give me the chance to help you operate a smooth-running, 'service with a smile' customer-service department."

2. Person looking for position as administrative assistant in hospital where vacancy may or may not exist: "Is your hospital drowning in paperwork? Let me jump in with both feet and clear up some of the confusion. Then you can go back to taking care of patients."

The second opening line may come across as a little brash to suit some tastes. It is important to use an opening line that suits your personality. A worksheet for writing a cover letter that can be adapted to any job is presented in Figure 17-2. The attention-grabbing opening line would be used as the start of paragraph 1, as shown in Figure 17-3.

Handling Yourself in a Job Interview

After a prospective employer has reacted favorably to your cover letter and résumé, the next step is to invite you for a job interview. The most

FIGURE 17–2. *COVER LETTER FORMAT DEVELOPED BY JOHN F. HITCHCOCK.*

Worksheet for Cover Letter

Your address
Town, street, zip code
Date

Name of person, Title (e.g., Human Resources Manager)
Name of firm
Address
Town, street, zip code

Dear Mr., Mrs., or Ms. Smith:
Paragraph 1: State the type of job that you want.
Paragraph 2: Summarize your qualifications.
Paragraph 3: Ask for interview. State your availability.
Paragraph 4: Do not forget "Thank you."

Yours truly,
Signature
Name typed out
Alternative address
location

important general strategy for performing well in a job interview is to present a positive, but accurate picture of yourself. Your chances of performing well in a job increase if you are suited for the job. "Tricking" a prospective employer into hiring you when you are not qualified is therefore a self-defeating tactic in terms of your career. Outright deception, such as falsifying one's educational or employment record, is widely practiced. However, if the person is hired and the deception is discovered later, that employee is subject to dismissal. Here we will describe a number of important tactics and strategies to keep in mind when being interviewed for a job you would like to obtain.

Look Relaxed and Make the Interviewer Feel Comfortable. By seeming "at home" during the interview, you move toward convincing the job interviewer that you will fit the job and the organization. Coming to the interview fully prepared to discuss yourself and your background and knowing something about the prospective employer will help you look relaxed.[7]

Establish a Link between You and the Employer. A good rapport builder between you and the prospective employer is to mention some plausible link between you and that firm. Organizations that serve the public, such as retail stores, supermarkets, hospitals and government agencies, provide natural opportunities for links between you and them.

FIGURE 17–3. *SAMPLE COVER LETTER.*

27 Buttercup Lane
Little Rock, AR 72203
Date

Mr. Bart Bertrand
President
South View Dodge
258 Princess Blvd.
Little Rock, AR 72201

Dear Mr. Bertrand:

Without a good service department, a new car dealership is in big trouble. An efficiency-mined person like myself who loves autos, and likes to help customers, can do wonders for your service department. Give me a chance, and I will help you maintain the high quality of after-sales service demanded by your customers.

The position you advertised in the *Dispatch* is an ideal fit for my background. Shortly, I will be graduating from Pine Valley Community College with an associate's degree in automotive technology. In addition, I was an automotive mechanics major at Monroe Vocational High.

My job experience includes three years of part-time general work at Manny's Mobil Service and two years of clerical work at Brandon's Chrysler-Plymouth. Besides this relevant experience, I'm the proud owner of a mint condition 1980 sports coupe I maintain myself.

I'm very stable in this community. A well-paying, secure job where I can make a contribution is important to me.

My enclosed résumé contains additional information about me. When might I have the opportunity to be interviewed?

Sincerely yours,

Rita Mae Jenkins

To illustrate, if being interviewed for a position at a Wal-Mart, one might say, "It's fun to visit the office part of Wal-Mart. Our family has been buying its housewares and garden supplies here for years."

Ask Perceptive Questions. During the job interview, it is important to ask some questions yourself. The best questions are sincere ones that reflect an interest in the content of the job and job performance, rather than benefits and social activities. Following are some questions that will usually be well received by the interviewer. Ask them during a period of silence or when you are asked if you have any questions. However, avoid making the interviewer feel uncomfortable by asking too many questions.

1. What kind of advancement opportunities are there in your firm for outstanding performers?
2. What personal qualities or characteristics are most important to success in this job?
3. What would you consider to be outstanding performance in this job?

Inevitably, the job applicant will want to ask about salary and benefits. In general, it is helpful to wait for the interviewer to take the initiative on this topic. If you are forced to take the initiative, ask about salary after you have talked about yourself and the job has been discussed. The reason for asking about salary at this point is that, if the company is sold on you, they may be willing to offer you a starting salary toward the top of the range.

The salary issue can be handled differently if you have previous full-time work experience at approximately the same level as the job for which you are applying. Just state your present or previous salary, and allow the interviewer to make an offer.[8]

Prepare in Advance. In addition to having good questions to ask during the job interview, it is necessary to prepare in advance in other ways. Be familiar with pertinent details about your background, including your social security number and names and addresses of references. Do your homework regarding your potential employer. It is important to know some basic facts about the firm in which you are seeking employment. Annual reports, brochures about the company, and sometimes newspaper and magazine articles should provide valuable information. A brief conversation with one or two current employees might provide some basic knowledge about the firm. Speaking to people who use the products or services of the firm can also provide valuable insights.

Be Ready to Discuss Your Strengths and Weaknesses. Most interviewers will ask you to discuss your strengths and weaknesses. It is therefore useful to prepare in advance for such questioning. Frequently asked questions are shown in Table 17-3. Everyone has weaknesses or at least needs to improve in certain areas. To deny them is to appear uninsightful or defensive. However, you may not want to reveal weaknesses that are unrelated to the job (such as a fear of drowning). A mildly evasive approach is to describe weaknesses that could be interpreted as strengths. A case in point: "I am so opposed to making mistakes, that I have been criticized for spending too much time with details." Do you think this approach is unethical?

Show How You Can Help the Employer. To repeat, use the "here is

TABLE 17–3. *QUESTIONS FREQUENTLY ASKED OF JOB CANDIDATES* _____

An important way of preparing for job interviews is to rehearse answers to the types of questions you will most likely be asked by the interviewer. The following questions are some of the same type found in most employment interviews. Rehearse answers to them prior to going out on job interviews. One good rehearsal method is to role play the employment interview with a friend who asks these typical questions, or videotape yourself.

1. Why did you apply for this job?
2. What are your career goals?
3. What do you expect to be doing five years from now?
4. What salary are you worth?
5. How much money do you expect to be earning ten years from now?
6. What are your strengths (or good points)?
7. What are your weaknesses (or areas of needed improvement)?
8. Why did you prepare for the career you did?
9. How would you describe yourself?
10. How would other people describe you?
11. Why should we hire you instead of other candidates for the same job?
12. How well do you work under pressure?
13. What makes you think you will be successful in business?
14. What do you know about our firm?

---

how I can help you" strategy at every stage of the job-finding process. Use this strategy to guide you in answering all employment interview questions.[9]

> Whatever the question, take a moment to think, "What details of my abilities and experience could be useful to them?" And you'll have your answers. You'll be giving the interviewers what they're looking for. They, in turn, will offer you want you came for—a good job.

Encourage the Interviewer To Talk. Frequently, the person interviewing you for a position would welcome the opportunity to talk about the company or himself or herself. At the right moment, ask the interviewer's opinion about the working conditions in the company, the future of the company, or what kind of work he or she does. As the interviewer says something that makes sense to you, subtly respond in this way: "You have a point there," or "It seems like you have given careful thought to this topic," or even "That's very informative."

Write a Follow-up Letter. Your responsibilities in the job-hunting process do not end with the employment interview. The vital next step is to mail a courteous follow-up letter several days after the interview, particularly if you want the job. You should state your attitudes toward the position and the company and summarize any conclusions reached about your discussion. A follow-up letter is a tip-off that you are truly interested in the position. Some employers remove from consideration those candidates who do not submit follow-up letters.

The approaches to improving your personal relationships on the job described in Part Three of this book can be regarded as ways of advancing your career. People who cultivate higher-ups and co-workers are in essence making plans for career advancement. The procedures for career goal setting described in Chapter 6 should also be regarded as an important strategy for advancing one's career. Here we will examine a number of other strategies and tactics for career advancement, divided into two groups. The methods in the first group relate to taking control over your own behavior, while those in the second relate to controlling the external environment.

Indiscriminate use of any method of career advancement may backfire. For example, if you overdo networking, you may spend so much time relating to people in your network that you will be neglecting your job. It is also important to choose methods of getting ahead that fit your circumstance and personal style. A case in point is the advice given later about taking risks. An adventuresome person without dependents would find this tactic to be ideal. A cautious person with dependents might find this tactic to be anxiety provoking.

Advancement through Taking Control of Yourself

The unifying theme for the strategies, tactics, and attitudes described in this section is that you attempt to control your own behavior.

Develop a Code of Professional Ethics. A good starting point in developing a career is to establish a personal ethical code. An ethical code determines what behavior is right or wrong, good or bad, based on values. The values may stem from cultural upbringing, religious teachings, and professional or industry standards. A code of professional ethics helps a person deal with such issues as accepting bribes, backstabbing a co-worker, or sexually harassing a subordinate or co-worker.

Make an Accurate Self-appraisal. A critical tactic for career advancement is to obtain an accurate picture of your strengths, areas for improvement, and preferences. Introspection is a good starting point in self-appraisal. The Self-Knowledge Questionnaire presented in Chapter 4 is a useful vehicle for introspection and self-analysis. In review, information for self-appraisal can also be obtained through career counselors, performance appraisals, personal growth groups, and peers.

> A sales representative constructed a brief form asking questions about himself, such as "What have I done this year that displeased you?" He gave the form to customers, his boss, and the office staff. The information he received helped him become more effective with others. In this regard, he learned that he was standing too close to people when he talked to them.

Develop Expertise and Build a Career around It. A starting point in getting ahead is to develop a useful job skill. This tactic is obvious if you are working as a specialist, such as a paralegal assistant. Being skilled at the task performed by the group is also a requirement for being promoted to a supervisory position. After being promoted to a supervisory or other managerial job, expertise is still important for further advancement. It helps a manager's reputation to be skilled in such things as memo writing, computer applications, preparing a budget, or developing a marketing plan. Another important skill is **troubleshooting,** the knack for pinpointing and analyzing snags in your department's work flow as they arise.

The surest path to career success is to identify your area or areas of expertise and then build a career around it or them. For example, the executives most in demand today have general experience, but at least one area of expertise, such as launching a new product.[10] Becoming wealthy and achieving recognition are by-products of making effective use of your talents.

Perform Well in Your Present Job. Common sense and research evidence support the idea that you have to be effective where you are before you can think about moving ahead.[11] Good job performance is the foundation on which you build your career. Job competence and talent are still the major success ingredients in all but the most political firms (those where favoritism outweighs merit). Before anybody is promoted in virtually every organization, the prospective new boss asks, "How well did this person perform for you?"

Good Performance Must Be Sustained. Consistency in performance helps the organization and therefore enhances one's career. The manager of a television station recalls, "Several years ago, I had to choose between promoting an employee who was competent and one who was spectacular. I promoted the competent woman because she was consistent. Her rival was only spectacular when the mood hit her. Because I couldn't schedule crises, I needed someone who could handle problems any time, not just when they coincided with her blazes of glory."[12]

Document Your Accomplishments. Keeping an accurate record of what you have accomplished in your career can be valuable when being considered for promotion. An astute person can point specifically to what he or she has accomplished in each position. Here are two examples from different types of jobs:

1. As ski shop store manager, increased sales to deaf skiers by 338 percent in one year by hiring an interpreter to work in our shop on Saturday mornings.
2. As industrial engineer, saved my company $72,000 in one year by switching from steel to nylon ball bearings in our line of bicycles and baby carriages.

Project a Professional Image. Your clothing, desk and work area, speech, and general knowledge should project the image of a professional, responsible person. Good grammar and sentence structure can give you the edge because so many people use highly informal patterns of speech. Being a knowledgeable person is important because today's professional businessperson is supposed to be aware of the external environment. Also, as noted by a human relations specialist, projecting a professional image hastens the development of trust and rapport in business relationships.[13]

Be Resilient. The ability to bounce back from adversity was described in Chapter 14 as an important leadership behavior. Resilience is also an important strategy for career advancement. The professional person accepts the fact that some setback is inevitable and learns how to profit from mistakes and misfortunes.

Job discrimination exemplifies a form of adversity that can block a person's career. Employers have overcome some discrimination through affirmative action and diversity awareness programs. Nevertheless, research and opinion suggest that many women and minority group members are still held back by invisible barriers. One study compared the career progress of more than 1,000 male and female managers in large business corporations. The data indicated that women lagged behind the men with respect to salary progression and frequency of job transfers.

The women in the study had "all the right stuff." In comparison to men, they had similar education, contributed the same percentage of family income, worked in similar industries, and were equally available for promotion. However, men still received higher salaries and favorable job transfers.[14] Faced with job discrimination, the person must be resilient enough to confront the issue or move on to a less discriminatory job environment.

Minimize Career Self-sabotage. Procrastination was described in Chapter 16 as a leading form of self-defeating behavior that can damage one's career. Many other behaviors can also defeat your own purposes and result in career self-sabotage. A way to overcome these behaviors is to solicit feedback from others on any aspect of your behavior under your control that could be harming your career. You would then attempt to overcome these behaviors on your own or get help through reading, attending seminars, or seeking professional assistance. Table 17-4 lists self-defeating behaviors that can result in career self-sabotage, thus blocking career advancement.

Hitch Your Wagon to Yourself. The ultimate strategy for developing career thrust is to have faith in what you are doing and to persist in doing it well. If you hitch your wagon to yourself, you will not be bothered by your critics. Eventually, your contributions will be recognized because what you are doing is worthwhile and of value to your employer or employers. Hitching your wagon to yourself is your career foundation. Other strategies for getting ahead are designed to supplement this basic strategy. If you lack technical, interpersonal, or administrative skills and ideas of your own, you are lacking the basis for a successful career.

TABLE 17–4. *COMMON FORMS OF CAREER SELF-SABOTAGE* —————

- Procrastination (carried out to the point that the person develops the reputation of being unreliable).
- Self-sabotaging life scripts (repeated patterns of messing up just when things are going well).
- Narcissism (wanting so hard to be liked that the person avoids necessary confrontations).
- Emotional immaturity (the person shows poor judgment and plays the role of office clown).
- Self-defeating beliefs (the person makes many negative self-statements).
- Unrealistic expectations (the person has such high goals that disappointment and discouragement are inevitable).
- Revenge (the person attempts to get even with the employer for reasons such as low salary increase or performance review).
- Attention seeking (the person will do almost anything to get attention, including being overcritical of management).
- Thrill seeking (just for kicks, the person might even make unauthorized use of company equipment).
- Excessive absenteeism and lateness (the person develops the reputation of being unprofessional and uninterested in career).
- Crossing swords with powerful people (the person argues too often with people who can damage his or her career).

Source: Gathered from information throughout Andrew J. DuBrin, *Your Own Worst Enemy: How to Prevent Career Self-sabotage* (New York: AMA COM, 1992).

Advancement through Exerting Control over the Environment

In this section we emphasize strategies and tactics requiring you to exert some control over the outside environment. If you do not fully control it, you can try to juggle it to your advantage.

Identify Growth Fields and Growth Companies. A sound strategy for career advancement is to seek jobs where possibilities for growth exist. Generally, this means seeking out growth industries, but it can also mean seeking out growth firms or areas of the country with plentiful job opportunities. Information about growth opportunities may be found in government publications (such as the *Occupational Outlook Handbook*), books on the topic, and the newspapers. Local banks and the chamber of commerce can be a valid source of information about growth firms in your area. A summary of good job opportunities for the 1990s is presented in Table 17-5.

Obtain Broad Experience. A widely accepted strategy for getting ahead in your career is to strengthen your credentials by broadening your experience. Broadening can come about by performing a variety of jobs or sometimes by performing essentially the same job for different firms. At one time it was believed that job hopping (moving from firm to firm) led to more rapid advancement than being loyal to one employer. Evidence collected during the last decade, however, points to the value of staying with one firm in order to advance your career. Managers who stay with the same firm tend to make more money and have bigger jobs than those who move from firm to firm.[15]

One practical way of obtaining broad experience is to become part of a management trainee program, where you rotate from department to department, after which you are permanently assigned to one department.

TABLE 17–5. *OCCUPATIONS ADDING THE MOST JOBS BY 2005* _____

Retail sales workers	+887,000
Registered nurses	+767,000
Cashiers	+685,000
Office clerks	+670,000
Truck drivers	+617,000
Executives, managers	+598,000
Nursing aides	+552,000
Waiters, waitresses	+449,000
Secondary school teachers	+437,000
Information clerks	+422,000
Systems analysts	+366,000
Child-care workers	+353,000
Gardeners	+348,000
Accountants	+340,000
Computer programmers	+317,000
Elementary school teachers	+313,000

Source: Data from U.S. Bureau of Labor Statistics, presented in *Human Resource Measurement,* published by Wonderlic Personnel Test, Inc., April 1992, p. 8.

Another way is to be assigned to or volunteer for committees and special projects.

Take Sensible Risks. People who make it big in their careers usually take several sensible risks on their journey to success. Among these risks would be to work for a fledgling company that offers big promises, but a modest starting salary, or to take an overseas assignment with no promise of a good job when you return. Industrial relations manager Michael Oliver offers this advice:

> If you want to achieve something really creative, thus enhancing your profession, then try a little risk taking. That doesn't mean you should pick up a lance and seek out a windmill. Balance your risk taking with good sense so you will be able to reach a new comfort level somewhere between the role of a bureaucratic follower and leaper of tall buildings. The goal should be to develop credibility without perpetrating a maverick reputation.[16]

Swim against the tide:
Take an unconventional path to career success.

Swim Against the Tide. One form of risk taking is to **swim against the tide**—take an unconventional path to career success. It involves placing yourself in a job setting where the competition might not be so overwhelming. Suppose that a man from Quebec City who is fluent in English and French is seeking a position in international marketing. He might be best advised to seek employment in a company not overloaded with people who can converse fluently in both English and French. Instead of seeking employment in Montreal, he might look for a job in Toronto or New York City. His background would then be at a premium. He would have the edge in competition for jobs dealing with French companies.

Swimming against the tide can also be applied to demographic characteristics. A rapidly growing occupation is hazardous waste (environmental) technician. So far, few women and minorities have entered this field. The director of an industrial health and safety program at Texas Technical Institute states that this is good reason for minorities and women to enter the field.[17]

The potential disadvantage of swimming against the tide is that a person pursuing an unconventional path may be blocked from advancement. A person who majored in business might have limited advancement opportunities in a company that promoted only engineers to key positions.

Find a Sponsor. A well-proved path to career advancement is to find somebody at a high place in the company who is impressed with your capabilities. A sponsor of this type can even be a blood relative or one by marriage. One reason that special assignments are so helpful to career progress is that they provide you with the opportunity to be seen by a variety of key people in your organization. Many an employee who has performed well in an activity such as the United Way has found a bigger job in the process. In general, any tactic that brings favorable attention to yourself can help you find a sponsor. Some of the suggestions made in Chapter 10 for impressing superiors fall into this category.

Mentor:
A boss who takes a subordinate under his or her wing and guides, teaches, or coaches him or her.

Find a Mentor. **Mentors** are bosses who take subordinates under their wings and guide, teach, and coach them. Mentorship is an important development process in many occupations: master–apprentice, physician–intern, teacher–student, and executive–junior executive. Most corporate presidents have had mentors who were an instrumental part of their success. An emotional tie exists between the less-experienced person (protégé) and the mentor. The mentor therefore serves as a positive model. A relationship with a sponsor involves much less teaching, coaching, and formation of emotional ties. It is possible to have more than one mentor at a given point in one's career.

Furthermore, peers can sometimes take over some of the functions performed by mentors. Peers can coach and counsel, provide critical information, and give support in handling personal problems and attaining professional growth.[18]

A study of about 600 business graduates shows that mentoring does help advance one's career. The people who received more extensive mentoring were promoted more frequently and had higher total income than those who received less mentoring.[19] Despite these advantages, mentoring does have its drawbacks. An executive placement specialist points out the danger of being a mentoree: "There is a real risk in allowing yourself to be identified as someone's protégé, and I've seen as many people get damaged by it as helped by it. If your mentor falls out of favor, the likelihood is that you will too."[20]

Use Your Network of Contacts. Networking has already been described as a major assist to finding a job. Members of your network can also help you by assisting with difficult job problems, providing emotional support, buying your products or services, and offering you good prices on their products and services. John Molloy studied hundreds of successful people in a variety of occupations. He notes: "The overwhelming majority of successful men and women we spoke to had a large network of friends."[21] In support of Molloy's findings, networking has become standard practice for advancing one's career.[22]

Capitalize on Luck. Few people do well in their careers without a good break along the way. Lucky events include your company suddenly expanding and therefore needing to promote people into key jobs, your boss quitting on short notice and you being asked to take over the job, or the industry in which you are working suddenly experiencing a boom, like roller blades in the 1990s. Despite these fortuitous-sounding events, it is difficult to capitalize on luck unless you are prepared. Luck, in fact, is sometimes defined as what happens when preparation meets opportunity.

A good strategy is not to simply wait for luck to come your way. Instead, manage luck to some extent by recognizing opportunities and taking advantage of them. A case in point is the man who became the national service manager in charge of service centers for small computers. He told a case writer:

> Several years ago a job opened up as national manager in charge of machine-repair centers for our company. Most of the hot-shots saw this as a dead-end job. They figured that repair work had no glamour. But I could see unlimited

possibilities. If people wanted to keep their home computer equipment running, they would need reliable service. Sure enough, our repair business expanded like mad. And my job became a true executive position.

Career plateau:
A point where it becomes evident that further job advancement is permanently or temporarily blocked.

Capitalize on Career Plateaus. A **career plateau** is a point where it becomes evident that further job advancement is permanently or temporarily blocked. The vast majority of the work force reaches a career plateau at least once or twice.[23] Some people reach an early plateau and stay there until retirement. Because of decreased opportunities for promotion today, plateaus are frequent. An important new trend in human resource management is to provide managers with varied assignments at the same level to keep them motivated and satisfied. For example, the food and beverage director at a large hotel would be given an opportunity to manage the front office and then to direct maintenance.

The best antidote to a plateau is to control your impatience and make constructive use of the time. Specifically, you might consider these strategies. First, learn to appreciate growth within your job. Develop new skills on your present job that will help you when you finally do receive a promotion. Second, since the demands on your time tend not to be excessive during a career plateau, invest some of that time in self-development. This would include reading in your field, attending workshops and seminars, increasing your formal education, and learning a second language to prepare you for the workplace of the future.

Career Switching

Career switching:
Changing from one career to another at any point during one's working life.

The process of changing from one career to another, or **career switching,** has become increasingly popular. Note that a career switch is a more profound change than simply making a job switch. People switch careers for such reason as boredom with the present career, being forced into early retirement, or being laid off and unable to find a job in one's present field. The many layoffs and early retirements created by large firms have resulted in thousands of people starting their own small businesses or purchasing franchises. For example, it is not unusual to find a former corporate executive running a yogurt store or the like.

Switching careers effectively requires long-range planning. Sometimes a long-term avocation can be converted into an occupation, assuming a high skill level has been developed. For example, a warehouse manager who made furniture as a hobby started a new career as a custom furniture maker.

To switch careers effectively, you should follow the suggestions for finding a field or first career. In addition, the potential career switcher is well advised to follow the advice offered in a current guide to finding another career. To avoid making what might turn out to be a costly and time-consuming error, you should:

1. Narrow your interests to a few specific areas or job titles.
2. Try part-time work in your desired area.
3. Get into an apprenticeship program (this usually requires completion of some specialized education).

4. Do volunteer work in your field of interest.
5. Take a course or two in the potential new field.
6. Determine if you should return to college full time or part time.[24]

BACK TO THE JOB TASKS

If your job task is to find a job, follow carefully the steps outlined in this chapter. Many people fail to find the job they want because they gloss over the necessary steps. If your task is to have a rewarding and satisfying career, follow the advice in this chapter and remember that success is achieved one step at a time.

Summary of Key Points

❏ You must accept the major responsibility for developing your career despite help offered by your employer. One reason is that you are likely to change employers either voluntarily or involuntarily.

❏ Career success can be defined in terms of both internal and external measures. Internal measures include job and life satisfaction. External measures include earnings, prestige, and progress.

❏ Finding a field and an occupation can be accomplished through a variety of formal and informal methods. Formal methods include counseling and/or testing and making systematic use of occupational information.

❏ Recommended job-hunting tactics include these: (1) identify your position objective(s), (2) identify your skills' potential contribution, (3) develop a comprehensive marketing strategy, (4) use networking to reach the internal job market, (5) be persistent, (6) take rejection in stride, (7) smile at network members and interviewers, and (8) avoid common mistakes such as overlooking your selling points.

❏ The purpose of a résumé is to help you to obtain a job interview. Employers today usually demand considerable detail in résumés, especially about skills and accomplishments. Three types of résumés are the chronological, functional (grouping of activities by the task performed), and targeted (focus on the job sought). A recommended résumé format is presented in Figure 17-1. A résumé should almost always be accompanied by a cover letter explaining how you can help the organization and why you are applying for this particular job.

❏ Keep the following points in mind when being interviewed for a job: (1) look relaxed and make the interviewer feel comfortable, (2) establish a link between yourself and the employer, (3) ask perceptive questions, (4) prepare in advance, (5) be ready to discuss your strengths and weaknesses, (6) show how you can help the employer, (7) encourage the interviewer to talk, and (8) write a follow-up letter.

❏ Building good personal relationships on the job and goal setting are important for career advancement. In addition, consider two other sets of strategies and tactics. One set of strategies and tactics for getting ahead can be placed in the category of taking control of your own behavior. Included here are the following:

1. Develop a code of professional ethics.
2. Make an accurate self-appraisal.

3. Develop expertise and build a career around it.
4. Perform well in your present job.
5. Document your accomplishments.
6. Project a professional image.
7. Be resilient.
8. Minimize career self-sabotage.
9. Hitch your wagon to yourself.

❑ Another set of strategies and tactics for getting ahead center around taking control of your environment, or at least adapting it to your advantage. Included here are the following:

1. Identify growth fields and growth companies.
2. Obtain broad experience.
3. Take sensible risks.
4. Swim against the tide (take an unconventional career path).
5. Find a sponsor.
6. Find a mentor.
7. Use your network of contacts.
8. Capitalize on luck.
9. Capitalize on career plateaus.

❑ Switching careers requires long-range planning and also involves many of the same approaches as finding an initial field. It is helpful to phase into a new career by trying it out part time and preparing for it educationally.

GUIDELINES FOR PERSONAL EFFECTIVENESS

1. Some people achieve career success (including both rewards and satisfaction) without a deliberate, planned effort. For the vast majority of people, attaining these ends requires careful planning. Planning is particularly helpful when you are getting started in your career and during its early stages. Planning includes choosing a field, finding a job, and using career-advancement tactics and strategies.
2. Should you be confronted with the task of finding a job, do not be overly apprehensive. Much useful information has been collected to aid you in the job-finding process. Following this information carefully will increase your chances of finding suitable employment.
3. Any of the strategies and tactics described in this chapter must be used with selectivity. A helpful approach is to select those suggestions that seem to fit your personality and preferences. Avoid those tactics and strategies that you think are in conflict with your values.

Discussion Questions and Activities

1. Do most people have satisfying and rewarding careers? What evidence do you have to support your opinion?
2. Why should employers be concerned whether or not their employees do an effective job of career management?
3. Which three measures of career success in Table 17-1 are the most important for you?

4. How does a newcomer to the job market know which skills he or she possesses?

5. Would you find any ethical problems with a professional résumé service preparing a résumé for you?

6. Assume that you are confident that a particular employer is very interested in hiring you. How would this affect your tactics as an interviewee?

7. Assume that a Native American with a business degree knows that many companies are eager to hire Native Americans because they are underrepresented in professional and technical jobs. How should this person use his or her heritage to advantage?

8. Assume you have a job interview for a position as the manager of a health club, and you know that while on duty the manager wears athletic attire. How would you dress for the interview?

9. Which three of the career-advancement strategies and tactics described in this chapter do you think are the most ethical and which three the least ethical?

10. Ask a successful person, "What should a person do to succeed in business?" Be prepared to discuss your findings in class.

A BUSINESS PSYCHOLOGY PROBLEM

Some Damaging Statistics

Congratulations, you have been hired as a human resources specialist at a large company. Your first assignment is employment interviewer, in which you will be screening hundreds of job applicants for your company. During your first several weeks on the job, you invest substantial time in reading human resources magazines and journals to acquire the appropriate knowledge. One day you come across a report furnished by the Certified Reference Checking Company, of St. Louis, Missouri, published in 1992.

According to their study of 1,200 job applicants, 34% of them embellished or lied about their background when applying for a job. The areas and frequency of misrepresentation included expertise, 22%; salary and job title, 12%; employment history, 11%; educational background, 9%; and self-employment, 4%.

You ponder over these facts carefully, and then decide to use the information.

1. How should this information influence company policy about hiring procedures?

2. How does the information fit your perception of whether or not people do inflate their credentials?

3. How does this report serve the interests of the Certified Reference Checking Company?

A BUSINESS PSYCHOLOGY PROBLEM

The Property Manager in Turmoil

Bonnie Fraser decided to cash in on her business school training and experience as an administrative assistant. She responded to this ad in a Pittsburgh newspaper for a job in Florida.

PROPERTY MANAGER

For 300 + apartment complex in Fort Lauderdale, Florida. Experience in all facets of multihousing, resident retention, marketing, rent collections, accounting, budget control, and sales ability. Self-motivated, take-charge person. Must be able to live on property. Excellent salary and fringe benefits.

Through pluck, luck, and an impassioned plea that she was a fast learner, Bonnie did get the job. She relocated to Florida and soon found she loved everything about Florida but her job. When her parents came down to visit her six months after her relocation, Bonnie gave them this tale of woe:

"Folks, I'm facing an early career crisis. Florida is more fun than I could have dreamed. Springtime in Ft. Lauderdale alone is worth a million bucks to me. I've made more good friends in six months here than I made in my last five years in Pittsburgh. When I'm not working, its nonstop fun and sun. But the job is the pits. It's too many headaches. I'm forever hustling for new reliable tenants and trying to collect rent from the existing tenants. Every problem on the property falls in my lap."

When her parents asked Bonnie why she didn't look for a new and less stressful job in the area, Bonnie answered:

"You don't understand my new life-style. I have a new car and an apartment full of furniture bought on time. This job pays much better than anything else around. And besides I live rent free. It seems like there is no turning back."

1. What career advice can you offer Bonnie?
2. To what extent do you think Bonnie has done a poor job of setting priorities for her values?
3. What concepts and methods of business psychology described in previous chapters would be relevant in helping Bonnie?

A BUSINESS PSYCHOLOGY ROLE PLAY

The Job Interview

As described in Table 17-3, a good way to prepare for a job interview is to rehearse answers to frequently asked questions. In this role play, one student will be the interviewer and one the interviewee. The job in question is that of property manager for a large apartment complex in Florida. (See the brief job description given previously.) Assume the interviewee really wants the job (just as Bonnie did). The interviewer, having taken a course in business psychology, will ask many of the questions shown in Table 17-3. The interviewer, however, will also have other specific questions, such as "Why do you want to work in Florida?"

Before proceeding with the role play, both people should review the information in this chapter about the job interview and in Chapter 15 about listening.

References

1. TIMOTHY E. GLAROS, "Play Your Way to the Top," *HRMagazine,* April 1992, p. 90.
2. C. BROOKLYN DERR, *Managing the New Careerists: The Diverse Career Success Orientation of Today's Workers* (San Francisco: Jossey-Bass, 1986), p. 1.

3. RICHARD N. BOLLES, *The 1993 What Color Is Your Parachute? A Practical Guide for Job Hunters and Career Changers* (Berkeley, CA: Ten Speed Press, published almost annually); J. I. Biegeleisen, *Make Your Job Interview a Success* (Englewood Cliffs, NJ: ARCO/Prentice Hall, 1991); *Navigator* (Job-finding software published by Drake Beam Morin, Inc.).

4. MARILYN MOATS KENNEDY, "How to Job Hunt," *Success,* October 1982, p. 30.

5. Quoted in "Job Hunt," *Business Week Careers,* February 1987, p. 77.

6. ROBERT B. NELSON, "10 Common Mistakes Job Hunters Make," *Business Week Careers,* November 1986, pp. 91–93.

7. SHIRLEY SLOAN FADER, "The Right Answers to Those Interview Questions," *The Honda How to Get a Job Guide,* published by *Business Week Careers,* 1987, p. 31.

8. JAMES E. CALLENGER, "10 Tough Interview Questions," *Business Week Careers,* April–May 1988, p. 25.

9. FADER, "The Right Answers to Those Interview Questions," p. 36.

10. KENNETH LABICH, "Take Control of Your Career," *Fortune,* November 18, 1991.

11. JOSPEH A. RAELIN, "First-job Efforts on Career Development," *Personnel Administrator,* April 1983, pp. 71–76.

12. JUDITH MEYERS, "Corporate Star Quality: How to Shine Brighter Than Your Competition," *Cosmopolitan,* August 1987, p. 162.

13. PHILLIP L. HUNSAKER, "Projecting the Appropriate Image," *Supervisory Management,* May 1989, p. 26.

14. LINDA K. STROH, JEANNE M. BRETT, AND ANNE H. REILLY, "All the Right Stuff: A Comparison of Female and Male Manager's Career Progression," *Journal of Applied Psychology,* June 1992, pp. 251–260.

15. CATHY A. GRAYSON, "Inside Moves: You Don't Have to Change Companies to Change Your Career," *Success,* November 1986, pp. 65–69.

16. MICHAEL L. OLIVER, "Taking Risks Will Get Your Career Moving," *Personnel Journal,* April 1983, p. 319.

17. DIANE KUNDE, "Ins-and-Outs Are Good Way to Attain Technical Expertise," *The Dallas Morning News,* December 26, 1990, p. 2D.

18. KATHY E. KRAM AND LYNN A. ISABELLA, "Mentoring Alternatives: The Role of Peer Relationships in Career Development," *Academy of Management Journal,* March 1985, p. 129.

19. WILLIAM WHITELY, THOMAS W. DOUGHERTY, AND GEORGE F. DREHER, "Relationship of Career Mentoring and Socioeconomic Origin to Managers' and Professionals' Early Career Progress," *Academy of Management Journal,* June 1991, pp. 331–351.

20. CLAUDIA H. DEUTSCH, "Guidance Counselors," *TWA Ambassador,* September 1983, p. 14.

21. JOHN T. MOLLOY, *Molloy's Live for Success* (New York: Bantam Books, 1982), p. 187.

22. "A Must-have Skill," *Executive Strategies,* June 1992, p. 2.

23. BEVERLY KAYE, "Are Plateaued Performers Productive?" *Personnel Journal,* August 1989, p. 57.

24. LINDA KLINE AND LLOYED L. FEINSTEIN, "Creative Thinking for Switching Careers," *Success,* March 1983, p. A2.

BENNETT, AMANDA. *The Death of the Organization Man*. New York: Simon & Schuster, 1991.

ETTORRE, BARBARA. "Breaking the Glass Ceiling … Or Just Window Dressing." *Management Review,* March 1992, pp. 16–22.

EYLER, DAVID R. *The Executive Moonlighter: Building Your Next Career without Leaving Your Present Job*. New York: Wiley, 1989.

KOLTNOW, EMILY, AND DUMAS, LYNNE. *Congratulations! You've Been Fired: Sound Advice for Women Who've Been Terminated, Pink-slipped, Downsized, and Otherwise Unemployed*. New York: Fawcett Columbine, 1990.

KUSHEL, GERALD. *Effective Thinking for Success*. New York: AMACOM, 1990.

MATTHES, KAREN. "Corporate Mentoring: Beyond the Blind Date." *HRfocus,* November 1991, p. 23.

MURRAY, MARGO (WITH OWEN, MARNA A.). *Beyond the Myths and Magic of Mentoring*. San Francisco: Jossey-Bass, 1991.

SANBORN, ROBERT. *How to Get a Job in Europe: The Insider's Guide*. New York: Surrey Books, 1991.

WEBBER, ROSS ARKELL. *Becoming a Courageous Manager: Overcoming Career Problems of New Managers*. Englewood Cliffs, NJ: Prentice Hall, 1991.

YAGER, JAN. *Business Protocol: How to Survive and Succeed in Business*. New York: Wiley, 1991.

GLOSSARY

Ability   A current capability that is partially based on native talent and experience.

Achievement motive   Finding joy in accomplishment for its own sake.

Action plan   A series of steps to be taken to achieve a goal.

Addictive behavior   A compulsion to use substances or engage in activities that lead to psychological dependence and withdrawal symptoms when use is discontinued.

Affective tone   A person's predisposition to be positive or negative.

Anger   A feeling of extreme hostility, indignation, or exasperation.

Anxiety   Generalized feelings of fear and apprehension that usually result from a perceived threat. Feelings of uneasiness and tension usually accompany anxiety.

Aptitude   A native ability to perform some task.

Assertiveness   Being forthright with one's demands, expressing both the specifics of what one wants done, and the feelings surrounding the demands.

Assertiveness training (AT)   A self-improvement training program that teaches people to express their feelings, and act with an appropriate degree of openness and assertiveness.

Authority   The right to control the actions of others; control that is sanctioned by the organization or society.

Autocratic leader   One who attempts to retain most of the authority granted to the group.

Balance theory   An explanation of interpersonal relationships contending that people tend to prefer relationships that are consistent or balanced.

Behavior modification   Changing behavior by rewarding the right responses, and/or punishing or ignoring the wrong responses.

Behavior shaping   *See shaping of behavior.*

Behavioral science   Any science concerned with the systematic study of human behavior. The primary behavioral sciences are psychology, sociology, and anthropology.

Behaviorism   A school of thought in psychology based on the assumption that psychologists should study overt behavior rather than mental states or other unobservable aspects of living things.

Blocking   An upward influence tactic involving work slowdowns or the threat thereof.

Body image   A person's perception of his or her own body.

Brainwriting (or **private brainstorming**)   Arriving at creative ideas by jotting them down oneself.

Brainstorm   A clever idea.

Brainstorming   A conference technique of solving specific problems, amassing information, and stimulating creative thinking. The basic technique is to encourage unrestrained and spontaneous participation by group members.

Brainwriting (or **solo brainstorming**)   Arriving at creative ideas by jotting them down yourself.

Bureaucracy   A rational, systematic, and precise form of organization in which rules, regulations, and techniques of control are precisely defined. A typical bureaucracy has many layers of management and many specialists.

Burnout   A state of exhaustion stemming from long-term stress.

Business psychology   The application of organized knowledge about human behavior to improve individual and organizational effectiveness in work settings.

Business etiquette   A special code of behavior required in work situations.

Career   A life-long series of experiences that form some kind of a coherent pattern.

Career-advancement strategy   Any systematic method or plan aimed at improving one's chances for success over the long range.

Career goal   A specific position, type of work, or income level that a person aspires to reach.

Career path   A sequence of positions necessary to achieve a career goal.

Career plateau   A point where it becomes evident that further job advancement is permanently or temporarily blocked.

Career success   Being able to live out the subjective and personal values one really believes in and to make contributions to the world of work.

Career switching   Changing from one career to another at any point during one's working life.

Cause-and-effect diagram   A decision-making technique widely used by quality-improvement teams.

Charisma   A person's charm or magnetism as perceived by others.

Chronological resume   A presentation of work experience, education, and interests, along with accomplishments in reverse chronological order.

Classical conditioning   A basic form of learning in which a stimulus that usually brings forth a given response is repeatedly paired with a neutral stimulus. Eventually the neutral stimulus will bring forth the response when presented by itself.

Coercive power   The leader's control over punishments.

Cognitive   Referring to the intellectual aspects of human behavior. A cognitive process is the means by which an individual becomes aware of objects and situations. It includes learning, reasoning, and problem solving.

Cognitive dissonance   A mental process by which people try to reduce or eliminate inconsistency in the information they receive.

Cognitive psychology   A movement within, or branch of, psychology that attempts to explain the behavior of human beings in terms of their intellectual, rational selves.

Cognitive resource theory   An explanation of leadership emphasizing that intelligent and competent leaders make more effective plans, decisions, and action strategies than do leaders with less intelligence or competence.

Common sense   Sound, practical judgment that is independent of specialized knowledge, training, or the like. Also natural wisdom not based on formal knowledge.

Communication   The sending, receiving, and understanding of messages.

Communication (or **information) overload**   A condition in which the individual is confronted with so much information to process that he or she becomes overwhelmed and therefore does a poor job of processing information.

Compensation   Working overly hard to reach a related goal when you are frustrated in reaching an original goal.

Competence   Job skills and social skills including the ability to solve problems and control anger.

Compulsiveness   A tendency to pay careful attention to detail and to be meticulous.

Computer shock (or **stress**)   A strong negative reaction to being forced to spend many more hours working at a computer than one desires.

Conflict   Simultaneous arousal of two or more incompatible motives, or demands.

Confrontation   Bringing forth a controversial topic or contradictory material in which the other party is personally involved.

Confrontation and problem solving   A method of identifying the true source of conflict and resolving it systematically.

Consensual leader   One who encourages group discussion about an issue and then makes a decision that reflects the consensus of group members.

Consultative leader   One who solicits opinions from the group before making a decision, yet does not feel obliged to accept the group's thinking.

Counterproductive person   One whose actions lead him or her away from achieving work goals, often because of a personality quirk.

Creative problem solving   The ability to overcome obstacles by approaching them in novel ways.

Creativity   The ability to develop good ideas that can be put into action.

Crisis manager   One who specializes in turning around failing organizations or rescuing them from a crisis.

Cumulative trauma disorder   Injuries caused by repetitive motions over prolonged periods of time.

Decision   A choice among two or more alternatives.

Decision making   The thought process that leads to a decision.

Decision-making software   Any computer program that helps the decision maker work through the problem-solving and decision-making steps.

Defensive communication   The tendency to receive messages in such a way that our self-esteem is protected.

Democratic leader   See *free-rein leader*.

Denial   A defense mechanism in which the person blocks out or denies that a particular event has taken place.

Dependent-care option   Any company-sponsored program that helps an employee take care of a family member.

Disarm the opposition   A technique of conflict resolution in which one person disarms another by agreeing with his or her criticism.

Distress   Negative stress.

Diversity awareness training   A training activity that provides an opportunity for employees to develop the skills necessary to deal effectively with each other and with customers in a diverse environment.

Downshifting   Investing more time in family and less in career.

Effectiveness   The extent to which an individual, organization, or machine achieves worthwhile or important results.

Electronic brainstorming   A problem-solving method in which group members simultaneously enter their suggestions into a computer, and their ideas are distributed to the screens of other group members.

Emotion   Any strong agitation of the feelings triggered by experiencing love, hate, fear, joy, and the like.

Empowerment   A manager sharing power with team members to help them achieve greater confidence in their abilities.

Employee abuse   Deliberate and malicious mistreatment that has an adverse effect on the employee's well-being.

Employee assistance program   A formal organization unit designed to help employees deal with personal problems that adversely affect their job performance.

Empowerment   The process by which a manager shares power with team members, thereby enhancing their feelings of self-efficacy.

Encounter group   A small therapy or training group that focuses on expressing feelings openly and honestly. Also referred to as a personal growth group.

Entrepreneur   A person who establishes and manages a business in an innovative manner.

Entrepreneurial pay   A share in the profits accruing from the new product.

Environmental determinism   The doctrine of behaviorism stating that our past history of reinforcement determines, or causes, our present behavior.

Ergonomics   The design of machinery, equipment, and the work environment to fit human characteristics, both physical and mental.

Esteem needs   Psychological needs relating to achieving self-respect.

Ethics   The moral choices a person makes.

Etiquette   A special code of behavior required in certain situations.

Eustress   Positive stress.

Exchange   The use of reciprocal favors in order to influence others.

Expectancy   The probability assigned by the individual that effort will lead to performing the task correctly.

Expectancy theory   An explanation of human motivation that centers around the idea that people will expend effort if they believe the effort will lead to a desired outcome.

Expert power   The ability to control others through knowledge relevant to the job as perceived by subordinates.

Expert system   A computer program that can "reason" and manipulate data in a manner similar to humans.

External locus of control   A belief that external forces control one's fate.

Fear of success   A conviction that success will bring with it some unwelcome outcomes, such as isolation or abandonment.

Feeling   Any emotional state or disposition, such as happiness or sadness.

Fight-or-flight response   The body's physiological and chemical battle against the stressor in which the person tries to cope with the adversity head-on, or tries to flee the scene.

Flexible working hours (flextime, flexitime)   A method of organizing the hours of work so that employees have flexibility in choosing their own hours.

Flow experience   The phenomenon of total absorption in one's work.

Fogging   A way of responding to manipulative criticism by openly accepting the criticism.

Formal communication pathway   The official path over which messages are supposed to travel in an organization.

Formal group   A collection of people deliberately formed by the organization to accomplish specific tasks and achieve objectives.

Formal organization   The job descriptions, organization charts, procedures, and other written documents which specify how individuals should work with each other.

Frame of reference   A perspective or vantage point for receiving information.

Free-rein leader   A person in charge who turns over virtually all the authority to the group.

Frustration   A blocking of a need, wish, or desire.

Frustration tolerance   The amount of frustration a given individual can handle without suffering adverse consequences.

Functionalism   An early school of psychological thought emphasizing the functions of the mind.

Functional resume   One that organizes skills and accomplishments into the functions or tasks that support the job sought.

g (general) factor   A major component of intelligence that contributes to problem-solving ability.

Gainsharing program   A profit-sharing plan in which employees are allowed to participate financially in the productivity gains they have achieved.

Game   A repeated series of exchanges between people that appears different on the surface from its true underlying motive.

General adaptation syndrome   The body's response to stress that occurs in three stages: alarm, resistance, and exhaustion.

Generation gap   A substantial difference in values between people that leads to conflict and misunderstanding.

Goal   The object or aims of a person's actions.

Goal-setting theory   A systematic explanation of how goal setting increases productivity.

Gossip   Idle talk or tidbits of information about people that are passed along informal communication channels.

Grapevine   The major informal communication channel or pathway in an organization.

Group   A collection of individuals who regularly interact with each other, who are psychologically aware of each other, and who perceive themselves to be a group.

Group norms   The unwritten set of expectations or standards of conduct telling group members what each person should do within the group.

Groupthink   A deterioration of mental efficiency, reality testing, and moral judgment in the interest of group solidarity.

Halo effect   An error in perception in which the favorableness or unfavorableness of our prime impression of another tends to make us see that person as all good or bad.

Hawthorne effect   The tendency for people to behave differently when they receive attention because they respond to the expectations of the situation.

Health psychology   The study and practice of how human behavior can be modified to prevent and treat illness.

Honesty testing   A method of determining if job applicants and present employees are telling the truth.

Human relations   The art and practice of using systematic knowledge about human behavior to achieve organizational and/or personal objectives.

Human relations movement   A concentrated effort by managers and their advisors to become more sensitive to the needs of employees or to treat them in a more humanistic manner.

Humanistic psychology   An approach to psychology that emphasizes the dignity and worth of people along with their many other positive but intangible or "soft' attributes.

Individual dominance   A problem in group decision making that occurs when one individual dominates the group thus negating the potential benefit of group input.

Industrial and organizational psychology   Basically, business psychology; the field of psychology that studies human behavior in a work environment. Overlaps considerably with organizational behavior.

Informal communication pathways   An unofficial network of communications used to supplement a formal pathway.

Informal group   A natural grouping of people in a work situation that evolves to take care of people's desires for friendship and companionship.

Informal organization   A pattern of work relationships that develops to both satisfy people's social needs and to get work accomplished.

Ingratiation   Getting somebody else to like you, often using political behaviors.

Insider system   A job-hunting technique in which a person searches for nonadvertised jobs that are usually offered to company insiders, friends, and relatives of insiders, or applicants who write unsolicited letters to the firm.

Insight   A depth of understanding that requires considerable intuition and common sense.

Instrumental learning   A type of learning in which the behavior of the individual leads to a specific consequence.

Instrumentality   The probability assigned by the individual that performance will lead to certain outcomes or rewards.

Instrumental learning   A type of learning in which the behavior of the individual leads to a specific consequence.

Intellectual style   The unique and characteristic way in which an individual solves problems, such as being reflective.

Intelligence   The capacity to acquire and apply knowledge, including solving problems.

Internal job market   The jobs that have not been advertised, and that are usually filled by word of mouth or through friends and acquaintances of employees.

Internal locus of control   The belief that fate is pretty much under one's control.

Intrapreneur   A company employee who engages in entrepreneurial thinking and behavior for the good of the company.

Intrinsic motivation   Motivation stemming from a person's belief about the extent to which an activity can satisfy his or her needs for competency and self-determination.

Introspection   A method of looking into one's conscious experience.

Intuition   A method of arriving at a conclusion by a quick judgment of "gut feel."

Job burnout   A condition of emotional, mental, and physical exhaustion, along with cynicism toward work, in response to long-term job stressors.

Job campaign   All the activities involved in finding a job.

Job design   The basic way in which a job is set up.

Job enrichment   Making a job more motivational and satisfying by adding variety and responsibility.

Job satisfaction   The amount of pleasure or contentment associated with a job.

Job sharing   An arrangement in which two people share one job by each working half time.

Job shock   Stress that occurs when a person's first full-time job fails to meet his or her expectations.

Lateral communication   Sending messages from one-co-worker to another.

Law of effect   In behavior modification, behavior that leads to a positive consequence for the individual tends to be repeated, while behavior that leads to a negative consequence tends not to be repeated.

Leading task   An easy warmup activity used to help avoid procrastination.

Leadership   The process of influencing other people to achieve certain objectives.

Leadership style   A leader's characteristic way of directing people in most situations.

Leading by example   Influencing group members by serving as a positive model.

Learning   A relatively permanent change in behavior based on practice or experience.

Learning style   The fact that people learn best in different ways.

Legitimate power   The ability to influence others that stems directly from the leader's position.

Life-change unit   A scale value of the impact of a given change in a person's life.

Management   Working with and through individuals and groups to accomplish organizational goals.

Management by objectives   A formal program of goal setting and review of performance against goals that is applied on an organizationwide basis.

Maslow's need hierarchy   A widely quoted and accepted theory of human motivation developed by Abraham Maslow, emphasizing that people strive to fulfill needs. These needs are arranged in a hierarchy of importance—physiological, safety, belongingness, esteem, and self-actualization. People tend to strive for satisfaction of needs at one level only after satisfaction has been achieved at the previous level.

Mentor   A boss who takes a subordinate under his or her wing and guides, teaches, or coaches him or her.

Meta-analysis   A study of studies combining quantitative information from them all.

Mind mapping   A creativity tool that produces a physical and conceptual map of a project.

Mirroring   (or posturing) A form of nonverbal communication used to establish rapport with another individual by imitating that person's physical behavior.

Mixed signals   The sending of different messages about the same topic to different audiences. Also, sending one message to an individual about desired behavior, yet behaving in another way yourself.

Modeling   A form of learning in which a person learns a complex skill by watching another person perform that skill. Also called learning by imitation.

Motivation   Work motivation is essentially motivation directed toward the attainment of organizational goals.

Motivational state   An inner state of arousal directed toward a goal.

Need   An internal striving or urge to do something.

Negative affectivity   A tendency to experience aversive emotional states.

Negative reinforcement   Being rewarded by being relieved of discomfort.

Negotiation and bargaining   Conferring with another person in order to resolve a problem.

Networking   Seeking friends and acquaintances and building systematically on these relationships to create a still wider set of contacts who might lead to employment.

Nominal group technique (NGT)   A group problem-solving method that calls people together in a structured meeting with limited interaction.

Nonverbal communication   The transmission of messages through means other than words.

Open-door policy   A situation when any employee can bring a gripe to higher management's attention without checking with his or her immediate manager.

Operant conditioning   Learning that takes place as a consequence of behavior. Also known as behavior modification or reinforcement learning.

Organizational citizenship behavior   Working for the good of the organization even without the promise of a specific reward.

Organizational culture   The predominant values of a firm that guide behavior.

Participative leader   A person in charge who shares decision-making authority with the group.

Passive aggressive   A person who expresses anger and hostility by not performing expected tasks.

Perceived control   The belief than an individual has at his or her disposal a response than can control the aversiveness of an event.

Perception   The various ways in which people interpret things in the external world and how they act on the basis of these perceptions.

Perceptual congruence   The degree to which people perceive things the same way.

Personal growth group   Small training or development groups similar in design and intent to encounter groups. People usually attend these groups to learn more about themselves.

Personal power   The ability to influence others based on personal characteristics and skills.

Personal productivity   An individual's level of efficiency and effectiveness.

Personality   An individual's characteristic way of behaving, feeling, and thinking.

Personality clash   An antagonistic relationship between two people based on differences in personal attributes, preferences, interests, values, and style.

Personality quirk   A persistent peculiarity of behavior that annoys or irritates other people.

Person-role conflict   A situation that occurs when the role that an organization assigns to an individual conflicts with his or her basic values.

Political factors   Factors other than merit that influence a decision, such as favoritism or attempting to please a key person.

Position power   The ability to influence others based on the formal position you occupy (the same as legitimate power).

Positive mental attitude   Expecting to succeed in a given undertaking.

Positive reinforcement   Receiving a reward for making a desired response, such as getting approval from a boss for being prompt.

Positive self-talk   Saying positive things about oneself to oneself.

Positive visual imagery   Imagining oneself performing well in an upcoming situation that represents a challenge.

Power   The ability to control resources, to influence important decisions, and to get other people to do things.

Practical intelligence   The concept that intelligence is composed of several varieties including academic intelligence and skills, creativity, and adaptation to the environment.

Prepotent   In reference to needs, one that must be satisfied before higher needs are activated.

Problem   A gap between an existing and desired situation.

Problem-solving ability   Mental ability or intelligence used to solve problems.

Procrastination   The delaying of action for no good reason.

Productivity   The amount of useful output achieved in comparison to the amount of input.

Proxemics   The placement of one's body in relation to someone else.

Primary reinforcer   A reinforcer that is rewarding by itself without association with other reinforcers, such as food.

Psychoanalysis   A type of long-term psychotherapy in which patients are encouraged to explore early memories and their unconscious. Also a theory of motivation that focuses on unconscious motivation.

Psychiatry A medical specialty that deals with the diagnosis and treatment of emotional problems and mental illness.

Psychological sabotage Deliberate behavior that interferes with the achievement of company goals, taking such forms as complaining and absenteeism.

Psychology The systematic study of behavior and all the factors that influence behavior.

Psychotherapist Any mental health professional who helps people with their emotional problems through conversation with them.

Public self What the person communicates about himself or herself, and what others actually perceive about the person.

Private self The actual person that one may be.

Punishment The introduction of an unpleasant stimulus as a consequence of the person having done something wrong.

Pygmalion effect The phenomenon that people perform according to expectations of them, particularly with respect to superior-subordinate relationships.

Quality improvement teams Groups of members who use problem-solving techniques to enhance customer satisfaction.

Rationalization Finding a plausible reason for doing something when the person cannot face up to the real reason.

Rationality Appealing to reason and logic.

Readiness In the situational model of leadership, the extent to which a group member has the ability and willingness to accomplish a specific task.

Receiver The person who is sent the message in an instance of communication.

Referent power The ability to control based on loyalty to the leader and the subordinates' desire to please that person.

Reinforcer A reward that is used to strengthen or reinforce a response in operant conditioning.

Relationship behavior The extent to which the leader engages in two-way or multi-way communication.

Relaxation response A bodily reaction in which you experience a slower respiration rate and heart rate and lowered blood pressure and metabolism.

Resilience The ability to withstand pressure and emerge stronger for it.

Reward power The leader's control over valuable rewards.

Role A set of behaviors a person is supposed to engage in because of his or her job situation or position within a group.

Role ambiguity A condition in which the job holder receives confusing or poorly defined expectations.

Role conflict Having to choose between competing demands or expectations.

Role confusion Being uncertain about what role you are carrying out.

Role overload Having too much to do.

Role underload Having too little to do.

Rote rehearsal In learning, reciting the information to yourself silently or out loud, several times.

Rumor   A message transmitted over the grapevine, although not based on official word.

s (special) factor   A specific component of intelligence that contributes to problem-solving ability.

Script   A program in the brain that orients a person in a particular direction toward solving a problem.

Secondary reinforcer   A reinforcer whose value must be learned through association with other reinforcers, such as money.

Security needs   Psychological needs for feeling emotionally and physically safe.

Selective perception   An unconscious process by which only selected aspects of a given stimulus are received and processed.

Self   The total being of the individual or the person.

Self-actualization   Making maximum use of the potential in oneself; like self-fulfillment.

Self-concept   What you think of you and who you think you are.

Self-confidence   A basic belief in one's ability to achieve the outcome he or she wants in many situations or in a specific situation.

Self-defeating behavior   A conscious or unconscious attempt to bring about personal failure.

Self-determination theory   The idea that people are motivated when they experience a sense of choice in initiating and regulating their actions.

Self-disclosure   The process of revealing your inner self to others.

Self-esteem   A sense of being worthwhile, similar to self-respect.

Self-fulfillment   The need to work toward making good or full use of one's potential.

Sender   The person who transmits a message in an instance of communication.

Sensory information   Information that is received by any of the senses, such as sight, hearing, smell, touch, or the muscle sense.

Serendipity   The gift of finding valuable things not sought for while looking for something else.

Sex role   Patterns of behavior attributed to whether a person is male or female.

Sexual harassment   Unwanted sexually oriented behavior in a work setting.

Shaping of behavior   The process of learning through approximations until the total skill is learned.

Skunk works   A secret place to conceive new products.

Social loafing   Shirking of individual responsibility in a group setting.

SQ3R method   A method of studying written material: survey, question, read, recite, and review.

Strain   The adverse effects of stress on an individual's mind, body, and actions.

Stress   The mental and physical condition that results from a perceived threat or demand that cannot be dealt with readily.

Stressor   The external or internal force that brings about the stress.

Style   A person's way of doing things.

Success cycle   A situation in which each little success builds self-confidence leading to more success and self-confidence.

Supervision   First-level management, or the overseeing of other workers.

Supportive leader   A person in charge who gives praise and encouragement to subordinates.

Suggestion program   A formal method for collecting and analyzing employee suggestions about processes, policies, product, and service.

SuperLeader   One who leads others to lead themselves.

Support network   A group of people who can listen to your problems and provide emotional support.

Swim against the tide   Taking an unconventional path to career success.

Synergy   A phenomenon of group effort whereby the whole is greater than the sum of the parts.

Target position   The ultimate goal a person seeks in a career path.

Targeted resume   A resume that focuses on a specific job target, or position and presents only information that supports the target.

Task force   A small group of individuals called together to solve a problem or explore and develop a new idea for an organization.

Technology   All the tools and ideas available for extending the natural physical and mental reach of people.

Telecommuter   An employee who performs regular work duties from home or at another location.

Tension   A feeling of internal uneasiness that is usually associated with stress or an unsatisfied need.

Theory X   Douglas McGregor's famous statement of the traditional management view that considers people as usually lazy and needing to be prodded by external rewards. A rigid and task-oriented approach to management.

Theory Y   Douglas McGregor's famous statement of an alternative to traditional management thinking. It emphasizes that people seek to fulfill higher-level needs on the job and that management must be flexible and humans relations oriented.

Time leaks   Anything you are doing or not doing that allows time to get away from you.

Total quality management   A system of management in which all activities are directed toward satisfying external and internal customers.

Transactional analysis   A set of procedures for improving interpersonal relationships that focuses on the transactions between people.

Transcendental meditation (TM)   A mental technique of establishing a physiological state of deep rest.

Transformational leader   One who helps organizations and people make positive changes.

Troubleshooting   The knack for pinpointing and analyzing snags in your department's work flow as they arise.

Type A behavior   A demanding, impatient, and overstriving pattern of behavior also characterized by free-floating hostility.

Type T personality   An individual driven to a life of constant stimulation and risk taking.

Upward appeal   Asking for help from a higher authority to resolve a dispute or conflict.

Valence   The value, or worth, or incentive value of an outcome.

Value   The importance a person attaches to something such as education, religion, or sports.

Variable pay   An incentive plan that intentionally pays good performers more money than poor performers.

VDT stress   An adverse physical and psychological reaction to prolonged work at a video display terminal.

Wellness   A formal approach to preventive health care.

Wellness program   A formal program to help employees stay well and avoid illness.

Win-win   The belief that after conflict has been resolved both sides should gain something of value.

Workaholic   A person addicted to work to the extent that it has adverse consequences for family and personal life.

Work ethic   A firm belief in the value and dignity of work.

Work-family conflict   A situation that occurs when an individual has to perform multiple roles: worker, spouse, and often parent.

Work habits   A person's characteristic approach to work, including such things as organization, handling of paper work, and the setting of priorities.

Work motivation   The expenditure of effort toward the accomplishment of a goal considered worthwhile by the organization.

Work teams   A small group with total responsibility for a task that manages itself to a large extent.

Ziegarnik effect   The phenomenon of uncompleted tasks creating a disturbing level of tension.

INDEXES